EDITING MUSIC IN EARLY MODERN GERMANY

To my parents

Editing Music in
Early Modern Germany

SUSAN LEWIS HAMMOND
University of Victoria, Canada

ASHGATE

Published by
Ashgate Publishing Limited
Gower House
Croft Road
Aldershot
Hampshire GU11 3HR
England

Ashgate Publishing Company
Suite 420
101 Cherry Street
Burlington, VT 05401-4405
USA

Ashgate website: http://www.ashgate.com

British Library Cataloguing in Publication Data
Lewis Hammond, Susan
  Editing Music in Early Modern Germany
  1. Music – Germany – Editing – History – 16th century. 2. Music – Germany – Editing
  – History - 17th century. 3. Music publishing – Germany – History – 16th century.
  4. Music publishing – Germany – History – 17th century. 5. Part songs, Italian –
  Germany – 16th century – History and criticism. 6. Part songs, Italian – Germany –
  17th century - History and criticism. I. Title
  780.1'49'0943'09031

Library of Congress Cataloging-in-Publication Data
Lewis Hammond, Susan.
  Editing Music in Early Modern Germany / by Susan Lewis-Hammond.
      p.   cm.
  Includes bibliographical references (p.   ) and index.
  1. Music – Editing – Germany – History – 16th century. 2.Music – Editing –
  Germany – History – 17th century. 3. Music publishing – Germany – History –
  16th century. 4. Music publishing – Germany – History – 17th century. 5. Part songs,
  Italian – Germany – 16th century – History and criticism. 6. Part songs, Italian –
  Germany – 17th century – History and criticism. 7. Lindner, Friedrich, ca. 1542–1597.
  I. Title.
  ML112.L62 2007
  780.1'490943–dc22   2007001206

ISBN 978-0-7546-5573-2

This volume has been printed on acid-free paper

Printed and bound in Great Britain by MPG Books Ltd, Bodmin, Cornwall.

Contents

List of Figures

List of Tables

List of Textual Examples

Acknowledgements

The completion of the present study would not have been possible without the financial support of the Herzog August Bibliothek at Wolfenbüttel, which enabled me to make an extended trip to Germany in 2005, during which time I completed much of the relevant research. Internal research grants from the University of Victoria funded shorter research trips to Germany (2003, 2005), and supported the purchase of microfilms, illustrations, and permissions for my book. The Helen Riaboff Whiteley Center at Friday Harbor provided an ideal setting for completing an early draft of the manuscript.

I am grateful to the libraries and archives that allowed me to use their materials, and to reproduce them here. The Deutsches Musikgeschichtliches Archiv proved a valuable resource for microfilm copies of printed music books from across German-speaking lands. I would like to thank the staff at the State and City Library of Augsburg, the Bayerische Staatsbibliothek in Munich, the Staatsbibliothek zu Berlin, Preußischer Kulturbesitz, The British Library, the Hamburg State and University Library, the Niedersächsische Staats- und Universitätsbibliothek at Göttingen, the University of Virginia, and Duke University for making their materials available to me. Dr. Gillian Bepler, Christian Hogrefe, and their colleagues at the Herzog August Bibliothek deserve special thanks for making their collections available, and easing my use of them. The staff of the McPherson Library at the University of Victoria handled my many requests for inter-library loan materials from North America and Europe. The Music Library kindly permitted me flexible access to reference materials.

A network of research colleagues shared their ideas and commented on my work at various stages, and they deserve special thanks here. The inspiration for the project dates back to Anthony Grafton's graduate seminar on early modern print culture, which first sparked my interest in the networks of authors, printers, editors, publishers, and agents that brought books to the public. Reports from the two anonymous readers for Ashgate provided valuable comments and suggestions that improved the final version of my study. Peter Wilton deserves special thanks for his careful proofreading. Mariacarla Gadebusch, Gregory Johnson, Mary Lewis, Alexander Fisher, and Mary Paquette-Abt commented on drafts and conference papers that helped shape the material presented here. Colleagues in early modern studies at the University of Victoria read an early version of Chapter 2 that significantly influenced my reworking of it here. Lloyd Howard assisted with translations of Italian poetry; Neil Rushton helped with the Latin texts; and Harald Krebs, Sharon Krebs, and Mitchell Lewis Hammond assisted with the many German translations. Students in my graduate seminars offered a venue for testing theories and issues of methodology. My colleagues in the School of Music offered encouragement and support at every step of the way.

My greatest debt lies with my family. My parents gave me continual support, and took over domestic duties of all sorts to free up my time to complete the project. My husband, Mitchell Lewis Hammond, lent his expertise as a translator and editor to early and late versions of the manuscript. Our son, Zachary, introduced me to the wonderful world of parenthood in the closing phase of the project. I am grateful for their love and support.

List of Abbreviations

A	alto, altus partbook
B	bass, bassus partbook
b.	born
c.	circa
col., cols	column, columns
edn	edition
fl	Florins
fol., fols	folio, folios
GBIÜ	*Göttinger Beiträge zur Internationalen Übersetzungs-forschung*
kr	Kreutzer
MGG	*Die Musik in Geschichte und Gegenwart*, ed. Friedrich Blume, 17 vols (Kassel: Bärenreiter, 1949-86)
MGG²	*Die Musik in Geschichte und Gegenwart*, 2nd edn, ed. Ludwig Finscher, Sachteil, vols 1-9, Personenteil, vols 1-15 (Kassel: Bärenreiter, 1994-)
MS	manuscript
nr.	near
New Grove II	*The New Grove Dictionary of Music and Musicians*, 2nd edn, eds Stanley Sadie and John Tyrrell (London Macmillan, 2001)
no., nos	number, numbers
NV	Emil Vogel, *Bibliothek der gedruckten weltlichen Vocalmusik Italiens, aus den Jahren 1500–1700* (Berlin, 1892; reprint Hildesheim: Georg Olms, 1962) [New Vogel].
r	recto
RISM	*Répertoire international des sources musicales*. AI/1-9. *Einzeldrucke vor 1800*, ed. Karlheinz Schlager (Kassel: Bärenreiter, 1971-92); B/I/1. *Recueils imprimés XVI-XVII siècles. Liste chronologique*, ed. François Lesure (Munich: G. Henle, 1960)
rule	printer's rule or straight line often used on title page to separate imprint and date
S	superius partbook
SLUB	Sächsische Landesbibliothek – Staats- und Universitäts-bibliothek Dresden
s.d.	no date indicated
s.l.	no place indicated
T	tenor, tenore partbook

v	verso
vv	voices
5	quinta, fifth-voice partbook
6	sexta, sixth-voice partbook

A Note on Spelling and Punctuation

Quoted passages follow the punctuation, orthography, and capitalization of the source, with the exception that repetitions of words have been dropped in textual examples. Contractions have been expanded in editorial brackets. Titles of music books follow spellings in RISM, while transcriptions of title pages are treated as quoted passages.

Introduction

Therefore anyone who wants to be a good pupil must not only do things well but must also make a constant effort to imitate and, if possible, exactly reproduce his master. And when he feels he has made some progress it is very profitable for him to observe different kinds of courtiers and, ruled by the good judgement that must always be his guide, take various qualities now from one man and now from another. Just as in the summer fields the bees wing their way among the plants from one flower to the next, so the courtier must acquire this grace from those who appear to possess it and take from each one the quality that seems most commendable.[1]

In this passage from *Il libro del cortegiano* (Venice, 1528) Balthasare Castiglione advises his courtier not only to gather and imitate, but to judge, select, and transform. His advice recalls Seneca, who recommended that "we should mingle all the various nectars we have tasted, and turn them into a single sweet substance, in such a way that, even if it is apparent where it originated, it appears quite different from what it was in its original state."[2] While Seneca emphasized the production of honey as the primary goal, Renaissance writers from Castiglione to Francis Bacon placed equal emphasis on the process of collecting itself, importing the metaphor of bees gathering honey to capture the renewed interest in selection and arrangement.[3]

The urge to collect lay at the root of the formation of early libraries, the origins of museums, and the cultivation of gardens that classified and stocked all known varieties of plant and flower species. The era was characterized by an interest in the natural world, an enthusiasm for antiquity manifest in the gathering of Roman coins, inscriptions, sculptures, and utensils, a fascination with the rare, strange, exotic, and technologically wondrous, and a passion for assembling these objects into cabinets, or *Kunstkammern*, as they became known in German-speaking lands.[4] The impetus to collect and arrange manifested itself musically in the compilation of anthologies, collections of pieces by several different composers. The history of the printed anthology is intimately linked to the history of music printing itself. Ottaviano Petrucci printed the first book of music in Venice in 1501, an anthology of *chansons* and other secular pieces known as *Harmonice musices Odhecaton A*.[5] Two

---

1   Baldesar Castiglione, *The Book of the Courtier*, trans. George Bull (New York: Penguin, 1967; reprint 1976), pp. 66–7.

2   Seneca, *Epistulae morales*, no. 84, quoted in Ann Moss, *Printed Commonplace-Books and the Structuring of Renaissance Thought* (Oxford: Clarendon Press, 1996), p. 12.

3   See Francis Bacon, *New Organon* [1620], trans. Michael Silverthorne, Cambridge Texts in the History of Philosophy (Cambridge: Cambridge University Press, 2000).

4   Mary W. Helms, "Essay on Objects: Interpretations of Distance Made Tangible," in Stuart B. Schwartz (ed.), *Implicit Understandings: Observing, Reporting, and Reflecting on the Encounters between Europeans and Other Peoples in the Early Modern Era* (New York: Cambridge University Press, 1994), p. 371.

5   *Harmonice musices Odhecaton A* (Venice: O. Petrucci, 1501; RISM B/I, 1501).

new editions of the anthology appeared within three years.[6] Inspired by Petrucci's success, anthologies figured prominently at presses across sixteenth-century Europe. Pierre Attaingnant in Paris, Girolamo Scotto and Angelo Gardano in Venice, Johannes Petreius, Johannes vom Berg and Ulrich Neuber, and their successor, Katharina Gerlach, in Nuremberg, all produced anthologies of new, old, or mixed repertory. Then, as now, printers recognized the commercial value of anthologies. They were cheap to produce (many were gathered from previously published pieces) and helped create interest in composers, old and new alike.

The figure at the heart of the printed anthology was the editor, the musical bee responsible for gathering and arranging sources, modifying them, and fashioning something new. Many anthologies were marketed as gardens, flowers, banquets, and *promptuarii* [storehouses]—titles that emphasize editorial processes of selection and arrangement. In contrast to editors of humanist and Classical texts, the music editor did not always stem from learned circles; he was often a skilled performer, composer, teacher, commercial printer, or poet. Editors straddled the commercial and artistic worlds of book production, bridging the needs of composers, printers, publishers, and their public. They relied on composers (directly or indirectly) for source material, while composers relied on them to communicate their work to the public, whose interests and abilities shaped and were shaped by editorial procedures. Printers and publishers imposed technological and financial constraints along the way.

As a publication type that depended upon the judicious selection and presentation of material, anthologies showcased editorial work. The story of who did this work, how they did it, and the value placed on it, is the subject of this book. It focuses on German-speaking lands, where editors had a profound impact on the transmission and reception of Italian secular song in the decades around 1600. The Italian madrigal was Italy's most successful musical export of the sixteenth century. Beyond the Alps, the genre circulated as a commercial product, a compositional model, a performance ideal, and an object for collection and exchange among rulers, patricians, merchants, students, and musicians. By the end of the century, the madrigal had become, in effect, a refined trans-European musical language (as Lorenzo Bianconi has called it), one that remained in use in the north long after its decline within Italy itself.[7] Beginning in the 1580s, editors used the anthology as a publishing strategy to introduce northern audiences to the music of Italian composers from across the peninsula.[8] Working predominantly from Venetian printed sources, German editors created what Bianconi dubs the "florilegio," an anthology compiled from previously published pieces.[9] As a compilation of pre-existing music, the florilegio bore traces

---

6   RISM B/I, 1503[2] and RISM B/I, 1504[2].

7   Lorenzo Bianconi, *Music in the Seventeenth Century*, trans. David Bryant (Cambridge: Cambridge University Press, 1987), p. 3.

8   For a statistical overview of all northern anthologies of Italian music, see Franco Piperno, "Madrigal Anthologies by Northern Printers and Monteverdi," in Silke Leopold (ed.), *Claudio Monteverdi und die Folgen: Bericht über das Internationale Symposium Detmold 1993* (Kassel: Bärenreiter, 1998), pp. 29–50.

9   Lorenzo Bianconi, "Il Cinquecento e il Seicento," in Alberto Asor Rosa (ed.), *Letteratura italiana* (Turin: Einaudi, 1982–90), vol. 6, p. 342, n. 21, cited in Giulio Ongaro,

of a rich, multi-layered printing and publishing history. As the madrigal crossed religious, linguistic, and geographic borders, the genre required the intervention of editors to shape it to suit its new speakers. German editors turned poets and translators as they reworked Italian secular songs to accommodate the linguistic and religious needs of an expanding, largely Lutheran market. Despite a sharp decline in the production of anthologies after 1620, the German market remained strong as consumers gathered and arranged music books into their own libraries and private collections. Consumers imitated editors as they judged, selected, and transformed music books into newly ordered libraries of books.

Towards a Historiography of the Early Modern Music Editor

The transmission of Italian models, and the role of German editors in reconstructing them, raise a number of issues that center on print as a medium for cultural transmission, transfer, and exchange. The language of transmission, and its related concepts of diffusion and influence, permeate Renaissance historiography, often with little acknowledgement of the heavy freight these terms carry.[10] Peter Burke offers one of the most cohesive interrogations of the terminology of influence, pointing out that words like "spread" impose a binary opposition between the source of an idea and those who adopt and transform it.[11] An assumption that Italians alone were active and creative in the process of cultural transmission is at the root of such models, which pervade early scholarship on the madrigal.[12] Building on a Jaussian theory of reception, Burke developed a methodology for studying the Italian Renaissance outside Italy that emphasized the processes of domestication and adaptation whereby receivers interpreted and contextualized Italian culture in the light of native traditions and local needs. Individuals practiced a form of *bricolage*—of selecting from the culture surrounding them whatever they find attractive, relevant, or useful,

---

"Venetian Printed Anthologies of Music in the 1560s and the Role of the Editor," in Hans Lenneberg (ed.), *The Dissemination of Music: Studies in the History of Music Publishing* (USA: Gordon and Breach, 1994), pp. 43–4. For a discussion of anthology types, see also Franco Piperno, *Gli 'Eccellentissimi musici della città di Bologna', con uno studio sull'antologia madrigalistica del Cinquecento* (Florence: Olschki, 1985), pp. 1–42; and Marco Giuliani, "Antologie, miscellanee, edizioni collettive nei secc. XVI–XVII," *Nuova rivista musicale italiana*, 22/1 (1988): 70–76.

10 See, for instance, Paul Oskar Kristeller, "The European Diffusion of Italian Humanism," *Italica*, 39 (1962): 1–20; and Roberto Weiss, *The Spread of Italian Humanism* (London: Hutchinson, 1964). Thomas DaCosta Kaufmann's preface to *Toward a Geography of Art* ([Chicago: Chicago University Press, 2004], pp. 187–216 and 423–31) is indicative of the critical stance found in more recent scholarship.

11 Peter Burke, "The Uses of Italy," in Roy Porter and Mukuláš Teich (eds), *The Renaissance in National Context* (Cambridge: Cambridge University Press, 1992), pp. 7–13.

12 Alfred Einstein focused exclusively on the origins and creation of the genre in Italy, leaving out its development outside Italy, in his otherwise comprehensive *The Italian Madrigal*, 3 vols (Princeton: Princeton University Press, 1949).

and assimilating it to what they already possess.[13] Renaissance transformations of Classical ideals and forms, for instance, represent deliberate artistic and intellectual choices rather than failed attempts to reproduce the source.[14] Burke's approach formed part of a broader shift, evident since the 1970s, that saw the reader and audience assume a central role in the field of literary theory and criticism.[15]

My study considers German editors as a "first audience" for madrigals and canzonettas, an audience that carefully selected attractive and suitable settings, and assimilated them into the cultural framework, be it a given city, religious institution, or court, in which they lived and worked. It applies Burke's function-based model of diffusion to the medium of print, a mode of communication that immediately raises its own issues of cultural transmission and control. Beginning in the late 1950s with Lucien Febvre and Henri-Jean Martin's *L'apparition du livre*, Martin, Roger Chartier, and Robert Darnton (among others) started to address such questions as how the medium of print structured the presentation and authorship of texts, and the ways texts were read and disseminated.[16] Roger Chartier describes this tension as the rub between the "strategies of writing and the author's intentions," and mechanisms that result from "publishing decisions or the constraints of the print shop."[17] Such lines of inquiry brought a range of social groups under scrutiny—authors, printers, editors, promoters, buyers, sellers, readers, and patrons—and the very networks of exchange that united and divided them.

Scholars outside of music have been quick to focus on anthologies as artifacts of these overlapping and complex layers of reception, print, and social histories. In the first full treatment of early modern anthologies Barbara Benedict argued that anthologies both shaped and were shaped by the literary culture in which they were produced, forming a living testament to the relationship between editors and

---

13   Hans-Robert Jauss, *Toward an Aesthetic of Reception*, trans. Timothy Bahti (Minneapolis: University of Minnesota Press, 1982). Peter Burke applies reception theory most extensively in *The Fortunes of the* Courtier*: The European Reception of Castiglione's* Cortegiano (Cambridge, UK: Polity Press, 1995).

14   Anthony Grafton, "Notes from Underground on Cultural Transmission," in Anthony Grafton and Ann Blair (eds), *The Transmission of Culture in Early Modern Europe* (Philadelphia: University of Pennsylvania Press, 1990), p. 2.

15   See, for example, Susan R. Suleiman and Inge Crosman (eds), *The Reader and the Text: Essays on Audience and Interpretation* (Princeton: Princeton University Press, 1980).

16   Lucien Febvre and Henri-Jean Martin, *L'apparition du livre* (Paris: Editions Albin Michel, 1958), trans. David Gerard as *The Coming of the Book: The Impact of Printing 1450–1800* (London: Verso, 1976); Roger Chartier (ed.), *The Culture of Print: Power and the Uses of Print in Early Modern Europe*, trans. Lydia G. Cochrane (Princeton: Princeton University Press, 1987); ibid., *Forms and Meanings: Texts, Performances and Audiences from Codex to Computer* (Philadelphia: University of Pennsylvania Press, 1995); and Robert Darnton, "What is the History of Books?" in his *The Kiss of Lamourette: Reflections in Cultural History* (New York: W.W. Norton, 1990), pp. 107–35.

17   Roger Chartier, *The Order of Books: Readers, Authors, and Libraries in Europe between the Fourteenth and Eighteenth Centuries*, trans. Lydia G. Cochrane (Stanford: Stanford University Press, 1994), p. 9. His work recalls Donald Francis McKenzie's *Bibliography and the Sociology of Texts, The Panizzi Lectures* (London: The British Library, 1986), especially ch. 1, "The Book as an Expressive Form," pp. 1–21.

their audiences.[18] As a venue for the publication of current literature and criticism, the anthology helped shape a canon while remaining flexible about its contents.[19] More recently, Adam Smyth argued that printed miscellanies (a bundling together of writings from diverse sources and authors) provide "moments of resistance" to macro narratives, including the rise of the author, the triumph of print over manuscript, the capacity of print to fix, set, and stabilize texts, and the separation of printed texts from ideas of social application and utility.[20] Leah Price tests perceived wisdom with her suggestion that editors' reproduction of old novels (through anthology, abridgment, expurgation, and collected works) shaped authors' production of new ones.[21] Their work is united by a sociological and cultural-materialist approach to textuality proposed by Jerome McGann and Donald Francis McKenzie in the 1980s.[22] Rather than an autonomous entity subject to the will and intentions of a single author, the work is a social artifact, whose meaning is embedded in its production, transmission, and consumption. For McGann, the socialization of a work in the production process, the act of communicating it to an audience, is an integral part of creating a work of art.

My study approaches music anthologies as social artifacts that reflect the needs and motivations of their producers and consumers. In the case of music books, we can consider multiple groups within these two categories. Editors collaborated, directly or indirectly, with composers, printers, and publishers to bring music to the public. As they worked, they kept in mind the interests of a diverse group of patrons, listeners, students, teachers, performers, and collectors.

Among these groups, I place special emphasis on the role of the anthologist, whose editorial decisions influenced and were influenced by the complete chain from composer to consumer. Scholars have examined Italian music anthologies from the perspectives of bibliography, genre, and printing history. Alfred Einstein published inventories of all anthologies of Italian secular music in a catalogue appended to the 1962 revision of Emil Vogel's *Bibliothek der gedruckten weltlichen Vocalmusik Italiens*.[23] Mary Lewis's and Jane Bernstein's monumental catalogues, of printers Antonio Gardano and Girolamo Scotto respectively, offer guides to single-

---

18   Barbara M. Benedict, *Making the Modern Reader: Cultural Mediation in Early Modern Literary Anthologies* (Princeton: Princeton University Press, 1996).

19   Ibid., p. 211.

20   Adam Smyth, *'Profit and Delight': Printed Miscellanies in England, 1640–1682* (Detroit: Wayne State University Press, 2004), p. 174.

21   Leah Price, *The Anthology and the Rise of the Novel: From Richardson to George Eliot* (Cambridge: Cambridge University Press, 2000).

22   See Jerome J. McGann, *A Critique of Modern Textual Criticism* (Chicago: University of Chicago Press, 1983) and McKenzie, *Bibliography and the Sociology of Texts*, passim.

23   Emil Vogel, *Bibliothek der gedruckten weltlichen Vocalmusik Italiens, aus den Jahren 1500–1700* (Berlin, 1892; reprint Hildesheim: Georg Olms, 1962). Einstein first brought out the inventory in instalments of *Music Library Association Notes* (1945–48). Anthologies are omitted in the third edition by François Lesure and Claudio Sartori, *Bibliografia della musica italiana profana, nuova ed. interamente rifatta e aumentata con gli indici dei musicisti, poeti, cantanti, dedicatari e dei capoversi dei testi letterari*, 3 vols (Pomezia: Staderini-Minkoff, 1977).

author volumes and anthologies from the mid-sixteenth century.[24] Giulio Ongaro's examination of the career of Giulio Bonagiunta, who earned a high reputation for his anthologies of motets, madrigals, and *canzoni alla napolitana* printed by Girolamo Scotto in the 1560s, demonstrates the new commercial focus placed on anthologies in the Venetian marketplace.[25]

Anthologies of Italian secular songs printed in German-speaking lands have been examined within the many valuable studies of the madrigal and canzonetta outside Italy.[26] As Ludwig Finscher admits, there are many gaps in our knowledge of the market for Italian madrigals printed in Germany.[27] The full impact of German editors on the reception of the madrigal and related genres remains to be shown. My study examines three sometimes overlapping categories of editors— compilers, translators, and poets—and gives particular attention to the environments in which they worked. In this respect, I build on a context-driven approach to musicology articulated by Gary Tomlinson as a "web of culture."[28] Adopting this approach, Martha Feldman's study of madrigals in Venice regards madrigals as products of the sociological, geographical, and urban contexts in which they were produced.[29] Even more significant for my work, Richard Freedman demonstrates ways that Protestants gave new meanings to Orlande de Lassus's French chansons by retexting them, inscribing them with new spiritual meanings.[30] Mary Lewis demonstrates the role of bibliography in the construction of cultural webs.[31] The metaphor of a web seems

---

24   Mary S. Lewis, *Antonio Gardano, Venetian Music Printer, 1538–1569: A Descriptive Bibliography and Historical Study*, 3 vols (New York: Garland, 1988–2005); and Jane A. Bernstein, *Music Printing in Renaissance Venice: The Scotto Press, 1539–1572* (New York: Oxford University Press, 1998).

25   Ongaro, "Venetian Printed Anthologies of Music, pp. 43–69.

26   Sara Dumont, *German Secular Polyphonic Song in Printed Editions, 1570–1630*, 2 vols (New York: Garland, 1989); Ludwig Finscher, "Lied and Madrigal, 1580–1600," in John Kmetz (ed.), *Music in the German Renaissance: Sources, Styles, and Contexts* (Cambridge: Cambridge University Press, 1994), pp. 182–92; Walther Dürr, "Die italienische Canzonette und das deutsche Lied im Ausgang des XVI. Jahrhunderts," in *Studi in onore di Lorenzo Bianchi* (Bologna: Zanichelli, 1960), pp. 71–102; and Basil Smallman, "Pastoralism, Parody and Pathos: The Madrigal in Germany, 1570–1630," in *Conspectus Carminis: Essays for David Galliver, Miscellanea Musicologica*, Adelaide Studies in Musicology, 15 (Adelaide: University of Adelaide Press, 1988), pp. 6–20.

27   Finscher, "Lied and Madrigal," p. 192.

28   Gary Tomlinson, "The Web of Culture: A Context for Musicology," *19th-Century Music*, 7 (1983–84): 350–62. Tomlinson applies this approach in his study *Monteverdi and the End of the Renaissance* (Berkeley: University of California Press, 1987), which reformulates the question of the relation of text and music in the Italian madrigal, working outward from the artifacts of the poem and its musical setting.

29   Martha Feldman, *City Culture and the Madrigal at Venice* (Berkeley: University of California Press, 1995).

30   Richard Freedman, *The Chansons of Orlando di Lasso: Music, Piety, and Print in Sixteenth-Century France*, Eastman Studies in Music, ed. Ralph P. Locke (Rochester: University of Rochester Press, 2000).

31   Mary S. Lewis, "The Printed Music Book in Context: Observations on Some Sixteenth-Century Editions," *Notes*, 46 (1990): 917–18.

aptly suited to a study of editors who worked predominantly with Venetian music books, sources that were first subject to editorial bias and selection in Venetian print shops prior to their export and subsequent editing north of the Alps.

Sources for a Study of Renaissance Editing

The central sources for such a study remain the music books themselves, the final products of editorial work. My approach to these sources draws much from the field of manuscript studies. The study of individual scribes and scriptoria presents a striking parallel to the printed anthology compiler and print shop. Stanley Boorman and Mary Lewis have drawn attention to the value of applying modes of inquiry, traditionally reserved for manuscript sources, to printed ones.[32] As Mary Lewis has shown, examinations of the concordance lists for the pieces in a printed book help us understand the contents, their transmission, and their reception.[33] The relative age of the repertory might suggest slow or quick access to recent music. A compiler's poetic choices may reinforce or depart from poets and poetic motives favored within Italy. Editors' efforts to depart from or slavishly follow their models indicate the extent of their intervention at the level of the verbal and musical texts.

The packaging of music books can also reveal much about their intended audience and the strategies editors employed to court them. There is growing interest in Renaissance liminary space or "paratext," to use Gerard Genette's term for the title pages, contents lists, indices, headings, and prefaces to early modern books.[34] While short opening and closing formulas gave sufficient details of the title and author of a manuscript written on commission, the competitive nature of the print industry necessitated a new approach to book packaging.[35] As a distinctive feature of printed books, title pages are good indicators of the values of early modern print culture in general, and the attitudes toward editorship in particular. The size of typeface and placement of text for an editor's name, for instance, reflect the priority placed on this knowledge. Further, as Brian Richardson has shown in his study of the interaction between written culture and the book industry of Renaissance Italy, the demand for editorial services came in part from readers who relied on the indices, tables, and prefaces supplied by editors to guide their use of books.[36] Thomas Corns compares this reliance to our own dependence on computer search engines to guide us on the World Wide Web, likening the early book editor to the modern-day web

---

32 Stanley Boorman, "Printed Music Books of the Italian Renaissance from the Point of View of Manuscript Study," *Revista de musicologia*, 16/5 (1993): 2587–2602; Mary S. Lewis, "The Printed Music Book in Context."

33 Mary S. Lewis, "The Printed Music Book in Context."

34 Gerard Genette, *Paratexts: Thresholds of Interpretation*, trans. Jane E. Lewin (Cambridge: Cambridge University Press, 1997); originally published as *Seuils* (Paris, Editions du Seuil, 1987).

35 Brian Richardson, *Printing, Writers and Readers in Renaissance Italy* (Cambridge: Cambridge University Press, 1999), p. 132. For an overview of the development of the title page, see Febvre and Martin, *The Coming of the Book*, pp. 83–6.

36 Richardson, *Printing, Writers and Readers*, pp. 130–31.

master working "behind the scenes" to make new technology more user-friendly.[37] Tables and indices created a visual order for the contents of an anthology, presenting hierarchies and frameworks for understanding the music contained within. This understanding was furthered by prefaces and dedications. As Martha Feldman has demonstrated, prefatory and dedicatory addresses functioned as dialogic genres (publications implying the use or suggestion of dialogue) that allowed authors to communicate directly with their audience, which included printers, publishers, and composers, alongside the more amorphous public that acquired the book.[38] My study of the use of these devices in music books will strengthen the dialogue between current musicological research, and scholarship on the history of the book.

My final category of sources comprises evidence of the commerce of books: publishers' catalogs, advertisements, inventories of libraries, and records of book purchases. The printing of books of Italian music in German-speaking lands presupposes a market for them, a market created first by the northern importation of other books from Venice. As Tim Carter has shown, it is important not only to examine what was printed in a given city or region, but also to analyse what was sold there.[39] Catalogs from the Frankfurt and Leipzig bookfairs document the availability of Italian music books in German-speaking lands, and the important role played by music publishers in the transfer of music across regions. How quick was the flow of music books from Venice to the north? Which composers and styles were imported the most? How did the imports shape the form and content of new German products? A related question concerns the tastes of consumers, a group that included such diverse parties as merchants, musicians, amateur and professional performers, students and teachers, religious and educational institutions, courts, and city councils. Analysis of the contents of their collections suggests ways that editorial work at once guided and responded to the tastes and abilities of consumers.

Outline of the Book

Chapters 1 and 5 frame the book with a consideration of the role of editors in the music book trade of early modern Europe (Chapter 1) and the consumer demand for their work (Chapter 5). The first chapter traces the cultural history of the music editor through a study of title pages, prefaces, and dedications—all signs of an editor's dialogue with composers, printers, publishers, patrons, and consumers. Examples from German-speaking lands are supplemented with others from across Europe to gather sufficient evidence to demonstrate that the first century of music printing witnessed a shift from anonymous editorship to the advertisement of an editor, and heavy reliance on his services. This is arguably strongest in German-speaking lands where demand for Italian music necessitated the reliance on editors to translate

---

37   Thomas N. Corns, "The Early Modern Search Engine: Indices, Title Pages, Marginalia and Contents," in Neil Rhodes and Jonathan Sawday (eds), *The Renaissance Computer: Knowledge Technology in the First Age of Print* (London: Routledge, 2000), pp. 95–105.

38   Feldman, *City Culture and the Madrigal at Venice*, pp. 47–82, esp. pp. 48–51.

39   Tim Carter, "Music-Selling in Late Sixteenth-Century Florence: The Bookshop of Piero di Giuliano Morosi," *Music and Letters*, 70 (1989): 483–504.

verbal texts into German and rewrite new texts appropriate for Protestant listeners. The chapter charts the growth of editorial additions—lengthy title pages, self-conscious prefatory texts, detailed tables, and indices—which reflect the importance of presenting music books visually in ways that helped performers, students, and teachers to use and consult them.

Chapters 2–4 consider editorial work through a series of focused explorations of particular music books and their editors: madrigal anthologies prepared in Nuremberg during the late sixteenth century; books of madrigals in which German poetry replaced the original Italian; and books that offer spiritual revisions of madrigal texts, in this instance conceived for the religious sensibilities of Lutheran musicians and listeners.

Chapter 2 tracks the career of Friedrich Lindner, one of the most prolific German editors of Italian music. Between 1588 and 1590, Lindner compiled a series of three volumes of secular songs titled *Gemma musicalis* for the Nuremberg printing and publishing firm of Katharina Gerlach. Despite their Latin titles, the trilogy included 185 madrigals and canzoni in Italian, making them the largest and among the earliest of their kind to be printed outside of Italy.[40] The contents and structure of Lindner's anthologies demonstrate the close connection between reception and editing. Lindner selected music on the basis of the reputation of a composer, his regional affiliation, a song's popularity, its level of difficulty, and poetic theme. The result was a series of anthologies whose size made them appealing to a range of consumers, but whose individual content reflected the tastes of Lindner's more immediate audience.

Lindner's trilogy created a market for Italian music that extended beyond consumers familiar with the Italian language. Chapter 3 focuses on Valentin Haussmann, who responded to demand for German translations of Italian songs. Beginning in 1606 Haussmann launched the first of seven volumes of German translations of Italian secular song, all published at the press of Paul Kauffmann in Nuremberg: a selection of three-voice villanellas and *canzoni alla napolitana* by Luca Marenzio (1606), a volume of canzonettas by Orazio Vecchi and Gemignani Capilupi (1606), tricinia by Giovanni Gastoldi (1607), five-voice balletts by Englishman Thomas Morley (1609), and three further volumes of Vecchi's canzonettas, all published in 1610. The series offers a German counterpart to the earlier, more famous anthologies of "madrigals Englished" issued by Nicholas Yonge, Thomas Watson, and Thomas Morley.[41] Haussmann's settings mark a critical juncture of musical and literary

---

40   They are preceded by Pierre Phalèse (ed.), *Musica divina di XIX. autori illustri, a IIII. V. VI. et VII. voci* (Antwerp: Pierre Phalèse and Jean Bellère, 1583; RISM B/I, 1583[15]); Andreas Pevernage (ed.), *Harmonia celeste di diversi eccellentissimi musici a IIII. V. VI. VII. et VIII. voci* (Antwerp: Pierre Phalèse and Jean Bellère, 1583; RISM B/I, 1583[14]); Giulio Gigli da Immola (ed.), *Sdegnosi ardori. Musica di diversi auttori, sopra un istesso soggetto di parole, a cinque voci* (Munich: Adam Berg, 1585; RISM B/I, 1585[17]); and Hubert Waelrant (ed.), *Symphonia angelica di diversi eccellentissimi musici a IIII. V. et VI. voci* (Antwerp: Pierre Phalèse and Jean Bellère, 1585; RISM B/I, 1585[19]).

41   Five anthologies of Italian madrigals in English translations appeared between 1588 and 1598: *Musica transalpina. Madrigals translated of foure, five and six parts* [...] *Published by N. Yonge* (London: Thomas East, 1588; RISM B/I, 1588[29]); *The first sett, of italian madrigalls englished* [...] *By Thomas Watson* (London: Thomas East, 1590; RISM

contact that represents an important facet of the reception of Italian culture in German-speaking lands, yet one that has been overlooked in the literature to date.[42] Haussmann's work can be best understood within the context of the debate among early modern translators between the relative merits of the source language and the target language. By freely adapting Italian texts to accommodate the artistic demands of the German language, Haussmann furthered the cause of German as a language for artistic expression and poetry.

Chapter 4 positions the work of editors within a broad context that actively considers intersections of histories of music, religion, and literary culture. Editors in Lutheran lands responded to the mounting tension between Catholics and Protestants in the years leading up to the Thirty Years War by adapting the madrigal and canzonetta for liturgical use and spiritual devotion. Chapter 4 argues that the high status given to music in Lutheran worship and praise influenced editorial strategies in the decades of confessional strife leading up to the war. While editors retained their enthusiasm for the sound of Italian music—they continued to borrow heavily from contemporary Italian music books—their selection of images, lyrics, and packaging remained deeply indebted to Luther's theology of music. The Lutheran poet and dramatist Martin Rinckart replaced the secular texts of the famous madrigal anthology *Il trionfo di Dori* (Venice, 1592) with sacred ones that championed the power of music, a central tenet of Lutheran theology. His extensive preface to *Triumphi de Dorothea: Laus Musicæ … Das ist, Geistliches, Musicalisches Triumph Cräntzlein* (Leipzig, 1619) uses citations from Classical authorities, church fathers, and reformers to comment on the music they frame. While Rinckart used Italian madrigals as his source, the Lutheran Cantor Petrus Neander brought the Italian canzonetta into direct contact with the tradition of psalm singing, which played an important role in Luther's liturgical and educational reforms, and their reception in the first century of the Reformation. Neander superimposed his own paraphrases of psalm texts from the Lutheran Bible onto 36 of Orazio Vecchi's widely popular canzonetta melodies, which he issued in two volumes (1614, 1620). As contrafacta (sacred texts substituted for existing, usually secular texts in songs), Rinckart's and Neander's texts demonstrates the value of transmitting "the word" through familiar, even popular tunes.

B/I, 1590[29]); *Canzonets. Or little short songs to foure voices* [...] *By T. Morley* (London: Peter Short, 1597; RISM B/I, 1597[23]); *Musica transalpina. The second booke of madrigalles, 5. to & 6. voices* [...] *newly published by Nicholas Yonge* (London: Thomas East, 1597; RISM B/I, 1597[24]); and *Madrigals to five voyces. Celected out of the best approved Italian authors. By Thomas Morley* (London: Thomas East, 1598; RISM B/I, 1598[15]).

42 Ludwig Finscher only alludes to the importance of translation in his study of the transformation of the German Tenorlied into madrigal- and canzonetta types of German song. He observes that "the simple and unassuming language and verse patterns of the villanelle suggested a similarity to the traditional, pre-madrigalian German song which facilitated translation and reception" but does not follow with an analysis of the translations themselves (Finscher, "Lied and madrigal," p. 191). Walther Dürr's important overview of the relationship between the Italian canzonetta and German Lied offers a starting point for my work ("Die italienische Canzonette und das deutsche Lied," pp. 73–102).

Chapter 5 shifts our focus from editors to their audiences. The print industry made music more accessible to larger and more diverse audiences than ever before. Yet rather than stimulating innovation, I argue that commercial printing promoted a long-term interest in late sixteenth-century Italian polyphonic song, as the contents of court, private, and institutional libraries in German-speaking lands attest. Building on the work of Jane Bernstein and Mary Lewis, I group German consumers into three categories.[43] First, we have individual collectors (nobility, merchants, patricians), who demonstrated a systematic approach to acquisitions. For members of the cultural elite, music books served a practical function—they provided repertory for performance at courtly and social gatherings—but they also served a symbolic role as a form of social capital. The possession of books and their assembly into early libraries formed part of a broader culture of collecting that united German patricians, merchants, and nobility in their pursuit of consumer and luxury goods of all kinds. The second group comprises music teachers, students, musicians, and performers—professionals with more limited resources, but the power to influence musical taste and fashion. The third category is made up of religious and educational institutions that followed Martin Luther's call to form sizable libraries.

The conclusion compares techniques for gathering and presenting material in anthologies from German-speaking lands with their counterparts from across Europe. It concludes that editing is a historically-defined practice whose product, an anthology, is a highly malleable publication type that is responsive to religious and political currents, the conditions of the local marketplace, the personal likes and dislikes of an editor, and the perceived tastes of a diverse range of consumers. In the case of German-speaking lands, there was a close relationship between editing and consumption. Editorial work explains the shift in buying habits of the northern public, which had little use for the madrigal prior to the period in question. Finally, I consider the extent to which editorial decision-making influenced the cultivation of particular styles, genres, composers, and audiences. Like their present-day counterparts, early modern editors played a vital role in the formation of a canon of musical works and genres.

Appendix A includes transcriptions of title pages, dedications, and a list of surviving copies of the anthologies selected as case studies for Chapters 2–4. Appendix B gives their contents, foliation, and earliest printed concordances or textual sources.

---

43   See, especially, Jane A. Bernstein, "Buyers and Collectors of Music Publications: Two Sixteenth-Century Music Libraries Recovered," in Jessie Ann Owens and Anthony Cummings (eds), *Music in Renaissance Cities and Courts: Studies in Honor of Lewis Lockwood* (Warren, MI: Harmonie Park Press, 1997), pp. 21–33; and Mary S. Lewis, "The Printed Music Book in Context."

Chapter 1

The Anthology and the Birth of the Professional Music Editor

Non est impius Medicus, qui tumorem ferit, qui putredinem secat & urit. Dolorem ingerit, ut perducat ad sanitatem. Molestus est, sed si non esset, utilis non esset.[1]
[A doctor who lances a tumor, cuts out the bad and cauterizes is not an evil man. He inflicts pain to restore health. He is troublesome, but if he were not, he would be of no use.]

On the title page of *Orthotypographia* (Leipzig, 1608), an early manual for editors, Hieronymus Hornschuch conjures up the laudable image of the editor as doctor, armed with a lance and ready to make careful incisions to the "monstrously faulty" (as he later grumbles) manuscripts of authors.[2] The doctor metaphor must have appealed to Hornschuch, who abandoned his medical studies in Jena when his funds ran out, and relocated to Leipzig to work as an editor at the firm of Michael Lantzenberg. Hornschuch's duties ranged from proofreading to the complete preparation of manuscripts, which entailed the compilation and ordering of sources, and their revision, emendation, or translation. Hornschuch's manual justified the employment of professional editors, with knowledge of languages, orthography, grammar, and subject expertise. Rather than wounding manuscripts, as Martin Luther, Erasmus, and Henri Estienne complained, Hornschuch's editor cured them of their afflictions.[3]

---

1   Philip Gaskell and Patricia Bradford (ed. and trans.), *Hornschuch's Orthotypographia, 1608* (Cambridge: The University Library, 1972), p. i.

2   "Nam cùm quotidie magis ferè cum manuscriptis mendosis & monstrosis, quàm typographorum erratis mihi esset depugnandum" (ibid., p. ix).

3   See Percy Simpson, *Proof-Reading in the Sixteenth, Seventeenth, and Eighteenth Centuries* (London: Oxford University Press, 1935; reprint 1970), p. 130 for Luther's complaints of misplaced letters in German Bibles. In the dedication of his edition of Jerome (Basel, 1516), Erasmus complained that "while trying to emend it [a perceived error] … he [the editor] introduces two mistakes in place of one, and while trying to cure a slight wound inflicts one that is incurable" (quoted in David McKitterick, *Print, Manuscript and the Search for Order, 1450–1830* [Cambridge: Cambridge University Press, 2003], p. 46 and p. 249 n. 86). Estienne complained of a corrector who "inflicted wounds on every passage in which he found the word *procos* [suitors], since he substituted 'porcos' [pigs] for it" in *Artis Typographicae querimonia*, in his *Pseudo-Cicero*, ed. F.W. Roloff (Halle, 1737), p. ccclxxvi (quoted in Anthony Grafton, "Correctores corruptores?: Notes on the Social History of Editing," in Glenn W. Most [ed.], *Editing Texts/Texte edieren*, Aporemata, Kritische Studien zur Philologiegeschichte, 2 [Göttingen: Vandenhoeck & Ruprecht, 1998], p. 70).

Hornschuch's treatise is representative of the intense debate over editorial work at the turn of the sixteenth to the seventeenth century. His defensive tone captures the tension between the work of the editor and the intent of the author, forces that in turn were subject to the technical and financial constraints of book printers and publishers. The battleground where these tensions often erupted was the title page, long recognized as a book's most important advertising tool. Nowhere is this conflict clearer than on the title pages of anthologies, works in which the editor assumed a defining role in the presentation of musical culture. The presence or absence of the editor's name on the title page is perhaps the strongest indicator of the value placed on his work. Corroborating evidence comes from the preliminary pages of anthologies—the dedications, prefaces, indices, and tables of contents—where the ordering of material imparted meaning to the music within. Beginning in the 1980s, literary historians Gérard Genette and Antoine Compagnon turned our attention to these paratextual moments, in recognition of the interdependent nature of the text and its frame.[4] Title pages and packaging launched texts onto the marketplace. This role makes them ideal windows for viewing changes to the value ascribed to editors in the music book trade of the sixteenth and seventeenth centuries.

The Editor on the Page

This section focuses on attribution practices during the first century of music printing, arguably the most important phase in the transformation of music into a commercial product or commodity for circulation. It traces the history of the attribution of anthologies by naming editors on title pages. My approach draws on the work of Martha Feldman, who has examined questions of attribution and anonymous circulation concerning individual madrigal settings in sixteenth-century anthologies.[5] The act of naming an editor served a dual purpose. It suggests ways that printers used the reputation of editors to promote books, and offers growing evidence of an authorial function bestowed upon editors.[6]

---

4   For Genette, the title, table of contents, dedication, preface, headings, notes, interviews, and correspondence constitute the paratext (Deborah N. Losse, *Sampling the Book: Renaissance Prologues and the French* Conteurs [Lewisburg: Bucknell University Press, 1994], p. 104 n. 1). See Gérard Genette, *Paratexts: Thresholds of Interpretation*, trans. Jane E. Lewin (Cambridge: Cambridge University Press, 1997); originally published as *Seuils* (Paris, Editions du Seuil, 1987). Antoine Compagnon uses the related term *périgraphie* [perigraphy] as the intermediate zone between the text itself and what is outside of the text, in *La Seconde Main ou le travail de la citation* (Paris: Editions du Seuil, 1979), p. 328.

5   Martha Feldman, "Authors and Anonyms: Recovering the Anonymous Subject in *Cinquecento* Vernacular Objects," in Kate van Orden (ed.), *Music and the Cultures of Print*, Critical and Cultural Musicology, 1 (New York: Garland, 2000), pp. 163–99.

6   Michel Foucault's famous essay "What Is an Author?" offers the more flexible construct of "author-function" as a substitute for the proto-Romantic sovereign author (Michel Foucault, "Qu'est-ce qu'un auteur?" *Bulletin de la Société française de Philosophie*, 44 [July–September 1969]: 73–104; trans. as "What Is an Author?" in Donald F. Bouchard [ed.], *Language, Counter-Memory, Practice: Selected Essays and Interviews* [Ithaca: Cornell University Press, 1977], pp. 113–38). For a response to Foucault, see Roger Chartier, "Figures

Title pages of early printed music anthologies show little effort to distinguish editorial activity from that of printer, publisher. bookseller, or composer. There was editorial work, but it remains unclear who did it, how they interacted with their collaborators, and how editorial practice influenced consumer demand. Take the case of Ottaviano Petrucci, the first to print polyphonic music from movable type using the multiple-impression technique, whereby the paper passed through the press once for the staff lines, once for the notes, and the final time for the text. Petrucci has become a household name among students of music history. The same cannot be said of his editor, the Dominican friar Petrus Castellanus, who both corrected proofs and supplied sources to Petrucci, whose name appears on the title pages, though he was not a musician himself, and Castellanus, if his work is mentioned at all, is relegated to the preface.[7] Valerio Dorico, in Rome, is another example of a music printer without specialist knowledge, who likely relied on both the network of contacts and technical expertise of an editor, though we are left to speculate about the identity of the editor and how he was compensated.[8]

The situation is mirrored across Europe in anthologies of all genres of music. From Paris the title pages of Pierre Attaingnant's nine anthologies of *Chansons nouvelles* (Paris, 1538–40) make no mention of their editorship. Working in Lyon, printer Jacques Moderne used organist and composer Antonio Francesco Layolle to edit sacred music, likely including the *Motetti del fiore* series, and composer P. de Villiers to edit the chanson series *Paragon*, but mentioned neither of them on the respective title pages of the anthologies.[9] Nuremberg printer Johannes Petreius expressed an equally ambivalent attitude. Petreius named Georg Forster as *selectore* [selecter, chooser] of the first volume of the motet anthology *Selectissimarum mutetarum partim quinque partim quatuor vocum* (Nuremberg, 1540), but left his name off the title pages of the *Tomus tertius psalmorum selectorum quatuor et quinque, et quidam plurium vocum* (Nuremberg, 1542) and two anthologies of secular *Teutscher Liedlein*.[10] The editorship of a further eight anthologies went

---

of the Author" in his *The Order of Books: Readers, Authors, and Libraries in Europe between the Fourteenth and Eighteenth Centuries*, trans. Lydia G. Cochrane (Stanford: Stanford University Press, 1994), pp. 25–59.

7   Bartolomeo Budrio's preface to *Harmonice musices Odhecaton A* (Venice: O. Petrucci, 1501; RISM B/I, 1501) names Petrus Castellanus and praises "cuius opera et diligentia centena haec carmina repurgata" [these hundred songs, corrected by his diligent labor] (Bonnie J. Blackburn, "Petrucci's Venetian Editor: Petrus Castellanus and His Musical Garden," *Musica disciplina*, 49 [1995]: 17).

8   Suzanne Cusick raises a number of questions about the editing of Dorico's music books, and points out that there is insufficient evidence to determine whether Dorico was a musician (Suzanne C. Cusick, *Valerio Dorico: Music Printer in Sixteenth-Century Rome*, Studies in Musicology, 43 [Ann Arbor: UMI Research Press, 1981], esp. pp. 77–92).

9   Samuel F. Pogue, *Jacques Moderne: Lyons Music Printer of the Sixteenth Century* (Geneva: Libraire Droz, 1969), pp. 34–44; cf. Cusick, *Valerio Dorico*, p. 90.

10   See *Ein Ausszug guter alter und newer teutscher Liedlein* (Nuremberg: Johannes Petreius, 1539; RISM B/I, 1539[27]) and *Der Ander Theil, kurtzweiliger guter frischer teutscher Liedlein* (Nuremberg: Johannes Petreius, 1540; RISM B/I, 1540[21]). For transcriptions of title pages and facsimiles of prefaces, see Mariko Teramoto and Armin Brinzing, *Katalog der*

unacknowledged on title pages during the same period at the Petreius firm. Hans Ott is another example of a German editor whose role was undermined on title pages of anthologies. Ott compiled and published the motet anthologies *Novum et insigne opus musicum, sex, quinque, et quatuor vocum* (Nuremberg, 1537) and *Secundus tomus novi operis musici, sex, quinque et quatuor vocum* (Nuremberg, 1538), with revised verbal texts to better suit his largely Protestant audience, and, more specifically, to honor members of the family of the dedicatee, King Ferdinand. Yet Ott, who commissioned the Nuremberg printer Hieronymus Formschneider (also known as Hieronymus Grapheus) to print the volumes, did not see fit to include his own name on their title pages.[11]

In the first half-century of music printing, editorial work lacked sufficient advertising cachet. By and large it was the printers and composers whose names dominated the title pages of music books, from the 1530s and the 1540s, single-author and anthology alike.[12] For volumes by multiple authors, this led to cases of what Giulio Ongaro dubs pseudo-anthologies, in which the composer featured on the title page is accorded only minimal representation in the anthology.[13] The strategy proved especially important for introducing new genres to the marketplace. The earliest Venetian madrigal books from the late 1530s and 1540s used the familiar names of composers Philippe Verdelot, Cipriano de Rore, and Jacques Arcadelt to sell anthologies that included madrigals by less well-known composers. In the case of Rore's madrigal books, his music often made up only a small portion of the contents. He authored only eight of a total 27 settings in *Di Cipriano il secondo libro de madregali a cinque voci insieme alcuni di M. Adriano et altri autori* (Venice, 1544). Verdelot composed only 11 of the 43 madrigals in *Le Dotte et eccellente compositioni de i madrigali de Verdelot, a cinque voci* (Venice, 1541).[14] Advertising composers in a lump category served a similar function. The tag "diversorum auctorum" [of diverse authors] was a pervasive device used by printers across Europe for chanson, madrigal, motet, and instrumental collections. It was used for the first time on the title page of an anthology of masses printed by Petrucci in Venice in 1509.[15] It

---

Musikdrucke des Johannes Petreius in Nürnberg, Catalogus Musicus, 14 (Kassel: Bärenreiter, 1993).

11   Royston Robert Gustavson examines their compilation, printing, and reception in "Hans Ott, Hieronymus Formschneider, and the *Novum et insigne opus musicum* (Nuremberg, 1537–1538)" (Ph.D. diss., University of Melbourne, 1998).

12   Only 56 music books, or roughly 12 per cent of Antonio Gardano's entire output, name no composer on their title page (Mary S. Lewis, *Antonio Gardano, Venetian Music Printer, 1538–1569: A Descriptive Bibliography and Historical Study*, 3 vols [New York: Garland, 1988-2005], vol. 1, p. 103).

13   Ongaro defines the pseudo-anthology as a single-composer volume with at least one addition by another composer (Giulio M. Ongaro, "Venetian Printed Anthologies of Music in the 1560s and the Role of the Editor," in Hans Lenneberg [ed.], *The Dissemination of Music: Studies in the History of Music Publishing* [USA: Gordon and Breach, 1994], p. 44).

14   Lewis, *Antonio Gardano, Venetian Music Printer*, vol. 1, p. 103 n. 2.

15   *Missarum diversorum auctorum liber primus. Si dedero Obreth. Dr Franza Philippus Basiron. Dringhs Brumel. Nastu pas Gaspar. De sancto Antonio Piero de la rue* (Venice: Ottaviano Petrucci, 1509; RISM B/I, 1509[1]).

appeared sporadically in the decades that followed and was commonplace by the 1540s.

While composers dominated book covers from the 1530s and 1540s, title pages of anthologies from the mid-century onward point to a growing interest in editorial work. The shift coincided with a steady increase in the amount of information found on title pages, where we start to find accounts of the gestation of the work, praise for its composers, descriptions of the verbal texts, and even performance suggestions.[16] Included in this new information age were greater occurrences of descriptions of editing and of claims of correctness. On the title pages of chanson books from the 1540s Tylman Susato, among the first musicians active in the print trade, designated himself "Imprimeur et Correcteur de Musique" [Printer and Corrector of Music].[17] Organist, printer, and editor Claudio Merulo highlighted his role as editor of a madrigal volume by Domenico Micheli with the phrase "con ogni diligenza revisti da Claudio da Correggio" [with every diligence edited by Claudio da Correggio].[18] His edition of Verdelot's first and second books of madrigals advertised works "da molti e importanti errori con ogni diligentia corretti da Claudi da Correggio" [with many important errors corrected with every diligence by Claudio da Correggio].[19] As Rebecca Edwards argues, Merulo was true to his word; his partbooks demonstrate an unusual level of accuracy and reliable copy.[20] Claims of accuracy became a mark of title pages from the Venetian firms of Antonio Gardano and Girolamo Scotto which regularly included the tag "con ogni diligentia corretti" [corrected with every diligence] from 1539 onward.[21]

---

16   Lucien Febvre and Henri-Jean Martin, *The Coming of the Book: The Impact of Printing 1450–1800*, trans. David Gerard (London: Verso, 1976), p. 82; originally published as *L'apparition du livre* (Paris: Editions Albin Michel, 1958).

17   Lothar Wolf, *Terminologische Untersuchungen zur Einführung des Buchdrucks im französischen Sprachgebiet*, Beihefte zur Zeitschrift für romanische Philologie, 174, series ed. Kurt Baldinger (Tübingen: Max Niemeyer, 1979), p. 183.   Susato also used the formulation "correctement imprimees en Anvers, par Tylman Susato" [correctly printed in Antwerp, by Tylman Susato].   For bibliographic descriptions of the chanson books, see Kristine K. Forney, "Tielman Susato, Sixteenth-Century Music Printer: An Archival and Typographical Investigation" (Ph.D. diss., University of Kentucky, 1979), pp. 279–322.

18   *Madrigali ... nuovamente dati in luce et con ogni diligenza revisti da Claudio da Correggio, a sei voci, libro terzo* (Venice: s.n., 1567; RISM A/I, M2678).   See Rebecca Edwards, "Claudio Merulo: Servant of the State and Musical Entrepreneur in Later Sixteenth-Century Venice (Ph.D. diss., Princeton University, 1990).

19   *Il madrigali del primo et secondo libro di Verdelot a quattro voci; nuovamente ristampati, et da molti e importanti errori con ogni diligentia corretti da Claudi da Correggio* (Venice: Claudio da Correggio, 1566; RISM A/I, V1238 and B/I, 1566²²).   See Alfred Einstein, "Claudio Merulo's Ausgabe der Madrigale des Verdelot," *Sammelbände der Internationalen Musikgesellschaft* 8/2 (1907): 220–54 for an account of Merulo's changes to Verdelot's settings, which included the placement of accidentals before the relevant note, adjustments to ligatures, text underlay, and corrections of printing errors.

20   Edwards, "Claudio Merulo: Servant of the State and Musical Entrepreneur," p. 198 n. 50.

21   For early examples, see *Il terzo libro de i madrigali novissimi di Archadelth a quattro voci, insieme con alchuni di Constantio Festa, & altri dieci bellissimi a voci mudate.*

Printers may have used such claims of editorial work to distinguish their volumes from rival publications. Scotto's shortened edition of the *Motetti del frutto a quatro voci* (Venice, 1562) uses the phrase "Novamente coretti e stampati" [newly corrected and published] to distinguish it from the first edition printed by Gardano in 1539, and Gardano's and Scotto's identical editions of 1549.[22] Antonio Gardano used the phrase "per Antonio Gardano stampati & corretti" [published and corrected by Antonio Gardano] to differentiate his own first edition of *Il primo libro de le Muse a cinque voci* (Venice, 1555) from the earlier Roman one by Antonio Barrè.[23] Gardano's attempt at credibility contrasts sharply with the ambivalent attitude toward editorship expressed earlier in his career. Mary Lewis proposes that in his first four years of activity in Venice Gardano edited two anthologies from the *Motetti del frutto* series (RISM B/I, 1538[4] and RISM B/I, 1539[3]), the chanson collection *Venticinque canzone francese* (RISM B/I, 1538[19]), and the first book of madrigals by various composers for five (RISM B/I, 1542[16]) and four (RISM B/I, 1542[17]) voices.[24] Yet Gardano left his name as editor off all title pages with the exception of *Venticinque canzone francese*. A change of attitude can be detected in German-speaking lands as well. In 1558 and 1559 the Nuremberg firm of Johannes vom Berg and Ulrich Neuber issued a three-volume motet anthology that reworked Hans Ott's *Novum et*

Novamente con ogni diligentia stampati, & corretti (Venice: Girolamo Scotto, 1539; RISM A/I, 1539[23]); *Il quarto libro di madrigali d'Archadelt a quarto voci composti ultimamente insieme con alcuni madrigali de altri autori novamente con ogni diligentia stampati et corretti* (Venice: A. Gardane, 1539; RISM B/I, 1539[24]); and *Il terzo libro de madrigali di Verdelotto insieme con alcuni altri bellissimi madrigali di Constantio Festa, et altri eccellentissimi auttori, novamente stampati, e con summa diligentia corretti* (Venice: Ottavio Scotto, 1537; RISM B/I, 1537[11]=RISM A/I, V1226). Lewis (*Antonio Gardano, Venetian Music Printer*, vol. 1, p. 13 and n. 53) notes two examples from Roman and Parisian music books of the 1520s.

22 See *Excellentiss. autorum diverse modulationes que sub titulo Fructus vagantur per orbem, ab Antonio Gardane nuper recognite. Liber primus cum quatuor vocibus* (Venice: Ant. Gardane, 1549; RISM B/I, 1549[10]); *Excelentiss. autorum diverse modulationes que sub titulo Fructus vagantur per orbem, a Hieronymo Scoto nuper recognite & edite. Liber primus cum quatuor vocibus* (Venice: G. Scotto, 1549; RISM B/I, 1549[10a]); and Bernstein, *Music Printing in Renaissance Venice*, catalogue no. 218, pp. 600–01.

23 *Il primo libro de le Muse a cinque voci composto da diversi eccellentissimi musici novamente per Antonio Gardano stampati & corretti con la gionta d'una canzon & uno madregale a otto voci* (Venice: A. Gardane, 1555; RISM B/I, 1555[25]) and *Primo libro delle muse a cinque voci madrigali de diversi authori* (Rome: A. Barré, 1555; RISM B/I, 1555[26]). Mary Lewis argues that Barrè's edition likely preceded Gardano's since the title page of the latter's advertises "with the addition of a canzon and a madrigal for eight voices" [con la gionta d'una canzon & uno madregale a otto voci] (*Antonio Gardano, Venetian Music Printer*, vol. 1, p. 60 and n. 5). To Barrè's volume, Gardano added Jachet Berchem's setting of Petrarch's sestina *Alla dolc'ombra* and the eight-voice madrigal *Madonna hor che direte*. On the complicated relationships of the *Muse* editions, see Lewis, *Antonio Gardano, Venetian Music Printer*, vol. 2, pp. 60–63 and John Steele, "Antonio Barrè: Madrigalist, Anthologist and Publisher in Rome—Some Preliminary Findings," in Richard Charteris (ed.), *Essays on Italian Music in the Cinquecento* (Sydney: Frederick May Foundation for Italian Studies and the Italian Institute for Culture, 1990), pp. 92–5.

24 Lewis, *Antonio Gardano, Venetian Music Printer*, vol. 1, p. 108.

insigne opus musicum (Nuremberg, 1537) and *Secundus tomus novi operis musici* (Nuremberg, 1538). Though Ott left his editorial involvement off the title pages in the 1530s, the title page of the first volume of the Berg/Neuber trilogy highlighted the editorial reworking, which included a reordering of the motets according to composer and the addition of 40 motets not found in Ott's earlier volumes.[25] Here the claim of extensive revision is accurate; among the 224 motets in three volumes, only 47 are taken from the first edition—30 motets from Ott's first volume and 17 from his second.[26]

At the same time composers expressed a renewed interest in the accuracy and reliability of editions of their music. Francesco Viola, Vincenzo Ruffo, Orlande de Lassus, and Leonhard Lechner each went to great lengths to see their works through the press, mirroring conditions found in the book world at large where it was not uncommon for authors to do their own proofreading.[27] More important, their editorial oversight was emphasized and distinguished from their role as composers on title pages of their works. The title page of Viola's first book of four-voice madrigals indicates the volume was "Autore corretto & dato in Luce" [corrected and brought to light (published) by the author] (Venice: Antonio Gardane, 1550).[28] Gardano's new edition of Ruffo's first book of chromatic madrigals (Venice, 1552) advertises works "newly reprinted and corrected with every diligence by the author" ["Autore Nouamente con ogni diligentia Ristampato & Corretto"].[29] The title page of Orlande de Lassus's third book of five-voice *Teutscher Lieder* boasts that the composer "corrected and prepared [the volume] for printing himself" ["selbst Corrigiert, unnd inn Truck verordnet worden"].[30] His student, Leonhard Lechner, followed with three-voice *Teutsche Lieder* that he "composed, corrected, and prepared for press"

---

25 *Novum et insigne opus musicum, sex, quinque, et quatuor vocum, cuius in Germania hactenus nihil simile usquam est editum* (Nuremberg: J. von Berg & U. Neuber, 1558; RISM B/I, 1558⁴). See RISM B/I, 1559¹ and RISM B/I, 1559² for the remaining volumes in the trilogy.

26 Gustavson compares the two editions in "Hans Ott, Hieronymus Formschneider," vol. 1, pp. 198–200.

27 For examples, see Simpson, *Proof-Reading in the Sixteenth, Seventeenth, and Eighteenth Centuries*, pp. 1–45; and Bernstein, *Music Printing in Renaissance Venice*, pp. 150–53. Cf. Georg Hoffman, "Writing without Leisure: Proofreading as Work in the Renaissance," *Journal of Medieval and Renaissance Studies*, 25 (1995): 17–31.

28 Lewis, *Antonio Gardano, Venetian Music Printer*, vol. 2, catalogue no. 150, pp. 187–9.

29 Ibid., vol. 2, catalogue no. 178, pp. 251–3 (*Il primo libro de madrigali cromatici a quatro voci con la gionta di alquanti madrigali del medesimo autore* Venice: Antonio Gardano, 1552; RISM A/I, R3067. On earlier editions, see the note for Gardano's edition of 1546 in ibid., vol. 1, catalogue no. 96, p. 538.

30 RISM A/I, L899. Lassus's attention to the appearance of his music in print likely dates back much earlier. Judging from the accuracy of the underlay of Italian texts, Donna Cardamone argues that Lassus may have corrected proofs for *Il primo libro dovesi contengono madrigali, vilanesche, canzoni francesi, e motetti a quattro voci* (Antwerp: Tylman Susato, 1555; RISM A/I, L756=RISM B/I, 1555²⁹), in Orlando di Lasso et al., *Canzoni villanesche and villanelle*, ed. Donna Cardamone, Recent Researches in the Music of the Renaissance, 82–3 (Madison, WI: A-R Editions Inc., 1991), p. xiv.

["Durch Leonardum Lechnerum Athesinum Componirt, Corrigirt, und inn Druck verfertigt"].[31]

Distinctions between the specializations of editing, printing, and composing created the necessary preconditions for the employment of professional editors, outside parties hired by printers for the express purpose of editing music books. Given the technical skills required for the job, professional editors tended to be either musicians or composers. Most held some form of regular employment at a court, city, educational, or religious institution. Their compensation for editing was flexible and often took the form of free copies of the edited book (which they could then sell off), other books from the shop, or some combination of cash and kind.[32] While some editors worked for multiple firms over the course of their career, others established long-term relationships with printers. The Venetian singer and composer Giulio Bonagiunta edited two sets of three-voice *canzoni alla napolitana*, eight anthologies of madrigals, and a collection of motets for the Scotto firm, all within the short span of 1565–68.[33] The employment of professionals like Bonagiunta reflected the increased specialization of roles evident in all aspects of the proto-industrial book trade of the late sixteenth century.[34] A good editor saved time, assured accuracy, and helped music pass from composer to consumer more efficiently. In the case of Bonagiunta, Jane Bernstein argues that the designation or its equivalent "Di novo posti in luce per Giulio Bonagionta da San Genesi" [Newly brought to light by Giulio Bonagionta of San Genesi] on title pages of some 15 Scotto editions indicates that his role extended to the sponsorship of music books as well.[35]

The benefits of using professional editors were most fully realized when music crossed cultural and linguistic regions, and hence required the hands of an editor to refashion it for a new audience. The transnational production of Italian music offers a compelling example of the critical role that editors played in the assembly,

---

31   RISM A/I, L1289.

32   See Harald Steiner, *Das Autorenhonorar – seine Entwicklungsgeschichte vom 17. bis 19. Jahrhundert* (Wiesbaden: Harrassowitz, 1998), pp. 257–67 and Walter Krieg, *Materialien zu einer Entwicklungsgeschichte der Bücher-Preise und des Autoren-Honorars vom 15. bis zum 20. Jahrhundert* (Vienna: Herbert Stubenrauch, 1953).

33   Music books edited by Bonagiunta are listed in Appendix 2 of Ongaro, "Venetian Printed Anthologies of Music," pp. 68–9. On the basis of similarities between some Scotto anthologies published between 1562 and 1565 and some of Bonagiunta's collections, Ongaro speculates that Bonagiunta "might have served as uncredited in-house editor" for the Scotto firm before 1565 (ibid., p. 63 n. 44). See RISM 1565[12], 1566[7], 1566[2], 1566[3], 1567[13], 1567[16], 1568[12], 1568[13], 1568[16], 1567[3], and a hitherto lost edition of *Il Gaudio, primo libro de madrigali … a tre voci* of 1567 (see Bernstein, *Music Printing in Renaissance Venice*, catalogue no. 297, pp. 727-9). Bonagiunta also edited volumes by Cipriano de Rore (1565[18], reprinted by Scotto in 1569 [R2515], and by his heirs in 1576 [R2516]), Orlande de Lassus (L786), Alessandro Striggio (1567[23]), and Giovanni Ferretti (F512).

34   Ongaro, "Venetian Printed Anthologies of Music," p. 57.

35   Bernstein, *Music Printing in Renaissance Venice*, pp. 143–4. Ongaro, "Venetian Printed Anthologies of Music," pp. 54–5 supports this hypothesis with evidence of a loan of 40 ducats, obtained on 25 September 1565 from the Procuratori of the church of St. Mark, that Bonagiunta may have used to underwrite music books.

adaptation, and marketing of music books. Northern editors anticipated the rate of musical literacy of the new target audience, to determine the level of difficulty of the contents, a suitable ordering scheme, how much or how little *musica ficta* to include, the level of precision required for text underlay and rules of prosody, and how much instruction should be given on technique and matters of taste. They assured the credibility of new, foreign music, thus greatly easing its reception in far-off places. Case studies of individual editors are discussed in Chapters 2–4. Here I will return to the title page, to analyze the effect of genre and geography on the rise in status of editors.

Title pages of the earliest northern madrigal anthologies from the 1580s all state the name of the editor. The Antwerp music printer Pierre Phalèse the Younger was the first to issue anthologies devoted to Italian secular song north of the Alps. Between 1583 and 1591 he printed four collections of madrigals; each featured music compiled by a different editor.[36] The title page of the first of the set, *Musica divina* (Antwerp, 1583), advertises works by 19 illustrious authors "raccolta da Pietro Phalesio" [collected by Pietro Phalesio]. For the three remaining anthologies, Phalèse farmed out the editorial work to local composers and musicians, Andreas Pevernage, Hubert Waelrant, and Englishman Peter Philips. Phalèse chose wisely. Pevernage may have served as music advisor to the master printer Christopher Plantin.[37] Waelrant was wellknown in the region as a madrigalist and, more importantly, as a professional music editor.[38] Between 1554 and 1558 he worked in partnership with the Antwerp-based printer Jean de Laet as the firm's publisher, bookseller, financial manager, and artistic director. Philips boasted a professional network that extended from his native England to Rome, where he made contacts with the English College. In 1591 he settled in Antwerp where he taught virginal lessons and formed associations with the city's key cultural backers.[39] The reputation of regional editors offset the

---

36 *Musica divina di XIX. autori illustri, a IIII. V. VI. et VII. voci, nuovamente raccolta da Pietro Phalesio, et data in luce. Nella quale si contengono i più excellenti madrigali che hoggidi si cantino* (Antwerp: P. Phalèse et J. Bellère, 1583; RISM B/I, 1583[15]); *Harmonia celeste di diversi eccellentissimi musici a IIII. V. VI. VII. et VIII. voci, nuovamente raccolta per Andrea Pevernage, et data in luce. Nella quale si contiene una scielta di migliori madrigali che hoggidi si cantino* (Antwerp: P. Phalèse & J. Bellère, 1583; RISM B/I, 1583[14]); *Symphonia angelica di diversi eccellentissimi musici a IIII. V. et VI. voci, nuovamente raccolta per Huberto Waelrant, et data in luce. Nella quale si contiene una scielta di migliori madrigali che hoggidi si cantino* (Antwerp: P. Phalèse & J. Bellère, 1585; RISM B/I, 1585[19]); and *Melodia olympica di diversi eccellentissimi musici a IIII. V. VI. et VIII. voci, nuovamente raccolta da Pietro Phillippi inglese, et data in luce. Nella quale si contengono i più eccellenti madrigali che hoggidi si cantino* (Antwerp: P. Phalèse et J. Bellère, 1591; RISM B/I, 1591[10]).

37 See Kristine K. Forney, "Pevernage, Andreas," in *The New Grove Dictionary of Music and Musicians*, 2nd edn, eds Stanley Sadie and John Tyrrell (London: Macmillan, 2001) [*New Grove II*], vol. 19, pp. 530–31.

38 Robert Weaver, "Waelrant, Hubert," in *New Grove II*, vol. 26, pp. 923–6. On his role in book production, see the same author's *Waelrant and Laet: Music Publishers in Antwerp's Golden Age* (Warren, MI: Harmonie Park Press, 1995).

39 John Steele: "Philips, Peter," *Grove Music Online*, ed. Laura Macy (Accessed 8 September 2006), <http://www.grovemusic.com>

relatively low recognition rate of foreign composers; none of them was named on the title pages, in marked contrast to the importance of composers' names on title pages of Venetian music books. These were anthologies compiled by and for a northern market.

A similar pattern of naming editors can be traced in motet anthologies from the early seventeenth century. The northern publication of motet anthologies was dominated by editors in German-speaking lands, where Venetian polychoral and Italian *concertato* idioms were highly prized.[40] Title pages of the 1610s–20s stressed the trope of the editor as collector, a designation that highlighted the process of gathering rather than later stages of editing. We find an early application of the term for Abraham Schadaeus, the editor of the first three parts of the motet series *Promptuarii musici* (Strasbourg, 1611–13).[41] The series attests to a continued German interest in late sixteenth-century polyphony and Venetian polychoral music, amidst the influx of the new Italian small *concertato* idiom. The title page to the first volume advertises motets "nunquam in Germania editis" [never before published in Germany] assembled by the rector of the grammar school at Speyer, Abraham Schadaeus, "Collectore" [Collector].[42] Here the metaphor of the editor as collector reinforced the claim that the motets appeared in Germany for the very first time—music gathered up by Schadaeus from far-off Italy. Schadaeus's associate and civic organist of Speyer, Caspar Vincentius, added a continuo part for the first three volumes and compiled all of the fourth part of the series in 1617, as its title page indicates: "Collegit vero et basi generali accommodavit Caspar Vincentius" [Collected and accommodated with a general bass by Caspar Vincentius].[43] By adopting Lodovico Viadana's technique of the figured bass (figures and other signs furnished above the bass line to indicate its harmonic realization), Vincentius guaranteed an expanded audience for the motets. A further three volumes of motets with basso continuo appeared under the same title, all by Johann Donfrid, "scholae Neccaro Rottenburgensium rectore" [Rector at the St Martin's school at Rottenburg]

---

40   See Table 5 of Jerome Roche, "'Aus den berühmbsten italiänischen Autoribus': Dissemination North of the Alps of the Early Baroque Italian Sacred Repertory Through Published Anthologies and Reprints," in Silke Leopold and Joachim Steinheuer (eds), *Claudio Monteverdi und die Folgen: Bericht über das Internationale Symposium Detmold 1993* (Kassel: Bärenreiter, 1998), pp. 26–7.

41   RISM B/I, 1611[1]; RISM B/I, 1612[3]; and RISM B/I, 1613[2].

42   Schadaeus was dismissed from the position of Rector in 1611; title pages for the rest of the series simply describe him as "senfftebergensi," from Senftenberg, Lusatia. The designation "Collectore" is retained on the title pages of parts 2–3.

43   *Promptuarii musici, sacras harmonias V. VI. VII. et VIII. vocum, e diversis, clarissimis huius et superioris aetatis authoribus, in Germania nusquam editis, collectas exhibentis. Pars quarta: quae exhibit Concentus varios selectioresque, qui omnibus a SS. Trinitatis Dominicis inclusivè inserviunt: cum spiritualibus Canticis, & sylva harmonica Deiparae Virgini sacra. Collegit vero et basi generali accommodavit Caspar Vincentius S. Andreae wormatiensis organoedus* (Strasbourg: A. Bertram, 1617; RISM B/I, 1617[1]). Vincentius produced and printed the third volume after Schadaeus had left Speyer (A Lindsey Kirwan, "Vincentius, Caspar," *New Grove II*, vol. 26, pp. 652–3).

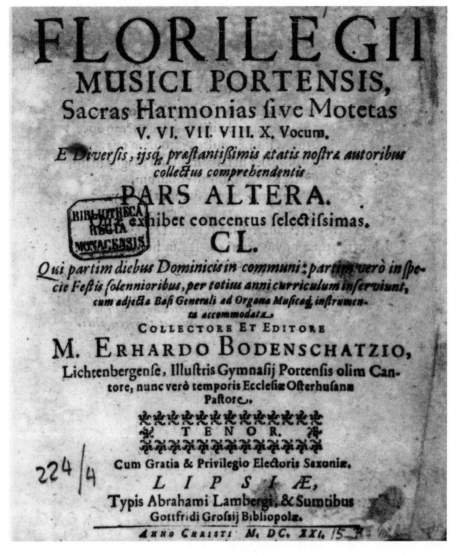

FLORILEGII
MUSICI PORTENSIS,
Sacras Harmonias five Motetas
V. VI. VII. VIII. X. Vocum.

E Diverfis, ijsq̃, præftantißimis ætatis noftræ autoribus
collectus comprehendentis

PARS ALTERA.

exhibet concentus felectifsimas.

CL.

Qui partim diebus Dominicis in communi: partim verò in fpe-
cie Feftis folennioribus, per totius anni curriculum inferviunt,
cum adjecta Bafi Generali ad Organa Muficæ, inftrumen-
ta accommodata.

COLLECTORE ET EDITORE

M. ERHARDO BODENSCHATZIO,

Lichtenbergenfe, Illuftris Gymnafij Portenfis olim Can-
tore, nunc verò temporis Ecclefiæ Ofterhufanæ
Paftore.

✿✿✿✿✿✿✿✿✿✿✿✿
TENOR.
✿✿✿✿✿✿✿✿✿✿✿✿

Cum Gratia & Privilegio Electoris Saxoniæ.

L I P S I Æ,

Typis Abrahami Lambergi, & Sumtibus
Gottfridi Grofsij Bibliopolæ.

ANNO CHRISTI M. DC. XXI.

Figure 1.1　　Title page of Erhard Bodenschatz, *Florilegii Musici Portensis ...*
Pars altera (Leipzig, 1621), Bayerische Staatsbibliothek München,
Musikabteilung: 4° Mus. pr. 1560

and "Collectore" [Collector] (Strasbourg, 1622–7).[44] The designation collector may
reflect the ambitious size of Donfrid's anthologies; he compiled huge volumes of
motets for two to four voices by Giovanni Francesco Anerio (75), Giacomo Finetti
(38), Antonio Cifra (47), Lodovico Viadana (40), Alessandro Grandi (21), Agostino

---

44　RISM B/I, 1622[2]; RISM B/I, 1623[2]; and RISM B/I, 1627[1]. Donfrid's profession and
role as "Collectore" are designated as such on the title pages of the first two volumes. The third
volume states simply "Opera et studio Joannis Donfrid, scholae Neccaro Rottenburgicae."

Agazzari (29), and Giovanni Nicolò Mezzogorri (9). The label is found again on the title page of the second part of *Florilegii Musici Portensis* (Leipzig, 1621), which designates Erhard Bodenschatz as "COLLECTORE ET EDITORE," indicating that he both compiled and published the volume (Figure 1.1).[45]

The titles of anthologies reinforced the collecting metaphors that described their editorship. The title of an anthology was a significant marketing tool; a catchy, prominently displayed title became the primary identification tag for the book. This was the name by which book agents referred to their wares, the name that appeared in publishers' catalogs, and what customers asked for when they came into the print shop. This importance did not go unnoticed by early commentators on the book industry. In his *Gepriesener Büchermacher* (Frankfurt, 1666), Aegidius Henning remarked "Was Ihr thut/ gebt mir dem Buch einen schönen Titul; So! So! Die Titul der Bücher/ nicht die Bücher selbst/ füllen deß Keuffers und Verteuffers Augen."[46] The title word *promptuarium* [storehouse, repository] strengthened the notion of the anthology as a container of musical objects. While growth metaphors such as *florilegium, flores, giardino,* and *hortus* evoked the image of Italian music literally transplanted onto northern soil.

Building on the growth imagery of its title, the title pages of the three-volume series *Hortus Musicalis* (1606–09) emphasized the editor's role in creating something new, an act of transformative imitation.[47] Their compiler, Michael Herrer, grouped five- and six-voice madrigals by Italian composers alongside contributions by Orlande de Lassus, Giaches de Wert, and Philippe de Monte—composers of northern origin but with strong Italian ties. Herrer substituted his own Latin sacred texts for the racier Italian originals to create pieces better suited to the religious sensibilities of his Catholic audience. As a Master of Arts, Augustinian canon, and dean of foundations in Baumberg, Suben am Inn, St Nicolai (near Passau), and Strassburg an der Gurk,

---

45 *Florilegii Musici Portensis, sacras harmonias sive motetas V. VI. VII. VIII. X. vocum. E diversis, iisque praestantissimis aetatis nostrae autoribus collectus comprehendentis. Pars altera. Quae exhibit concentus selectissimas … Collectore et editore M. Erhardo Bodenschatzio, …* (Leipzig: A. Lamberg, 1621; RISM B/I, 1621[2]).

46 "Whatever you do, give me a book with an appealing title; Yes! Yes! The title of a book, not the book itself, fills the eyes of buyers and sellers" (Aegidius Henning, *Gepriesener Büchermacher, Oder Von Bückern / und Bücher machen* [Frankfurt, 1666]; reprint in *Das Buchwesen im Barock* [Munich: Kraus, 1981], pp. 154–5 [pp. 106–7 of the original]).

47 *Hortus musicalis, variis antea diversorum authorum Italiae floribus consitus, jam verò latinos fructus, mira suavitate quinque vocibus concinendos, piè & artificiosè germinans. Authore R. P. Michaele Herrerio, ad S. Nicolai Strasburgi praeposito. Liber primus* (Passau: M. Nenninger, 1606; RISM B/I, 1606[6]); *Hortus musicalis, variis antea diversorum authorum Italiae floribus consitus, jam verò latinos fructus, mira suavitate quinque & sex vocibus concinendos, piè & artificiosè parturiens. Authore R. P. Michaele Herrerio, ad S. Nicolai Strasburgi praeposito. Liber secundus* (Munich: A. Berg, 1609; RISM B/I, 1609[14]); and *Hortus musicalis, variis antea diversorum authorum Italiae floribus consitus, jam verò latinos fructus, mira suavitate & artificio. V. VI. VII. VIII. & pluribus vocibus concinendos, piè & religiosè parturiens. Authore R. P. Michaele Herrerio, … Liber tertius, …* (Munich: A. Berg, 1609; RISM B/I, 1609[15]).

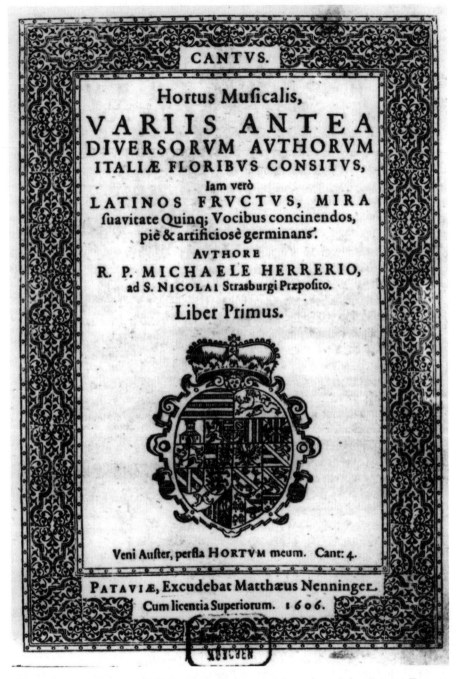

Figure 1.2   Title page of Michael Herrer, *Hortus Musicalis ... Liber Primus* (Passau, 1606), Bayerische Staatsbibliothek München, Musikabteilung: 4° Mus. pr. 24

Herrer's name lent credibility to the newly compiled contrafacta.[48] To promote the series, Herrer's name appears centerd on the title page of each anthology, in a single line of text in Roman capital letters. The mere act of placing the editor's name on a single line using a consistent font contrasts with earlier title pages that divide even major words with hyphens and freely mix type sizes.[49] An even more telling tribute is the designation "AVTHORE" [author] on the title pages of all three volumes (Figure 1.2). Here we find the complete transfer of authorial function from the composer to the editor.

Title pages of sixteenth-century music books chart a growing interest in editorial work and greater public recognition for the editor who completed it. The importation and reproduction of music by Italian composers accelerated the rise of the professional editor in German-speaking lands, where title pages used rhetorical strategies to emphasize the editor's role in collecting music for publication, and the novelty produced from his new mixture. Some of these strategies were not new, to be sure. The tag "never before published in Germany" recalls earlier claims of music "nuovamente dati in luce" [newly brought to light].[50] Likewise, advertising the music of diverse composers was a commonplace gesture in the Venetian book trade from the mid-century onward. Yet the occurrence of such tags, alongside the naming of the editor, testifies to an appreciation for editorial work that is most pronounced in German-speaking lands. The naming of an editor became highly functional as a guarantee of a book's worth and status in the German music book trade, replacing the condition of anonymity that characterized early editing.

The highlighting of authorship and the strategies of persuasion first seen on title pages were reinforced upon opening an anthology and finding the dedicatory preface and address to the reader, which appeared under various headings "Ad lectorem," "An den Leser," "Günstiger Leser," and "Ad Musicum benevolum." Scholars have been quick to dismiss prefaces as unreliable indicators of the editorial practices that they frame.[51] Early modern book dedications are laden with formulas, rhetorical tropes, and strategies of persuasion that only rarely depart from the convention of obligatory bows to patrons, humble offerings of artistic endeavors, and requests for their acceptance. Yet their perceived status as commonplace appendages overshadows

---

48   For biography, see Horst Leuchtmann and A. Lindsey Kirwan, "Herrer, Michael," *New Grove II*, vol. 11, p. 438.

49   Walter J. Ong explores the organization of sixteenth-century title pages, which he characterizes as a shift from hearing-dominance to sight-dominance, in *Orality and Literacy: The Technologizing of the Word* (London: Routledge, 1988; reprint of London: Methuen, 1982), pp. 117–23.

50   Ott made the claim in *Novum et insigne opus musicum ... cuius in Germania hactenus nihil simile usquam est editum* (Nuremberg: Formschneider, 1537), though eight of the motets had already appeared in the *Liber selectarum cantionum* (Augsburg, 1530) (Gustavson, "Hans Ott, Hieronymus Formschneider," vol. 1, pp. 210–11 and p. 211 n. 6).

51   Leah Price, *The Anthology and the Rise of the Novel: From Richardson to George Eliot* (New York: Cambridge University Press, 2000), p. 12. An exception is Dagmar Schnell, *In lucem edidit: Der deutsche Notendruck der ersten Hälfte des 17. Jahrhunderts als Kommunikationsmedium. Dargestellt an den Vorreden* (Osnabrück: Der Andere Verlag, 2003), which remains the most extensive study of German music book prefaces.

evidence that contemporaries regarded dedicatory prefaces as tools of cultural power—commodities of exchange that served the needs of both their authors and recipients. Martha Feldman argues that dedications and dedicatory prefaces formed part of a broader "literary dialogics" that involved speaking to and among patrons, composers, enemies, followers, teachers, students, and potential consumers.[52] Genette argues that book prefaces served two main functions: to convince us of the book's worth and use (a goal that can be traced back to Cicero's *De inventione* and *Rhetorica ad Herennium*) and to guide the book's readers.[53] The analysis of dedications and prefaces is especially important for the study of anthologies since it can shed light on an editor's attitude toward his work, his perception of its reception, how an editor acquired his sources, and how he thought they should be performed.

Dedications and Prefaces

Dedications and prefatory letters to music books inherited a rich literary history. Manuals on letter-writing made the formula of dedicatory address accessible to literate audiences across German-speaking lands.[54] One of the most widely circulated texts was Tobiam Hinzium's *Epistel und Verbungsbüchlein*, which first appeared in Leipzig in 1627, and by 1646 had received its fourth edition. It offers 438 pages of advice and tips, complete with a 25-page index with subject headings leading the user to examples for daily use, ranging from formulas for weddings, baptisms, and funerals, to "Von Brieffen darinnen man bittet" [Letters of Supplication] and "Von Brieffen darinn man jemandes dancket" [Letters of Thanks]. Hinzium groups examples according to the five structural elements of a letter: (1) salutation; (2) preface; (3) the subject of the letter; (4) petition; and (5) conclusion. These categories constitute the basic formulas for dedicatory address in the Renaissance, as codified in Justus Lipsius's *Epistolica Institutio* [Principles of Letter-Writing] of 1591.[55]

The dedicatory letter was framed by a conventional salutation and conclusion. Most important for its visual impact, the opening salutation publicized the patron's name in large type at the head of the dedicatory letter. The act of naming was followed by a territorial mapping, often comprised of a lengthy list of regions under the dedicatee's jurisdiction. Editor Michael Herrer systematically mapped the territories of the Archduke of Austria at the start of his preface to the madrigal anthology *Hortus Musicalis [...] Liber Secundus* (Munich: Adam Berg, 1609):

---

52   Martha Feldman, *City Culture and the Madrigal at Venice* (Berkeley: University of California Press, 1995), p. 48.

53   See Losse, *Sampling the Book*, pp. 12–13 for Cicero and pp. 57–78, 115–18 for Genette, citing his *Seuils* (Paris: Editions du Seuil, 1987), p. 183.

54   Reinhard Nickisch counts 76 letter-writing handbooks from the seventeenth century (*Die Stilprinzipien in den deutschen Briefstellern des 17. und 18. Jahrhunderts: Mit einer Bibliographie zur Briefschreiblehre (1474–1800)* [Göttingen: Vandenhoeck & Ruprecht, 1969], pp. 160–280, quoted in Blake Lee Spahr, "The Letter as a Literary Sub-Genre in the German Baroque," *Chloe*, 6 [Amsterdam: Rodopi, 1987]: 654).

55   Justus Lipsius's *Epistolica Institutio*, eds and trans R.V. Young and M. Thomas Hester (Carbondale: Southern Illinois University Press, 1996).

TO THE MOST SERENE AND MOST REVEREND LORD, LORD LEOPOLD,
Archduke of Austria, Duke of Burgundy, Styria, Carinthia, Carniola, and Slavonia, etc.
Bishop of Strasbourg and Passau, to His Most Kind Lord.[56]

The conclusion of the dedication reinforced the opening with an offering of servitude
"To Your Serenity, from your most obedient servant, Michael Herrer" ["Seren: Tuae
seruus obedientiss. Michaël Herrerius"].

But it was in the intervening preface, narration, and petition that the dedicatory
letter achieved its primary goals of convincing us of the book's worth and guiding
its readers. Not all dedications evoked the same rhetorical strategies to the same
degree to achieve these ends. While some editors turned to the musical content to
demonstrate the book's worth, others argued for the larger role of music in social
and religious contexts. Likewise the amount and type of guidance depended on the
target audience. An assessment must consider both the motivation of editors and the
cultural contexts in which they worked.

Editors used the narration and petition to ward off criticism over the perceived
frivolousness and cheap profit of their activities. Anthologies compiled from
previously printed works became a target for criticism. One defence was to pen
the dedicatory text in Latin, a language that lent scholarly weight and authority to
music books of all kinds. Nuremberg printer Paul Kauffmann used Latin in his
address "Omnibus Musices amatoribus" [To All Music Lovers] that prefaces the
madrigal anthology *Fiori del giardino* (Nuremberg, 1597).[57] Here Kauffmann asks
for protection "In order that the rules of judgment ... not condemn these songs which
were seized from similar books, and throw them away as something which should
be censored."[58] In his negotiation with readers, Kauffmann claims to have their
interests at heart: "I would rather arrange in this most praised musical art and would
rather collect chiefly those songs ... which I recall were previously printed in Italy,
but whose copies either because they sold too quickly never reached these borders,
or because they were able to frighten buyers, not without cause, by their excessive
price."[59] Finally, Kauffmann professes that he was urged by others, a common

---

56   RISM B/I, 1609[14]. "SERENISSIMO ET REVERENDISSIMO PRINCIPI AC
DOMINO, DOMINO LEOPOLDO ARCHDUCI Austriae, Duci Burgundiae, Styriae,
Carinthinae, Carniolae, et Sclavoniae, etc. Episcopo Argentinensei et Passaviensi Domino
suo Clementissimo" (Harrison Powley III, "*Il trionfo di Dori:* A Critical Edition," 3 vols [Ph.
D. diss., University of Rochester, Eastman School of Music, 1974], vol. 2, p. 84).

57   *Fiori del giardino di diversi eccellentissimi autori à quattro, cinque, sei, sette,
otto, et novi voci. Raccolte con molta diligentia e novamente date in luce* (Nuremberg: P.
Kauffmann, 1597; RISM B/I, 1597[13]). The preface is signed "Typographus," which suggests
that Kauffmann may have had a hand in the anthology's compilation as well.

58   RISM B/I, 1597[13], fol. 1v: "ne judicii præcipites, (ut sæpè experiri cogimur)
comprehensas eimodi libris cantiones contemnant & velut deculpatas abjiciant" (Bayerische
Staatsbibliothek München, Musikabteilung, 4° Mus. pr. 2724/7). All English translations of
excerpts of the preface are taken from Powley, *Il trionfo di Dori*, vol. 2, p. 49.

59   RISM B/I, 1597[13], fol. 1v: "horas meas subsecivas vix possum, quin in hac laudatiβima
arte Musica collocem, easque potiβimum cantiones colligam, ac velut sub signa quasque
sua revocem, quæ quidem in Italiâ terrâ, Musicæ velut unicâ ætatis nostræ nutriculâ, prius
impressæ sunt, sed quarem vel exemplaria nimis cito vendita ad hos oras non pervênere,

defence mechanism, that here doubles as an advertisement for past and future work from his shop:

> After I published in past years three song books, musical jewels printed with my type [*Gemma musicalis I–III* (Nuremberg: Katharina Gerlach, 1588–90)], thereupon I am still daily urged, even by the demand of many distinguished men, to continue such efforts. [...] Because I firmly believe that my plan will be proven correct by as many prudent men and supporters of music as possible, I wish to receive suggestions, either singly or all together, from those into whose hands the present work or others like it may have come. [...] if you will sing those songs more often and most attentively with friends, whereby it will come so that you may be able to proclaim of their goodness better and more equally, and also even courage is given me to prepare similar works in the future. Farewell.[60]

Kauffmann creates a line of communication that extends back to his predecessor, Katharina Gerlach, and forward to the firm's success of the early seventeenth century.

Validation was also sought through interlocutors, including Minerva, the Roman goddess of wisdom, medicine, the arts, science, trade, and war. Minerva made frequent appearances in early modern music books. Herrer petitioned to Archduke Leopold so that "the nakedness of this little work will be clothed with Your Serenity's most honorable title and indeed it will be able to defend itself more quickly from the affronts and maliciousness of Momus."[61] Anthologist Christian Hildebrand addressed Minerva directly in an elaborate dedicatory defence "Ad Momum" (Figure 1.3) for his instrumental anthology *Ander Theil, ausserlesener lieblicher Paduanen, und* [...] *Galliarden* (Hamburg, 1609).[62]

---

aut pretio nimio emtorem non immeritò absterrere postuerunt" (Bayerische Staatsbibliothek München, Musikabteilung, 4° Mus. pr. 2724/7).

60 RISM B/I, 1597[13], fol. 1v: "POSTEA QVAM SVPERIORIBVS annis tres Cantionum libros, GEMMAE MVSICALIS nomine proscriptos typis meis in publicum volgavi, & exinde etiam cotidiano velut flagitio multorum præstantium virorum ad labores ejuscemodi perseverandos instigatus sum; [...] Quod meum consilium quam plurimis cordatis viris & Musices cultoribus omnino me probaturum confido, omnes simul & singulos, in quorum manus hoc præsens opus, eique alia consimilia pervenient [...] si eas sæpius & attentiβimè cum amicis cecineris, quo fiet, ut & melius æquiusque de illarum bonitate pronunciare poβis, & mihi etiam in consimilibus operibus porrò quoq[ue] adornandis animus addatur: vale" (Bayerische Staatsbibliothek München, Musikabteilung, 4° Mus. pr. 2724/7).

61 RISM B/I, 1609[14]: "Tvae nomen ac praeclarum patrocinium suppleatur, Hinc enim fiat, vt nuditas huius Opusculi, Sere: Tvae honorisicentissimo titulo vestita, se alacrius ab injurijs et claumnijs Momorum edfendere valeat," cited in Powley, *Il trionfo di Dori*, vol. 2, p. 85 with English translation.

62 *Ander Theil, ausserlesener lieblicher Paduanen, und auch so viel Galliarden, mit fünff Stimmen, auff allerley Instrumenten, und insonderheit auff Fiolen zu gebrauchen. Hiebevor im Druck nie aussgangen. Jetzt aber allen der edlen Music Liebhabern (so den Text nicht brauchen) zu Nutz und frommen colligirt, und mit Verlegung an Tag gegeben, durch Christian Hildebrand, ...* (Hamburg: P. von Ohr Erben, 1609; RISM B/I, 1609[30]).

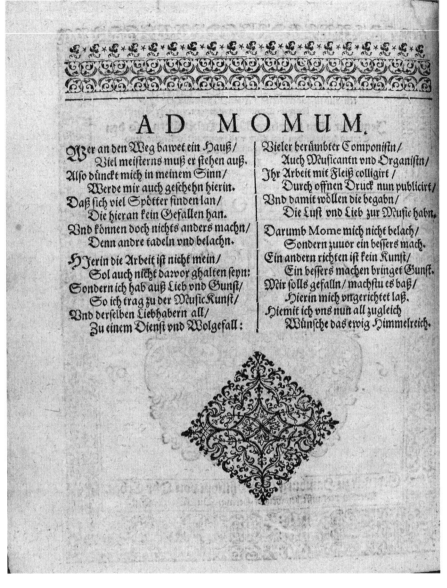

Figure 1.3   "Ad Momum," from Christian Hildebrand, *Ander Theil, ausserlesener lieblicher Paduanen* (Hamburg, 1609), fol. 1v, Herzog August Bibliothek Wolfenbüttel: 1.3.5 Musica (13)

Hildebrand's defence rests with claims of diligence ["mit Fleiß colligirt"] and novelty ["Durch offnen Druck nun publicirt"]—all for the enjoyment of lovers of music ["Liebhabern"].

Minerva is evoked again by Valentin Diezel in his preface to *Erster Theil lieblicher, welscher Madrigalien* (Nuremberg, 1624), an anthology of Italian madrigals with secular German texts by Diezel.[63] Diezel dedicated the anthology to the Greater Council (naming members Paul Pessler the Elder, Paul Sidelmann, and Leonhard Beer), the merchants, and music lovers of Nuremberg, where he worked as Cantor at the school of St. Sebald. Here he faults critics like Momus and Zoilius "that soon undertake everything themselves, and turn around what otherwise had good intentions, to infer, to criticize others ... to despise."[64] In the introduction to the address Diezel explained the gestation of the volume:

> these present foreign madrigals I collected many years ago, when I was still unmarried, and not as I am now, as many wish to have supposed, having set secular German words to the music, and more recently adorned them with Latin captions. For many reasons, at that time I was neither inclined nor motivated to publish the same through the public press, but rather was following an old and common proverb: Whoever wants to live in the street, will have to face up to defeat.[65]

Genette labels such mention of future criticism *paratonnerres* [lightning rods], a protective device for warding off or pre-empting possible disapproval.[66] Each critical remark is systematically met with a possible defence:

> And they might finally say: It would be a trifling thing to underlay foreign madrigals with German texts. The following should be their answer, as was said by Terrence [*Phormio* 16]: "That the prize is offered to all who cultivate the art of poetry."[67]

---

63 *Erster Theil lieblicher, welscher Madrigalien, auss den berühmtesten Musicis italicis mit allem Fleiss zusammen colligirt, mit 3. 4. 5. 6. 7. unnd 8 Stimmen, darunter deutsche weltliche Text applicirt, auch mit lateinischen Lemmatibus gezieret, und in Druck verfertiget, durch Valentinum Diezelium witzenhusanum Hassum* ... (Nuremberg: S. Halbmayer, 1624; RISM B/I, 1624[16]).

64 RISM B/I, 1624[16], cantus partbook, fol. 2v: "die alles/ was sonsten an vnd für sich gut gemeynet/ miß zu deuten/ zu tadeln/ bey andern ... zu verachten." Exemplar Uppsala, Universitetsbiblioteket: Utl. vok. Mus. i tr. 184. All English translations of this preface are taken from Powley, *Il trionfo di Dori*, vol. 2, pp. 320–22.

65 RISM B/I, 1624[16], cantus partbook, fol. 2r: "diese gegenwertige Welsche *Madrigalien* hab ich vor vielen abgewichenen Jahren/ da ich noch außer Ehestandts gewesen/ vnd nicht allererst jetzt/ wie es wol etliche darfür holten möchten/ zusammen *colligirt*, mit Teutschen weltlichen Texten damals vnterlegt/ vnd newlicher Zeit mit Lateinischen *Lemmatibus* gezieret/ bin aber niemals/ vieler Vrsachen halber/ weder gesinnet noch gewillet gewesen/ dieselbigen durch den öffentlichen Druck zu *publi*ciren/ sonderlich aber/ weil mir wol bewust/ daß es gehe nach dem alten gemeinen Sprichwort: Wer will bawenan die Strassen/ Der muß die Leute redden lassen."

66 Losse, *Sampling the Book*, p. 66, citing Genette, *Seuils*, p. 192.

67 RISM B/I, 1624[16], cantus partbook, fols 2v–3r: "Sie möchten auch endlich für geben: Es were ein gerings Ding, deutsche Text unter Welsche Madrigalien appliciren. So sollen sie

Here Diezel reminds the reader of his dual role as editor and poet.

The anxiety over the reception of translated work reflected a growing fear among editors in response to the expanding commerce of books, the rise of unauthorized editions, and book censorship by the Church.[68] Such concerns may have prompted Daniel Lyttich to pen a lengthy dedicatory preface to *Musicalische Streitkräntzelein* (Nuremberg, 1612), an anthology based on *Il trionfo di Dori* (Venice, 1592) now "written with gracious favor and with amusing artful German texts."[69] Lyttich felt pressure to defend the work on the basis that it was his brother, Johannes, "who took the pains upon himself to create a new and charming German text."[70] As Daniel explains, upon Johannes's death, he published the volume with the encouragement of "others well-versed in the art, who found it most useful."[71] Given his limited authorial role, Daniel rests the legitimacy of his work first on the value of music itself, "which, thanks to God, has risen so high in favor that many think it be the highest [art]."[72] Second, he praises his source, the "remarkable text" ["sonderlichen Text"] *Il trionfo di Dori*, which despite its high acclaim is "nevertheless unknown to us Germans, and hence somewhat inconvenient" ["vnnd aber vns Teutschen solche Welsche Text unbekannt/ vnnd derwegen etwas vnbequem"].[73] These rhetorical strategies of persuasion were amplified in the sequel, *Rest Musicalisches Streitkränzleins* (Nuremberg, 1613).[74] The volume opens with a Latin epigram

---

ihnen das zur antwort haben, was Terentius sagt: In medio omnibus palmam esse positam, qui artem tractant Musicam."

68   Losse, *Sampling the Book*, p. 63.

69   "zu günstigem gefallen/ mit lustigen Politischen Teutschen Texten," from the title page of *Musicalische Streitkränzlein: hiebevorn von den allerfürtrefflichsten unnd berühmtesten Componisten, in welscher Sprach, pro certamine, mit sonderlichem Fleiss, und auffs künnstlichst, mit 6. Stimmen auffgesetzt, und dannenhero Triumphi di Dori oder Dorothea genennet, und in Druck verfertiget, durch Johannen Lyttichium, ...* (Nuremberg: A. Wagenmann, 1612; RISM B/I, 1612[13]), fol. 1r. All examples are taken from the tenor partbook of the exemplar at Staatsbibliothek zu Berlin – Preußischer Kulturbesitz, Musikabteilung mit Mendelssohn-Archiv: Mus. ant. pract. L 1200.

70   RISM B/I, 1612[13], tenor partbook, fol. 2v: "als hat mein Bruder seeliger/ JOHANNES LITTICHIUS, Cantor zu Eißleben/ solche mühe auff sich genommen/ vnd neue Teutsche anmutige Text/ also daß die gantze Harmonia für sich bleibet/ vnd keine nota verendert wirdt/ drunter bracht/ daß sie also mit besserm verstande vnnd grössern lust können gebraucht werden." English trans. Powley, *Il trionfo di Dori*, vol. 2, p. 105.

71   RISM B/I, 1612[13], tenor partbook, fol. 2v: "Wann aber ich solche meines Brudern seeligen Arbeit andern/ welche dieser Kunst wol erfahren/ gezeiget/ vnnd ihr judicium darüber begehret/ die es für nützlich," (English trans. Powley, *Il trionfo di Dori*, vol. 2, p. 105).

72   RISM B/I, 1612[13], tenor partbook, fol. 2r: "ist die Musica nicht die geringste/ welche nun mehr/ GOTT lob/ so hoch gestiegen ist/ daß sichs von vielen ansehen lesset/ als wenn sie nicht mehr höher kommen köndte" (English trans. Powley, *Il trionfo di Dori*, vol. 2, p. 104).

73   RISM B/I, 1612[13], tenor partbook, fol. 2v (English trans. Powley, *Il trionfo di Dori*, vol. 2, p. 105).

74   *Rest musicalisches Streitkränzleins: hiebevorn von den allerfürtrefflichsten unnd berühmtesten Componisten, in welscher Sprach, pro certamine, mit sonderlichem Fleiss, und auffs künstlichst, mit 6. Stimmen auffgesetzt, und dannenhero Triomphi di Dori oder de*

penned by the theologian Martin Rinckart.[75] Rinckart addresses Salomon Engelhart, teacher at the Gymnasium in Eisleben and Cantor at St. Andreas church, who "legally acquired their entirety after the death of Johannes Lyttich, and put forth in print" ["nach absterben Herrn JOHANNIS LYTTICHII vollendt absolviert/ vnd in Druck gefördert/"].[76] Rinckart draws on the authority of Sethus Calvisius (1556–1615), his teacher and the most influential German theorist of his time, to confirm the credibility of Engelhart as a musician and leader.

> That choir of yours (I repeat) has no inconstancy but has all skill, even justly great enough for Calvisius, and also this work neither has the power of Venus nor the filth of impure Gods. So whoever you are, sing this work with pious dignity.[77]

Finally, he assures us of the textual purity of the volume, which made it suitable for use at the Gymnasium.

For sacred music the discourse of legitimacy manifests itself in references to Martin Luther and quotations from the Bible that affirmed the role of music in worship and praise. Burckhard Grossmann crafted an extended preface to his motet anthology *Angst der Hellen und Friede der Seelen* (Jena, 1623) that firmly established a scriptural authority for music.[78] Grossmann addressed the *Præfatio* to the volume's 16 contributors, his "dear, noble, and valued friends" ["Meinen besonders günstigen geliebten Herren, und fürnehmen werthen Freunden"], whom he commissioned to set the text of Psalm 116 of the Lutheran Bible. As a blessing for deliverance from death, the psalm text had special meaning for Grossmann, who was saved from a near-death illness in 1616.[79] Grossmann carefully annotated his preface with citations for Biblical and classical sources that reveal a rich scriptural tradition. His description of his trade, music, interweaves citations from 1 Chronicles 26, Sirach 40, Samuel, and Psalms 33, 34, 71, and 150, which give rise to a general call for praise: "Da ist es denn an ein Dancken vnd Loben gangen/ mit Singen und Klingen/

Dorothea genennet. ... in Druck gefördert, durch Solomonem Engelhart, ... (Nuremberg: B. Scherff, 1613; RISM B/I, 1613[13]).

75   Rinckart later set the *Trionfo di Dori* tunes to sacred texts as *Triumphi de Dorothea* (Leipzig: L. Köber, 1619; RISM B/I, 1619[16]). See Chapter 4.

76   RISM B/I, 1613[13], tenor partbook, title page, fol. 1r. All examples are taken from the exemplar at SLUB Dresden: Mus gri 22,2.

77   RISM B/I, 1613[13], tenor partbook, fol. 1v: "Nil levitatis habet (repeto) chorus iste, sed ARTIS OMNIA, sat magna judice CALVISIO. Nec valet hîc Veneris, spurcarum aut lerna Dearum; Quisquis es ergò, piâ hîc cum gravitate canis" (English trans. Powley, *Il trionfo di Dori*, vol. 2, p. 159).

78   *Angst der Hellen und Friede der Seelen, das ist: der CXVI. Psalm Davids durch etzliche vornehme Musicos im Chur und Fürstenthumb Sachsen, sehr künstlich und anmuhtig auff den Text gerichtet, mit V. IIII. und III. Stimmen componiret und von ihnen durch freundschrifftliches Süchen und Bitten impetrirt, colligirt ... zum Druck verlegt durch Burckhard Grossman, fürstl. Sächs. Amptschössern zu Jehna und Burgaw* (Jena: J. Weidner, 1623; RISM B/I, 1623[14]).

79   Christoph Wolff with Daniel R. Malamed (eds), *Anguish of Hell and Peace of Soul/ Angst der Hellen und Friede der Seelen, compiled by Burckhard Grossmann (Jena, 1623)*, Harvard Publications in Music, 18 (Cambridge: Harvard University Press, 1994), p. ix n. 2.

mit Harpffen/ auff dem Psalter mit zehen Seiten/ mit Posaunen/ Seiten/ Pfeiffen/ Cymbeln/ die wol geklungen/ ja alles was Odem gehabt ha in solchem Chor/ Gott Dancken/ Loben und Preisen müssen."[80] These musically rich passages reappear in various guises in Lutheran music prefaces of the early seventeenth century.[81]

Grossmann's commitment to God's praise in music is demonstrated by his inclusion of instructions on how to perform the motets. Following the *Præfatio*, Grossmann inserted performance instructions from one of the volume's contributors, Michael Praetorius:

> The late author Herr Praetorius [d. 1621], in transmitting this psalm, also provided a detailed *Ordinantz* and several variations indicating how he wanted the same performed; [...] Inasmuch as he passed away shortly thereafter and was transported into the heavenly *Capelle*, and after this work presumably composed not another note more, I have neglected neither this, his final farewell and swan song, nor, to his ever praiseworthy memory and in dutiful gratitude, his *Ordinantz*, which I should and have caused to be printed here, just as he sent it to me in his own hand.[82]

Praetorius's *Ordinantz* notes that his psalm motet is intended to be sung by five voices alone, but can accommodate five additional instrumental parts and/or *pro capella plena* [another choir] to strengthen the tutti passages.[83] Praetorius's flexible approach to performance resources was necessitated by the turmoil of the Thirty Years War, which Grossmann bemoaned earlier with an allusion to Saul's spear:

> I pass by the fact that in some towns and places where music formerly flourished and one praised God on Sundays and feast days with 16 and more voices in two, three, or more

---

80   *Præfatio*, fol. 3v, from the facsimile in Wolff, *Anguish of Hell*, plate 6. Grossmann most clearly adheres to Psalm 150, verses 3-5: "Praise him with the sound of the trumpet: praise him with the psaltery and harp. Praise him with the timbrel and dance: praise him with stringed instruments and organs. Praise him upon the loud cymbals: praise him upon the high sounding cymbals" (*The Holy Bible*, King James version [New York: Harper, 1995], p. 604).

81   See Chapter 4 for a discussion of Martin Rinckart's prefatory material to *Triumphi de Dorothea* (Leipzig, 1619).

82   RISM B/I, 1623[14], quinta vox partbook, p. ix: "Demnach seelig folgender Herr Author Prætorius, bey vbersendung dieses Psalms auch eine feine Ordinantz vnd etzliche Variationes auffgesetzet/ wie er denselben musicirt haben wil/ [...] Inmassen er denn kurtz darauff selig verstorben vnd in die Himlische Capell transferirt worden/ das vermuthlich er nach solcher Composition keine Noten mehr auffgesetzet/ Als hab ich zu seinem seeligen ewiglobwürdigen Gedächtniß/ vnd zu schuldiger Danckbarkeit/ dieses seines letzten Willens *Valete* und Schwanengesangs hierbey nicht vergessen/ sondern seine Ordinantz/ wie er dieselbe mir vnter seiner eigenen Hand zugeschicht/ anhero præfigiren lassen wollen vnd sollen," quoted from the facsimile in Wolff, *Anguish of Hell*, plate 18 with English trans., p. 255.

83   RISM B/I, 1623[14], quinta vox partbook, p. x: "Dieser 116. Psalm ist erstlich auff 5. *Vocal*-Stimmen zum singen allein gesetzet worden. Darnach kan er auch mit fünff *Instrumental*-Stimmen darzu gemacht werden/ und also werden es X. Stimmen [...] Man kan auch *pro Capella plena* noch einen andern Chor lassen herausser schreiben an dem Ort/ da das Wort *Tutti* gefunden: Dadurch denn die Music mercklichen gestercket wird," quoted from the facsimile in Wolff, *Anguish of Hell*, plate 19 with English trans., pp. 256–7.

choirs, one can now only engage an old unaccompanied quartet; that the cantors and organists, for whom the keys stick and the bellows freeze, complain and say: "What else is the cause but that the trustees of the church property or the church father flourish and bear Saul's spear of ignorance and contempt, and hate music as they hate poison?"[84]

Such conditions made Grossmann's commission appealing to composers of Saxony and Thuringia whose publishing opportunities were significantly compromised during wartime.

Far from being mere jargon-laden bows to patrons, prefaces contextualized music books by positioning them within the social, economic, and cultural milieu of their time. This was especially important for anthologies of repertory whose grouping and arrangement required explanation and, at times, a defence.

While prefaces provided a verbal introduction to music books, tables and indices offered a visual snapshot of the anthology. They gave consumers their first full glimpse of the volume's contents from the perspective of the editors who assembled them. The use of tables and indices presents a strong point of continuity with manuscript practices. Working with fourteenth-century sources, Emma Dillon has demonstrated the attention given to page layout and finding aids such as alphabetization, marginalia, and letter size, to locate and retrieve information in the *Roman de Fauvel*,[85] while Mary and Richard Rouse remind us that the fifteenth-century revival of the monastic scriptoria in Austria, Germany, and the Low Countries anticipated the attention to order and layout associated with the coming of the printed book.[86] Tables, indices, and other finding aids made the new technology of the printed music book easier to use. Their compilation was a vital part of editorial work that reinforced priorities of the anthology—the choice of composers, poetry, performance medium, and tonal structure. Individual approaches to compilation and working with sources—the editorial strategies for deciding what to include and how to revise and order it— will be addressed in detailed case studies in Chapters 2–4. Here, I will present a more general account of the methods of organizing music anthologies and their accompanying finding guides, that compares practices in German-speaking lands with models from across Europe.

---

84   RISM B/I, 1623[14], *Præfatio*, fol. 5r: "Davon lasse ich nun in manchen Städten und Ortern/ da vorweilen die *Musica floriret*, vnd man mit 16. vnd mehr Stimmen auff zwey drey vnd mehr Chören alle Son= vnd Festtage/ Gott angesungen/ gelobet vn[d] gepriesen/ jetzo aber nehrlich ein altes *Quatuor* vngesawet *figuriren* vnd bestellan kan/ *Cantores* vnd Organisten/ denen die *Claves* bestecken vnd die Bälge einfrieren/ klagen vn[d] sagen/ was machts anders/ denn daß die Vorsteher der Kirchengüter oder Kirchväter Sauls Spieß der *ignorantiae & contemptus* schwingen vnd führen/ vnd der Music Spinnenfeind seynd," quoted from the facsimile in Wolff, *Anguish of Hell*, plate 9, with English trans., p. x.

85   Emma Dillon, *Medieval Music-Making and the* Roman de Fauvel (Cambridge: Cambridge University Press, 2002).

86   Mary A. Rouse and Richard H. Rouse, "*Statim invenire*: Schools, Preachers, and New Attitudes to the Page," in Robert L. Benson and Giles Constable (eds), *Renaissance and Renewal in the Twelfth Century* (Cambridge: Harvard University Press, 1982), pp. 201–25.

The Order of Music Books

The most significant structural difference between Italian and German anthologies is the number of performance parts they contained. Italian music anthologies grouped repertory for a single ensemble size, be it two, three, four, or more parts. The average Venetian anthology of the mid-to-late sixteenth century counted only 16–24 leaves per partbook, making it much smaller than a contemporary German anthology, that often exceeded 60 folios. This meant that consumers of Venetian anthologies purchased a relatively small volume to suit their immediate performance needs. By contrast, German anthologies included music for a range of performance combinations that gave consumers access to a large quantity of music in a single volume. This ordering scheme was first used in German-speaking lands for the *Liber selectarum cantionum* (Augsburg, 1521), which grouped motets for six, five, and four voices.[87] The structure was retained for anthologies of sacred and secular music, though motet books from later in the century tend to group music according to the liturgical calendar for either Catholic or Protestant practice.[88]

Though the technique of grouping by ensemble size did not immediately catch on, Hans Ott made it standard practice for his motet anthologies of the late 1530s. Ott was an innovative editor whose ordering habits remained in use for decades to follow. He issued the two-volume *Novum opus et insigne musicum* (Nuremberg, 1537–38) with each part divided into three sections of six-, five-, and four-voice Latin motets.[89] Within each section Ott ordered the contents according to composer, a procedure found earlier in his *Der erst Teil. Hundert und ainundzweintzig newe Lieder* (RISM B/I, 1534[17]) and *Schöne auszerlesne Lieder* (RISM B/I, 1536[9]). The opening and closing positions of an anthology were devoted to the most popular composers or individual pieces, in this case Josquin des Prez, whom Ott praised as "the champion of this art" ["celeberrimu(s) huius artis Heroem"] in his preface to his first volume.[90] Each of the six-, five-, and four-voice sections opens with two or three motets attributed to Josquin; the final three motets of the first volume, and the final motet of the second, are likewise reserved for the master. Ott mentioned two other composers in his preface—Heinrich Isaac and Ludwig Senfl, whose works are

---

87   *Liber selectarum cantionum quas vulgo Mutetas appellant sex quinque et quatuor vocum* (Augsburg: Grimm & Wyrsung, 1520; RISM B/I, 1520[4]) (Gustavson, "Hans Ott, Hieronymus Formschneider," vol. 1, p. 223).

88   Each of Friedrich Lindner's three motet anthologies in the *Sacrarum Cantionum* series (Nuremberg: Katharina Gerlach, 1585–90) follows the liturgical year, beginning with Nativity and Circumcision, and ending with Advent. Johann Donfrid arranged the motets for *Promptuarii musici* (RISM B/I, 1622[2]; RISM B/I, 1623[2]; and RISM B/I, 1627[1]) in a liturgical cycle according to Catholic practice covering the entire church year in vols 1–2 and individual feasts and saints' days in vol. 3.

89   *Novum et insigne opus musicum, sex, quinque, et quatuor vocum, cuius in Germania hactenus nihil simile usquam est editum* (Nuremberg: H. Grapheus [Formschneider], 1537; RISM B/I, 1537[1]) and *Secundus tomus novi operis musici, sex, quinque et quatuor vocum, nunc recens in lucem editus ...* (Nuremberg: H. Grapheus, 1538; RISM B/I, 1538[3]).

90   See the facsimile and translation in Gustavson, "Hans Ott, Hieronymus Formschneider," vol. 2, Appendix 3, pp. 561–8.

positioned in close proximity to Josquin's motets. Ott hid the music of the lesser-known composers—Leonhard Päminger, Haydenhaymer, and Johannes Heugel—in the middle of the volumes, at a comfortable distance for a potential buyer browsing the front contents. Each of Ott's anthologies contained a numbered list of the motets in the front matter printed in the tenor partbook.[91] The Index followed the order of the volume, and included composer attributions, which confirms that identities of composers were a key selling feature.

Ordering strategies for anthologies of motets and madrigals of the mid-sixteenth century attest to a renewed interest in the modal classification of polyphonic music, occasioned by the publication of Pietro Aaron's *Trattato della natura et cognitione di tutti gli tuoni di canto figurato* (Venice, 1525).[92] Drawing examples from actual polyphonic pieces, Aaron demonstrated that music could be assigned to one of the eight church modes of Gregorian chant theory. This interest in post-compositional classification was taken up by editors as they ordered the contents of anthologies. The most ambitious case is the 15-volume series of Latin motets entitled *Liber ... ecclesiasticarum cantionum* printed in Antwerp by Tylman Susato from 1553 onward.[93] Evidently Susato felt the modal structure of the series worth advertising to the public. Title pages to Books V and VI advertise motets "(omnes) primi toni" [(all) in mode one], while Books VII, VIII, X, XI, XII, XIV call for motets "de uno tono" [all in one mode]. The result is an order that matches the sequence of the eight church modes.

Modal ordering was largely dependent on the personal taste and interest of printers or editors. Such interest tended to wax and wane. Beginning in 1536, Pierre Attaingnant ordered his chanson anthologies according to modal pairs—protus, deuterus, tritus, tetrardus—a strict modal plan that few followed with such rigor.[94] Antonio Gardano proved more ambivalent. In 1539 Gardano published two anthologies of motets titled *Fior de mottetti tratti dalli mottetti del fiore*; both consisted entirely of music drawn from Jacques Moderne's six books of *Motetti del fiore* (Lyons, 1532–39).[95] While Moderne's volumes lack any overriding ordering

---

91 It was common for mid-century publications in German-speaking lands to include the full title page, preliminaries, and colophon in the tenor partbook only of each volume (Gustavson, "Hans Ott, Hieronymus Formschneider," vol. 1, p. 282).

92 Harold S. Powers, "Tonal Types and Modal Categories in Renaissance Polyphony," *Journal of the American Musicological Society*, 34 (1981): 433. My account of modal systems and sixteenth-century polyphonic music is based on Powers.

93 See Table 15 of Powers, "Tonal Types and Modal Categories," pp. 468–9.

94 Howard Mayer Brown, "Theory and Practice in the Sixteenth Century: Preliminary Notes on Attaingnant's Modally Ordered Chansonniers," in Lewis Lockwood and Edward Roesner (eds), *Essays in Musicology: A Tribute to Alvin Johnson* ([n.p.]: American Musicological Society, 1990), pp. 75-100 cited in Lewis, *Antonio Gardano, Venetian Music Printer*, vol. 2, p. 123.

95 *Primus liber cum quatuor vocibus. Fior de mottetti tratti dalli mottetti del fiore.* (Venice: A. Gardane, 1539; RISM B/I, 1539[12]); *Secundus liber cum quinque vocibus. Fior de mottetti tratti dalli Mottetti del fiore* (Venice: A. Gardane, 1539; RISM B/I, 1539[6]).

scheme, Gardano selected and positioned the motets according to modal principles.[96]
Yet Gardano later "undid" the modal plan of Antonio Barré's Roman *Il primo libro
delle muse, a quattro voci* (RISM B/I, 1555[27]), which opens with madrigals in the
Dorian mode, followed by settings in the Phrygian, Mixolydian, and Lydian modes.
Gardano substituted madrigals and completely changed their order in his *Madregali
ariosi ... Libro primo delle Muse a quatro voci* (RISM B/I, 1557[17]).[97] Rather than
mode, most of Gardano's editions were organized either around the ambitus of the
pieces (the relative high or low range of pitches, indicated by the use of high or low
clefs) or by system (the presence or absence of a flat in the signature), with tonal
type or mode and final functioning as subgroups of these two attributes.[98] The
most frequent arrangement was by ambitus first, then by system. This ordering
assembled all pieces for a similar combination of voices together, making it practical
for singers, and grouped pieces in *cantus mollis* or *cantus durus* one after the other to
aid sightsinging. Gardano used the procedure for *Mottetti del frutto a quatro* (RISM
B/I, 1539[13]), *Le Dotte et eccellente compositioni ... di Verdelot* (RISM B/I, 1541[17]),
Il primo libro d'i madrigali de diversi quatuor vocum (RISM B/I, 1542[17]), *Il primo
libro d'i madrigali de diversi a quatro voci* (RISM B/I, 1546[15]), *Madrigali ariosi a
quatro voci* (RISM B/I, 1557[17]), *Il secondo libro de le Muse a cinque voci* (RISM
B/I, 1559[16]), and *De diversi autori il quatro libro de madrigali a quatro voci* (RISM
B/I, 1554[28]). Only rarely did Gardano stick to a strict modal scheme.[99] Antwerp-
based printer Pierre Phalèse demonstrated northern interest in modal ordering in the
madrigal anthology *Il vago alboreto di madrigali et canzoni a quattro voci* (Antwerp,
1597), which groups works according to the eight-mode system.[100]

German editors appear far less interested in arrangement by mode or tonal
type than their counterparts in Italy and the Low Countries. The arrangement of
anthologies remained largely composer driven, as it had under Hans Ott in the late
1530s. To be sure, grouping by composer was not unique to Germany. Girolamo
Scotto's *Le dotte et eccellente compositioni dei i madrigali a cinque voci* (RISM
B/I, 1540[18]) named Adrian Willaert, Leonardo Barro (his student), Philippe Verdelot,
Costanzo Festa, Jacques Arcadelt, Francesco Corteccia, and Jacquet de Berchem on

---

96   Gardano's contents are listed in Samuel F. Pogue, "A Sixteenth-Century Editor at
Work: Gardane and Moderne," *Journal of Musicology*, 1 (1982): 237–8.

97   Steele, "Antonio Barré," pp. 100–102. Steele compares the ordering of Barré's and
Gardano's editions on pp. 111–12.

98   Harold Powers terms "tonal type" a particular combination of system signature,
ambitus or cleffing, and final sonority. The following is based on Lewis, *Antonio Gardano,
Venetian Music Printer*, vol. 2, pp. 123–49.

99   Gardano reordered *Madrigali di Verdelot et de altri autori a sei voci* (RISM B/I,
1546[19]) to create a rare case of clear, modally-ordered groupings. His attention to modal
ordering contrasts with his earlier ordering of the same music in *La piu divina, et piu bella
musica [...] madrigali, a sei voci [...] Verdelot* (RISM B/I, 1541[16]) (Lewis, *Antonio Gardano,
Venetian Music Printer*, vol. 2, pp. 135–6).

100 See Stephen Thomson Moore, *"Il vago alboreto* (Antwerp, 1597): An Edition and
Commentary on the Unpublished Works," (DMA, Stanford University, 1982), pp. 18–20 for
the table of contents with voice ranges and finals.

its title page, with the contents arranged by composer following this order.[101] Scotto ordered the two-volume *I dolci & harmoniosi concenti a cinque voci* (RISM B/I, 1562[5-6]) by composer, a fitting schema for a series promoting madrigals by Venetian musicians.[102] But the technique was practiced by Nuremberg firms with a degree of consistency not found elsewhere. The Nuremberg houses of Petreius, Ott, Berg and Neuber, Gerlach, and Kauffmann all relied on authorial groupings to create order in their large collections, a plan distinct from those found in the original anthologies from which many of the works were drawn. Rank determined the ordering of the composers—Josquin for Ott's *Novum et insigne opus musicum* (1537–38), Clemens non Papa, Gombert, and their contemporaries for Berg and Neuber's motet anthologies, and Marenzio for Friedrich Lindner's madrigal collections (see Chapter 2). Within an authorial grouping, pride of place might be given to a popular setting such as Marenzio's *Liquide perle* which heads the set of 23 five-voice madrigals by the composer in Lindner's *Gemma musicalis I* (Nuremberg, 1588). Another factor was poetic unity; poetic cycles were retained within an authorial grouping rather than scattered or missing altogether. When small groups of settings in the same mode or tonal type did occur, it often resulted from the editor's borrowing of a slate of madrigals from the same source, and thus transplanting the set ordering with it.[103]

Authorial groupings were emphasized visually in the design of tables at the front of German anthologies. Tables followed the ordering of the volume, thus giving consumers a glimpse of the composer groupings within. Berg and Neuber used brackets to reinforce these groupings in the table to *Novum et insigne opus musicvm, sex, quinque et quatuor vocum* (RISM B/I, 1558[4]), and coupled brackets with line divisions for the *Secunda pars magni operis musici … Quinque vocum* (RISM B/I, 1559[1]) and *Tertia pars magni operis musici … Quatuor vocum* (RISM B/I, 1559[2]) (Figure 1.4).

The technique of bracketing persisted under Berg's followers. Friedrich Lindner used brackets for *Gemma musicalis I* and *III* (Nuremberg, 1588, 1590). Katharina Gerlach's grandson and successor, Paul Kauffmann, used brackets for both volumes of *Fiori del giardino*.[104] The uniform design of tables created a recognizable house style for all music books from the Nuremberg firms.

Indices to Venetian and Antwerp music anthologies showed greater variety in their layout, possibly a result of their appearance at the end of the volume, where consumers might turn to "look something up" in a number of ways. Rather than following the order of the volume, indices to many anthologies by Gardano and

---

101 Bernstein, *Music Printing in Renaissance Venice*, catalogue no. 15, pp. 255–7.

102 Ibid., catalogue nos 219–20, pp. 601–604.

103 Lindner groups Marenzio's madrigals by system and ambitus as he transfers the settings from the composer's first, second, and third madrigal books for five voices into *Gemma musicalis I* (Nuremberg, 1588).

104 RISM B/I, 1597[13] and *De'fiori del giardino di diversi eccellentissimi autori. Seconda parte, à quatro, cinque et sei voci. Raccolti con molta diligenza et novamente date in luce* (Nuremberg: Paul Kauffmann, 1604; RISM B/I, 1604[12]).

Figure 1.4   Table of contents from Johannes vom Berg, *Tertia pars magni operis musici* (Nuremberg, 1559), dicantus partbook, fol. 2r, Staatsbibliothek zu Berlin–Preuβischer Kulturbesitz, Musikabteilung mit Mendelssohn-Archiv: Mus. ant. Pract. B 440-3

Scotto are ordered alphabetically by text incipit, which suggests the book was targeted at consumers fluent in (or at least more familiar with) the language of the contents. Consumers of madrigals may have searched by poem rather than composer. There are cases where the names of composers are left off the index altogether. The alphabetical ordering by text marks a clear difference between anthologies of madrigals published in Venice and those issued in German-speaking lands where the Italian language was less familiar.

One final point of comparison concerns "collected editions"—anthologies of works devoted to the music of a single composer. Reprint editions that grouped earlier books of music by Orlande de Lassus attest to the popularity of the composer's motets long after their first printing. In the hands of later editors, Lassus's motets were subject to much reshuffling and retexting. Antonio Gardano reordered Lassus's motet collection *Sacrae cantiones quinque vocum* (Munich: Adam Berg, July 1562) according to system-clef combinations, apparently unaware that the composer had already arranged the works in the cycle of the eight church modes.[105]   Working

105 *Sacrae cantiones (vulgo motecta appellatae) quinque vocum, tum viva voce tum omnis generis instrumentis cantatu commodissimae, liber primus* (Venice: Antonio Gardano,

Figure 1.5 *Liquide perle*, from Luca Marenzio, *Madrigalia* (Nuremberg, 1601), canto partbook, fol. 4r, Herzog August Bibliothek Wolfenbüttel: 2.2.7 Musica

from motet books dating back to 1562, Katharina Gerlach published a reprint collection of Lassus's motets that arranged them in modal order within each voice

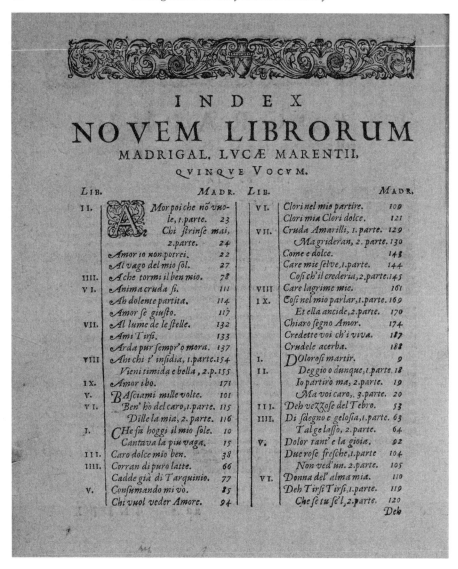

Figure 1.6   Table of contents from Luca Marenzio, *Madrigalia* (Nuremberg, 1601), canto partbook, fol. 2v, Herzog August Bibliothek Wolfenbüttel: 2.2.7 Musica

grouping.[106] As Richard Freedman has shown, modal order played an important role in the organization of later French editions of Lassus's secular chansons as well.[107] Editorial reshuffling and reworking perpetuated the circulation of popular music, decades after its first printing.

The madrigals of Luca Marenzio were prime candidates for compilation in collected series. They appeared in collected editions printed in Venice, Nuremberg, and Antwerp. It is instructive to compare the collected editions of Pierre Phalèse and Paul Kauffmann, since both editors relied on Venetian editions, but differed considerably in their approach to the assembly and presentation of Marenzio's music. Phalèse scattered madrigals across his collected edition of Marenzio's first five books of five-voice settings, with no regard for their order of appearance in Venetian editions (Venice, 1580–85).[108] By contrast, Kauffmann emphasized a steady progression through all nine books of Marenzio's five-voice madrigals (Venice, 1580–99).[109] His title page drew attention to the Venetian origins of the volume with the text "Anteà VENETIIS, diversis temporibus, novem separatis edita libris, jam verò, commodioris usus cauβâ, uno volumine conjuntim excusa" [previously appearing in Venice at various points as nine separate books, now, for ease of use, released together in one volume].[110] Kauffmann gave clear section headings to mark the progression from Books 1 through 9. He opened with *Liquide perle*, the first madrigal to appear in the composer's *Il primo libro de' madrigali a cinque voci* (Venice: Angelo Gardano, 1580) and perhaps his most famous (Figure 1.5). The table at the front of the volume lists contents in alphabetical order, a departure from German practice but one justified in the context of a volume devoted to music by a single composer. The table includes a column indicating the source book, information that also appears in the headline to each setting (Figure 1.6).

The display of sources and bracketing of composer groupings characteristic of German anthologies speaks to a broader interest in method and display evident in didactic treatises, manuals, and textbooks. With its concern for practical strategies of argumentation, Rodolphus Agricola's *De inventione dialectica* (c.1479; published in 1515) paved the way for Peter Ramus to popularize the dichotomous method

---

106 *Fasciculi aliquot sacrarum cantionum cum quatuor, quinque, sex et octo vocibus, antea quidem separatim excusi, nunc vero auctoris consensu in unum corpus redacti* (Nuremberg: Gerlach, 1582; RISM A/I, L937) (Powers, "Tonal Types and Modal Categories," pp. 462–4).

107 Richard Freedman, *The Chansons of Orlando di Lasso and Their Protestant Listeners: Music, Piety, and Print in Sixteenth-Century France*, Eastman Studies in Music, ed. Ralph P. Locke (Rochester: University of Rochester Press, 2000), pp. 142–66.

108 *Madrigali a cinque voci, ridotti in un corpo ... & con ogni diligentia corretti* (Antwerp: Pierre Phaèse & Jean Bellère, 1593; RISM A/I, M572). Phalèse follows the ordering of Books 1–5 for his collection of Marenzio's three-voice villanellas and *canzonette alla napolitana* of 1610 (RISM A/I, M612).

109 *Madrigalia quinque vocum, antea Venetiis, diversis temporibus, novem separatis edita libris jam vero, commodioris usus caussa, uno volumine, conjunctim excusa* (Nuremberg: Paul Kauffmann, 1601; RISM A/I, M576=RISM B/I, 1601¹²).

110 Canto partbook, fol. 1r. Exemplar Herzog August Bibliothek Wolfenbüttel: 2.2.7 Musica.

(the display of material) as the ideal method of presentation.[111] According to this method, the teacher begins with the most general definition of the subject, followed by its division into two parts, then proceeds to display the material under each head in tabular form; the process always moves from the general to the particular. The method became the standard way to present material in lectures, textbooks, and manuals. Ramist ideas remained intensely popular in Germany at the close of the sixteenth century: 83 editions of his *Dialecticae institutiones* were published there between 1581 and 1600, more than in all other countries combined during the same period.[112] It is tempting to link the visual "look" of German music books to the reception of Ramist ideas in German-speaking lands.

Walter Ong argues that visual representations like tables and indices form an integral part of the long-developing transfer from discourse (coded symbols representing oral record) approached through hearing, to spatial models approached chiefly in terms of vision.[113] Yet a more balanced assessment that works well for performance-based texts like music and theatrical plays unites the senses: vision works in the service of hearing. A well-ordered table helped performers select music more quickly and locate it faster. The table complemented rather than replaced practical use. As such tables highlight the rub between editor and consumer. Search engines gave more flexibility to consumers to experience a music book, to quickly assess the use of the volume for their needs. Consumers turned editors themselves. Yet at the same time tables and indices imparted an editor's judgment on, and assessment of the contents of the volume.

Conclusion

Editors played a critical role not only in selecting the contents of anthologies, but also in their packaging and marketing. There was growing recognition of this role in the first century of music printing, as anonymous editorship gave way to the advertisement and heavy reliance on editorial services. Genre and geography also influenced what editorial work was done, and how. Editors in German-speaking lands gathered foreign music, ordered it according to composer preference, translated it for native audiences, and packaged it with prefaces and tables to guide users. With the "birth" of the professional music editor, anthologists can assume their rightful place in the historiography of the production and consumption of printed music books.

---

111 Walter J. Ong, *Ramus: Method and the Decay of Dialogue: From the Art of Discourse to the Art of Reason* (Cambridge: Harvard University Press, 1958). For a useful summary, see Lisa Jardine, "Humanistic Logic," in Quentin Skinner and Eckhard Kessler (eds), *The Cambridge History of Renaissance Philosophy* (Cambridge: Cambridge University Press, 1988), pp. 173–98.

112 Ong, *Ramus: Method and the Decay of Dialogue*, p. 296.

113 Ong, *Orality and Literacy*, passim.

Chapter 2

Friedrich Lindner: Working for a Local Clientele

One of the most prolific German editors of Italian music was Friedrich Lindner (c. 1542–97), cantor at the church of St. Egidien in Nuremberg. Between 1588 and 1590 Lindner compiled a trilogy of Italian secular songs that appeared under the Latin title *Gemma musicalis,* and included 185 madrigals and canzoni in their original language. *Gemma musicalis I-III* are the largest and among the earliest northern anthologies devoted to Italian-texted repertory. The series was printed and published in Nuremberg by Katharina Gerlach, who commissioned Lindner to edit a total of nine anthologies of sacred and secular music from 1585 until her death in 1591.

This chapter uses the three *Gemma musicalis* anthologies as a case study to examine Lindner's editorial habits—how he selected and ordered repertory, and what his methods suggest about his role in shaping the German reception of Italian music. It also presents compelling evidence of the influence of the local conditions in which an editor worked on the product of that work. Lindner's anthologies shaped and were shaped by the literary and musical culture in which they were produced. His success hinged on his knowledge and his contacts with composers, printers, publishers, and consumers, whose interests (financial or artistic) affected his decision-making at every step.

The Market for Italian Music in Renaissance Nuremberg

Lindner's *Gemma musicalis* presumed a consumer audience familiar with the Italian language. The size and expense of the *Gemma musicalis* anthologies point to a ready-made market. This section charts the reception of Italian music in late sixteenth-century German-speaking lands in the years leading up to Lindner's trilogy.

A turn toward Italian music can be traced back to the 1560s, with the confluence of the importation of Venetian music books, the activity of Italian composers at German courts, and the German printing of Italian and Italianate music. Prior to this, the northern market was limited to a handful of collectors, such as the Hewart, Welser, and Fugger families of Augsburg.[1] The most important venue for the exchange of books between northern and southern publishers was the Frankfurt bookfair, which took place twice yearly from 1485 to the eighteenth century. Beginning in 1564,

---

1   Mary S. Lewis, *Antonio Gardano, Venetian Music Printer: 1539–1569: A Descriptive Bibliography and Historical Study*, 3 vols (New York: Routledge, 1988–2005), vol. 3, p. 21. See also Lewis's forthcoming article "The Dissemination of Italian Music in Germany in the Mid-Sixteenth Century."

Augsburg printer and publisher Georg Willer issued catalogs of books for sale at the fall and spring fairs at Frankfurt.[2] Organized first by language and book format—strong indicators of how consumers purchased music—it is possible to gauge changes in available stock within the field of music, and, more specifically, at the level of genre. Venetian firms dominated this early phase of distribution; Girolamo Scotto and Antonio Gardano figured prominently among them. As Jane Bernstein points out, they focused their efforts on Latin-texted motets, a linguistically safe bet for the European marketplace.[3] Italian-texted repertory appeared only sporadically in the 1560s. An entry from the fall fair of 1565 included Lassus's madrigals for four and five voices in three volumes each, two volumes of *canzoni alla napolitana* by Leonardo Primavera, Books 1–3 of "Madrigalia diversorum autorum," and single volumes of madrigals by Jacques Arcadelt, Cipriano de Rore, Pietro Vinci, and Filippo Azzaiolo.[4] Entries for fall 1567 offered a more diverse selection, with volumes by Claudio Merulo, Hubert Waelrant, Cypriano de Rore, Alessandro Striggio, Leonardo Primavera, Baltassare Donato, Stephani Rossetti, Philippe Verdelot, Adrian Willaert, Jhan Gero, and anthologies edited by Giulio Bonagiunta.[5] Books appeared in Willer's catalogs within a few years of their printing, indicating that music made it from Venice to the Frankfurt fairs quickly and efficiently.

This early importation of madrigals and *canzoni alla napolitana* coincided with the vogue for Italian music at the courts of Dresden, Munich, and Prague, where composers of Italian birth or training held the top posts. Their presence sparked the first publications devoted to Italian-texted music in Germany. Table 2.1 lists Italian-texted secular songs printed in German-speaking lands between 1566 and 1587, one year before Lindner's *Gemma musicalis*.

2   Georg Willer, *Die Messkataloge Georg Willers [1564–1600]*, ed. Bernhard Fabian, Die Messkataloge des sechzehnten Jahrhunderts, 5 vols (Hildesheim: Georg Olms, 1972–2001).

3   Jane A. Bernstein, *Music Printing in Renaissance Venice: The Scotto Press (1539–1572)* (New York: Oxford University Press, 1998), p. 128.

4   Willer, *Die Messkataloge*, vol. 1, p. 64. For details of the editions, see Bernstein, *Music Printing in Renaissance Venice*, p. 129.

5   Willer, *Die Messkataloge*, vol. 1, pp. 124–5.

Table 2.1 Italian-Texted Madrigals & Related Genres Printed in German-Speaking Lands, 1566–1587

DATE	RISM	COMPOSER/SHORT TITLE	PLACE	PRINTER
1541	1541[2]	*Trium vocum cantiones centum … Tomi primi*	Nuremberg	Johann Petreius
1544	1544[20]	*Hundert und fünfftzehen guter newer Liedlein, mit vier, fünff, sechs Stimmen*	Nuremberg	Hans Ott
[s.d.]	[1560][1]	*Selectissimorum triciniorum*	Nuremberg	Johannes vom Berg & Ulrich Neuber
1566	S1146	Antonio Scandello, *El primo libro de le canzoni napoletane a IIII. voci* 2nd edn/1572 (RISM A/I, S1147), Nuremberg, Heirs of Ulrich Neuber 3rd edn/1583 (RISM A/I, S1148), Nuremberg, Katharina Gerlach & Berg's heirs	Nuremberg	Ulrich Neuber & Dietrich Gerlach
1567	1567[2]	*Tricinia sacra ex diversis et probatis autoribus collecta*	Nuremberg	Dietrich Gerlach
1573	L860	Orlande de Lassus, *Sex cantiones latinae quatuor … Sechs teutsche Lieder mit vier … Six chansons françoises nouvelles a quatre … Sei madrigali nuovi a quarto, con un dialogo a otto voci*	Munich	Adam Berg
1574	R738	Jacob Regnart, *Il primo libro delle canzone italiane a cinque voci* 2nd edn/1580 (RISM A/I, R739), Nuremberg, [Katharina Gerlach] 3rd edn/1585 (RISM A/I, R740), Nuremberg, [Katharina Gerlach]	Vienna	Johann Mair

DATE	RISM	COMPOSER/SHORT TITLE	PLACE	PRINTER
1577	R1295	Teodore Riccio, *Il primo libro delle canzone alla napolitana a cinque voci*	Nuremberg	Katharina Gerlach & Berg's heirs
1577	S1156	Antonio Scandello, *Il secondo libro dele canzone napolitane, a quatro & a cinque voci*	Munich	Adam Berg
1579	L1293	Lechner/Regnart, *Newe Teutsche Lieder, Erstlich durch ... Jacobum Regnart ... Componirt mit drey stimmen, nach art der Welschen Villanellen. Jetzund aber ... mit fünff Stimmen gesetzet durch Leonardum Lechnerum Athesinum. Con alchuni madrigali in lingua Italiana* 2nd edn/1586 (RISM A/I, L1294), Nuremberg, Katharina Gerlach	Nuremberg	Katharina Gerlach & Berg's heirs
1581	R753	Jacob Regnart, *Il secundo libro delle canzone italiane a cinque voci*	Nuremberg	Katharina Gerlach & Berg's heirs
1585	L960	Orlande de Lassus, *Madrigali: novamente composti a cinque voci*	Nuremberg	Katharina Gerlach
1585	1585[17]	*Sdegnosi ardori. Musica di diversi auttori ... a cinque voci, raccolti insieme da Giulio Gigli da Immola*	Munich	Adam Berg
1587	L981	Orlande de Lassus, *Madrigali: a quattro, cinque et sei voci*	Nuremberg	Katharina Gerlach

Composers can be divided into two categories: Italian musicians active at German courts, and northerners who either apprenticed or worked in Italy. Antonio Scandello's *Il primo libro de le canzoni napolitana* (Nuremberg, 1566) for four voices heads the list as the first German publication of a volume of Italian texts. Scandello joined the Dresden court as a trumpeter in 1549, and succeeded Matthaeus Le Maistre as court chapelmaster in 1566, a position Scandello held until his death in 1580.[6] Further north, Teodore Riccio spent the majority of his career in the service of Margrave Georg Friedrich of Ansbach-Brandenburg, first in Ansbach, and, from 1578–86 in Königsberg, before returning once again to Ansbach as court chapelmaster.[7] In 1577, Katharina Gerlach issued his *primo libro delle canzone alla napolitana*, based on the Venetian edition of the same year.[8]

Among northerners, Orlande de Lassus was pivotal for the early reception of the madrigal in German-speaking lands. Ludwig Finscher credits Lassus's Italianate *Neue teütsche Lieder mit fünff Stimmen* (Munich, 1567) with challenging the dominance of the German Tenorlied, a genre whose strength of tradition arguably thwarted an early reception of the Italian madrigal in German-speaking lands.[9] Lassus spent much of his youth and early career in Italy before issuing his first Italian pieces in *Le quatoirsiesme livre a quatre parties* (Antwerp: Susato, 1555), a collection of madrigals, *villanesche*, French chansons, and motets for four voices. In 1556 Lassus joined the Bavarian court as a tenor and succeeded Ludwig Daser as chapelmaster in 1563, a position Lassus held until his death in 1594. During his long tenure, Lassus worked at one time or another with 52 Italian musicians at the Munich court including the singer and instrumentalist Giulio Gigli da Immola.[10] In 1585 Immola compiled *Sdegnosi ardori*, an anthology of 31 settings of Giovanni Battista Guarini's madrigal *Ardo sì*.[11] Roughly half of the anthology is devoted to

---

6   Dane O. Heuchemer: "Scandello, Antonio," *Grove Music Online*, ed. Laura Macy (Accessed 10 September 2006), <http://www.grovemusic.com>

7   Walter Blankenburg/Norburt Dubowy: "Riccio, Teodore," *Grove Music Online*, ed. Laura Macy (Accessed 10 September 2006), <http://www.grovemusic.com>

8   *Il primo libro delle canzone alla napolitana a cinque voci, con alcune mascherate nel fine a cinque et a sei* (Nuremberg: Katharina Gerlach & Johann Bergs Erben, 1577; RISM A/I, R1295).

9   Ludwig Finscher, "Lied and Madrigal, 1580–1600," in John Kmetz (ed.), *Music in the German Renaissance: Sources, Styles and Contexts* (Cambridge: Cambridge University Press, 1994), p. 182. Cf. Basil Smallman, "Pastoralism, Parody and Pathos: The Madrigal in Germany, 1570–1630," in *Conspectus Carminis: Essays for David Galliver, Miscellanea Musicologica*, Adelaide Studies in Musicology, 15 (Adelaide: University of Adelaide Press, 1988), p. 17.

10   Sara E. Dumont, *German Secular Polyphonic Song in Printed Editions, 1570–1630: Italian Influences on the Poetry and Music*, 2 vols (New York: Garland, 1989), vol. 1, p. 73, citing Wolfgang Boetticher, *Orlando di Lasso und seine Zeit, 1532–1594: Repertoire-Untersuchungen zu der Musik der Spätrenaissance* (Kassel: Bärenreiter, 1958), pp. 331–8, 431–2, and 533–6, and Adolf Sandberger, *Beiträge zur Geschichte der bayerischen Hofkapelle unter Orlando di Lasso* (Leipzig: Breitkopf & Härtel, 1894–95).

11   *Sdegnosi ardori. Musica di diversi auttori, sopra un istesso soggetto di parole, a cinque voci, raccolti insieme da Giulio Gigli da Immola* (Munich: A. Berg, 1585; RISM B/I, 1585[17]).

music by Gigli's colleagues, with Lassus heading the list of music by members of the ducal chapel.

The imperial court of Emperor Maximilian rivaled Munich for its Italianate tastes. After two years of study in Italy (1568–October 1570), Jacob Regnart returned north to assume the post of music teacher to the imperial chapel choristers.[12] The fruits of his study were born out in *Il primo libro delle canzone italiane a cinque voci* (Vienna, 1574).[13]

Equally important for the long-term success of Italian and Italianate music were the sophisticated urban elites. Nuremberg's dominance as a center for trade and commerce assured the city a rich cultural life as well.[14] Cultural life during the third quarter of the century was dominated by the city's patricians, a class that was well-traveled, highly educated, and (in many cases) musically knowledgeable. Nuremberg's patricians came from two groups: families from which the members of the City Council were selected, and *Ehrbarkeit*—officials, judges, lawyers, and those who married into patrician families. Patricians held 34 of the 42 seats on the Small Council, giving them a powerful position in Nuremberg's political and social order as well.[15] The names of patrician families and illustrations of their crests are presented in the "Topochronographia reipublicae Norimbergensis," a bound manuscript volume dating from the late seventeenth century.[16] It includes guidelines for appropriate patrician behavior, confirming that formal study and foreign travel continued to be prized attributes of a patrician's formative years. To this end, many Nurembergers sent their sons abroad, either to study, or to live with foreign business partners. Paul Behaim II spent extended periods in Italy, and studied law at the University of Padua in the mid-late 1570s. In a letter home to his mother, one of many to request funds, Behaim showed a particular passion for musical developments from the south:

> ... as at the "Herrenmarkt" at home, the most distinguished persons in Verona meet to practice the lute, the clavier, singing, and the viol. ... besides my lessons I may get to meet other fine people from whom I may learn some other things. (Verona, 20 April 1577)[17]

---

12   Walter Pass, "Regnart, Jacob," *New Grove II*, vol. 21, p. 118.

13   Regnart drew many of the texts from Giovan Leonardo Primavera's *Il primo libro de canzone napolitane a tre voci* (Venice: Girolamo Scotto, 1565) (Rudolf Velten, *Das Ältere Deutsche Gesellschaftslied unter dem Einfluss der Italienischen Musik*, Beiträge zur Neueren Literaturgeschichte, Neue Folge, Heft 5 [Heidelberg: Carl Winters Universitäts-Buchhandlungen, 1914], p. 28).

14   For a comprehensive English-language study of the city, see Gerald Strauss, *Nuremberg in the Sixteenth Century: City Politics and Life between Middle Ages and Modern Times* (Bloomington: Indiana University Press, 1976).

15   The remaining eight, non-voting seats were held by artisans representing the cloth makers, tanners, brewers, edging makers, butchers, tailors, and metal works (Susan Gattuso, "16th-Century Nuremberg," in Iain Fenlon [ed.], *The Renaissance: From the 1470s to the End of the 16th Century* [Englewood Cliffs, NJ: Prentice Hall, 1989], p. 287).

16   The manuscript survives at Nuremberg, Bibliothek des Germanischen National-Museums, Hs. 7178, and is discussed in John Edward Lindberg, "Origins and Development of the Sixteenth Century Tricinium" (Ph.D., diss., University of Cincinnati, 1989), pp. 76–7.

17   "wie bei euch auf den herrenmark die stadtlichsten edelleut in Verona zusammen komen und sich da üben: einer auf der lauten, der ander auf dem instrument, der dritt in

Here Behaim connects the music academies of Verona with Nuremberg's own music societies, that offered their members formal venues for musical and literary discussion, including the early transmission of Italian song and poetry.[18]

The earliest group formed on 31 October 1568 at the home of patrician Nicolaus Nützel.[19] Totaling 22 members, the group was made up of teachers, clergymen, doctors, lawyers, businessmen, and city officials. At least two groups were active in the 1570s. Though they did not employ musicians on a regular basis, we can learn something about their musical and literary tastes from dedications of music books, both to the groups and to their individual members. In 1572 composer Ivo de Vento dedicated his four-voice *Schöne auserlesene newe Teutsche Lieder* to the famous *Sodalicium Musicum*, a society of councilmen in Nuremberg. De Vento used the term *newe* [new] to highlight his combination of native, strophic song with the Italian style, a style he likely learned at first hand in Venice, and at the Italophile court of Duke Albrecht V at Munich where the volume was printed. Jacob Regnart perfected the mixed style, fully transfering Italian 11-syllable verse to the German language in *Kurtzweilige teutsche Lieder zu dreyen Stimmen. Nach art der Neapolitanen oder Welschen Villanellen* (Nuremberg, 1574).

The *neue Lieder* of Jacob Regnart and Leonhard Lechner became a staple of the south German music presses (Table 2.2). Their simple harmonies, homophonic textures, strophic forms, and rustic quality made them suitable for amateur performance at the music societies.Leonhard Lechner may have studied in Italy before spending ten years in Nuremberg (1575–85) as assistant teacher at the St. Lorenz, the largest grammar school in the city.[20]

---

dem singen, der viert auf den geigen ... damit ich neben dem lehrnen auch ander edelleut kundtschaft überkomen möge und bei solchen etwas anders lehrnen möge" (Nuremberg, Bibliothek des Germanischen National-Museums, Behaim Briefwechsel, cited with trans. in Bartlett R. Butler, "Liturgical Music in Sixteenth-Century Nuremberg: A Socio-Musical Study" [Ph.D. diss., University of Illinois at Urbana-Champaign, 1970], pp. 512–13 and p. 513 n. 11).

18   For an overview, see Gattuso, "16th-century Nuremberg," pp. 286–303 and Butler, "Liturgical Music in Sixteenth-Century Nuremberg," pp. 509–24. The definitive study remains Uwe Martin, "Die Nürnberger Musikgesellschaften," *Mitteilungen des Vereins für Geschichte der Stadt Nürnberg*, 49 (1959): 185–225.

19   See Martin, "Die Nürnberger Musikgesellschaften," pp. 188–94.

20   Konrad Ameln, "Lechner, Leonhard," in *New Grove II*, vol. 14, p. 441. Lechner's whereabouts in the early 1570s is unknown. In the preface to his Latin motet volume of 1581, he writes that he had once "roved far and wide, visiting various places," a comment that, in addition to evidence of his own musical style, suggests he apprenticed in Italy (ibid., p. 441).

Table 2.2 German Imitations of Italian Secular Song by Regnart & Lechner, 1576–1590

DATE	RISM	COMPOSER/SHORT TITLE[a]	PLACE	PRINTER
1574	R742	Jacob Regnart, *Kurtzweilige teutsche Lieder zu dreyen Stimmen. Nach art der Neapolitanen oder Welschen Villanellen* 2nd edn/1576 (RISM A/I, R743), Nuremberg, Katharina Gerlach & Berg's heirs	Nuremberg	Dietrich Gerlach
1576	L1288	Leonhard Lechner, *Neue teutsche Lieder zu drey Stimmen, Nach art der Welschen Villanellen* 2nd edn/1577 (RISM A/I, L1289)	Nuremberg	Katharina Gerlach & Berg's heirs
1577	L1290	Leonhard Lechner, *Der ander Theyl Neuer Teutscher Lieder zu drey Stimmen, Nach art der Welschen Villanellen*	Nuremberg	Nicolaus Knorr
1577	L1291	Leonhard Lechner, *Neue Teutsche Lieder, mit Vier und Fünf Stimmen*	Nuremberg	Nicolaus Knorr
1577	R746	Jacob Regnart, *Der ander Theyl Kurtzweiliger teutscher Lieder zu dreyen Stimmen. Nach art der Neapolitanen oder Welschen Villanellen* 2nd edn/1578 (RISM A/I, R747); 3rd edn/1580 (RISM A/I, R748)	Nuremberg	Katharina Gerlach & Berg's heirs
1578	R744	Jacob Regnart, *Der erste Theyl Schöner Kurtzweiliger Teutscher Lieder zu dreyen Stimmen* 2nd edn/1580 (RISM A/I, R745)	Nuremberg	Katharina Gerlach & Berg's heirs

DATE	RISM	COMPOSER/SHORT TITLE	PLACE	PRINTER
1579	R749	Jacob Regnart, *Der dritter Theil Schöner Kurtzweiliger Teutscher Lieder zu dreyen Stimmen. Nach art der Neapolitanen oder Welschen Villanellen* 2nd edn/1580 (RISM A/I, R750)	Nuremberg	Katharina Gerlach & Berg's heirs
1579	L1293	Lechner/Regnart, *Newe Teutsche Lieder; Erstlich durch ... Jacobum Regnart ... Componirt mit drey stimmen, nach art der Welschen Villanellen. Jetzund aber ... mit fünff Stimmen gesetzet durch Leonardum Lechnerum Athesinum. Con alchuni madrigali in lingua Italiana* 2nd edn/1586 (RISM A/I, L1294), Nuremberg, Katharina Gerlach	Nuremberg	Katharina Gerlach & Berg's heirs
1580	R751	Jacob Regnart, *Neue Kurtzweilige Teutsche Lieder mit fünff stimme* 2nd edn/1586 (RISM A/I, R752), Nuremberg, Katharina Gerlach	Nuremberg	Katharina Gerlach & Berg's heirs
1582	L1296	Leonhard Lechner, *Neue Teutsche Lieder mit fünff und vier Stimmen*	Nuremberg	Katharina Gerlach & Berg's heirs
1583	R755	Jacob Regnart, *Teutsche Lieder mit dreyen stimmen nach art der Neapolitanen oder Welschen Villanellen ... in ein Opus zusamen druckt.* Collected edition of Books 1 (1576), 2 (1577), and 3 (1579) Reprinted in 1587, 1590, 1597, and 1611	Munich	Adam Berg

DATE	RISM	COMPOSER/SHORT TITLE	PLACE	PRINTER
1584	R756	Jacob Regnart, *Tricinia. Kurtzweilige teutsche Lieder zu dreyen stimmen nach art der Neapolitanen oder Welschen Villanellen* Reprinted twice at the firm up to 1593	Nuremberg	Katharina Gerlach
1586	L1299	Leonhard Lechner, *Der erst und ander Theil Der Teutschen Villanellen … mit dreyen Stimmen* 2nd edn/1590 (RISM A/I, L1300)	Nuremberg	Katharina Gerlach
1586	L1301	Leonhard Lechner, *Neue lustige Teutsche Lieder nach art der Welschen Canzonen mit vier stimmen Componirt*	Nuremberg	Katharina Gerlach
1588	L1302	Leonhard Lechner, *Neue lustige Teutsche Lieder, nach art der Welschen Canzonen, mit vier Stimmen componirt*	Nuremberg	Katharina Gerlach
1589	L1304	Leonhard Lechner, *Neue Geistliche und Weltliche Teutsche Lieder mit fünff und vier stimmen*	Nuremberg	Katharina Gerlach

[a] Subsequent editions were printed by the same printer as the first edition unless indicated otherwise.

During this decade Lechner dedicated three editions of his three-part German villanellas to members of the Nuremberg City Council, who were also participants in the music society. Lechner dedicated one volume each of the three-part *Newe Teutsche Lieder ... nach art der Welschen Villanellen* to Anton Geuder (Nuremberg, 1577) and Hans Pfinzing (Nuremberg, 1576). His *Newe Teutsche Lieder mit vier und fünnf Stimmen* of 1577 is addressed to a third music society, to seven young men of high social standing: Johann Nützel, Gabriel Nützel, Gabriel Scheurl, brothers Gabriel and Franz Schleicher, Johann Unterholtzer, Nicolaus Rottengatter.[21] The City Council repaid Lechner with the title of *archimusicus*, and an annual salary of 90 florins.[22]

In addition to their interest in strophic poetry, the music societies also showed an early interest in the more elevated madrigal. De Vento's polyglot *Quinque motetae, duo madrigalia, Gallicae cantiones duae, et quatuor Germanicae* (Munich: Adam Berg, 1575) dedicates a setting to each of the 11 members of the society of city councilmen. The list included Hieronymus Baumgartner, an avid collector of Italian madrigal books. His private library included 17 books of madrigals printed in Italy between 1570 and 1584.[23] The title page of Lechner's five-voice versions of Regnart's three-part *Lieder* boldly advertises "Con alchuni madrigali in lingua Italiana" ["with some madrigals in the Italian language"] (Figure 2.1).[24] Lechner's additional voices elevated the light tone of Regnart's original settings with the chromaticism of *Come nave ch'in mezzo all'onde sia combattuta da venti* and *Così son io nel piant'aspro et amaro* (second part), and the imitative textures of *Fato, fortuna, predestinatione, caso, ventura son di quelle cose* and Petrarch's *Che più d'un giorno è la vita mortale nubilo breve*.[25] Lechner dedicated the volume to

---

21 Martin, "Die Nürnberger Musikgesellschaften," pp. 201, 206.

22 Ameln, "Lechner, Leonhard," p. 441

23 Numbers extracted from Heinz Zirnbauer, *Der Notenbestand der Reichsstädtisch Nürnbergischen Ratsmusik: Eine bibliographische Rekonstruktion* (Nuremberg: Stadtbibliothek, 1959). Baumgartner's music library is examined in Chapter 5.

24 Martin ("Die Nürnberger Musikgesellschaften," pp. 209–10) speculates that two of the Italian madrigal texts may be by the composer-poet Paul Melissus Schede (1539–1602), whose stay in Nuremberg in 1577, while en route to Italy, makes his association with the volume likely. Schede subsequently penned a poem in praise of Lechner that appears in the composer's *Sacrarum Cantionum*, bk. 21 (Nuremberg, 1581), and a dedicatory ode to Lechner's new patron, Count Eitelfriedrich IV von Hohenzollern-Hechingen, that prefaces Lechner's *Liber Missarvm*, (Nuremberg, 1584).

25 For a modern edition, see Jacob Regnart, *Deutsche dreistimmige Lieder nach Art der Neapolitanen, nebst Leonhard Lechner's fünfstimmiger Bearbeitung*, ed. Robert Eitner, Publikation Aelterer Praktischer und Theoretischer Musikwerke, 19 (Leipzig, 1895; reprint New York: Boude Brothers, 1966), pp. 100–16.

"Einer Erbarn Musicalischen versamlung" [To the Honorable Musical Assembly] (naming all 12 members), thereby confirming an early interest in madrigals among Nuremberg's cultural elite.[26]

Figure 2.1   Title page of Leonhard Lechner, *Newe Teutsche Lieder* (Nuremberg, 1579), Herzog August Bibliothek Wolfenbüttel: 18.1 Mus. Coll. Inc. (11)

In addition to his contribution as a madrigalist, Lechner proved an important figure for the reception of Italian music through his activity as editor at the Gerlach firm. Between 1579 and 1583 Lechner edited one volume of masses and two volumes of motets by his teacher, Lassus, and *Harmoniae miscellae cantionum sacrarum*, an anthology of predominantly Italian sacred music.[27] The revived commercial interest in Lassus's music may be linked to the composer's visit to Nuremberg in 1581, when he likely participated in the city's music societies.[28] Gerlach's *Catalogvs Librorvm*

---

26   Fol. 2r, "Den Ehrnuesten/ Fürsichtigen/ Erbarn vnnd Weisen Herrn/ Bartholomeo Pömer/ Joachim Pömer/ Joachim Nützel/ Christophen Fürer/ Hansen Pfintzing/ Hieronymo Schürstab/ des Innern Raths: Auch Antonio Geuder/ Jobsten Lochner/ Sebalden Münsterer/ Johann Newdörffer/ Georgen Keulhaw/ vnnd Niclausen Nützel/ des grössern Raths der Stadt Nürmberg/ Einer Erbarn Musicalischen versamlung" (Altus partbook, Herzog August Bibliothek Wolfenbüttel: 18.1 Mus. Coll. Inc. [11]).

27   RISM A/I, L915; RISM A/I, L916; RISM A/I, L924; and RISM B/I, 1583².

28   Martin, "Die Nürnberger Musikgesellschaften," p. 217.

(c. 1582–83) shows six volumes of Lassus's sacred music.[29] As Latin motets, the volumes heightened awareness of Lassus's music within a familiar linguistic context. Gerlach may have used them to generate interest in Lassus's Italian madrigals, which soon followed in collected editions for five (1585) and four to six voices (1587).[30]

The taste for Italian music spawned the formation of a new music society in 1588 that replaced the earlier patrician groups.[31] Its founder, the patrician Paulus Koler, stemmed from a learned background, having studied at universities in Wittenberg, Jena, Ingolstadt, Padua, Bologna, and Sienna.[32] Members Paul Behaim II and Georg Volckamer II both spent extended periods of time in Italy before returning to Nuremberg to join the group.[33] Unlike its predecessors, which sponsored professional musicians on an ad hoc basis, this group employed full-time professional musicians: Friedrich Lindner, Kaspar Hassler (organist at the St. Lorenz), and two of the city musicians, Jacob von der Hooven and Martin Baumann. Each received a semi-annual fee of 5 gulden in exchange for providing instrumental music for the society's afternoon meetings, which were held on alternate Sundays.[34] All four are named in the ordinance book of the society, which also confirms the date of Lindner's death as 13 September 1597.[35]

Lindner was a prime candidate for support from a society with musical tastes strongly rooted in Italian styles. He developed an early knowledge of Italian music during his years as a choirboy at the Dresden court.[36] During his decade of service at the Ansbach court, first as tenor (from 1564–5) and from 1573 as vice-chapelmaster, Lindner supplemented his income through what Harold Love terms "entrepreneurial

---

29   It is reproduced in Konrad Ameln, "Ein Nürnberger Verlegerplakat aus dem 16. Jahrhundert," in Richard Baum and Wolfgang Rehm (eds), *Musik und Verlag: Karl Vötterle zum 65. Geburtstag am 12. April 1968* (Kassel: Bärenreiter, 1968), pp. 132–42.

30   RISM A/I, L959 and RISM A/I, L981.

31   The demise of the earlier groups was likely the result of the plague (Martin, "Die Nürnberger Musikgesellschaften," p. 224).

32   Friedhelm Brusniak, "Nürnberger Schülerlisten des 16. Jahrhunderts als Musik-, Schul- und Sozialgeschichtliche Quellen," *Mitteilungen des Vereins für Geschichte der Stadt Nürnberg*, 69 (1982): 31.

33   See above regarding Paul Behaim's travels to Italy (1575–77 and later). Georg Volckamer (1560–1633) studied at Altdorf and then in Italy for two years (G.A. Will, *Nürnbergisches Gelehrten-Lexicon*, 4 vols [Nuremberg, 1755–58; reprint Neustadt an der Aisch: Schmidt, 1997], vol. 4, p. 119, cited in Butler, "Liturgical Music in Sixteenth-Century Nuremberg," p. 521 n. 37).

34   Willibald Nagel, "Die Nürnberger Musikgesellschaft (1588–1629)," *Monatshefte für Musik-Geschichte*, 27 (1895): 3.

35   The protocol book survives at The British Library: MS. Add. 25716. For the date of Lindner's death, see Bartlett, "Liturgical Music in Sixteenth-Century Nuremberg," p. 584 n. 222.

36   For biography, see Franz Krautwurst, "Lindner, Friedrich," in *Die Musik in Geschichte und Gegenwart* [*MGG*], ed. Friedrich Blume, 17 vols (Kassel: Bärenreiter, 1949-86), vol. 8 (1960), cols 894–7 and Thomas Röder, "Lindner, Friedrich," in *Die Musik in Geschichte und Gegenwart*, 2nd edn [*MGG²*], ed. Ludwig Finscher, Personenteil, 15 vols (Kassel: Bärenreiter, 1994–), vol. 11, cols 161–2.

publication," the copying of manuscripts for sale by a third party.[37] Lindner sent copies of choirbooks to ducal courts and imperial cities in exchange for dedicatory fees, and it is in this context that he had his first contact with his future residence of Nuremberg. In 1566 Lindner sent the City Council a copy of a Passion setting, which was returned to him on the grounds that the churches were already well supplied with such music.[38] Lindner's skills as a copyist surely motivated the church administrator, Hieronymus Baumgartner the Younger, to recruit Lindner for the position of Cantor at Nuremberg's Gymnasium and Church of St. Egidien in 1574, a post Lindner held until his death in 1597.[39] Baumgartner enlisted Lindner to copy large codices of liturgical music for a supplement of about 17 florins per codex, a significant increase to his base salary of 76 florins.[40] Seventeen of the volumes survive, most with the coat-of-arms of the Baumgärtner family tooled on the original leather covers.[41] Lindner's activities as a copyist and manuscript compiler enhanced his contacts with composers on both sides of the Alps, an important factor for his later service as music advisor to the Gerlach publishing house.

The founding of the music society in 1588 coincided with the publication of the first volume of Lindner's *Gemma musicalis*. It is tempting to speculate that Lindner had the group's interests, abilities, and tastes in mind as he compiled the anthology. In fact there is evidence that the title for the series originated with the group. Though Lindner used the first volume to pay homage to the Electoral court, he dedicated the remaining volumes to patricians and merchants. Lindner addressed the second volume to the Florentine merchant Carlo Albertinello, a long-time participant in Nuremberg's music societies.[42] The city's strategic position on overland trade routes made Nuremberg an attractive base for foreign merchants and businessmen like Albertinello. His niece, Isabella, married Carl Imhoff, thereby uniting the Albertinello

---

37   Harold Love, *Scribal Publication in Seventeenth-Century England* (Oxford: Clarendon Press, 1993), p. 47.

38   Ratsverlässe, 2 April 1566, cited in Butler, "Liturgical Music in Sixteenth-Century Nuremberg," p. 577 n. 202.

39   The following is based on the detailed account of the hiring in Butler, "Liturgical Music in Sixteenth-Century Nuremberg," pp. 573–84.

40   Lindner heckled and petitioned, and eventually raised his income to 100 florins, with the addition of an approved subsidy of 4 florins, and compensation of 20 florins for performing polyphonic music on the holy days of the year (ibid., p. 583).

41   Eleven of the 'Lindner choirbooks' are now in Nuremberg, Bibliotheken beim Landeskirchlichen Archiv: MS. Fenitzer IV. 2° 227, St. Egidien 19, 27, 33 (Masses); Fenitzer IV. 2° 222 and 226, St. Egidien 20, 28, and 29 (motets); Fenitzer IV. 2° 224 and St. Egidien 30 (Vespers music). Six manuscripts are in D-Ngm: 8820 Q (Masses); 8820 B, 8820 N, and 8820 X (motets); 8820 Z (Masses and motets); and 8820 T (*Magnificat* settings). See Charles Hamm and Jerry Call: "Sources, MS, §IX, 21: 16th-century German sources of Catholic music," *Grove Music Online*, ed. Laura Macy (Accessed 20 February 2006), <http://www.grovemusic.com> They are examined in Walter H. Rubsamen, "The International 'Catholic' Repertoire of a Lutheran Church in Nürnberg (1574–1597)," *Annales Musicologiques*, 5 (1957): 229–327.

42   Röder, "Lindner, Friedrich," col. 162. Carlo officially joined the society in 1596 (Butler, "Liturgical Music in Sixteenth-Century Nuremberg," p. 521).

family with one of the most prominent patricians in the city.[43] In Lindner's dedication we learn that Albertinello inspired the title of the trilogy. Lindner offered the volume "titulo, cujus tu ipse autor fuisti Gemmænimirum Musicalis" [titled, as you yourself made Gemmænimirum Musicalis].[44] Lindner dedicated the third volume to a merchant patrician, Onofrius Zollikofer of Saint Gall. Once again, Lindner emphasized patrician music-making in the home, for which Zollikofer was well-known:

> Cogitanti vero mihi, cui hanc Tertiam partem inscriberem, quò & ipsa, sicut priores duæ, non sine patrono emitteretur, venit ante alios mihi in mentem tua praestantia, ornatißime Domine Onophri, quòd nobis exercendæ Musicæ gratia congregatis, sæpenumero depræhenderim [sic] te & Autores, quorum opera hac parte continentur, ob singularem in hac arte suavitatem atque usum, vehementer probare, & eorum cantiones, quoties per negocia atq[ue] occupationes licet, non canendo tantum, sed & Musicis instrumentis accommodatas non sine singulari voluptate privatim atq[ue] domi tuæ exercere. [Canto partbook, fols 2r–v, Bayerische Staatsbibliothek München, Musikabteilung: 4° Mus. pr. 2718/2]

> [And so, as I considered to whom I should dedicate this third book—in order, as well, not to send it out without a patron—I thought of you before all others, most splendid Lord Onophri, since, in our musical gatherings I have often noted that you contribute enthusiastic praise and find great enjoyment in the authors whose works are contained in this book, [and that you] practice their canzonettas at home with singing or instrumental transcriptions, as often as the time left over for music allows.]

The dedicatory texts solidified Lindner's allegiances to court and patrician patrons. Now we will examine what Lindner selected for these groups.

Lindner as Editor: A Rationale for the *Gemma musicalis*

Lindner both shaped and was shaped by his cultural and professional environment. The tastes of Nuremberg's music societies and the printing program of the Gerlach firm established a framework for anthologies that mixed Italian and German traditions. This is most strongly felt in the combination of the familiar style of the *canzoni alla napolitana* with the more serious madrigals. Both genres are named directly on the title pages of the *Gemma musicalis*: "CANTIONES (VVLGO ITALIS MADRIGALI ET NAPOLITANE DICVNTVR" (Figure 2.2).

---

43   They announced their intent to marry on 15 July 1596 (Stadtarchiv Nürnberg, Rep. B 14/III, Nr. 2, Heiratsnotelbuch Nr. 2, 1566–1600, fols 96r–v).

44   Canto partbook, Bayerische Staatsbibliothek München, Musikabteilung: 4° Mus. pr. 2718/1, fol. 2v.

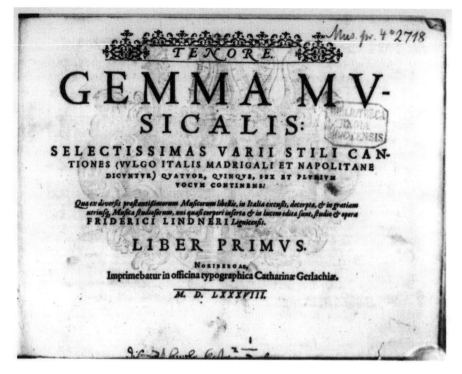

Figure 2.2   Title page of Friedrich Lindner, *Gemma Musicalis ... Liber primus* (Nuremberg, 1588), Bayerische Staatsbibliothek München, Musikabteilung: 4° Mus. Pr. 2718

The use of Latin-texted title pages made the anthologies easier for German audiences to read and understand. Gerlach and her successor, Paul Kauffmann, retained the strategy on title pages of Luca Marenzio's *Madrigalia quinque vocum* (1601) and *Madrigalia sex vocum* (1608) and Orazio Vecchi's *Convivium musicale* (1598) and *Noctes Iudicrae cio è Le veglie di Siena* (1605).[45]

Lindner arranged each anthology in descending order of the vocal forces required by the pieces it contained: music for 12 parts came before music for 11, 10, 9, etc. This method suited both printers and consumers, since all pieces for a single ensemble size were grouped together. Each anthology comprises 60–62 folios, averaging 63 pieces. The volumes departed from Venetian norms in terms of both their inclusion of multiple voice groups and their large size.[46] Scholars have turned instead to Antwerp as a potential source of Lindner's inspiration. Ludwig Finscher and Joseph Kerman argue that Lindner imitated Pierre Phalèse's anthologies *Musica divina* (Antwerp, 1583), *Harmonia celeste* (Antwerp, 1583), and *Symphonia angelica* (Antwerp, 1585), pointing to their large size, multiple voice

---

45   See RISM B/I, 1601[12] (=RISM A/I, M576); RISM A/I, M523; RISM A/I, V1051; and RISM A/I, V1054.

46   Methods of ordering anthologies are discussed in Chapter 1.

parts, and the presence of 13 settings concordant with the *Gemma musicalis*.[47] Yet, as Kristine Forney points out, the formula of a large group of works, nearly equally divided between four-, five-, and six-voiced compositions, may in fact be of German origin.[48] Forney proposes Melchior Kriesstein's *Selectissimae cantiones* (Augsburg, 1540), an anthology of chansons, lieder, motets, and madrigals for various numbers of voices, as a likely model. Yet the formula extends back even further to Hans Ott's *Novum opus et insigne musicum* (Nuremberg: Formschneider, 1537–38), with each part divided into three sections of six-, five-, and four-voice Latin motets. The practice was continued under Johannes vom Berg and Ulrich Neuber, who built the family business around large collections that featured a range of composers, styles, and performance options. The *Evangelia Dominicorum et Festorum* series of 1554–56 included motets for four to eight voices, offering an in-house model for Lindner.[49] As he compiled the *Gemma musicalis* anthologies, Lindner used a well-known structure to introduce new repertory to northern consumers.

Working within the framework of a large-scale compendium, Lindner's editorial choices were in the first place dictated by his access to Italian music. With two decades of experience as a music copyist and manuscript compiler, Lindner had well established networks that connected him with northern and southern cities, courts, religious institutions, and composers. Judging from his own words, Lindner had close contacts with Italian composers. In the dedication of *Gemma musicalis I* to the Saxon Duke Christian I, he boasts:

> However from colleges at this time many men have given me inspiration and advice as to the names of the great men from whom we should select these songs from the most distinguished musical compilations of our time, and from Italy they have sent them to me [...].[50]

Lindner made similar claims in the dedicatory preface to *Sacrae Cantiones* (Nuremberg, 1585), the first of his three anthologies of Latin motets by Italian and northern composers.[51] Alongside their printed works, in dedications to *Gemma musicalis II* and *III*, Lindner claims that composers sent him "songs which have

---

47 Finscher, "Lied and Madrigal," p. 187; *Die Musik des 15. und 16. Jahrhunderts*, ed. Ludwig Finscher, Neues Handbuch der Musikwissenschaft, 3/2, ed. Carl Dahlhaus (Laaber: Laaber-Verlag, 1990), p. 492; and Joseph Kerman, *The Elizabethan Madrigal: A Comparative Study* ([New York]: American Musicological Society, 1962), p. 49.

48 Kristine K. Forney, "Antwerp's Role in the Reception and Dissemination of the Madrigal in the North," in Angelo Pompilio et al. (eds), *IMS 14th Congress 1987. Round Table IV. Produzione e distribuzione di musica nella società del XVI e XVII secolo*, 3 vols (Turin: Edizioni di Torino, 1990), vol. 1, p. 248.

49 RISM B/I, 1554[10], RISM B/I, 1555[10–12], and RISM B/I, 1556[9]. The fifth volume includes 44 motets for five voices (RISM B/I, 1556[8]).

50 Collegi autem hoc tempore, instinctu & monitis quorundam magni nominis Virorum, selectissimas quasdam Cantilenas, à præstantissimis nostræ ætatis Musicis compositas, & ex Italia ad me allatas [...]. Tenor partbook, Bayerische Staatsbibliothek München, Musikabteilung: 4° Mus. pr. 2718, fol. 2r. Thanks to Neil Rushton for his assistance with the translation of this passage.

51 RISM B/I, 1585[1].

not been written down", and "originalia" [manuscripts?], suggesting that composers sent him manuscript copies of their works as well.[52] To these direct contacts can be added those fostered through intermediaries. In the dedication of *Liber secundus Gemmae musicalis*, Lindner writes that he received songs "from Italy which through friendly communications with friends [Albertinello?] I have accepted."[53] The lack of evidence that Lindner himself traveled south of the Alps puts greater weight on his close relationships with musicians, patricians, and merchants, like Albertinello, who did.

Lindner's Contents and Selection Criteria

The contents and earliest printed concordances for the *Gemma musicalis* are listed in Appendix B (pp. 210–30). Most of the earliest concordances are Venetian, and date from the early to mid 1580s, factors that lend force to Lindner's claims of direct and speedy transmission. Of course, many of Lindner's sources (printed and manuscript alike) have not survived. The list of earliest printed concordances confirms only that the vast majority of the contents were already in circulation. Lindner tells us this much in his dedication of *Liber secundus Gemmae musicalis*:

> In part [this collection] has been previously made in Italy, because certainly we should attempt to reach out at this time in order to publish a great collection; And with singular favor and approbation I will hopefully have seen as many music books as possible: and then without delay we have painstakingly reconciled these [songs] into print, carrying this out with as little delay as possible.[54]

---

52   See *Liber secundus Gemmae musicalis* (Nuremberg, 1589; RISM B/I, 1589[8]), canto partbook, fols 2r–v: "& aliquot hactenus non impressarum, non tamen minus suavium cantionum acceßione auxi, typis evulgare" [and other songs which have not been written down but nevertheless are no less sweet and so should be acquired, put into print and published] (exemplar Bayerische Staatsbibliothek München, Musikabteilung: 4° Mus. pr. 173/4); and *Tertius Gemmae musicalis* (Nuremberg, 1590; RISM B/I, 1590[20]), canto partbook, fol. 2r: "Passus igitur sum me impelli, ut tertiæ quoq[ue] partis (in qua florem eiusmodi cantionum complexus mihi videor) collectionem atq[ue] editionem adgrederer, præsertim cum intelligam, hoc meum studium ab ipsis etiam Autoribus in Italia non improbari, ut qui & originalia (ut vocant) ad me mittant, & exemplaria hîc excusa, magno numero ad se reportari curent" [And thus I have allowed myself to be persuaded to undertake the collection and editing of a third volume (which, I believe, contains the best and most beautiful canzonettas of this sort), especially since I observe that the Italian composers themselves approve of my work, in that in great numbers they send me their compositions, as they demand exemplars printed here] (exemplar Bayerische Staatsbibliothek München, Musikabteilung: 4° Mus. pr. 2718/2).

53   RISM B/I, 1589[8], canto partbook, fol. 2v: "si quid eiusmodi cantionum ex Italia ab amicis accepisti, eas mecum benigne communicaris" (exemplar Bayerische Staatsbibliothek München, Musikabteilung: 4° Mus. pr. 173/4).

54   RISM B/I, 1589[8], canto partbook, fol. 2r: "partem, ex præcipuorum in Italia artificum, quæ quidem hoc tempore ad nos pervenere, monumentis collectam, edidissem; eamq[ue] singulari favore & approbatione Philomusorum exceptam esse animadvertissem" (exemplar Bayerische Staatsbibliothek München, Musikabteilung: 4° Mus. pr. 173/4).

Lindner's dedicatory prefaces conveyed the impression of a resourceful editor who aimed to bring music to market quickly.

Like his Nuremberg predecessors, Lindner adopted a composer-based approach to anthology compilation. A handful of composers dominate the series. Table 2.3 lists composers represented in the *Gemma musicalis* trilogy. Across the series, there are 45 works by Marenzio alone. For *Liber secundus Gemmae musicalis*, Lindner drew 45 of a total of 88 pieces from only five volumes of music by as many different composers: Girolamo Conversi, Giovanni Ferretti, Andrea Gabrieli, Giovanni Gabrieli, and Luca Marenzio.

Table 2.3 Composers: Their Geographic Origin and Representation in *Gemma musicalis I–III*

COMPOSER	REGION OF ORIGIN/ACTIVITY	# OF PIECES
Anerio, Felice	Rome	1
Antegnati, Costanzo	Brescia	2
Antinori, Cavallier	unknown	2
d'Aranda, Sessa	composer active in Italy; from Aranda, Spain or Portugal?	1
Bertani, Lelio	Brescia; Padua 1598–1604	7
Biffi, Gioseffi	b. Cesena; chapelmaster for Zsigmond Báthory; composer for Friedrich I, Duke of Württemburg	3
Cedraro, Francesco da	Disciple of Sessa d'Aranda	2
Coma, Annibale	Mantua	2
Conversi, Girolamo	b. Correggio; in the service of Cardinal Granvelle, Viceroy of Naples	7
Croce, Giovanni	Venice; posts at San Marco	1
Donato, Baldassaro	Venice; posts at San Marco	3
Duc, Filippo	b. Flanders; active at Padua?	2
Eremita, Giulio	b. Ferrara; active at Rome	3
Faignient, Noë	b. Flanders; Antwerp, from 1580 active at 's-Hertogenbosch	1
Ferabosco, Domenico	Bologna; Rome; Paris	1
Ferretti, Giovanni	Italian; Ancona, Loreto, Gemona, Friuli, Rome?	12
Gabrieli, Andrea	Venice, San Marco; 1562 in service of Albrecht V	24
Gabrieli, Giovanni	Venice; 1575–79? Munich, San Marco, San Rocco	5

COMPOSER	REGION OF ORIGIN/ACTIVITY	# OF PIECES
Gastoldi, Giovanni Giacomo	b. Carravaggio, Mantua	8
Lassus, Orlande de	b. Mons, Hainaut; Mantua-Milan-Naples, Rome, Antwerp, from 1566 at the Bavarian Court at Munich	1
Macque, Giovanni de	b. Valenciennes; Vienna, Rome, Naples	2
Marenzio, Luca	b. Coccaglio, nr. Brescia; mainly Rome	45
Marni, Paolo	unknown	1
Merulo, Claudio	b. Correggio; Brescia, Venice, Parma	2
Monte, Philippe de	b. Mechelen; Vienna, Prague	2
Moscaglia, Giovanni	Rome	1
Nanino, Giovanni Maria	b. Tivoli; active in Rome	1
Palestrina, Giovanni Pierluigi da	b. Palestrina, nr. Rome; Rome	4
Pallavicino, Benedetto	b. Cremona; Mantua	23
Pallavicino, Germano	Cremona; brother of Benedetto	3
Pratoneri, Gaspari	active at Reggio nell'Emilia	1
Renaldi, Giulio	active at Padua	2
Rore, Cipriano de	b. Ronse, Flanders; Brescia, Ferrara, Parma	1
Sabino, Ippolito	Lanciano; Cathedral of Ortona	2
Soriano, Francesco	b. Soriano; Rome, Mantua	1
Spontini, Bartholomeo	unknown	1
Striggio, Alessandro	Mantua; Florence 1560s; Bavaria and Austria; Mantua	4
Vecchi, Orazio	Modena, Correggio	22
Waelrant, Hubert	Flemish composer; Antwerp	1
Wert, Giaches de	Flemish composer in Italy; Mantua, Ferrara	17
Zoilo, Annibale	Rome, Loreto	1

Within sections of a single composer's music, Lindner frequently ordered the settings according to the sources he used, a technique borrowed from manuscript compilation. In this respect Lindner departed from the Venetian practice of grouping pieces by ambitus (cleffing), system (presence or absence of a flat in the signature), mode, or final. Instead Lindner mimicked single-composer editions by creating subsections devoted to the music of one composer. This is most striking in *Gemma musicalis I*, with 23 consecutive settings by Luca Marenzio drawn from the composer's first two books of five-voice madrigals and his first book of spiritual madrigals (See Appendix B, pp. 214–16). For *Gemma musicalis I*, Lindner transferred seven madrigals by Lelio Bertani directly from the opening of the composer's first book of madrigals for six voices. Lindner headed the five-voice section of *Tertius Gemmae musicalis liber* with the opening six madrigals from Benedetto Pallavicino's second book of five-voice madrigals; he followed them with a further five madrigals by Pallavicino, taken in order from the fourth book. Ease of access may best explain Lindner's inclusion of 23 madrigals by Pallavicino, whose music was little known outside of Italy at the time.

Lindner's emphasis on composer selection and presentation reveals much about how he thought the *Gemma musicalis* would be used. Arrangement by composer was a pragmatic approach that may have served an instructional purpose, by making the music and styles of individual composers available for study and emulation.[55] Lindner selected composers whose music demonstrated the primary attributes of the *canzoni alla napolitana*, canzonetta, and madrigal genres; thus, they might serve as models for German poets and composers. Giovanni Ferretti's and Girolamo Conversi's five-voice *canzoni alla napolitana* exemplify the form's first stage of development in the late 1560s and early 1570s.[56] During this phase, there is little relation between the content of the text and its musical setting—a stylistic quality that would not be missed by audiences less familiar with the Italian language. Vecchi was the first to use the term canzonetta on the title page of the second edition of his *Canzonette ... libro primo a quattro voci* (Venice, 1580). Vecchi's books met with instant success. Book 1 reached six numbered editions, five for Book 2, three for Book 3, and two for Book 4 between 1578–79 and 1613.[57] As a poet-composer, Vecchi wrote simple strophic poems of stanzas of 3 to 6 lines, with lines of 7 and 11 syllables freely intermixed. They inspired imitators like Christoph von Schallenberg, Cesare de Zacharia, Valentin Haussmann, Hans Leo Hassler, and Theobald Höck, whose German translations of Vecchi's poems established new standards of German verse poetry that paved the way for the reforms of Martin Opitz.[58] Their stanza forms, homophonic or lightly imitative textures, and simple harmonies offered models for German composers as well.

For the madrigal, Marenzio's ten books of five-voice madrigals quickly established the composer's reputation across Europe. English composer, theorist, and print entrepreneur Thomas Morley commended Marenzio for his "good ayre and fine invention" in *A Plaine and Easie Introduction to Practicall Musicke* (London, 1597).[59] Writing in 1619, German composer and theorist Michael Praetorius singled out Marenzio as a defining example of madrigal technique: "a composer may at times use the same text for one part and on other occasions divide it between two

---

55 Lindner may be alluding to an established tradition of printing didactic music anthologies in Nuremberg. See Cristle Collins Judd, *Reading Renaissance Music Theory: Hearing with the Eyes* (Cambridge: Cambridge University Press, 2000), pp. 82–114.

56 Ruth I. DeFord: "Canzonetta," *Grove Music Online*, ed. Laura Macy (Accessed 20 February 2006), <http://www.grovemusic.com>

57 Orazio Vecchi, *Orazio Vecchi: The Four-Voice Canzonettas. With Original Texts and Contrafacta by Valentin Haussmann and Others*, ed. Ruth I. DeFord, Recent Researches in the Music of the Renaissance, 92–3 (Madison, WI: A-R Editions Inc., 1993), part 1, pp. 1–2.

58 See Chapter 3.

59 James Chater, "Marenzio, Luca (4)," *Grove Music Online*, ed. Laura Macy (Accessed 28 May 2006), <http://www.grovemusic.com>

parts, as is amply borne out by Luca Marenzio and other composers."[60] He goes on to praise Marenzio's spiritual madrigals for their exemplary use of mensuration signs and part-writing.[61]

Beyond offering northern consumers model compositions in all three subgenres of Italian secular song, Lindner hoped to create a market for subsequent single-author volumes. By retaining a sense of composer independence, the *Gemma musicalis* built interest in the stylistic identity of individual authors. Marenzio's strong showing in the *Gemma musicalis* anthologies paved the way for the success of Paul Kauffmann's compendiums of his madrigals for five (1601) and six (1608) voices.[62] Here, Kauffmann followed a marketing plan already proven by his northern rival Pierre Phalèse, whose collected editions of Marenzio's five- (1593) and six-voice (1594) madrigals followed the appearance of Marenzio in the Antwerp anthologies *Musica divina*, *Harmonia celeste*, *Symphonia angelica*, and *Melodia olympica*.[63] Orazio Vecchi offers the most convincing example at the Nuremberg firm of early anthology transmission, followed by later success with single-author publication. Following the transmission of 22 canzonettas by Vecchi in the *Gemma musicalis* anthologies, the shop issued five volumes of music devoted to Vecchi's Italian-texted works, three volumes of his canzonettas in German translation, and one dual collection of canzonettas by Vecchi and his pupil Gemignano Capilupi in both Italian and German translation (Table 2.4).

Table 2.4 Orazio Vecchi at the Gerlach-Kauffmann Firm

DATE	RISM	SHORT TITLE & DERIVATION
1593	V1029	*Canzonette a quattro voci ... raccolte insieme* Contents=RISM A/I, V1010; RISM A/I, V1017; RISM A/I, V1022; RISM A/I, V1027 (Books I–IV, for four voices, Venice: Angelo Gardano, 1580–90), together with an appendix of 18 pieces from *Selva di varia ricreatione* (RISM A/I, V1044) and a five-voice madrigal from *De floridi virtuosi d'Italia, il primo libro de madrigali a cinque voci* (RISM B/I, 1583[11])

---

60   Michael Praetorius, *Syntagma Musicum III* (Wolfenbüttel, 1619), p. 12. Trans. in Michael Praetorius, *Syntagma Musicum III*, ed./trans. Jeffery Kite-Powell, Oxford Early Music Series (Oxford: Oxford University Press, 2004), pp. 26–7.

61   Michael Praetorius, *Syntagma Musicum III*, pp. 33, 50–52, ed./trans. Kite-Powell, *Syntagma Musicum III*, pp. 51, 69–72.

62   RISM A/I, M576 (=RISM B/I, 1601[12]) and RISM A/I, M523.

63   *Madrigali a cinque voci, ridotti in un corpo ... & con ogni diligentia corretti* (Antwerp: Pierre Phalèse & Jean Bellère, 1593; RISM A/I, M572); and *Madrigali a sei voci, in un corpo ridotti, Nuovamente posti in luce, & con ogni diligentia corretti. Aggiuntovi di più uno madrigale del istesso authore a dieci voci* (Antwerp: Pierre Phalèse & Jean Bellère, 1594; RISM A/I, M522 [=RISM B/I, 1594[14]]).

DATE	RISM	SHORT TITLE & DERIVATION

1594 V1047 *Piu e diversi madrigali e canzonette a 5.6.7.8.9. & 10. voci, per*
avanti separatamente iti in luce, & ora insieme raccolti
Contents=21 settings from RISM A/I, V1026; 20 pieces from
RISM A/I, V1040; 21 settings from RISM A/I, V1043; 30 pieces
from RISM A/I, V1044; 4 settings from RISM A/I, V1050; a
five-voice madrigal from *De floridi virtuosi d'Italia, il primo*
libro de madrigali a cinque voci (RISM B/I, 1583[11]); three six-
voice madrigals from *Trionfo di musica di diversi ... Libro primo*
(RISM B/I, 1579[3]); a seven-voice madrigal from *Dialoghi*
musicali de diversi eccellentissimi autori (RISM B/I, 1590[11]);
and a seven-voice *Dialogo* from *Liber secundus Gemmae*
musicalis (RISM B/I, 1589[8])

1597 V1033 *Canzonette a tre voci di Horatio Vecchi, et di Gemignano Capi*
=1597[22] *Lupi da Modena*
Contents=RISM A/I, V1032=RISM B/I, 1597[21]

1598 V1051 *Convivium musicale ... ternis, quaternis, quinis, senis, septenis,*
& octonis vocibus
Contents=RISM A/I, V1050

1600/ V1030 *Canzonette a quattro voci ... con aggiunta di altre a 5.4. e 3. voci*
1601 canto partbook dated 1600; alto, tenor, bass dated 1601
Contents=RISM A/I, V1029, together with an appendix of
19 settings for 3–5 parts from RISM A/I, V1047

1605 V1054 *Noctes Iudicrae cio è Le veglie di Siena*
Contents=*Le veglie di Siena ... a tre a 4. a 5. & a 6. voci*
(RISM A/I, V1053)

1606 V1034 *Canzonette, mit dreyen Stimmen, Horatii Vecchi unnd*
Gemignani Capi Lupi ... mit teutschen Texten belegt,
=1606[13] *und inn Truck gegeben durch Valentin Haussmann*
Musical Contents=RISM B/I, 1597[21]=RISM A/I, V1032

1610 V1035 *Die erste Class Der vierstimmigen Canzonetten ... mit*
=1610[19] *unterlegung Teutscher Texte auffs neue inn Druck gebracht,*
durch Valentinum Haussmann
Contents=28 pieces from RISM A/I, V1030, with an opening
"Prooemium" set to music by Valentin Haussmann

DATE	RISM	SHORT TITLE & DERIVATION
1610	V1036	*Die ander Class Der vierstimmigen Canzonetten ... mit unterlegung Teutscher Texte auffs neue inn Druck gebracht, durch Valentinum Haussmann* Contents=28 pieces from RISM A/I, V1030
1610	V1037	*Die dritte Class Der vierstimmigen Canzonetten ... mit unterlegung Teutscher Texte auffs neue inn Druck gebracht, durch Valentinum Haussmann* Contents=34 pieces from RISM A/I, V1030

Regional affiliation also influenced Lindner's selection process. With a combined total of 29 settings, the prominence of Andrea and Giovanni Gabrieli across the series as a whole is a mark of the status of the Venetian tradition and the authority Germans invested in it. Both Andrea and Giovanni had ties to south German courts and cities, which created a regional interest in their music and eased Lindner's receipt of it. Andrea joined the retinue of Duke Albrecht V with Lassus to attend the coronation of Emperor Maximilian II in Frankfurt in fall 1562.[64] Years later Giovanni became an assistant to Lassus in Munich from 1575–79. The Cathedral of St Mark was the pearl of the Venetian musical crown. Andrea's association with the cathedral may date back to 1536 when he studied there under master Adrian Willaert and sang in the chapel. After two decades as second organist, Andrea advanced to first organist from 1585, with his nephew Giovanni as second. Giovanni succeeded his uncle the following year, and retained the post for the rest of his life. At the seat of arguably the most prestigious musical institution of Europe, the Gabrielis came into contact with German travelers, students, and dignitaries. The Nuremberg merchant and music patron, Georg Gruber, had close ties with Venice, where he met both Andrea and Giovanni Gabrieli. Giovanni became a close personal friend, and even composed the six-part madrigal *Scherza Amarilli e Clori* for Gruber's wedding to Helen Joanna Kolmann in 1600.[65] The Cathedral became an important training ground for German musicians, thereby reinforcing the pattern of Italian study observable among patricians and merchants. Giovanni Gabrieli taught a generation of German students, including Gregor Aichinger, Christoph Kegel, Heinrich Schütz, Christoph Clemsee, and Johann Grabbe.[66]

---

64 David Bryant: "Gabrieli, Andrea," *Grove Music Online*, ed. Laura Macy (Accessed 28 May 2006), <http://www.grovemusic.com>

65 David Bryant, "Gabrieli, Giovanni," *Grove Music Online*, ed. Laura Macy (Accessed 20 February 2006), <http://www.grovemusic.com>

66 On Giovanni's students, see Siegfried Schmalzriedt, *Heinrich Schütz und andere zeitgenössische Musiker in der Lehre Giovanni Gabrielis* (Neuhausen: Hänssler-Verlag,

Lindner's selection of Andrea Gabrieli's music complemented his inclusion of the composer in his motet anthologies. Lindner included 17 motets by Andrea Gabrieli in the *Continuatio cantionum sacrarum* (RISM B/I, 1588²), and a further seven in the *Corollarium cantionum sacrarum* (RISM B/I, 1590⁵). Following Andrea's appearance in the *Gemma musicalis*, his nephew, Giovanni, remained a recurring presence in anthologies from the Gerlach-Kauffmann firm. Kaspar Hassler included 23 of his motets in the anthology series *Sacrae Symphoniae* (RISM B/I, 1598²; RISM B/I, 1600²), and Gruber paid tribute to him by editing the *Reliquiae Sacrorum Concentuum* (RISM B/I, 1615²), an anthology of motets by Hans Leo Hassler and Giovanni Gabrieli.

Lindner extracted all but one of the Gabrieli settings from a single volume, the *Concerti ... Continenti musica di chiesa, madrigali, & altro* (Venice, 1587).[67] Giovanni Gabrieli edited the volume shortly after his uncle's death in 1585, and devoted it to large-scale sacred, secular, and instrumental pieces by both Gabrielis. Lindner opened *Liber secundus Gemmae musicalis* with Giovanni Gabrieli's 12-voice *Sacri di Giove augei* on a text (by Giovanni himself?) that honors the Fugger family of Augsburg, with whom Giovanni was closely connected. Giovanni dedicated the *Concerti* to Jacob Fugger and presented his later *Sacrae Symphoniae* (Venice: Angelo Gardano, 1597) as a gift for the quadruple wedding of the brothers Georg, Anton, Philipp, and Albert Fugger.[68] *Sacri di Giovi augei* ends with the text "Focchari, a voi ch'havete il simulacro, Di fama eterna i miei concenti i'sacro" [Focchari, to you who are the image, of eternal fame I dedicate my harmonies].[69] The inclusion of a madrigal dedicated to an Augsburg patriarch intensified the regional appeal of the *Gemma musicalis* series.

Lindner opened *Gemma musicalis I* with Andrea Gabrieli's 12-voice *Ecco Vinegia bella*, a polychoral madrigal on a text that spread the virtues of the city of Venice far and wide. The text reinforces the propaganda of Venetian publicists Francesco Sansovino, Gasparo Contarini, Giovanni Botero, and Paolo Sarpi, who constructed a mythic vision of the city that took hold across Europe. The setting was

---

1972); and Denis Arnold, *Giovanni Gabrieli and the Music of the Venetian High Renaissance* (London: Oxford University Press, 1979), pp. 211–30.

67 *Concerti di Andrea, et di Gio. Gabrieli organisti della sereniss. sig. di Venetia. Continenti musica di chiesa, madrigali, & altro, per voci, & stromenti musicali, à 6. 7. 8. 10. 12. & 16. Novamente con ogni diligentia dati in luce. Libro primo et secondo* (Venice: Angelo Gardano, 1587; RISM B/I, 1587¹⁶=RISM A/I, G58=RISM A/I, G85).

68 There is some debate concerning whether Giovanni Gabrieli attended the Fugger wedding. See Holger Eichhorn, "Der Deutsche Gabrieli: Zur Überlieferung des Spätwerks von Giovanni Gabrieli unter vorrangigem Betracht deutscher Rezeption und Quellenlage im 17. Jahrhundert," *Giovanni Gabrieli: Quantus vir*, Musik-Konzepte, 105 (1999): 35 n. 2. Cf. Butler, "Liturgical Music in Sixteenth-Century Nuremberg," p. 522 n. 39, who notes that Giovanni Gabrieli and Gregor Aichinger were hosted by the Nuremberg music society in May 1597.

69 Richard Charteris, *Giovanni Gabrieli (ca. 1555–1612): A Thematic Catalogue of his Music with a Guide to the Source Materials and Translations of his Vocal Texts*, Thematic Catalogues, 20, general ed. Barry S. Brook (Stuyvesant, NY: Pendragon Press, 1996), p. 182.

occasioned by the visit to Venice of the new king of France, Henry III, in July 1574.[70] The poem tells the allegorical story of Hercules, here the fictitious brother of Venice, who comes to rest from his labors in his sister's bosom (Example 2.1).

Example 2.1 Andrea Gabrieli, *Ecco Vinegia bella*. The text is published in *Andrea Gabrieli: Complete Madrigals*, 12. Edited by A. Tilmann Merritt. Recent Researches in the Music of the Renaissance, vol. 52. Madison, WI: A-R Editions, Inc. 1981. Used with permission.

Ecco Vinegia bella—
Che chi domò tant'Hidre, e tant'estinse
Mostri, e fe' tante e sì notabil prove,
Sol per piacer al suo gran padre Giove,
Ch'ancor fanciul lo spinse
Ad alt'imprese ov'egli sempre vinse,
In gremb'a te, che sua fida sorella
Con pur'affett'appella,
S'acqueta, e'l mal de la passata via
Ne le tue bracc'accolto homai s'oblia—
Tu, scopr'intanto le tue gioie, e mostra
Quanto gradir t'aggrada
A lui che venne a te per lunga strada.
E come vibra a te per lunga strada.
Da la stellata chiostra
I suoi lucenti rai,
Quasi che sì gran Re, tant'a Dio caro,
Voglia honorar col suo bel lume chiaro;
Così tu spiega le tue pomp', e'n mille
Modi e col dolce suon, col dolce canto,
Col ribombar di squille
E col tuonar de' cavi bronzi, segno
Porgi pront'e amico
Ch'al suo paterno Regno
Godi ch'ascenda il glorioso Henrico.

Lo, beautiful Venice—he who subdued so many hydras, destroyed so many monsters, and performed so many and such remarkable feats, solely to please his great father Jove, who, when [his son] was still a child, pushed him to lofty exploits in which he was always victorious: he has now become calm in your bosom, you whom with pure affection he calls his faithful sister; and, welcomed to your arms, he forgets the misfortunes of his past career—you, then, reveal your joys and show how pleased you are to welcome him who came by such a long way to visit you. And, as from its starry cloister heaven darts its rays, shining far more than usual, as if it wishes with its beautiful, clear light to honor such a great king so dear to God, so you [Venice] unfold your splendor and, in a thousand ways, with sweet sound and sweet song,

---

70 On the celebrations honoring the visit, see Ellen Rosand, "Music in the Myth of Venice," *Renaissance Quarterly*, 30 (1977): 530–31.

with the clanging of bells and thundering of cannons, you give a ready and friendly signal that you rejoice in the ascent of the glorious Henry to his paternal throne.

Lindner selected a textual theme that resonated with the interest Venice held for Nuremberg patricians and merchants. Reminders of the victories of Venice, its splendor, and famed music reinforced messages transmitted in travel literature, histories, and political commentaries on the city. *Ecco Vinegia bella* enhanced the stylistic diversity of the series, and solidified the close ties between the two cities.

The popularity of individual settings further guided Lindner's selection process. Among the earliest repertory in the series, Lindner chose settings that had already acquired much fame. Examples include Cipriano de Rore's *Anchor che col partire*, Giovanni Pierluigi da Palestrina's *Vestiva i colli*, and Domenico Ferrabosco's *Io mi son giovinetta*. Each of these madrigals had already appeared in madrigal books and instrumental arrangements, some dating back to the 1550s.[71] The transmission of *Io mi son giovinetta* and *Anchor che col partire* in German instrumental anthologies by Melchior Newsidler, Bernhard Schmid, and Elias Nicolaus Ammerbach may have sparked interest in their transmission—with texts—in *Gemma musicalis I*. Luca Marenzio's *Liquide perle* created an immediate splash after its publication in the composer's *Il primo libro de madrigali a cinque voci* (Venice: Angelo Gardano, 1580). It served as the model for the text of Antonio Bicci's *Candide perle*, published as the third madrigal in Marenzio's *Il quinto libro de madrigali a sei voci* (Venice: Angelo Gardano,1591).[72] In 1583 it made its northern debut in the Antwerp anthology *Musica divina*, and was included in all reprints of the anthology through 1634. In 1588 it appeared both in *Gemma musicalis I*, and in English translation as *Liquid and wat'ry tears*, in the first volume of Nicholas Yonge's *Musica transalpina* (London, 1588). Paul Kauffmann opened his anthology of Marenzio's five-voice madrigals

---

71 Instrumental arrangements of Ferrabosco's *Io mi son giovinetta* had already appeared in RISM B/I, 1563[7]; RISM B/I, 1566[2]; RISM B/I, 1568[2]; RISM B/I, 1571[6]; RISM B/I, 1572[1]; RISM B/I, 1573[1]; RISM B/I, 1574[6]; RISM B/I, 1577[6]; RISM B/I, 1583[2]; RISM B/I, 1584[3]; RISM B/I, 1584[5]; and RISM B/I, 1584[6] (Howard Mayer Brown, *Instrumental Music Printed Before 1600: A Bibliography* [Cambridge: Harvard University Press, 1965; reprint London: iUniverse.com, 2000], p. 525). The madrigal appeared in two northern anthologies, Pierre Phalèse the Elder's *Livre de meslanges* (RISM B/I, 1575[4]), and his son's *Musica divina* (RISM B/I, 1583[15]). Palestrina's *Vestiva i colli* was equally popular. For vocal and instrumental transmissions, see Clara Marvin, *Giovanni Pierluigi da Palestrina: A Guide to Research*, Composer Resource Manuals, 56 (New York: Routledge, 2002), p. 461. Rore's *Anchor che col partire* first appeared in the composer's *Primo libro de Madrigali a quatro voci* (Ferrara: Giovanni de Buglhat, et Antonio Hucher, 1550), a volume subsequently issued by the Venetian firms of Girolamo Scotto, Antonio (and later Angelo) Gardano, Francesco Rampazetto, and Giorgio Angelieri. Phalèse included it in *Musica divina* (RISM B/I, 1583[15]), and it appeared in instrumental arrangements in RISM B/I, 1560[3]; RISM B/I, 1563[12]; RISM B/I, 1568[1]; RISM B/I, 1568[2]; RISM B/I, 1568[7]; RISM B/I, 1571[6]; RISM B/I, 1574[5]; RISM B/I, 1577[5]; RISM B/ I, 1577[6]; RISM B/I, 1578[3]; RISM B/I, 1583[2]; RISM B/I, 1584[2]; and RISM B/I, 1584[6] (Brown, *Instrumental Music*, p. 500).

72 James Chater, *Luca Marenzio and the Italian Madrigal, 1577–1593*, Studies in British Musicology, ed. Nigel Fortune, 2 vols (Ann Arbor: UMI Research Press, 1981), vol. 1, p. 26.

(Nuremberg, 1601) with *Liquide perle*.[73] The multiple transmissions of *Liquide perle* guaranteed the madrigal a lasting position in the repertory, and justified Pietro della Valle singling it out as an example of Marenzio's *grazie* [grace] in his treatise *Della musica dell'età nostra* (1640).[74]

Lindner was keenly aware that his target audience included amateur musicians. He avoided the highly chromatic madrigals of Carlo Gesualdo and the virtuosity of Luzzascho Luzzaschi, that would be too challenging for the amateur music market. Instead, he chose homorhythmic and homophonic settings like *Io vo gridando* and *Poi che m'hai tolto* from Conversi's first book of *Canzone* (Venice, 1572), and Vecchi's four-voice canzonettas with their simple internal forms (AABCC or AABB) and conventional harmonies. Lindner includes only the initial stanzas of multi-verse canzoni, thereby removing the problem of text underlay for subsequent verses. Even in cases of larger ensemble music, Lindner chose selections like Vecchi's *Io son restato* and *Io v'ho servita*, that grouped the six voices into upper and lower parts.

Lindner's editorial work was further informed by his literary taste. Across the series one can detect his preference for pastoral poetry, by Jacopo Sannazaro, Francesco Petrarch, and Giovanni Battista Guarini. Inspired by Classical models such as Virgil's *Eclogues*, Sannazaro's *Arcadia* (1504) is the first non-dramatic Renaissance pastoral. Sannazaro cast the pastoral in a series of 12 chapters of prose discourse, each ending with a poetic eclogue, and framed by a prose prologue and prose epilogue. It tells the story of the frustrated love of Sincero for Phyllis. *Arcadia* was immensely popular, with 66 editions appearing between 1504 and 1600.[75] Madrigals from *Arcadia* inspired a steady number of musical settings from the early 1540s through 1600, by Marenzio, Giovanni Piero Manenti, Ruggiero Giovannelli, Alfonso Ferrabosco, Jacques Arcadelt, Claudio Monteverdi, Giaches de Wert, Andrea Gabrieli, Philippe de Monte, Giovan Leonardo Primavera, Giovanni de Macque, and Orlande de Lassus.[76] Lindner's choice of 10 texts by Sannazaro, all set by Marenzio (who set a total of 26 madrigals by the poet), suggests that poetic taste may have shaped Lindner's selection of music within a single composer's *oeuvre*.

Lindner included ten settings of Petrarch's poetry set by Andrea Gabrieli (4), Giovanni Gabrieli (1), Wert (2), Marenzio (2), and Lassus (1). Petrarch enjoyed a revival in Italy, following Pietro Bembo's edition of the poet's *Canzoniere* (Venice, 1501) and Bembo's subsequent study of the sound quality of Petrarch's poetry in *Prose della volgar lingua* (Venice, 1525). Though more of his madrigals were set to music in the first two thirds of the century, reprints and commentaries on the *Canzoniere* kept the poet's style in vogue long after. Writing in 1597, Thomas Morley defined the madrigal as "a kinde of musicke made upon songs and sonnets, such as

---

73   See Chapter 1, Figure 1.6, p. 42.

74   James Chater: "Marenzio, Luca (4)," *Grove Music Online*, ed. Laura Macy (Accessed 28 May 2006), <http://www.grovemusic.com>

75   Alfredo Mauro (ed.), *Iacopo Sannazaro, Opere volgari*, Scrittori d'Italia, 220 (Bari: G. Laterza, 1961), p. 427, cited in Chater, *Luca Marenzio*, vol. 1, p. 28.

76   Musical settings are listed in Silke Leopold, "Madrigali sulle egloghe sdrucciole di Iacopo Sannazaro," *Rivista italiana di musicologia*, 14 (1979): 102–27.

Petrarcha and many Poets of our time have excelled in."[77] German audiences were first exposed to Petrarch's madrigal texts in Leonhard Lechner's five-voice versions of Jacob Regnart's three-part *Lieder ... Con alchuni madrigali in lingua Italiana* (Nuremberg, 1579) and Lassus's five-voice *Madrigali* (Nuremberg, 1585). The high proportion of Petrarchan settings in the *Gemma musicalis* anthologies may have been a calculated move by Lindner to include poetry that was not readily available in German-speaking lands. Their presence strengthens the evidence that music books served both musical and literary audiences.

Scholars have undermined the poetic taste of northern editors by pointing to the many cases of editors including only the first or second part of a poem, thereby breaking the textual unity.[78] Lindner distinguished himself from his northern counterparts by transmitting complete settings of a poem. Lindner included five complete settings of Guarini's three-part *Tirsi morir volea*, set by Marenzio, Andrea Gabrieli, Pallavicino, Wert, and Monte. The madrigal text first appeared in the first part of Torquato Tasso's *Rime* (Venice, 1581), and only much later in Guarini's own *Rime* (Venice, 1598). Lindner's passion for the text built on pan-European interest in Guarini's lyrics, which were a major source for composers writing in the decades around 1600.[79] Guarini's madrigal *Ardo sì, ma non t'amo* inspired 31 competitive settings, compiled by the Bavarian court composer Giulio Gigli da Immola and published as *Sdegnosi ardori* (Munich: Adam Berg, 1585), the first anthology of Italian madrigals printed in Germany. Guarini's *Tirsi morir volea* proved equally popular. It was set by 27 different composers between 1578 and 1633.[80] Composers and editors were drawn to the text's blatant imagery—eyes, burning, death metaphors—images that made the characteristic word painting of the Italian madrigal immediately audible for German audiences (Example 2.2). The text was infused with dramatic possibility. Andrea Gabrieli cast the dialogue for two choruses. He assigned the narrative to the second chorus (alto, tenors 1 and 2, bass) and the role of the shepherdess to the first (canto 1

---

77 Thomas Morley, *A Plaine and Easie Introduction to Practicall Musicke* (London, 1597), pg. 180, quoted in Chater, *Luca Marenzio*, vol. 1, pp. 19, 21.

78 In Franco Piperno, "Polifonisti dell'Italia Meridionale nelle Antologie Madrigalistiche d'Oltralpe (1601–1616)," *La musica a Napoli durante il Seicento. Atti del Convegno Internazionale di Studi Napoli*, Miscellanea Musicologica, 2 (Rome: Edizioni Torre d'Orfeo, 1987), pp. 83–4, Piperno concludes that variety and heterogeneity seemed to be the rule among northern anthologists.

79 See the bibliography of musical compositions whose verbal text is based on or inspired by passages from *Il pastor fido* in James Chater, "*Il pastor fido* and Music: A Bibliography," in Angelo Pompilio (ed.), *Guarini, la musica, i musicisti*, Con Natazioni 3, series ed. Paolo Fabbri (Lucca: Libreria Musicale Italiana Editrice, 1997), pp. 157–83. For *Rime* set to music, see Antonio Vassalli and Angelo Pompilio, "Indice delle rime di Battista Guarini poste in musica," pp. 185–225 in the same volume.

80 Vassalli and Pompilio, "Indice delle rime," p. 221. Alfred Einstein (*The Italian Madrigal*, 3 vols [Princeton: Princeton University Press, 1949], vol. 2, p. 542) described it as "the madrigal text most frequently composed during the so-called Golden Age of the genre" (quoted in George C. Schuetze [ed.], *Settings of* Ardo si *and Its Related Texts*, Recent Researches in the Music of the Renaissance, 78–9 [Madison, WI: A-R Editions Inc., 1990], part I, p. xxxvii n. 2).

and 2, tenor) with the choruses joining forces at the end of the madrigal (mm. 63–80 of the modern edition).[81]

Example 2.2 Giovanni Battista Guarini, *Tirsi morir volea*. The text is published in *Andrea Gabrieli: Complete Madrigals*, 9–10. Edited by A. Tilmann Merritt. Recent Researches in the Music of the Renaissance, vols 49–50. Madison, WI: A-R Editions, Inc., 1983. Used with permission.

Dialogo

Dialogue

Tirsi morir volea,
Gl'occhi mirando di colei ch'adora;
Quand'ella, che di lui non meno ardea,
Li disse: "Oimè, ben mio,
Deh, non morir ancora,
Chè teco bramo di morir anch'io."
Frenò Tirsi il desio,
C'hebbe di pur sua vit'alhor finire;
Ma sentia mort'in non poter morire.
E mentre'l guardo suo fisso tenea
Ne' begl'occhi divini
E'l nettare amoroso indi bevea,
La bella Ninfa sua, che già vicini
Sentia i messi d'Amore,
Disse con occhi languidi e tremanti:
"Mori cor mio, ch'io moro."
Cui rispose il Pastore:
"Et io, mia vita, moro."
Così moriro i fortunati amanti
Di morte sì soave e sì gradita,
Che per anco morir tornaro in vita.

Thyrsis was wanting to die, gazing into the eyes of her whom he adores, when she, who was no less burning for him, said to him, "Alas, my sweet, pray don't die yet, for I want to die with you." Thyrsis controlled the desire that he had to finish off his life, but he was feeling death in not being able to die. And while he kept his gaze fixed in her beautiful, divine eyes, and drank the amorous nectar, his beautiful nymph, who was already conscious of the messengers of Love at hand, said with languid and trembling eyes, "Die, my love, for I am dying." To whom the shepherd answered, "And I, too, my life, am dying." Thus the fortunate lovers died a death so sweet and welcome, that in order to die again they came back to life.

The early transmission of Guarini's poetry in the *Gemma musicalis* anthologies reminds us that music books served an important function as anthologies of poetry as well. It is likely that interest in Guarini and other Italian poets may have fuelled the German market for Italian music books.

Having considered Lindner's selection of contents for the *Gemma musicalis* anthologies, brief mention can be made of how he worked with these materials. In all likelihood Lindner proofread the volumes himself; it was common for composers or their representatives to correct commissioned publications of their own works.[82]

---

81   See *Andrea Gabrieli: Complete Madrigals*, 9–10, ed. A. Tillman Merritt, Recent Researches in the Music of the Renaissance, 49–50 (Madison, WI: A-R Editions Inc., 1983), pp. 206–16.

82   Printers may have done this themselves for anthologies that were not commissioned (without editor) (Bernstein, *Music Printing in Renaissance Venice*, p. 59).

In keeping with European norms of production, minor or insignificant errors, such as turned letters in the text, designation of the wrong vocal part in the heading, and errors in pagination and signatures remained uncorrected. For instance, Giovanni Gabrieli's *Lieto godea* (à 8) appears in *Gemma musicalis I* with the first choir of the bass part incorrectly labeled "Sec.", as it had appeared in *Concerti ... continenti musica di chiesa, madrigali, & altro* (Venice, 1587).[83] Lindner did not make substantive changes to the music that he copied. His editorial work falls between what Mary Lewis categorizes as "direct copying" and "revised copying," which includes some evidence of direct copying alongside editorial emendations.[84] Lindner does not change any of the pitches, and retains all accidentals. His biggest changes were at line endings, especially in cases that involved a shift from upright format for the printed concordances to oblong format for the *Gemma musicalis* anthologies. Lindner took great care with text underlay, a critical issue for foreign readers of Italian. Syllables within melismatic phrases are located directly beneath the notes to which they are to be sung. While one might expect to find cases of misspellings and errors in the Italian texts, the accuracy of Lindner's edition demonstrates his own facility with the Italian language.

Conclusion

Gerlach's decision to commission a professional editor paid off. Lindner's name provided a professional stamp of authority, advertised for all to see, on the title pages of the *Gemma musicalis* anthologies. Lindner's reputation was earned through a series of appointments at German courts, his long-standing service at Nuremberg's St Egidien, and his position as music advisor for the city's music society. These positions brought him into close contact with Italian music and composers, and necessitated the early development of his editorial skills. Building on growing interest in Italian-texted music among German patrician and amateur musicians, Lindner adopted the familiar form of the large-scale compendium to educate German audiences on the styles, types, and models of Italian secular song.

Though the size and combination of genres in the *Gemma musicalis* anthologies departed from Venetian practices of anthology compilation, Lindner's selection criteria for composers and individual settings did not. The reputation of an individual composer, his contacts with the printing locale, and the popularity of individual settings were important factors for editors working across Europe. By grouping his selections by composer, Lindner exerted a lasting influence on the reception of individual composers in German-speaking lands.

Lindner's career strengthens the evidence for the growing professionalization of music editing in northern Europe at the end of the sixteenth century. His editorial voice is always present, whether in the dedications, or in the tone, form, and shape

---

83 RISM A/I, G58=RISM A/I, G85=RISM B/I, 1587[16]. This error is discussed in Charteris, *Giovanni Gabrieli (ca. 1555–1612): A Thematic Catalogue*, p. 173.

84 Mary S. Lewis, "Twins, Cousins, and Heirs: Relationships among Editions of Music Printed in Sixteenth-Century Venice," in John Knowles (ed.), *Critica Musica: Essays in Honor of Paul Brainard* (Amsterdam: Gordon and Breach, 1996), p. 199.

of the music that followed them. Lindner selected and ordered Italian music to suit the needs, interests, and abilities of his clientele, both actual and potential. His efforts represent an important preparatory step toward the broader German reception of Italian secular song. The *Gemma musicalis* anthologies educated Nuremberg audiences and shaped their esthetic tastes as consumers. The presence of Italian models inspired vernacular translations and adaptations of a range of poetic forms that will be explored in the next chapter.

Chapter 3

Editors and the Germanization
of Italian Song

This chapter examines the intersections of editing, translation, and reception in the decades around 1600, as the growing interest in Italian culture sparked a demand for translations of Italian works into German. Translation holds a special place in the history of cultural exchange between Italy and Germany. The sixteenth century witnessed an increased demand for translated books, a demand based initially on religious works, but soon extending to literary, cultural, historical, and political topics as well. The etiquette manuals of Balthassare Castiglione, Giovanni della Casa, and Stefano Guazzo enjoyed long lives in German translations well into the seventeenth century.[1] Hieronymus Megiser's 1602 translation of Donato Gianotti's *Libro della repubblica di Venezia* transferred Venetian ideas of rulership and governance to German readers.[2] The early decades of the seventeenth century saw an intense interest in Italian literature, with translations of works by Tomaso Garzoni (1618), Giovanni Battista Gelli (1619), Giovanni Battista Guarini (1619), and Torquato Tasso (1626).[3] Poet-composers Giovanni Battista Pinello, Abraham Ratz, Cesare de Zacharia, Andreas Myller, and Valentin Haussmann translated Italian madrigals, canzonettas, and villanellas into German "for the better use of those who do not understand the Italian language" ["so der Italienischen Sprach nicht kundig/ zu besserm gebrauch"], as Haussmann wrote on the title page of his translated edition of Luca Marenzio's villanellas.[4]

As a topic of Renaissance studies, translation has attracted much scholarly attention since the 1980s.[5] Three issues have shaped the literature: the conflict between free and literal renderings of the text; the predilections of individual translators, a manifestation of what Armin Paul Frank dubs a given translator's

---

1   Frank-Rutger Hausmann, *Bibliographie der deutschen Übersetzungen aus dem Italienischen von den Anfängen bis 1730*, 2 vols (Tübingen, Niemeyer, 1992), vol. 1/1, nos 0265 (Castiglione), 0364 (della Casa), and 0530 (Guazzo).

2   Ibid., vol. 1/1, no. 0473.

3   Ibid., vol. 1/1, nos 0462 (Garzoni), 0467 (Gelli), 0522 (Guarini); vol. 1/2, nos 1101 and 1105 (Tasso).

4   Title page of *Ausszug auss Lucæ Marentii … Villanellen und Napolitanen … von Valentino Haußmanno Gerbipol* (Nuremberg: Paul Kauffmann, 1606; RISM A/I, M611). It is transcribed in full in Appendix A, p. 194.

5   The range of approaches is demonstrated in the volume of essays on Renaissance translation in *Canadian Review of Comparative Literature*, 8 (1981).

ethos; and assessments of "fit" between the original and target languages.[6] Such considerations are heightened in the case of translated poetry set to music, since the pre-existing musical model had its own impact on the meaning, rhythm, and syntax of the verbal text. The work of Valentin Haussmann offers a case study for examining these issues. After an ambitious career as a poet-composer, he compiled and translated seven volumes of canzonettas and villanellas by Luca Marenzio, Orazio Vecchi, Giovanni Giacomo Gastoldi, Thomas Morley, and others (1606–10). They were published in Nuremberg at the firm of Paul Kauffmann, who may have personally encouraged Haussmann in his endeavor.

In what follows I position the work of editor-translators within the broader shift in the esthetics of translation in the latter half of the sixteenth and early seventeenth centuries, as the artistic merits of the target language came to outweigh the importance of fidelity to the source. From this perspective, the work of Haussmann stands at a critical juncture, that anticipates Martin Opitz's call for the vernacular as a literary and poetic language.

Renaissance Theories of Translation and Imitation

The growing demand for vernacular translations brought with it considerations bearing on artistic quality, rhetoric, and style that increasingly privileged the final product over the literal rendering of the original, and led to the rise of vernacular languages in the linguistic hierarchy.[7] Translators of the late sixteenth and early seventeenth centuries turned to theories of imitation rooted in the peculiarities of the target language, with little consideration given to the style and words of the original source work.[8] The French debate was fuelled by Joachim Du Bellay whose *La deffence et illustration de la langue françoise* (Paris, 1549) urged poets to avoid direct translation, from which their own literature could not benefit, and

---

6   As Frank argues, a translator's *ethos* reflects his coming to terms with working conditions including his own and other's views of the work to be translated, his or the publisher's objectives, his concept of translation, and the dictionaries and reference works he used or failed to use (Armin Paul Frank, "Towards a Cultural History of Literary Translation: 'Histories,' 'Systems,' and Other Forms of Synthesizing Research," in Harald Kittel [ed.], *Geschichte, System, Literarische Übersetzung / Histories, Systems, Literary Translations, Göttinger Beiträge zur Internationalen Übersetzungsforschung [GBIÜ]*, 5 [Berlin: Erich Schmidt, 1992], pp. 371–2).

7   Significant studies of non-music books include Werner Schwarz, "The Theory of Translation in Sixteenth Century Germany," *The Modern Language Review*, 40 (1945): 289–99; Thomas Greene, *The Light in Troy: Imitation and Discovery in Renaissance Poetry* (New Haven: Yale University Press, 1982); G.W. Pigman III, "Versions of Imitation in the Renaissance," *Renaissance Quarterly*, 33 (1980): 1–32; and Theo Hermans, "Renaissance Translation between Literalism and Imitation," in Kittel (ed.), *Geschichte, System, Literarische Übersetzung*, pp. 95–116.

8   Schwarz, "The Theory of Translation," pp. 298–9. Cf. Wilibald Pirckheimer, who warns against the tendency for translation to turn into paraphrase in his *Thetrum Virtutis & Honoris* (Nuremberg, 1606), pp. 112–13, quoted in Schwarz, "The Theory of Translation," p. 299.

to adopt the method of imitation. Du Bellay uses a digestive metaphor calling his countrymen "to transform ourselves into them [borrowed works], devour them and, having digested them well, convert them into blood and nourishment."[9] For German translators, Martin Luther's "Circular Letter on Translation" (1530) and his "Defence of the Translation of the Psalms" (1531–33) emphasized the missionary task that necessitated adaptation to make God's Word accessible to the reader. Luther used the verb *verdeutschen* [to germanize] to capture the essence of his work.

Unlike translation, imitation constituted a fundamental and prestigious category of the humanist poetic, with an established discourse and pedigree that stretched back to Quintilian, Cicero, and Aristotle. The most important source for Haussmann and his colleagues was Quintilian's *Institutiones oratoriae* (first century CE), which treats methods of imitation in Book X, Chapter 2:

> From the study of these authors, and of others worth reading, one should acquire a copious vocabulary, a variety of metaphors, and a method of composition; then attention should further be given to the copying of all their good qualities. For undoubtedly a great part of art consists in imitation; since, while invention came first and is most important, it is helpful to copy the things that have in the past been well invented. For the whole conduct of life is based on this: that what we admire in others we desire to do ourselves.[10]

Quintilian's closing observation recalls Castiglione's advice to the courtier to observe the behavior of different kinds of courtiers, and, taking the best qualities from each of them, fashion his own identity in their likeness.

The imitation of models was central to the fields of Renaissance literature, pedagogy, grammar, rhetoric, esthetics, the visual arts, music, historiography, politics, and philosophy.[11] Yet there is good reason to link the technique of imitation to music pedagogy and composition more closely. Imitation was the primary means for teaching the principles of music composition. Students practiced by imitating the structure of a model, the organization of individual sections, the transitions between them, and the overall argument, all techniques familiar from the study of rhetoric, as prescribed in Erasmus's *De duplici copia verborum acierum*, the most widely disseminated rhetoric textbook of the sixteenth century.[12] Imitation remained an important device over the course of a composer's career. The imitation, or parody mass, whereby a new composition is derived from multiple parts of a polyphonic model, constituted the most important type of mass of the sixteenth century. Imitation

9   Du Bellay, *La deffence et illustration de la langue françoise* (Paris, 1549), ed. H. Chamard (Paris: Didier, 1948), p. 42: "se transformant en eux, les devorant, et apres les avoir bien digerez, les convertissant en sang et nourriture," quoted in Hermans, "Renaissance Translation between Literalism and Imitation," p. 111.

10   Quintilian, *Institutiones oratoriae*, Book X, Chapter 2, ii, *De imitatione*, quoted in Walter L. Bullock, "The Precept of Plagiarism in the Cinquecento," *Modern Philology*, 25 (1928): 296.

11   Greene, *The Light in Troy*, p. 1.

12   Michelle Fromson, "A Conjunction of Rhetoric and Music: Structural Modelling in the Italian Counter-Reformation Motet," *Journal of the Royal Musical Association*, 117 (1992): 239–42. On Erasmus, see Terence Cave, *The Cornucopian Text: Problems of Writing in the French Renaissance* (Oxford: Clarendon, 1979), pp. 3–34.

lay at the root of competitive settings, such as the string of masses on the *L'homme armé* tune and the 31 versions of Giovanni Battista Guarini's *Ardo sì* in Giulio Gigli's madrigal anthology *Sdegnosi ardori* (Munich, 1585). Music theorists, from the second half of the sixteenth century onward, included discussions of imitation in their treatises. Nicola Vicentino (1555), Gioseffo Zarlino (1558), and Pietro Pontio (1588 and 1595) made early reference to the technique of parody, using the term *imitatio*.[13] German theorist Joachim Burmeister included the chapter *De Imitatione* in his treatise *Musica poetica* (Rostock, 1606), advising composers to be mindful of the four genera of style—low, grand, middle, and mixed—being sure to recognize the style of the model and to follow it.[14] Their reference to *imitatio* lends weight to Howard Mayer Brown's argument that the technique of basing new works on pre-existing models is rooted in the rhetorical tradition of *imitatio*.[15]

German adaptations of Italian song form part of this rich tradition. Citing authorities from Quintilian to Joseph Scalinger, the Jena Cantor and schoolmaster Georg Quitschreiber (1569–1638) delineated four categories of imitation in his short pamphlet *De parodia tractatus musicalis* (Jena, 1611).[16] Listed first are modern versions of older pieces such as a parody mass or motet; second, the reduction or increase in the number of voices of a pre-existing work, such as Leonhard Lechner's five-voice expansion of Jacob Regnart's three-voice German songs (Nuremberg, 1579); third, stylistic copying; and finally, the substitution of new texts. For the final category, Quitschreiber cited Valentin Haussmann as an example:

> But no fault has been imputed to our Valentinus Haussmann for having adorned the music of Italians and others with German texts. Elsewhere different kinds of *parodia* are very common and usual, as far as the form or tone of some song is concerned, as when I fit a new song with a joyful, serious, or sad mode--not to mention the custom of song-writers

13   Sixteenth-century music theorists used the term *imitatio* to denote a technique of composition that involved the use of pre-existing material (Suzanne G. Cusick: "Imitation," *Grove Music Online*, ed. Laura Macy [Accessed 22 February 2006], <http://www.grovemusic.com>). Theorists now use the term parody for this technique (Michael Tilmouth and Richard Sherr: "Parody [i]," *Grove Music Online*, ed. Laura Macy [Accessed 22 February 2006], <http://www.grovemusic.com>).

14   Joachim Burmeister, *Musical Poetics*, trans. Benito V. Rivera, Music Theory Translation Series, Claude V. Palisca (ed.) (New Haven: Yale University Press, 1993), pp. 206–11.

15   Howard Mayer Brown, "Emulation, Competition, and Homage: Imitation and Theories of Imitation in the Renaissance," *Journal of the American Musicological Society*, 35 (1982): 1–48. For an alternative view, see Honey Meconi, "Does Imitatio Exist?" *Journal of Musicology*, 12 (1994): 152–78.

16   The most thorough discussion of his work remains Klaus Wolfgang Niemöller, "Parodia-Imitatio: Zu Georg Quitschreibers Schrift von 1611," in Annegrit Laubenthal (ed.), *Studien zur Musikgeschichte: eine Festschrift für Ludwig Finscher* (Kassel: Bärenreiter, 1995), pp. 174–80; and Kristin M. Sponheim, "The Anthologies of Ambrosius Profe (1589–1661) and the Transmission of Italian Music in Germany" (Ph.D. diss., Yale University, 1995), pp. 93–128 esp. pp. 104–11.

who take a text (poetry or prose, German or Latin)--at their pleasure from anywhere, or compose one from scratch.[17]

For Haussmann the primary consideration in working with an existing musical and textual model was how closely it fit with native sensibilities of poetic verse and song. Gunilla Anderson characterizes this relationship as the tension between the need to establish ties between the target text and its source (the adequacy factor) and the need to formulate a text in the target language (the acceptability factor).[18] This relationship has been examined along almost exclusively disciplinary lines, with little room for comparisons across musical and non-musical texts. The following section brings the special considerations of musical settings of translated poetry into the debate.

---

17 Georg Quitschreiber, *De Parodia* (Jena, 1611): "Imo Valentino nostro Haussmanno nondum vitio datum fuit, quod Italorum & aliorum harmonias germanicis textibus adornaverit. Aliàs, Parodia alia, quoad formam vel Tonum alicijus cantionis, communis & usitatissima est, ut, quando juxta hilarem, gravem aut tristem Modem, novum concinno cantum. Jam non dicam, Melopoeos solutum aut ligatum textum, latinum vel germanicum, alicunde pro arbitrio desumere, aut de novo componere solere," cited and translated in Sponheim, "The Anthologies of Ambrosius Profe," p. 107.

18 Gunilla Anderson, "Drama Translation," in Mona Baker (ed.), *Routledge Encyclopedia of Translation Studies* (New York: Routledge, 1998), p. 71.

Table 3.1 Secular Translations of Italian Canzonettas, 1584–1624[a]

RISM	TRANSLATOR	SHORT TITLE	PLACE	DATE
P2389	Pinello, Giovanni Battista	*Nawe Kurtzweilige Deutsche Lieder*, 5vv	Dresden	1584
Z8	Zacharia, Cesare de	*Soave et dilettevole canzonette*, 4vv	Munich	1590
R741	Ratz, Abraham	*Threni amorum. Der erste Theil Lustiger weltlicher lieder … Jacobo Regnarto*, 5vv	Nuremberg	1595
R754	Ratz, Abraham	*Threni amorum. Der ander Theil. Lustiger weltlicher … lieder Jacobo Regnarto*, 5vv	Nuremberg	1595
M611	Haussmann, Valentin	*Auszug auss Lucae Marentii vier Theilen seiner Italianischen … Villanellen und Napolitanen*, 3vv	Nuremberg	1606
1606[13] =V1034	Haussmann, Valentin	*Canzonette … Horatii Vecchi unnd Gemignani Capi Lupi*, 3vv	Nuremberg	1606

RISM	TRANSLATOR	SHORT TITLE	PLACE	DATE
1607[25] =GG553a	Haussmann, Valentin	*Johann-Jacobi Gastoldi und anderer Autorn Tricinia, 3vv*	Nuremberg	1607
M8249 =1608[22]	Myller, Andreas	*Newe teutsche Canzonetten … von den fürtrefflichsten italianischen Componisten, 3vv*	Frankfurt	1608
M3700	Haussmann, Valentin	*Liebliche Fröhliche Ballette … Thoma Morlei, 5vv*	Nuremberg	1609
V1035 =1610[19]	Haussmann, Valentin	*Die erste Class … Canzonetten Horatii Vecchi, 4vv*	Nuremberg	1610
V1036	Haussmann, Valentin	*Die ander Class … Canzonetten Horatii Vecchi, 4vv*	Nuremberg	1610

RISM	TRANSLATOR	SHORT TITLE	PLACE	DATE
V1037	Haussmann, Valentin	*Die dritte Class ... Canzonetten Horatii Vecchi*, 4vv	Nuremberg	1610
F1951	Friderici, Daniel	*Thomae Morley Angli, ... Weltliche Liedlein*, 3vv	Rostock	1624

[a] Table 3.1 is assembled from Walther Dürr, "Die italienische Canzonette und das deutsche Lied im Ausgang des XVI. Jahrhunderts," in *Studi in onore di Lorenzo Bianchi* (Bologna: Zanichelli, 1960), pp. 101–102. My table omits volumes with only partial contents devoted to translations, such as Jacob Regnart's *Kurtzweilige Teutsche Lieder, zu dreyen Stimmen* (Nuremberg, 1576), which contains translations of one canzonetta by each of Orazio Vecchi and Leonardo Primavera (Alberto Martino, *Die italienische Literatur im deutschen Sprachraum: Ergänzungen und Berichtigungen zu Frank–Rutger Hausmanns Bibliographie, Chloe.* Beihefte zum Daphnis, 17 [Amsterdam: Rodopi, 1994], p. 221). Table 3.1 excludes sacred transformations of canzonettas and translations of madrigals; both topics are addressed in Chapter 4.

German Translations & Imitations of Italian Song

German poets and musicians turned to Italian verse forms as models for the artistic renewal of the German language (Table 3.1). An understanding of the Italian model allows for a closer assessment of the fit between the original and the target languages. German poets and translators preferred the strophic, schematic verse forms of the villanella or *canzone alla napolitana*, canzonetta, and balletto to the freer madrigal, which permitted variable length and free arrangement of terminal rhymes.[19] Villanella texts exploited the pairing of male frustration with female deceit, often in the form of a parody of the more serious madrigal. Evoking a pastoral setting, the object of love for both villanella and madrigal texts was often a peasant girl or shepherdess. The villanella earns Alfred Einstein's classification as a "lighter form" for its predilection for stock character types including imprudent maidens, domineering guardians, devious courtesans, duped husbands, brazen old men, and jealous suitors.[20] Among the most rustic Italian poems, *villanesca* texts derived their form from the *strambotto*, and consisted of four two-line stanzas, rhymed AB AB AB CC or AB AB AB AB, each followed by a refrain of one to four lines.[21] Around 1560, the refrain structure was abandoned, and the generic designation changed to villanella or *canzone alla napolitana*. Though these terms continued to be applied even after the specifically Neapolitan character was lost, the more general terms canzone and canzonetta became increasingly common at the close of the sixteenth century.[22] By about 1580 the standard form used in all of the light genres was a simple strophic poem with 3 or 4 lines per stanza, with lines of 7 and 11 syllables freely intermixed (in imitation of the Petrarchan style of madrigal verse), and rhymed couplets. Ruth DeFord refers to poems of this type as "canzonetta texts."[23] Giovanni Giacomo Gastoldi's *Balletti a cinque voci* (Venice, 1591) offered an alternative textual model for northerners.[24] Most of Gastoldi's *balletti* set strophic texts consisting of two repeated strains (AABB), with sections of nonsense syllables ("fa-la," "li-rum") interpolated at the ends of couplets or tercets. His five-voice *Balletti* was reprinted 30 times in Venetian and northern editions as late as 1657, and attracted parodies by Thomas Morley,

---

19   Don Harrán, "Verse Types in the Early Madrigal," *Journal of the American Musicological Society*, 22 (1969): 37. German adaptations of Italian madrigals are addressed in my Chapter 4.

20   Cardamone, Donna G., "Villanella," *Grove Music Online*, ed. Laura Macy (Accessed 30 May 2006), <http://www.grovemusic.com>

21   Ruth I. DeFord, "Musical Relationships between the Italian Madrigal and Light Genres in the Sixteenth Century," *Musica Disciplina*, 39 (1985): 110–11. For further discussion of text forms, see Donna G. Cardamone, *The Canzone Villanesca alla Napolitana and Related Forms, 1537–1570*, 2 vols (Ann Arbor: UMI Research Press, 1981), vol. 1, pp. 67–92.

22   Ruth I. DeFord, "The Influence of the Madrigal on Canzonetta Texts of the Late Sixteenth Century," *Acta Musicologica*, 59 (1987): 127. On definitions and terminology, see p. 127 n. 2–3.

23   DeFord, "Musical Relationships between the Italian Madrigal and Light Genres," p.111.

24   Suzanne G. Cusick: "Balletto (2)," *Grove Music Online*, ed. Laura Macy (Accessed 22 February 2006), <http://www.grovemusic.com>

Hans Leo Hassler, and Haussmann. German poets were equally inspired: Theobald Hoeck included many "fa-la-la" refrains in imitation of the balletto in his *Schönes Blumenfeldt* (1601).

Yet working within these stanzaic frameworks, the structure and content of German poetry were ill-suited to the subtleties of Romance languages. Sara Dumont summarizes the sharp differences between Italian and German poetry as follows:

> German poetry used strong accented metres in lines of usually four or eight syllables, and its concerns were those of hunting, drinking, springtime, courtly love and the narration of stories; Italian poetry used quantitative metres in lines of six, seven, ten or eleven syllables and engaged in extravagant Petrarchan modes of expression and references to classical and/or mythological figures.[25]

While German meter depended upon stress, the metrical character of Romance languages was determined by the number of syllables in a line. In Italian poetry, lines of 7 (*settenari*) and 11 syllables (*endecasillabi*) were the most common.[26] Syllable count was complicated by conventions concerning the pronunciation of consecutive vowels, and the position of the tonic accent in the final word. Consecutive vowels could be fused or separated, either within a single word (*sineresi, dierse*), or as the final and initial letters of two different words (*sinalefe, dialefe*). Apocopation allowed for the suppression of the entire final vowel of a word. Further, syllable count was affected by the position of the tonic accent in the final word. In accordance with poetic theory, all lines are classified as *versi piani* (with the accent on the penultimate syllable); one counted the number of syllables up to and including the first unstressed syllable following the final accent.

The problems of poetic translation were heightened when poetry was set to music since the musical gestures were designed to reinforce the grammar, syntax, punctuation, and tonic accent of the original language. The relationships of word and tone attracted much interest on the part of Renaissance theorists.[27] Gioseffo Zarlino included two short chapters on text-setting in part IV of *Le Istitutioni harmoniche* (Venice, 1558), which formed the basis of formulations by northern theorists Sethus Calvisius, Thomas Morley, and Johann Andreas Herbst.[28] Citing Plato and Horace, Zarlino argues that the harmony and rhythm should follow the words: "For if a text, whether by way of narrative or imitation, deals with subjects that are cheerful or sad, grave or without gravity, and modest or lascivious, a choice of harmony and rhythm

---

25　Sara Dumont, "Valentin Haussmann's Canzonettas: The Italian Connection," *Music and Letters*, 63 (1982): 63.

26　For a useful summary of the principles of Italian versification, see John Whenham, *Duet and Dialogue in the Age of Monteverdi* (Ann Arbor: UMI Research Press, 1982), pp. 19–28, upon which the following is based.

27　For a historical survey, see Don Harrán, *Word-Tone Relations in Musical Thought: From Antiquity to the Seventeenth Century*, Musicological Studies & Documents, 40, ed. Armen Carapetyan (Stuttgart: American Institute of Musicology/Hänssler-Verlag, 1986).

28　Chapters 32 and 33 of Gioseffo Zarlino, *On the Modes: Part Four of* Le Istitutioni Harmoniche, *1558*, trans. Vered Cohen, Music Theory Translation Series, ed. Claude V. Palisca (New Haven: Yale University Press, 1983), pp. 94–9.

must be made in accordance with the nature of the subject matter contained in the text, in order that these things, combined with proportion, may result in music that is suited to the purpose."[29] He followed the general hierarchy with more specific rules for the particular disposition of notes and syllables. Here, he warns against the "barbarism" of faulty accentuation (short notes on long syllables or vice versa) and textual syntax (when rests and cadences were placed in disregard of natural syntactical divisions).[30] German theorists expressed particular concern over accentuation. Writing in 1592, Calvisius warned that such errors should be "avoided with utmost care"; almost 50 years later, Herbst considered faulty accentuation especially laughable.[31]

Given the complexity of Italian versification, it is not surprising that the earliest German translations of Italian songs were by native Italians active in Germany. Giovanni Battista Pinello and Cesare de Zacharia illustrate the bias toward the source language held by early translators. Both musicians were active in southern Germany. After a period of service as a singer at the Habsburg chapel in Innsbruck, Pinello served as chapelmater at the electoral court in Dresden from 1580–84, and subsequently as *Knabenpräceptor* [instructor of the choirboys] at the imperial court in Prague until his death in 1587.[32] Zacharia was active in Munich (1590) before assuming the post of chapelmaster at the Hohenzollern court of Hechingen (1596–97).[33] The texts of Pinello's five-voice *Nawe Kurtzweilige Deutsche Lieder*, (Dresden, 1584) are translations of his earlier *Libro primo de napolitane*, (Dresden, 1584), also for five voices.[34] Though the *Libro primo* is now lost, Rudolf Velten identified two Italian texts from other sources, *O sol', o luna o giorno* (Pinello, no. 8, *O Sonn', O Mond, O lichter Tag*) and *Un temp'ogn'hor piangeva* (Pinello, no. 14, *All stund*

---

29   Ibid., p. 94.

30   Ibid., p. 96.

31   Sethus Calvisius, *Melopoeia sive melodiae condendae ratio* (Erfurt: Georg Baumann, 1592), fol. I 4v, quoted in Harrán, *Word-Tone Relations in Musical Thought*, p. 268; Johann Andreas Herbst, *Musica poetica* (Nuremberg: Jeremia Dümler, 1643), p. 112: "Letzlich *quantitas syllabarum*, oder *Prosodia*, das ist: der *accent*, welche Sylben lang oder kurtz seyn/ soll und muß sonderlich in acht genommen werden: Denn sonsten nichts lächerlichers ist/ wenn solches nicht *observiret* wird" ["Finally *quantitas syllabarum*, or *Prosodia*, that is: the *accent*, which syllables are long or short, should and must be taken into particular consideration. For nothing is more laughable than when this is not observed"] (quoted with English translation in Kerala J. Snyder, "Text and Tone in Hassler's German Songs and Their Sacred Parodies," in Nancy Kovaleff Baker and Barbara Russano Hanning [eds], *Musical Humanism and Its Legacy: Essays in Honor of Claude V. Palisca* [Stuyvesant: Pendragon Press, 1992], 265 and n. 28).

32   Dane O. Heuchemer: "Pinello di Ghirardi, Giovanni Battista," *Grove Music Online*, ed. Laura Macy (Accessed 22 February 2006), <http://www.grovemusic.com>

33   Murray C. Bradshaw: "Zacharia, Cesare de," *Grove Music Online*, ed. Laura Macy (Accessed 22 February 2006), <http://www.grovemusic.com>

34   *Nawe Kurtzweilige Deutsche Lieder, mit fünff stimmen aus welscher Sprach verdeutschet, welche nach Neapolitanischer Art gantz lieblich zu singen und auff allerley Instrumenten zugebrauchen* (Dresden: Matthäus Stöckel, 1584; RISM A/I, P2389).

BENIGNO LETTORE,

NON si mara uíglíar' che queste Canzonette Italiane siano tradutte in Rime Alemane, che à d'altro non è fatto se non per quelle persone, che non sono intelligenti de la Língua Italiana, & che hauerebbeno a caro intendere il sentimento d'esse, Et acciò anco si poscia aplicare'tal parole Alemane' sotto le Note, è stato constretto di non obseruare'più silabe di quello che nelli versi Italiani sono, essedo impossibile('si'come dice'oratio, Nec verbum verbo curabit reddere fidus interpres) di obseruare le regule che sono nella Poesia Alemana, & si come sano quelli ch' in ambe le Lingue inteligenti sono; Non ti dispiacia questa opera, Vale.

Bün-

Figure 3.1 "BENIGNO LETTORE," from Cesare de Zacharia, *Soave et dilettevole canzonette* (Munich, 1590), fol. 4r, Bayerische Staatsbibliothek München, Musikabteilung: 4°. Mus. pr. 88

Günstiger Leser.

ES soll dich nit wunder vnd frembdt nemen / das dise Italianische Liedlein in Teutsche Reymen gebracht sind. Dann solches allein darumb geschehen / damit den jenigen / so der Italianischen Sprach vnerfaren / vnd diesen Gesängen Innhalt zu wissen begeren / gedienet vnnd geholffen würde. Damit aber die teutschen Wort auch / vnder die Noten künden gesungen werden / hat man / nit mehr oder weniger Sylben in die Reymen wöllen setzen / dann souil die Italianischen in sich begreiffen (Darumb auch nit wol müglich gewesen (nach der lehr Horatij, der da sagt: Nec verbum verbo curabit reddere fidus interpres) die Regulen der Teutschen Prosodia zu obseruiren, wie dann denen wol bewüst / so in beyden diesen sprachen erfahren seyn. Lasz dir disz Werck nit missfallen / Vale.

Figure 3.2 "Günstiger Leser," from Cesare de Zacharia, *Soave et dilettevole canzonette* (Munich, 1590), fol. 4v, Bayerische Staatsbibliothek München, Musikabteilung: 4°. Mus. pr. 88

Figure 3.3 *Vola vola pensier fuor del mio petto/Fleug hin fleug hin von mir, gedenck für die thür*, from Cesare de Zacharia, *Soave et dilettevole canzonette* (Munich, 1590), fols 8v–9r, Bayerische Staatsbibliothek München, Musikabteilung: 4°. Mus. pr. 88

ich weinet kleglich).[35] Velten's analysis demonstrates Pinello's practice of word-by-word translation at the expense of the natural declamation of the German language.

Pinello's compatriot, Zacharia, shared this approach to translation. Zacharia's *Soave et dilettevole canzonette* (Munich, 1590) is a collection of four-voice canzonettas in simple, homophonic style that remains the only bilingual edition from the period.[36] Zacharia gives us a clue to his intentions in the bilingual preface addressed "BENIGNO LETTORE" (fol. 4r) or "Gunstiger Leser" (fol. 4v) [To the reader] (Figures 3.1–3.2). Here Zacharia states that the German translations may be used to assist one in understanding the Italian words, or they may be sung on their own:

> One should not take it as a curiosity or oddity that these Italian songs have been set in German rhymes; for this has been done solely for the benefit of those who are unversed in the Italian language yet who desire to understand the content of these songs. However, so that the German words also might be sung with the notes, I did not wish to set more or fewer syllables to the rhyme than the amount contained in the Italian. Thus it has also not been possible ... to observe the rules of German prosody, as will be obvious to those who are fluent in both languages. May this work not displease you. Be well.

Zacharia's defensive tone was well warranted. Translators faced the challenge of working with two poetics. The different vowel and consonant distributions of the two languages made end rhyme difficult to translate. The word order governing syntax varied between Italian and German, which created stresses on unsuitable words or beats. What is most striking about the volume is that Zacharia invites these comparisons by including the German translations directly under the Italian texts for the first verses, with remaining verses printed at the end of each setting, Italian on the left side and German on the right (Figure 3.3). By underlaying both texts, Zaccharia's *Soave et dilettevole canzonette* may have functioned as a pedagogical tool for teaching Germans the principles of Italian versification, particularly the rules for counting syllables. As Alfred Noe points out, such notable poet-composers as Valentin Haussmann later drew Italian texts from the volume.[37]

But the difficulty of translating onomatopoeic devices, stylized expressions, nonsense words, metaphorical language, and Petrarchan antitheses, so typical of

---

35 Rudolf Velten, *Das Ältere Deutsche Gesellschaftslied unter dem Einfluss der Italienischen Musik*, Beiträge zur Neueren Literaturgeschichte, ed. Max Freiherr von Waldberg, Neue Folge, Heft 5 (Heidelberg: Carl Winters Universitäts-Buchhandlungen, 1914), pp. 52–7.

36 RISM A/I, Z8.

37 Zacharia's opening *Canzon, vane volando/Geh hin, trauriger Gsang* and the fourth setting, *Vola, vola pensier/Fleug hin, mein sinn und gdancken* appear with new German texts in Haussmann's *Neue Teutsche weltliche Canzonetten* (Nuremberg, 1596) (Alfred Noe, "Cesare Zaccarias Zweisprachige Canzonetten-Sammlung von 1590," in Norbert Bachleitner, Alfred Noe, and Hans-Gert Roloff [eds], *Beiträge zu Komparatistik und Sozialgeschichte der Literatur: Festschrift für Alberto Martino*, Chloe. Beihefte zum Daphnis, 26 [Amsterdam: Rodopi, 1997], p. 232).

Italian poetry, made the word-by-word method untenable in the long-term.[38] The challenge of setting translated texts to music only heightened the tension between the artistic merits of the original and target languages. In his *Bericht von der Didactica oder Lehrkunst* (Magdeburg, 1621), Wolfgang Ratich forcefully argues for the importance of a translator's knowledge of both the source and target languages:

> He who wants to translate something from one language to another must fully understand the language from which he translates, so that he can grasp the correct meaning or understanding of the author; but for the language into which he brings the translation, he must not only correctly understand [it], but [he must] also be so capable that he has a great storehouse of varied *phrases* and expressions of speech, through which he might express his meaning in the most diverse ways, and have [his] choice among words.[39]

This new attitude toward the German vernacular occasioned a host of guides for its proper use and spelling. Johann Sattler's *Teutsche Orthographey* (Basel, 1607) opens with a history of the German language, then embarks on extended rules of orthography, word separation, phrase structure, and the use of common words.[40] Proper German spelling became a desideratum of printed books. Hieronymus Hornschuch's manual for correctors echoes Ratich's demand for higher standards in the vernacular, asking: " ...why ... do we not care a jot about accuracy in our own language? ... Certainly if the intelligence of a nation can be judged from it[s] language, (and it is agreed that the more refined and civilized they are the more cultivated and uniform a language they possess), it is certainly obvious to an intelligent person what judgement is to be made of the Germans."[41]

The new linguistic hierarchy is illustrated in *Threni amorum ... Lustiger weltlicher Lieder I–II* (Nuremberg: Paul Kauffmann, 1595), an edition of Jacob Regnart's two

---

38   Velten raises these criticisms of Zacharia's translations in *Das Ältere Deutsche Gesellschaftslied*, pp. 62–5. For a more sympathetic view, see Noe, "Cesare Zaccarias Zweisprachige Canzonetten-Sammlung von 1590," pp. 211–32.

39   "Denn welcher aus einer Sprach in die ander etwas dolmetschen wil/ muß die Sprach/ daraus er dolmetscht/ völlig verstehen/ damit er den rechten Sinn oder Verstandt des Autorn fassen kan/ die Sprach aber/ in welche er die Dolmetschung bringt/ muß er nit allein recht verstehen/ sondern ihrer auch so weit mechtig seyn/ daß er einen grossen Vorrath von allerley *Phrasibus* oder Formulen zu reden/ darinnen habe/ auff daß er seine Meinung auff vnterschiedliche Art könne auß reden/ vnd vnter den Worten die Wahl haben," Wolfgang Ratich, *Bericht von der Didactica oder Lehrkunst* (Magdeburg, 1621), p. 30. Exemplar Herzog August Bibliothek Wolfenbüttel: 34.1 Gram (2).

40   For a full listing of German vocabulary books and dictionaries, see Franz Claes, *Bibliographisches Verzeichnis der deutschen Vokabulare und Worterbücher, gedruckt bis 1600* (Hildesheim: Georg Olms Verlag, 1977).

41   Hieronymus Hornschuch, *Orthotypographia 1608*, eds and trans Philip Gaskell and Patricia Bradford (Cambridge: The University Library, 1972), pp. 20–21: "Cæterum ... quod reliquis in lingvis sanctè, & jure quidem, cavetur, ne scribendi ratio negliagatur, aut literæ aliæ pro aliis temerè usurpentur; ... cur, quæso, in nostra vernacula id flocci facimus? ... Profectò, si de ingeniis populorum judicium ferri potest ex eorum lingva: (siquidem constat quò illi humaniores sunt & mansvetiores, eò lingvam quoque habere excultiorem & æquabiliorem) de Germanis certè quid sit judicandum sapienti cuiq[ue]; patet."

books of five-voice *canzoni alla napolitana* with German texts by Abraham Ratz, "Musicum zur Naumburg an der Sahla" as he stylized himself on the title pages of both volumes.[42] Rather than being enslaved by the original texts, Ratz usurps their authority to demonstrate that the German language and culture were en par with the Italian. Ratz justifies his work in the preface to the volume, where he provides a detailed account of his method of translation:

> But I did not wish to set the Italian text word-for-word [*ad verbum*], since the German language, in meter and many other respects, has a different style and dialect than the Italian, and accordingly I had to rely much more upon my ingenuity and *influentien* in this case, and had to follow the tone of the composition and harmony so that they remained everywhere and completely undisturbed and so that my German text might fit no less charmingly under the notes than the original. Thus I have also not only observed the *genera carminum*[43] of the former Italian texts, but have also improved [it] with the insertion of lines in many places. And since these Italian rhythms are very uneven, since one line might have eleven syllables, the one following it five, another one six, or more or fewer syllables (whereas, in contrast, the Germans count their meters and rhythms precisely in even and exact [numbers of] feet); also [since] often in the Italian texts an entire syllable is elided and removed at the end of a word, so that a word pronounced at one time with two syllables soon thereafter is pronounced with one, such as *sempre* and *sempr'*, and *sospir' sospire* etc., which the German language does not permit: for this reason I have, in truth, had no small trouble, in those places where elisions occur, to invent and place many monosyllabic words, or at least such German words, which, according to the circumstances of the Italian words and *Notulen*, accommodate elisions, and, which may be applied and pronounced daintily and with refinement both in bi- and in monosyllabic form, in such a manner that not a single note might be adjusted, but rather the composition remains correct and unchanged throughout.[44]

---

42   Ratz's first book translated Jacob Regnart's *Il primo libro delle canzone italiane a cinque voci* (Vienna: Johann Meir, 1574; RISM A/I, R738), while his second volume adapted Regnart's *Il secondo libro delle canzone italiano a cinque voci* (Nuremberg: Katharina Gerlach & Johann Bergs Erben, 1581; RISM A/I, R753).

43   The term *carmen* carried various meanings in the sixteenth century. Ratz evokes the medieval Latin use of the word for lyric poetry. See David Fallows: "Carmen," *Grove Music Online*, ed. Laura Macy (Accessed 30 May 2006), <http://www.grovemusic.com>

44   "hab aber die Wälschen Text darumb *ad verbum* nicht vertiren wollen/ weil die Teutsche sprach *in prolatione* vnd sonsten auch vil eine andere art vnd *dialectos* hat als die Italianische/ und ich dahero vil mehr meinem *ingenio* und *influentien* dißfals folgen/ vn[d] mich *cum decere* nach der *composition* vn[d] *Harmonien reguliren* müssen/ damit dieselbe allenthalben vnd durchauß vnverruckt bliben/ vnd meine teutschen *Textus* nichts minders als die *nativs* sein lieblich vnter die noten fuessen mügen. So hab ich auch die *genera carminum* der vorigen Wälschen Texten nicht allein *observiret*; sondern auch an vilen orten mit mehren *versibus* ersetzt vnnd verbessert. Vnd weil dieselben Italianischen *rhythmi* sehr vngleich/ sintemal ein vers zuweilen eilff/ der andere darauff folgend/ fünff/ bald einer sechs/ auch wol mehr vnd weniger syllaben hat (da hiergegen die Teutschen ire *metra* vnd *rhythmos* auff gleiche vn[d] gewisse *pedes exactè dimetiren*) auch offtmals in den Wälschen Texten *in fine verborum* eine gantze *syllaba elidiret* vnd abgeworffen/ also das ein wort bißweilen mit zwo *syllaben* außgesprochen/ bald hernach mit einer syllaben *pronuncieret* wirdt/ als *sempre* vnd *sempr'*/ Item/ *sospir' sospiri & c.* welchs die Teutsche Sprach nicht leidet: So hat mirs

Ratz's preface echoes Quintilian's call for imitation to surpass its model: "imitation in itself is not enough ... even those who do not aspire to the highest achievement should try to excel rather than merely follow their model."[45] Ratz's solution represents the middle ground between translation and original composition. In *Dir und mir geschicht groß leiden* Ratz alters the meaning of the original poem, *Di pensier, in pensier io vo pensando* to create an artistic unit in the target language while preserving musical integrity (Examples 3.1–3.2). Consumers of Ratz's translations must have favored this technique, for the title pages of both volumes advertise settings "ohn einige verenderung der composition" [without any changes to the composition].[46]

Example 3.1 Jacob Regnart, *Di pensier, in pensier io vo pensando*[47]

Di pensier, in pensier io uo pensando,
poi ch'altro che pensar, non m'e restato,

O duro caso, o cruda, o cruda sorte,
penso ch'el mio, pensier mi darà morte.

From thought to thought I go thinking
since other than thinking nothing has been left to me

Oh hard event, oh cruel, oh cruel fate
I think that is mine, the thought will give me death.

---

fürwar nicht wenig mühe gemacht/ das ich so vil *monosyllabica* oder doch solche Teutsche wort/ an denen orten da *elisiones* einfallen/ erfunden vnd gesatzt/ welche nach gelegenheit der Wälschen wörter vnd *Notulen*, die *elisiones* leiden/ vnd sich zwey vnnd einsyllabig fein zierlich vnd gelinde *appliciren* vnnd außsprechen lassen/ auch der gestalt kein einige *Nota* nicht *resolviret* werden dürffen/ sondern die *composition* durchauß richtig vnd vnverendert bliben," Abraham Ratz, *Threni Amorum, Der erste Theil* (Nuremberg, 1595), tenor partbook, fols 2r–v. Exemplar Staatsbibliothek zu Berlin – Preußischer Kulturbesitz, Musikabteilung mit Mendelssohn-Archiv: Mus. ant. pract. R 255. Thanks to Harald Krebs for his assistance with the translation of this passage.

45   Quintilian, *Institutiones oratoriae*, Book X, Chapter 2, ii, *De imitatione*, quoted in Bullock, "The Precept of Plagiarism," p. 296.

46   For further comparisons of Regnart and Ratz, see Dürr, "Die italienische Canzonette," pp. 92–5; and Velten, *Das Ältere Deutsche Gesellschaftslied*, pp. 22–3, 128–30.

47   Jacob Regnart, *Il primo libro delle canzone italiane a cinque voci* (Nuremberg, 2nd edn/1580), superius partbook, fol. 8r. Exemplar Bayerische Staatsbibliothek München, Musikabteilung: 4° Mus. pr. 162. Thanks to Lloyd Howard for his assistance with the translation of this example.

Example 3.2 Abraham Ratz, *Dir und mir, dir und mir geschicht groß leiden*[48]

Dir vnd mir dir vnd mir geschicht groß
leiden/
für vnd für für vnd für einander meiden/
das macht on vnterlaß in meinem hertzen/
gar grossen schmertzen/
das mit dir nit mer soll freundlich schertzen.

You and I, you and I, are being stricken by
great suffering.
Forever and forever to avoid one another:
that constantly causes me
such great pain in my heart,
[my heart] that is no longer to jest amiably
with you.

This freer approach to translation coincided with a movement to model new German verse on Italianate principles. Jacob Regnart was one of the first to transfer Italianate 11-syllable versification to the German language in his widely popular *Kurtzweiligen Teutschen Lieder, nach Art der Neapolitanen oder welschen Villanellen* for three voices (3 vols, Nuremberg, 1576, 1577, 1579). The first volume includes translations of texts by Orazio Vecchi and Leonardo Primavera and newly-conceived German texts modeled after the principles of Italian versification. The inaugural volume shows the deepest Italian influence of the three. It features a high proportion of Italian poetic forms such as AAA, ABA, ABB (with lines of 11 syllables) and AA, BB, CC.[49] The subsequent volumes combine Italian forms with the older Germanic Tenorlied, and also contain texts that mix German and Italian elements. Such a combination typified the collections of Leonhard Lechner, whose two volumes of villanellas (Nuremberg, 1576 and 1577) use mostly Tenorlied texts from song-books of Georg Forster and Hans Ott.[50]

It was not until the 1590s that the full influence of Italian poetic forms was felt, with a string of four- and five-voice volumes "nach Art der Italienischen Canzonetten" [according to the style of Italian canzonettas] by Franz Joachim Brechtel, Johann Knöfel, Christoph Demantius, Paul Sartorius, Hans Leo Hassler, and Valentin Haussmann. Among the most famous, Hassler learned Italian poetic and musical forms during his trip of 1584–85 to Venice where he studied composition and organ-playing under Andrea Gabrieli. The fruits of this direct contact are born in Hassler's collection of Italian-texted *Canzonette* (Nuremberg, 1590), a volume of Italian *Madrigali* (Augsburg, 1596), the *Neüe teütsche Gesang* (Augsburg, 1596), and *Lustgarten neuer teutscher Gesäng* (Nuremberg, 1601). Seven- and eleven-syllable lines dominate the German-texted *Neüe teütsche Gesang* and *Lustgarten*, with textual themes ranging from songs of love, joy, anger, the pain of rejection, and drinking, to dancing or singing.[51] Gastoldi's presence is felt in eight balletti with "fa-la-la" refrains, included in the *Lustgarten*. Alongside Hassler's Italianate German

---

48   Abraham Ratz, *Threni amorum I* (Nuremberg, 1595), discantus partbook, fol. 7r. Thanks to Sharon Krebs for her assistance with the translation of this passage.

49   Walter Pass, "Regnart, Jacob," in *New Grove II*, vol. 21, p. 119.

50   Sara E. Dumont, *German Secular Polyphonic Song in Printed Editions, 1570–1630: Italian Influences on the Poetry and Music*, Outstanding Dissertations in Music from British Universities, 2 vols (New York: Garland, 1989), vol. 1, p. 169.

51   Snyder, "Text and Tone in Hassler's German Songs," p. 255.

texts were his translations of Italian poetry by Orazio Vecchi, Luca Marenzio, Giovanni Battista Guarini, and Torquato Tasso, including Guarini's *Ardo sì, ma non t'amo* with Tasso's *risposta, Ardi e gela à tua voglia.*[52] In the dedication to *Neüe teütsche Gesang*, Hassler claimed that he was "urged to compose some German songs and to publish them" as a counterpart to the many "beautiful songs" in Latin and Italian already in print.[53]

Hassler's contemporary, Valentin Haussmann, became the strongest proponent of German poems in Italian forms. Haussmann exemplifies a new, freelance kind of music professional. He never held a permanent position at a court, church, or educational institution, instead earning his living from music publications, commissions, occasional teaching, and dedications of printed and manuscript copies of his music.[54] This freelance existence led Dumont to characterize Haussmann as "a bohemian musical enthusiast," a description that undermines Haussmann's humanist background and business acumen.[55] Haussmann showed an early and lasting interest in Italian music and poetry. Between 1592 and 1597 he completed four volumes of *teutsche Lieder* and one book of *teutsche Canzonette*, all printed by the Gerlach-Kauffmann firm in Nuremberg (Table 3.2).[56]

---

52 Ibid., pp. 256–7. Rudolf Schwartz compares Hassler's work against Italian models in "Hans Leo Haßler unter dem Einfluß der italiänischen Madrigalisten," *Vierteljahrsschrift für Musikwissenschaft*, 9 (1893): 51–61, esp. pp. 51–5.

53 Hans Leo Hassler, *Canzonette von 1590 und Neüe Teütsche Gesang von 1596*, Rudolf Schwartz (ed.), Denkmäler der Tonkunst in Bayern, V/2 (Leipzig: Breitkopf und Härtel, 1904), p. 65: "Diewehl aber auch sonsten täglich vil schöner Gesang von berümbten Musicis und Componisten in obgemeldten sprachen in Truck außgehen/ und hergegen wenig in Teütscher sprach sich zu Componieren begeben/ so doch nit jederman Lateinisch unnd Welsch verstehet" [But since every day much more beautiful songs are published in these languages (Latin and Italian) by famous musicians and composers, and on the contrary little is composed in the German language, even though not everyone understands Latin and Italian] (quoted with translation in Snyder, "Text and Tone in Hassler's German Songs," p. 256 and p. 256 n. 8).

54 For biography, see Klaus-Peter Koch, "Documentary Biography," in Robert B. Lynn, *Valentin Haussmann (1565/70–ca.1614): A Thematic-Documentary Catalogue of His Works*, Thematic Catalogues, 25, Barry S. Brook (ed.) (Stuyvesant, NY: Pendragon Press, 1997), pp. 1–52.

55 Dumont, "Valentin Haussmann's Canzonettas," p. 61.

56 Sara Dumont has studied this material in detail in "Valentin Haussmann's Canzonettas," and in her *German Secular Polyphonic Song*, vol. 1, pp. 191–244.

Table 3.2 Valentin Haussmann's German Secular Songs, 1592–1597

RISM	SHORT TITLE	PLACE	DATE
H2379	*Neue Teutsche Weltliche Lieder*, 5vv	Nuremberg	1592
H2380	*Neue Teutsche weltliche Canzonette*, 4vv	Nuremberg	1596
H2381	*Eine fast liebliche art ...* *Teutschen weltlichen Lieder*, 5vv	Nuremberg	1594
H2382	*Neue Teutsche Weltliche Lieder*, 5vv	Nuremberg	1597
H2383	*Andere noch mehr Neue* *Teutsche Weltliche Lieder*, 4vv	Nuremberg	1597

Considering Haussmannn ever traveled to Italy, his complete assimilation of Italian musical and poetic styles in these volumes has been described by Dumont as "remarkable".[57] Yet Haussmann's early education offered the ideal training for his future vocation. After preliminary study of Latin, organ, and keyboard at the Gymnasium in Quedlinburg and the Lyceum in Wernigeröde, Haussmann entered the Gymnasium Poeticum in the free imperial city of Regensburg. Though student lists and financial records from 1584–90 do not survive, Haussmann's dedication in the manuscript "Magnificat" (1 June 1591) mentions that he studied under Andreas Raselius (c. 1563–1602), who served as Cantor of the Gymnasium Poeticum from 1584–1600.[58] Haussmann dedicated the work to the town fathers of Regensburg, and signed it from "Ratisponae." This puts his period of study at the Gymnasium Poeticum between 1584, when Raselius arrived, and 1591. Judging from an early school ordinance from the rectorship of Agricola (1551–62), Raselius taught Haussmann principles of voice-leading, cadences, notation, the art of singing, solmization, transposition, and elements of melody and harmony.[59] Haussmann's musical studies were complemented by a humanist curriculum that emphasized language acquisition, a combination that proved critical for his career as poet and translator. Students at the Gymnasium Poeticum learned German grammar in conjunction with Latin, with

---

57   Dumont, "Valentin Haussmann's Canzonettas," p. 62.

58   Raselius is best known for his treatise *Hexachordum seu Questiones musicae practicae ... in welchem viva exempla Dodechachordi Glareani in utraque scala gefunden werden* (Nuremberg, 1591), which remained a required text at the Gymnasium until 1664 (August Scharnagl, "Raselius, Andreas," *MGG*, vol. 11, col. 3).

59   *Agricola, Lib. E. 3. a & b*, cited in J. Auer, "M. Andreas Raselius Ambergensis, sein Leben und seine Werke," *Beilage zu den Monatsheften für Musikgeschichte*, 24 (1892): 12.

exercises consisting mainly of translation of Latin and Greek authors into German, the writing of a German letter, and the composition of a German poem.[60] According to the study plan of 1610, instruction in Latin and German formed the mainstay of the curriculum, with 23, 17, 14, 12, and 8 hours per week of instruction, in the second through sixth years of study, respectively.[61] The curriculum conformed to Renaissance pedagogical practice, both for the teaching of the Classical languages, and, in the literary sphere, for the training of the aspiring writer. Students started with strict translation, followed by paraphrase technique, and, finally, exercises in imitative and original composition.[62]

As a poet-composer Haussmann applied his systematic training in translation and imitation to German secular song poetry. Unlike Regnart, who authored much of the poetry that he set to music, Haussmann relied on either Italian poems or texts clearly derived from Regnart and Zacharia.[63] Though his volumes from the 1590s retained the combination of purely Italianate, mixed, and Germanic forms (like Regnart and Lechner before him), my examples focus on Haussmann's early translations of Italian poetry, which form a basis for his later translated editions of 1606–10.

Haussmann was faced with four options when adapting foreign texts: (1) to give a direct, word-by-word translation; (2) to change as little as possible; (3) to create a new poem with the same *Affekt* or overall mood, perhaps using a few of the same words; and (4) to write a completely different poem with a different *Affekt*, while preserving the number of syllables and rhyme scheme of the original. His early adaptations of Italian poems show a marked preference for the second method, retaining as much of the original meaning as possible. The five-voice *Eine fast liebliche art ... Teutschen weltlichen Lieder* (Nuremberg, 1594) includes a translation of Torquato Tasso's madrigal *Se'l vostro volto è d'un'aria gentile* from *Rime d'amore, Libro III*.[64] Haussmann based his translation of Tasso's poem on its appearance in the fifth edition of Oracio Vecchi's first book of four-voice canzonettas (Venice, 1591) (Example 3.3).[65] The resultant *Wann dein gesicht, das mich ansicht* (no. 11 in Haussmann's volume) features lines of seven and eight syllables set in light imitation across the parts (Example 3.4). With short phrases and conventional

---

60   Christian Heinrich Kleinstäuber, "Geschichte des evangelischen reichstädtischen Gymnasii poetici, part 1 (1538–1811)," *Verhandlungen des historischen Vereins von Oberpfalz und Regensburg*, 35–6, Neue Folge, 27–8 (1880; 1882): 47.

61   Ibid., p. 25.

62   Hermans, "Renaissance Translation between Literalism and Imitation," p. 95.

63   Dumont, *German Secular Polyphonic Song*, vol. 1, p. 201. Velten identified five of Haussmann's *Neue Teutsche weltliche Canzonette* (Nuremberg, 1596) as translations of Italian poems found earlier in Zacharia's bilingual collection (Velten, *Das Ältere Deutsche Gesellschaftslied*, pp. 91–100). Haussmann's settings appear in modern edition in Dumont, *German Secular Polyphonic Song*, vol. 2, pp. 227, 232, 262, 264, and 272.

64   Martino, *Die italienische Literatur im deutschen Sprachraum*, p. 438. For a modern edition, see Dumont, *German Secular Polyphonic Song*, vol. 2, pp. 183–4.

65   *Canzonette ... libro primo a quattro voci, novamente ristampate. ... quinta impressione* (Venice: Angelo Gardano, 1591; RISM A/I, V1014). Martino, *Die italienische Literatur im deutschen Sprachraum*, pp. 438–9.

harmonies, the setting aptly suited performance at gatherings hosted by the volume's dedicatees, the members of Nuremberg's music societies.[66]

Example 3.3 Torquato Tasso (as set by Orazio Vecchi), *Se 'l vostro volto è d'un'aria gentile*. The text is published in *Orazio Vecchi: The Four-Voice Canzonettas. With Original Texts and Contrafacta by Valentin Haussmann and Others*, edited by Ruth I. DeFord. 2 vols. (R92 and R93) Recent Researches in the Music of the Renaissance, vol. 92. Madison, WI: A-R Editions, Inc. 1993. Used with permission.

Se'l vostro volto è d'un'aria gentile,	If your face is made of gentle air, and your
E i bei vostri occhi son due fiamme ardenti,	lovely eyes are two burning flames, then
In voi dunque ci sono due elementi.	there are two elements in you.
Et se quessi occhi hor sono fonti e fiumi,	And if my eyes are fountains and rivers,
Et cenere io mio cor, dunque diremo	and my heart ashes, then we can say that
Che voi et io quattro elementi semo.	you and I are four elements.
Et se voi sete un'aria e dolce foco,	And if you are air and sweet fire, and I am
Acqua amara son io, cenere, e terra,	bitter water, ashes, and earth, why is there
Perche frà noi ci nasce tanta guerra?	such great war beween us?
Ma se volesse il fato e la mia sorte	But if fate and my destiny wished that all
Che tutti quattro fussimo una cosa,	four of us were one thing, o what a happy
O che vita felice e gloriosa!	and glorious life it would be!

Example 3.4 Valentin Haussmann, *Wann dein gesicht, das mich ansicht*[67]

Wann dein gesicht / das mich ansicht,	When your face, which gazes upon me
wie Wolken solche schweben,	like hovering clouds,
und dein euglein / der sternen schein	and [when] your eyes give forth the
	shining of the stars
mit i[h]ren stralen geben:	with their beams:
so wern in dir / o schöne zier,	so in you, oh sweet adornment,
zwey element gar eben.	two elements would be evenly balanced.
Wann wie ein quell / mein augen hell	If, as a spring, my bright eyes,
sich solten beid ergießen	should both pour forth [tears],

---

66 The dedication reads "Den Edlen/ Ehrnbesten/ Hochge= | lehrten/ Fürsichtigen/ Erbarn vn[d] Weisen Herrn: Christof- An= | dree Gugel beider Rechten Doctor/ Paulusen Koler/ Hansen Nützel/ Paulusen Be= | haim/ Georgen Volckhamer/ des kleinern Raths der Statt Nürmberg &c. Gabrieln Scheurl/ Wilhel= | men im Hof/ Wolffen Harsdorffer/ Erckenbrechten Koler/ Niclausen Rotengatter/ des grössern Raths &c. | auch ChristoffenTaig/ vnd Georgen Hasen &c. einer Erbarn löblichen gesellschafft | des Musickräntzels daselbs" (as transcribed in Lynn, *Valentin Haussmann*, p. 81).

67 No. 11 of *Eine fast liebliche art ... Teutschen weltlichen Lieder*, (Nuremberg, 1594). Haussmann's German text is given in Velten, *Das Ältere Deutsche Gesellschaftslied*, pp. 88–9. Thanks to Sharon Krebs for her assistance with the translation of this passage.

und wer mein hertz / sag ich on schertz,	and were my heart, I say without jest,
wie aschen zu den füssen;	like ashes at our feet,
so trügen wir / glaub gentzlich mir,	then, believe me utterly, we would carry
vier element mit wissen.	knowingly [all] four elements.
So dich nun zart / des luftes art	If you are gently then adorned with the nature of air
auch lieblichs feuer zieret,	and [with] lovely fire,
aber bey mir / Erdenmanier	but within me, earthly character
mit bitterm brunn regieret:	reigns along with a bitter wellspring:
was mag dann sein / das uns mit Pein	What may it be, then, that
in Widerwillen füret?	leads us into painful strife?
Wann Gottes gunst / und liebesbrunst	When God's favor and fire of love
uns endlich beiden gweret,	is finally granted to both of us,
daß in eins b[e]hend / die element	so that nimbly into one the four elements
all vier würden verkeret,	would be transformed,
wie könnte baß / freud one maß	then how could joy without measure
bei uns beiden werden gmeret.	be [further] increased within both of us?

Haussmann penned an extended text that retained the principle textual content and themes of Tasso's madrigal—praise of the beloved's face and eyes amidst painful strife resolved by destiny (in Tasso's case) and by God's will (in Haussmann's). It was typical for poet-translators to require "more space" when working from Italian to accommodate the syntactical demands of the German language. Haussmann's adherence to textual meaning is further demonstrated in five translations of Italian poems (set earlier by Zacharia in his *Soave e dilettevole canzonette*) found in Haussmann's four-voice *Neue Teutsche weltliche Canzonetten* (Nuremberg, 1596).[68] In his comparison of translations by Zacharia and Haussmann, Velten argued that the latter was the superior translator.[69] Dumont concurs that Haussmann's *Canzonetten* demonstrate his complete absorption of Italian style, both musical and poetic, as an integral part of his own compositional language.[70]

The second part of Haussmann's *Neue Teutsche Weltliche Lieder* (Nuremberg, 1597) reveals the more interpretative side of translating. Working from Vecchi's *Sembr'il mio corp'un legno in alto mare*, Haussmann creates a new strophe from each of the poem's first four lines (Example 3.5).

---

68   See n. 63 above. Haussmann's texts are no. 3, *O zartes bild*, no. 6, *Mit seuffzen und mit klag*, no. 21, *Fleug hin, mein sinn und gdancken*, no. 22, *Auß eurer schön und gdancken*, and no. 26, *Geh hin, trauriger gesang*.

69   Velten, *Das Ältere Deutsche Gesellschaftslied*, pp. 97–8.

70   Dumont, "Valentin Haussmann's Canzonettas," p. 68.

Example 3.5 Orazio Vecchi, *Sembra il mio corpo*. The text is published in *Orazio Vecchi: The Four-Voice Canzonettas. With Original Texts and Contrafacta by Valentin Haussmann and Others*, edited by Ruth I. DeFord. 2 vols. (R92 and R93) Recent Researches in the Music of the Renaissance, vol. 92. Madison, WI: A-R Editions, Inc. 1993. Used with permission.

Sembra il mio corp'un legno in alto mare;	My body seems like a boat on a high sea:
Le mie lagrime amare	my bitter tears are the waters, my torment
Son l'acque, e'l mio tormento	cruel fortune, and my sighs the wind.
Cruda fortuna, e i miei sospiri il vento.	

Building on only the first line of Vecchi's text, Haussmann constructs his first verse (Example 3.6).

Example 3.6 Valentin Haussmann, *Mein hertz, das tut sich krenken* (first stanza)[71]

Mein hertz, das tut sich krenken	My heart is aggrieved,
Mit lieb sehr hart verwundt,	sorely wounded by love.
wann ich das recht bedenke,	If I honestly consider it,
dünkt mich zu aller stunt,	methinks in every hour
daß es gleich einem Schiff,	that it is like a ship,
das in dem Wasser tieff	which in deep water
in g[e]fahr und großen nöten	in danger and great distress,
gantz in der irre lieff.	has completely gone astray.

Haussmann builds his stanza from Vecchi's comparison of a distressed heart to the ups-and-downs of a ship at sea. This freer approach to translation reflects the natural progression of a translator, from strict adherence to the original to flexible imitation of it. Working in the 1590s, Haussmann exemplified the overriding emphasis on the artistic qualities of the target language, a feature retained in his translated editions from the next decade.

Valentin Haussmann as Editor and Imitator, 1606–1610

Haussmann's activity as an editor-translator came at the end of a long career as poet and composer. His motivation for translating Italian music likely stemmed from close contact with the printer, Paul Kauffmann, whose firm issued all of Haussmann's secular and instrumental music books. Their personal contact dates back at least to the Leipzig book fair of fall 1597, where Haussmann was "reminded by the Hr. Paul Kauffmann ... to complete something of new merry dances and to send them

---

71   No. 21 of *Neue Teutsche Weltliche Lieder*, (Nuremberg, 1597). Haussmann's text is taken from Velten, *Das Ältere Deutsche Gesellschaftslied*, p. 101. Thanks to Sharon Krebs for her assistance with the translation of this passage.

to him."[72] Further mention of the printer appears in prefaces to *Extract Auß ... der Teutschen Weltlichen Lieder I* (Nuremberg, 1603) and *Extract auß ... der Teutschen Weltlichen Lieder II* (Nuremberg, 1603), both compilations of previously published works.[73] References to Paul Kauffmann continue in the dedications of Haussmann's translated editions of Marenzio, Gastoldi, and Vecchi/Capilupi. Haussmann makes Kauffmann's involvement clear in his dedication of *Ausszug auss Lucæ Marentii ... Villanellen und Napolitanen* (Nuremberg, 1606) to city councillor Wolff Rehlein, where he notes that he was "moved by the instruction of my good friend of typography" [So habe ich auß meines guten Freundes deß *Typographi* anleitung mich bewegen lassen].[74] Beyond encouragement, Paul Kauffmann may have provided financial backing for at least part of the series. Haussmann's translations of Vecchi's four-voice canzonettas lack dedicatory prefaces, suggesting that the printer-publisher financed them himself.

The selection of composers and texts for the series conforms to trends in composer reception at the Kauffmann firm. Haussmann initiated the series with a compendium of 51 settings drawn from Luca Marenzio's first four books of villanellas (1584–87).[75] Marenzio's "Roman style" villanellas offered appealing and accessible melodies that attracted the attention of English theorist and composer Thomas Morley, who observed: "If you think [villanellas] worthy of your pains to compose them, you have a pattern of them in Luca Marenzio and John Ferretti."[76] The volumes went through a total of 26 Italian editions from 1584 to 1605, immediately prior to Haussmann's setting of 51 of them to German texts.[77] The Kauffmann firm had established a reputation for printing and distributing Marenzio's music. Building on the strong showing of Marenzio's works in the *Gemma musicalis* anthologies, Kauffmann issued a compendium of selections from his nine books of five-voice madrigals in 1601.[78] The move to three-voice, German-texted repertory in 1606

---

72   His presence at the fair is noted in the dedication of *Neue artige und liebliche Täntzen* (Nuremberg, 1598): "... im nechstverschienen Leiptziger Herbstmarckt/ bin ich von Herrn Paul Kauffmann/ Buchhändlern vnd Buchdruckern zu Nürnberg/ abermals erinnert worden/ etwas von neuen lustigen Täntzen zuverfertigen/ vnnd jhme zu überschicken" [... in the previous Leipzig autumn market, I was reminded again by the Hr. Paul Kauffmann, book dealer and book printer in Nuremberg, to complete something of new merry dances and to send them to him], quoted in Koch, "Documentary Biography," p. 10, with English translation on p. 34.

73   For transcriptions of the prefaces, see Lynn, *Valentin Haussmann*, p. 146 and pp. 150–51, respectively.

74   Valentin Haussmann/Luca Marenzio, *Ausszug auss Lucæ Marentii ... Villanellen und Napolitanen* (Nuremberg: Paul Kauffmann, 1606; RISM A/I, M611), cantus partbook, fol. 2r (Faksimile-Edition Schermar-Bibliothek Ulm, 24 [Stuttgart: Cornetto-Verlag, 1997]).

75   RISM A/I, M587; RISM A/I, M594; RISM A/I, M599; and RISM A/I, M604. They are discussed in Ruth I. DeFord, "Marenzio and the *villanella alla romana*," *Early Music*, 27 (1999): 535–52. For a modern edition, see Luca Marenzio, *I cinque libri di Canzonette, Villanelle et arie alla Napolitana a tre voci di Luca Marenzio (in tre quaderni)*, ed. Marco Giuliani (Trent: Edizioni Nova Scuola Musicale, 1995–96).

76   Donna G. Cardamone: "Villanella," *Grove Music Online*, ed. Laura Macy (Accessed 30 May 2006]), <http://www.grovemusic.com>

77   DeFord, "Marenzio and the *villanella alla romana*," p. 535.

78   RISM A/I, M576=RISM B/I, 1601[12].

signals an attempt to reach a wider audience that did not understand Italian, yet enjoyed singing Italian songs, as Haussmann explained in the dedication of *Ausszug auss Lucæ Marentii … Villanellen und Napolitanen* (Nuremberg, 1606). Kauffmann tapped into an established market for three-voice, *tricinium* editions that appeared steadily from the Nuremberg firms of Hieronymus Formschneider, Johann Petreius, Johannes vom Berg and Ulrich Neuber, and Dietrich and Katharina Gerlach from the mid-sixteenth century onward. Kauffmann's Antwerp-based counterpart, Pierre Phalèse, shared his appreciation for three-voice repertory in simple, homophonic settings, with an anthology of three-voice *Canzonette alla romana* (1607) and an edition of Marenzio's three-voice villanellas and *canzonette alla napolitana* (1610) appearing simultaneously with Kauffmann's translated volumes.[79]

Martin Ruhnke observes that the strophic form of the villanella made it challenging for Haussmann to create a close musical-textual relationship.[80] Working within this constraint, Haussmann preserved the musical setting and metrical structure of the poems, but freely paraphrased them to create more realistic texts that conformed to Germanic rather than Italian norms of courtship.[81] Haussmann retained the metric accent and rhyme scheme of Marenzio's *Chi vuol vedere, Amanti*, but transformed the poem to address a single "Jungfrau" (Examples 3.7–3.8).

Example 3.7 Luca Marenzio, *Che vuol vedere, Amanti* (first stanza). Jerome and Elizabeth Roche (eds.), Barbara Reynolds, translator: *Light Madrigals and Villanellas.* The Flower of the Italian Madrigal, 3 (New York: Gaudia Music and Arts, 1995, Schaffner Publishing Co., sole agent).

Chi vuol vedere, Amanti, in terra il cielo,	Lovers, if heaven on earth you wish to see,
Venghi a vedere costei che è per me un gelo,	Come look on her who is so cold to me:
Che porta nel bel viso	Who in her visage bears
Quanto ha di bello e vago il Paradiso.	All that is beautiful in Paradise.

79 *Canzonette alla romana de diversi eccellentissimi musici romani a tre voci. Nuovamente raccolte & date in luce* (Antwerp: P. Phalèse, 1607; RISM B/I, 1607[14]); *Il primo, secondo, terzo, quarto & quinto libro delle villanelle, et canzonette alla napolitana, a tre voci, nuovamente stampate & in un corpo ridotte* (Antwerp: Pierre Phalèse, 1610; RISM A/I, M612).

80 Martin Ruhnke, "Zum Wort-Ton-Verhältnis in den mehrstrophigen Villanellen von Luca Marenzio und ihren Umtextierungen durch Valentin Haußmann," in Martin Just and Reinhard Wiesend (eds), *Liedstudien: Wolfgang Osthoff zum 60. Geburtstag* (Tutzing: Hans Schneider, 1989), pp. 137–51.

81 They are discussed in Maria Teresa Rosa Barezzani, "Le villanelle e la loro diffusione in Italia e all'estero," in Maria Teresa Rosa Barezzani and Manella Sala (eds), *Luca Marenzio musicista europeo*, Fondazione Civiltà Bresciana, 2 (Brescia: Edizioni di Storia Bresciana, 1989), pp. 134–7.

Example 3.8 Valentin Haussmann, *Jungfrau was habet ir an mir für tadel* (first stanza)[82]

Jungfrau was habet ir an mir für tadel/	Maiden, what do you find to rebuke in me,
vnd stecht auff mich gleich als	and poke at me as if with a needle?
mit einer Nadel?	
Wenn ich euch nicht bin eben/	If I don't suit you,
thut mir doch solche Stich ohn Blut nicht	don't keep giving me such bloodless stabs.
geben.	

While Marenzio's text praises physical beauty, Haussmann's adaptation asks the maiden not to taunt if he is not the object of her affection.

Two further volumes of three-voice repertory followed—translations of canzonettas by Orazio Vecchi and Gemignani Capilupi, and an anthology of 47 tricinia by Gastoldi (15), Marenzio (3), Vecchi (3), Mariano Tantucci (under the pseudonymn "Dell'Affetuoso," 10), Tomaso Pecci (signed "Dell'Invaghito," 11), and Haussmann himself (5). The status of the dedicatees of the three-voice volumes indicates a departure from territorial princes and regional rulers that characterize madrigal book dedications from the late sixteenth century. Instead the simplicity of the music and its setting to native texts points to an audience that included both courtly and urban contexts.[83] All dedicatees were citizens of Nuremberg. While Wolff Rehlein (the dedicatee of Marenzio's villanellas) was a member of the Greater Council, brothers Hans and Georg Losen (the dedicatees of the Vecchi/Capilupi volume) had no affiliation with city government. Haussmann dedicated *Johann-Jacobi Gastoldi und anderer Autorn Tricinia* (1607) to the Nuremberg merchant Georg Gruber and signed it "Euer guter Freund" [your good friend], an indication of their close relationship. Gruber was a noted amateur musician, and head of music-making at Nuremberg's Frauenkirche. This, coupled with Gruber's strong ties to Venice (see Chapter 2), made him an apt choice for dedicatee.

Haussmann's translated editions exhibit a range of approaches to compilation and ordering. While he had selected villanellas from across Marenzio's three volumes, for the Vecchi/Capilupi anthology Haussmann retained the ordering of contents found in Angelo Gardano's *Canzonette a tre voci di Horatio Vecchi, et di Gemignano Capi Lupi da Modona* (Venice, 1597), and Paul Kauffmann's Nuremberg edition of the same title and year.[84] The ordering of the 34 pieces is consistent across all three editions, with the exception of Haussmann's reversal of the final pair of canzonettas. Haussmann's *Johann-Jacobi Gastoldi und anderer Autorn Tricinia* of 1607 returns to

---

82   RISM A/I, M611, cantus partbook, fol. 12r (Faksimile-Edition Schermar-Bibliothek Ulm, 24 (Stuttgart: Cornetto-Verlag, 1997). Thanks to Sharon Krebs for her assistance with the translation of this passage.

83   Melchior Franck's *Tricinia nova lieblicher amorosischer gesänge* (Nuremberg: Abraham Wagenmann, 1611) bears a dedication to brothers Johann Ernst and Friderich, Dukes of Saxony, which confirms that three-voice Italianate repertory remained popular at court as well.

84   RISM B/I, 1597[21] (Venice) and RISM B/I, 1597[22] (Nuremberg).

the pattern of compilation from multiple sources. He selected works from Gastoldi's first book of *Canzonette a tre voci*, a joint volume of *Canzonette a tre voci* by Pecci and Tantucci, and Marenzio's *Il secondo libro delle canzonette alla napolitana* and *Il quarto libro delle villanelle a tre voci*.[85] Following Nuremberg practice, Haussmann orders the anthology by composer, opening with 15 settings by Gastoldi, a combined 21 pieces by Tantucci and Pecci (interspersed with two by Vecchi near the end), three settings by Marenzio, a further setting by Vecchi, and five by Haussmann himself to close. Haussmann's *Liebliche Fröliche Ballette ... von Thoma Morlei* (1609) adapts poetry from Morley's *Il primo libro delle Ballette a cinque voci* (London, 1595), a volume first released earlier that year with English texts.[86] Morley arranged the volume in modal order: nos 1–8 in G Mixolydian, no. 9 in C Ionian, 10–12 in G Dorian, 13 in A Aeolian, and 14–15 in F Ionian; the closing six pieces (nos 16–21) are canzonettas and a dialogue, a genre shift indicated by Morley's return to G Mixolydian for nos 16–17, A Aeolian for no. 18, and G Dorian for nos 19–21.[87] Haussmann retained Morley's systematic arrangement, demonstrating an interest in modal ordering, atypical of German editors (see Chapter 1). Haussmann based his final translated editions on Vecchi's four volumes of canzonettas, at times scattering their contents across the trilogy, at other times borrowing in blocks of up to five settings. This flexible approach suggests that Haussmann worked on the contents to all three volumes at roughly the same time, a chronology confirmed by the quick succession of the volumes in 1610.

As a translator, Haussmann exercised much flexibility in working with Italian poetry. From their study of Haussmann's translations, Morricone and Salottolo demonstrate that he modified the order of verses and text accentuation as needed, adjusted the metrical structure (syllable count per line), and amplified the meaning of the source poem.[88] Gastoldi's *Ahi chi mi tien'il core*, for instance, is transformed from four strophes of four lines each to three strophes of six lines each; the opening accented syllable of Tantucci's **Caro** *albergo d'amore* becomes an unaccented syllable in Haussmann's *Amor, ich bin gefangen.*[89] Haussmann generally retained

---

85   Lynn, *Valentin Haussmann*, pp. 254–62. *Canzonette a tre voci ... libro primo ... in miglior forma ristampate* (Venice: Ricciardo Amadino, 1595; RISM A/I, G551); *Canzonette a tre voci nuovamente composte, et date in luce* (Venice: G. Vincenti, 1599; RISM B/I, 1599[11]=RISM A/I, P1102); *Il secondo libro delle canzonette alla napolitana a tre voci ... raccolte per Attilio Gualtieri* (Venice: Giacomo Vincenti & Ricciardo Amadino, 1585; RISM A/I, M594); and *Il quarto libro delle villanelle a tre voci ... raccolte per Attilio Gualtieri* (Venice: Giacomo Vincenti, 1587; RISM A/I, M604).

86   *Il primo libro delle ballette a cinque voci* (London: Thomas East, 1595; RISM A/I, M3698) and *The first booke of balletts to five voyces* (London: Thomas East, 1595; RISM A/I, M3697). Haussmann's German edition is not listed in the works list in Philip Brett: "Morley, Thomas," *Grove Music Online*, ed. Laura Macy (Accessed 1 April 2006]), <http://www.grovemusic.com>

87   Lionel Pike, *Pills to Purge Melancholy: The Evolution of the English Ballett* (Aldershot: Ashgate, 2004), p. 43.

88   Clotilde Morricone and Adriana Salottolo, "Valentin Haussmann trascrittore e le canzonette italiane in Germania," *Rivista di musicologia*, 5 (1970): 73–98.

89   Ibid., pp. 77–8.

the amorous themes of his source texts, but often tempered them to suit German sensibilities, as in his *Als ich bey meinem schönen Bulen ware*, based on Pecci's *Mentre stava Mirtillo in braccio a Clori*.[90] Musically, Haussmann departed from Abraham Ratz's prized faithfulness to the music, by neutralizing dissonant intervals, and implementing minor changes in rhythm and ornamentation to accommodate textual adjustments.[91]

Haussmann's adaptations of Thomas Morley's ballettos demonstrate an intermingling of cultural influences. Morley's ballettos were themselves based on earlier settings by Gastoldi, Vecchi, Marenzio, Trofeo, Ferretti, and Croce.[92] Leonel Pike divides them into four categories: the dance type (a short balletto that adheres closely to a dance pattern), the imitative type, the contrasting type (pieces that change from *note nere* to *note bianche* for expressive purposes), and those evoking a "chase" (often a close canon) between two voices.[93] Prior to this volume, Haussmann's awareness of English practice was largely restricted to instrumental music. He came into contact with English musicians in Hamburg in 1601, and the fruits of this exchange appeared in his *Neue Intrade ... Nach disen sind etliche Englische Paduan und Galliarde anderer Composition zu finden* (Nuremberg, 1604) for viol consort, and *Neue fünffstimmige Paduane und Galliarde* (Nuremberg, 1604).[94] Through contact with Hamburg, Haussmann may have learned of Morley's English edition of the *Ballette*, which Joseph Kerman argues was Haussmann's source for nos 4, 8, and 15 of the *Liebliche Fröliche Ballette*.[95] The connection with the English edition is strongest in the case of no. 15 (Examples 3.9–3.11).

90 Ibid., pp. 82–3.

91 Ibid., pp. 89–95.

92 The contents of Morley's English and Italian editions of ballettos (both printed in London in 1595), along with their sources, are given in Table XIII of Joseph Kerman, *The Elizabethan Madrigal: A Comparative Study* ([New York]: American Musicological Society, 1962), p. 140.

93 Pike, *Pills to Purge Melancholy*, pp. 43–4. Morley's 1595 ballettos and their models are examined in ibid., pp. 39–131.

94 See Koch, "Documentary Biography," pp. 36–7 on the Hamburg connection. For a broader discussion, see Werner Braun, *Britannia Abundans: Deutsch-Englisch Musikbeziehungen zur Shakespearezeit* (Tutzing: Hans Schneider, 1977), esp. pp. 196–7, 247–52, 346–51.

95 Kerman, *The Elizabethan Madrigal*, p. 138 n.1.

Example 3.9 Valentin Haussmann, *Hoja, hoja, wo da?*[96]

Hoja hoja,	Heyo, heyo, where there, fa la.
wo da?	where there?
Fa la.	Fa la.
Ach helfft ach helfft,	Oh help, oh help
mein hertz brin[n]t mir in meinem liebe/	my heart burns me with my desire
nach einem außerwelten schönen Weibe/	for a gorgeous girl,
Fa la ...	Fa la ...

Example 3.10 Thomas Morley, *Fyer! Fyer! My heart!*[97]

Fyer! Fyer!
My heart!
Fa la.
O help, alas, O help!
Ay me: I sit and cry me,
And call for help,
Alas, but none comes nigh me.
Fa la.

Example 3.11 Thomas Morley, *A la strada*[98]

A la strada	To the road
A dio.	Good-bye
Fa la.	Fa la.
Aiut' aiut' aiut' aiut'	Help, help help help
Ohime ch'io son tradita	Alas that I am betrayed [female subject]
O poverino	Oh poor one [male subject]
Me ch'io son ferito.	I who am wounded [male subject]
Fa la.	Fa la.

While the presence and positioning of the "fa-la" refrains are consistent across all three examples, Haussmann's opening call and plea for help (line 4) more closely mirror Morley's English version.

The remainder of this chapter focuses on Haussmann's three translated volumes of Vecchi's canzonettas, which illustrate both the predilections of Haussmann as a

---

96   No. 15 of *Liebliche Fröliche Ballette ... von Thoma Morlei* (Nuremberg, 1609), cantus partbook, fol. 12r. Exemplar Staats- und Universitätsbibliothek, Hamburg: 1 an Scrin. A/580.

97   No. 14 of *The First Booke of Balletts* (London, 1595). The text is taken from Pike, *Pills to Purge Melancholy*, p. 110.

98   From *Il primo libro delle ballette* (London, 1595); originally set by Luca Marenzio in *Il secondo libro delle canzonette alla napolitana* (Venice, 1585). The text for the first stanza is taken from ibid. Thanks to Lloyd Howard for his assistance with the English translation.

translator and the broader shift of approach that his work represents. The contents of the trilogy appear in Appendix B (pp. 230–36). Haussmann translated all but two of Vecchi's 90 four-voice canzonettas, music that had become a veritable cash cow for the Gardano printing firm. Beginning before 1580 and continuing through 1613, Angelo Gardano and his heirs issued six editions of Book 1, five editions of Book 2, three of Book 3, and two of Book 4. Katharina Gerlach issued the complete set in a single volume in 1593; her grandson and successor, Paul Kauffmann, reissued them in 1600-01.

Haussmann launched the Vecchi trilogy with one of his own canzonettas that paid tribute to his audience (Example 3.12):

Example 3.12 Valentin Haussmann, "Prœmium," *Die Canzonetten wir vorehrn euch Venusknaben*. The text is published in *Orazio Vecchi: The Four-Voice Canzonettas. With Original Texts and Contrafacta by Valentin Haussmann and Others*, edited by Ruth I. DeFord. 2 vols. (R92 and R93) Recent Researches in Music of the Renaissance, vol. 92. Madison, WI: A-R Editions, Inc. 1993. Used with permission.

Die Canzonetten wir vorehrn euch, Venusknaben;
Darinnen werdet ihr eurs hertzen meinung haben.
Thut ihnen lieb beweisen;
Das werck wirdt selber seinen Meister preisen.

We present these little songs to you, sons of Venus; in them you will find your heart's desires. Treat them with love; the work itself will honor its creator.

The pronoun "wir" [we] symbolizes the collaborative efforts of composer, editor-translator, printer, and performer in bringing the work to the public.

Haussmann's adaptations of Vecchi's texts exploit the potential "fit" between the original and the target languages. Haussmann retains the ABAB rhyme scheme and alternation of seven and 11-syllable lines that pervade Vecchi's canzonettas. The strongest cases of borrowing occur on the two occasions that Haussmann follows Vecchi's refrain structure as well. Haussmann's *Amor, ich geb mich deiner macht gefangen* adopts the refrain structure of Vecchi's *Amor con ogni imper e gran possanza*, to create a close relationship between the model and its reworking (Examples 3.13–3.14).

Example 3.13 Orazio Vecchi, *Amor con ogni impero e gran possanza*. The text is published in *Orazio Vecchi: The Four-Voice Canzonettas. With Original Texts and Contrafacta by Valentin Haussmann and Others*, edited by Ruth I. DeFord. 2 vols. (R92 and R93) Recent Researches in the Music of the Renaissance, vol. 92. Madison, WI: A-R Editions, Inc. 1993. Used with permission.

Amor con ogni impero e gran possanza
S'è mosso con furor per assediarmi,
A suon di Trombe e di Tamburri e d'armi.

Love, with all authority and great power, moved in fury to lay siege to me, to the sound of trumpets and drums and arms.

Già scorre il campo con grand'ordinanza,
Contro di me gridando: "à l'armi, à l'armi,"
A suon di Trombe e di Tamburri e d'armi.

Already he is running through the camp with great commands shouting against me, "to arms, to arms," to the sound of trumpets and drums and arms.

Sopra un corsiero porta scudo e lanza,
Con la quale hà giurato d'atterrarmi,
A suon di Trombe e di Tamburri e d'armi.

Above a steed he carries a shield and a lance, with which he has vowed to lay me low, to the sound of trumpets and drums and arms.

E d'ogni libertà, d'ogni speranza
Privarmi, e fiamme e fuoco al cor gettarmi,
A suon di Trombe e di Tamburri e d'armi.

And to deprive me of all liberty and all hope, and to throw fire and flames at my heart, to the sound of trumpets and drums and arms.

Example 3.14 Valentin Haussmann, *Amor, ich geb mich deiner macht gefangen*. The text is published in *Orazio Vecchi: The Four-Voice Canzonettas. With Original Texts and Contrafacta by Valentin Haussmann and Others*, edited by Ruth I. DeFord. 2 vols. (R92 and R93) Recent Researches in the Music of the Renaissance, vol. 92. Madison, WI: A-R Editions, Inc. 1993. Used with permission.

Amor, ich geb mich deiner macht gefangen;
Du hast mich inn gewalt ein mal bekommen.
Laß schlagn alarma mit pfeiffen und mit trommen!

Love, I give myself up to your power; you have won me by force. Sound the alarm with pipes and drums

Ich hab mich wider dich so lang gewehret,
Biß du die waffen all mir hast genommen.
Laß schlagn alarma mit pfeiffen vnd mit trommen!

I have defended myself against you for so long that you have taken all my weapons from me. Sound the alarm with pipes and drums!

Jetzt lig ich hie, und bin so hart verwundet.
Den schaden hab ich nun; du hast den frommen.

Now I lie here and am wounded deeply. I have the wounds; you have your faithful servant.

Laß schlagn alarma mit pfeiffen vnd mit trommen!   Sound the alarm with pipes and
                                                             drums!

This is Haussmann's strongest case of borrowing the structure and textual content of the model. Musically, the refrain is cast with triadic pronouncements in the tonic of F major, a passage that aptly suits both composers' call to arms.

In the second example of refrain borrowing, Haussmann transforms Vecchi's dialogue *Lucilla, io vo morire* into a dialogue between a "Jungfrau" [young maiden] and her beloved (Examples 3.15–3.16).

Example 3.15 Orazio Vecchi, *Lucilla, io vo morire*. The text is published in *Orazio Vecchi: The Four-Voice Canzonettas. With Original Texts and Contrafacta by Valentin Haussmann and Others*, edited by Ruth I. DeFord. 2 vols. (R92 and R93) Recent Researches in the Music of the Renaissance, vol. 92. Madison, WI: A-R Editions, Inc. 1993. Used with permission.

"Lucilla, io vo morire."   "Lucilla, I want to die." "Do not die, my
[L.] "Deh non morir, cor mio."   love." "Why should I live?" "To await the
"Perche viver debb'io?"   good that will come." Alas, my miserable
[L.] "Per aspettar il ben c'hà da venire."   heart! Its pain is certain; its joy is
Ahi misero mio core!   doubtful, Love
Ha certo il duol; dubbia la gioia, Amore.

"Tienmi tu dunque in vita."   "Then you keep me alive." "How, my
[L.] "Ma come, anima mia?"   beloved?" "By being more merciful to
"Co l'essermi più pia."   me." "Wait, someday I will help you."
[L.] "Aspetta, ch'anco un di ti darò aita."   Alas, my miserable heart! He who is
Ahi misero mio core!   dying cannot well wait for help.
Mal può aspettare aiuto chi si more.

"Dunque debbo aspettare?"   "Then I must wait?" "Yes, my dear, as you
[L.] "Si, ben mio, come fai."   are doing." "But if it never comes?" "It
"Ma se non viene mai?"   will come, believe me, do not doubt."
 [L.] "Verrà, credilo à me, non dubitare."   Alas, my miserable heart!
Ahi misero mio core!   He who dies loving well has a good end.
Un bel fin fa chi ben amando more.

Example 3.16 Valentin Haussmann, *Jungfrau, dein Lieb mich brinnet*. The text is published in *Orazio Vecchi: The Four-Voice Canzonettas. With Original Texts and Contrafacta by Valentin Haussmann and Others*, edited by Ruth I. DeFord. 2 vols. (R92 and R93) Recent Researches in the Music of the Renaissance, vol. 92. Madison, WI: A-R Editions, Inc. 1993. Used with permission.

Dialogus:

[I.] "Jungfrau, dein Lieb mich brinnet."
[P.] "Wo ist sie denn herkommen?"
[I.] "Von Venus feur und flammen."
[P.] "Was ist denn Venus gegen dir gesinnet?"
[I.] "Ach weh, mein armes hertze!
Das ängstigt sie gar sehr mit liebes schmertze."

I. "Köndt ich doch hülff erlangen."
P. "Wer solte dir denn helffen?"
I. "Du, durch mein flehn unnd gelffen."
P. "Wenn ich es thett, hett ich auch feur gefangen."
I. "Ach weh, mein armes hertze
Ist ohne hülff und trost in liebes schmertze."

I. "Gott g'segn dich, ich muß sterben."
P. "Wer spricht dir ab das leben?"
I. "Das feur der lieb thuts eben."
P. "So will ich helffn beklagen dein verderben."
I. "O weh, mein junges hertze
Deintwegn verdirbt, und stirbt in liebes schmertze."

Dialogue:

[I.] "Young lady, your love burns me." [P.] "Where did it come from?" [I.] "From Venus's fire and flames." [P.] "What does Venus have against you?" [I.] "Alas, my poor heart! It is frightened greatly with the pain of love."

I. "If only I could get help!" P. "Who should help you?" I. "You, from my pleading and sobbing." P. "If I did it, I would catch fire, too." I. "Alas, my poor heart is without help or comfort in the pain of love."

I. "God bless you, I must die." P. "Who is taking away your young life?" I. "The fire of love is doing it." P. "Then I will help to mourn your death." I. "Alas, my young heart is destroyed by you and dies in the pain of love."

The two texts share the common theme of the pain of love. They contrast in their response to the pain. The refrain of Vecchi's third stanza resolves "He who dies loving well has a good end," while Haussmann's lover interjects a reference to God as he "dies in the pain of love." Such religious references permeate Haussmann's love poetry, and infuse the series with a tone more befitting German sensibilities. Growing religious tensions created an ideological divide between secular song texts in the Italian tradition and Protestant audiences.

Haussmann responded by incorporating spiritual themes and toning down Vecchi's overt sexual imagery. The first volume includes *Eur schöne jugent* (Example 3.17), a setting of Tasso's *Se'l vostro volto è d'un aria gentile*, a poem translated earlier as *Wann dein gesicht, das mich ansicht* in Haussmann's *Eine fast liebliche art ... Teutschen weltlichen Lieder* of 1594 (see Examples 3.3–3.4).

Example 3.17 Valentin Haussmann, *Eur schöne jugent* (first stanza). The text is published in *Orazio Vecchi: The Four-Voice Canzonettas. With Original Texts and Contrafacta by Valentin Haussmann and Others*, edited by Ruth I. DeFord. 2 vols. (R92 and R93) Recent Researches in the Music of the Renaissance, vol. 92. Madison, WI: A-R Editions, Inc. 1993. Used with permission.

Eur schöne jugent,	Your beautiful youth and your noble
Eur Adeliche tugent,	virtue alone draw me to you with
Allein zu euch mit lieb vnd gunst mich treiben.	love and good will. I cannot resist
Ich weiß für grosser liebe nicht zu bleiben.	such great love.

Haussmann departs from the specific imagery of Tasso's poem to enhance the purity of his version through praise of maidenly virtue and good will. As Ruth DeFord speculates, Haussmann's texts seem to be pitched at prospective brides, a sharp contrast to the courtesan atmosphere of Vecchi's canzonettas.[99]

Haussmann's more chaste vision manifests itself in multiple guises. His *Ach ihr Liedlein der Liebe* (Example 3.19), and its model, Vecchi's *Canzonette d'Amore* (Example 3.18), share the common theme of love songs. From the start, Vecchi's poem focuses on their recipient, Cloris. By contrast, Haussmann's first stanza directs attention to the source of the love songs, Venus (first stanza), then to the singers themselves (second stanza).

Example 3.18 Orazio Vecchi, *Canzonette d'Amore* (first and second stanzas). The text is published in *Orazio Vecchi: The Four-Voice Canzonettas. With Original Texts and Contrafacta by Valentin Haussmann and Others*, edited by Ruth I. DeFord. 2 vols. (R92 and R93) Recent Researches in the Music of the Renaissance, vol. 92. Madison, WI: A-R Editions, Inc. 1993. Used with permission.

Canzonette d'Amore	Little songs of Love that go forth
Che m'uscite del core,	from my heart, tell of my pains,
Contate i miei dolori,	kissing the hands of my lovely
Le man baciando alla mia bella Clori.	Cloris.
Ivi liete e vezzose,	There happy and pretty, crowned
Coronate di rose,	with roses, tell of my pains, kissing
Contate i miei dolori,	the hands of my lovely Cloris.
Le man baciando alla mia bella Clori.	

---

99 Orazio Vecchi, *Orazio Vecchi: The Four-Voice Canzonettas. With Original Texts and Contrafacta by Valentin Haussmann and Others*, ed. Ruth I. DeFord, Recent Researches in the Music of the Renaissance, 92–3 (Madison, WI: A-R Editions, Inc. 1993), part 1 (vol. 92), p. 7.

Example 3.19 Valentin Haussmann, *Ach ihr Liedlein der Liebe* (first and second stanzas). The text is published in *Orazio Vecchi: The Four-Voice Canzonettas. With Original Texts and Contrafacta by Valentin Haussmann and Others*, edited by Ruth I. DeFord. 2 vols. (R92 and R93) Recent Researches in the Music of the Renaissance, vol. 92. Madison, WI: A-R Editions, Inc. 1993. Used with permission.

Ach ihr liedlein der Liebe,	Oh you little songs of love that come
Kommt auß Venus getriebe,	from Venus, sing of the great pain
Singt von dem grossen schmertzen,	that the prettiest one gives me in my
Den mir die schönst thut an inn meinem hertzen.	heart.

O ihr Stimmlein so süsse,	Oh you sweet little voices, do not be
Euch last es nicht verdriessen;	annoyed, but be glad that you can
Thut euch lieblich bequemen,	warm the heart of the gentle one.
Daß ir der zartn ihr hertzlein könnt einnemen.	

For the final stanza (Examples 3.20–3.21), both Vecchi and Haussmann turn their attention to the respective recipient of the love songs. While Vecchi praises the physical beauty of Cloris, Haussmann replaces Vecchi's explicit sexual overtones with laments of unrequited love for the "honored lady."

Example 3.20 Orazio Vecchi, *Canzonette d'Amore* (third stanza). The text is published in *Orazio Vecchi: The Four-Voice Canzonettas. With Original Texts and Contrafacta by Valentin Haussmann and Others*, edited by Ruth I. DeFord. 2 vols. (R92 and R93) Recent Researches in the Music of the Renaissance, vol. 92. Madison, WI: A-R Editions, Inc. 1993. Used with permission.

Poi mirando il bel seno	Then looking at her lovely breast and
E'l suo viso sereno,	her serene face, tell of my pains,
Contate i miei dolori,	kissing the hands of my lovely
Le man baciando alla mia bella Clori.	Cloris.

Example 3.21 Valentin Haussmann, *Ach ihr Liedlein der Liebe* (third stanza). The text is published in *Orazio Vecchi: The Four-Voice Canzonettas. With Original Texts and Contrafacta by Valentin Haussmann and Others*, edited by Ruth I. DeFord. 2 vols. (R92 and R93) Recent Researches in the Music of the Renaissance, vol. 92. Madison, WI: A-R Editions, Inc. 1993. Used with permission.

Ach holdselig geehret,	Oh most honored lady, you wound
Die mich mit lieb versehret,	me with love; listen attentively, and
Hör zu mit allem fleisse,	see how I suffer for you.
Und betracht, wie ich sitz	
deintwegn im schweisse.	

Ach holdselig geehret/	Oh most honored lady, you wound
Die mich mit lieb versehret/	me with love; listen attentively, and
Hör zu mit allem fleisse/	see how I suffer for you.
Und betracht, wie ich sitz deintwegn	
im schweisse.	

Haussmann's adaptation preserves the general meaning of Vecchi's poem, while freely altering individual words.

Haussmann's most frequent form of spiritual cleansing was word substitution. A strong case can be found in *Die mir mein hertz besessen* (Example 3.23), an adaptation of Vecchi's *Se pensando al partire* (Example 3.22). Here Haussmann removes the overt word-play on "morire" [death, dying], and replaces it with a more chaste nostalgia.

Example 3.22 Orazio Vecchi, *Se pensando al partire* (first stanza). The text is published in *Orazio Vecchi: The Four-Voice Canzonettas. With Original Texts and Contrafacta by Valentin Haussmann and Others*, edited by Ruth I. DeFord. 2 vols. (R92 and R93) Recent Researches in the Music of the Renaissance, vol. 92. Madison, WI: A-R Editions, Inc. 1993. Used with permission.

Se pensando al partire	If in thinking of parting I feel myself dying,
Io mi sento morire,	what should I do, alas, since you are the
Che far ahime deggio io,	only cause of my life?
Se sola sei cagion del viver mio?	

Example 3.23 Valentin Haussmann, *Die mir mein hertz besessen* (first stanza). The text is published in *Orazio Vecchi: The Four-Voice Canzonettas. With Original Texts and Contrafacta by Valentin Haussmann and Others*, edited by Ruth I. DeFord. 2 vols. (R92 and R93) Recent Researches in the Music of the Renaissance, vol. 92. Madison, WI: A-R Editions, Inc. 1993. Used with permission.

Die mir mein hertz besessen,	I cannot forget the one who has taken my
Ihr kan ich nicht vergessen.	heart. I have given myself to her, because
Ihr hab ich mich ergeben,	she gives joy to my heart, my mind, and my life.
Denn sie erfreut mein hertz, mein sinn .	
und leben.	

Haussmann's technique was partly consumer-driven. By rendering neutral the more racey imagery of Italian secular poetry, he created songs that suited the tastes and sensibilities of the German marketplace.

As Haussmann adapted Vecchi's texts, he did so with little concern for the music-tone relationship. In *Im grünen Wald* (Examples 3.24–3.25) Haussmann retains Vecchi's opening image of verdant fields, but transforms the pastoral scene to feature birds praising God with song.

Example 3.24 Orazio Vecchi, *Trà verdi campi*. The text is published in *Orazio Vecchi: The Four-Voice Canzonettas. With Original Texts and Contrafacta by Valentin Haussmann and Others*, edited by Ruth I. DeFord. 2 vols. (R92 and R93) Recent Researches in the Music of the Renaissance, vol. 92. Madison, WI: A-R Editions, Inc. 1993. Used with permission.

Trà verdi campi a la stagion novella
Vince ogni fior una vermiglia rosa.
 Veggiola di lontano,
 Ma stendo in vano
 L'ardita mano.

Among the green fields in the springtime one red rose surpasses every flower. I see her from afar, but I extend my ardent hand in vain.

Famosi fiumi, e tu, Colonia bella,
Quanto di bene ha'l mondo in voi si posa.
 Veggiola di lontano,
 Ma stendo in vano
 L'ardita mano.

Famous rivers, and you, lovely Colonia, all that is good in the world is in you I see her from afar, but I extend my ardent hand in vain.

Cogliete i fiori in questa parte e in quella,
Ninfe, à honorar di voi la piu famosa.
 Veggiola di lontano,
 Ma stendo in vano
 L'ardita mano.

Gather the flowers from all over, nymphs, to honor the most famous among you, I see her from afar and extend my ardent in vain.

Et voi, felici e cari umbrii Pastori,
Cantate in rime i suoi celesti honori;
 Veggiola di lontano,
 Beltà infinita,
 Dammi la vita.

And you, dear, happy, Umbrian shepherds, sing her heavenly honors in rhymes; I see her from afar, infinite beauty, give me life.

Example 3.25 Valentin Haussmann, *Im grünen Wald*. The text is published in *Orazio Vecchi: The Four-Voice Canzonettas. With Original Texts and Contrafacta by Valentin Haussmann and Others*, edited by Ruth I. DeFord. 2 vols. (R92 and R93) Recent Researches in the Music of the Renaissance, vol. 92. Madison, WI: A-R Editions, Inc. 1993. Used with permission.

Im grünen Wald ich neulich gieng spatzieren,
Zu hören wie die vöglein lieblich singen,
Wie sie zu Gott dem Herren
Ihr zünglein kehren,
Mit g'sang ihn ehren.

In a green wood I recently went for a walk to hear the sweet singing of the birds, how they turn their tongues to the Lord God and praise him with song.

Da hört ich vnter allen jubiliren
Ein kleines Vöglein, sang mit hellem schalle
So wunder vnd so schone
Ein süssen Tone,
Es bracht mir wonne.

There I heard among others
a little bird rejoice; it sang clear,
sweet tones so beautifully that
it brought me great pleasure.

Nun sing, daß dich der liebe Gott behüte,
Du kleines Vöglein, meisterin im singen.
Dein Melodey und weise
Ich lob unnd preise
Mit gantzem fleisse.

Now sing, so that God will protect you,
you little bird, mistress of song. I praise
your tune with all my heart.

Haussmann transforms Vecchi's poem of worldly love into one of spiritual love, captured through the song of birds. Though Haussmann's bird imagery is not realized in the musical setting—creating a disparity in the music-tone relationship—its inclusion served a broader purpose: it built on a common theme of spiritual poetry from German-speaking lands where Martin Luther's praise of birds permeated the texts of sacred songs (see Chapter 4).

Conclusion

Haussmann was the first music editor to achieve fame as a translator. In his treatise *De parodia tractatus musicalis* (Jena, 1611), theorist Georg Quitschreiber lauded Haussmann's work as a model of translation. Four years later, the chapelmaster at the Sachsen-Coburg court, Melchior Franck, praised Haussmann's "Italian Tricinia, of Marentio, H. Vecchi, and Gastoldi, under which he placed charming German texts so that they might be better known in Germany."[100] Upon Haussmann's death, Johannes Jeep composed an elegy where *Musica* claims "ein stein ist der dich nicht beweint, groß lob hast du erworben" [he is a stone, who does not weep for you; you have earned great praise].[101] Martin Zeuner included 14 of Haussmann's translated settings in his songbook *Schöne teutsche weltliche Stücklein mit vier und fünff Stimmen* (Nuremberg, 1617).[102]

But Haussmann's translations made a more lasting contribution to German poetics than these tributes alone suggest. The profusion of translations and adaptations of Italian texts may be connected with contemporary German efforts to overtake foreign influences, in an attempt to forge a national identity amidst growing regional

---

100 " ... etliche Italienische Tricinia, als Marentii, H. Vecchi, vnd Gastoldi, darunter er anmütige Teutsche Text/ damit sie in Teutschland auch desto besser bekannt würden/ gelegt/ publiciren lassen," from the dedication of Melchior Franck, *Delitiae amoris* (Nuremberg, 1615), quoted with English translation in Koch, "Documentary Biography," pp. 18, 42.

101 From the final stanza of *Mortuus Hausmannus vivit in aede poli*, from the fourth edition of Johannes Jeep, *Studentengärtleins Ander Theil, Neuer lustiger Weltlicher Liedlein, mit 4. und 5. Stimmen* (Nuremberg: Abraham Wagenmann, 1614; RISM A/I, J513). Quoted with English translation in Koch, "Documentary Biography", p. 44.

102 Velten, *Das Ältere Deutsche Gesellschaftslied*, p. 137.

and transnational conflict. Though scholars have examined music's contribution to German images of nationhood and identity in the nineteenth and twentieth centuries, the search for such imagery dates back to the seventeenth century, when poets, musicians, and composers demonstrated intense interest in issues of national identity.[103] Georg Schmidt has argued that an attempt to construct a "German nation" took hold in the decades around 1600, as regional and transnational conflicts encouraged nationalist reactions.[104] The development of a national identity took a different shape in Germany in comparison with neighboring England, France, and Spain, all kingdoms with a central court. As a conglomeration of smaller principalities, duchies, electorates, and city-states, any concept of "Germany" was by definition one of political and linguistic fragmentation.[105] Artists, musicians, and poets attempted to join these fragments through a conscious effort to create a cultural identity distinct from *Welschland*, which subsumed both francophone and italophone regions.[106]

The emergence of German as a literary language was an important part of this movement. Taken together, Haussmann's translations demonstrate his skilful development of German verse in the years before the reforms of Martin Opitz and his followers. As translated anthologies, Haussmann's editions promoted interest in Italian music and poetry (the source language), while at the same time providing new impetus to the target language.[107] For Martin Opitz, recognized as the pioneer of German poetics, the German language needed to assert itself against both Latin and the neighboring vernaculars—a feat complicated by the infiltration of loan words, and, in artistic endeavors, the predilection for preferring foreign languages to German.[108] Basil Smallman has pointed out the paradox of this cultural exchange.[109] Yet, as the work of Valentin Haussmann suggests, the adoption of Italian models played a vital role in the very construction of a German poetic language for music.

---

103 Celia Applegate and Pamela Potter (eds), *Music and German National Identity* (Chicago: University of Chicago Press, 2002) ignores music's role in constructing images of the nation and identity in the seventeenth century.

104 Georg Schmidt, "Die frühneuzeitliche Idee 'deutsche Nation': Mehrkonfessionalität und säkulare Werte," in Heinz-Gerhard Haupt and Dieter Langewiesche (eds), *Nation und Religion in der Deutschen Geschichte* (Frankfurt: Campus, 2001), pp. 33–67.

105 Mara R. Wade and Glenn Ehrstine, "Der, die, das Fremde: Alterity in Medieval and Early Modern German Studies," *Daphnis*, 33 (1–2) (2004): 17.

106 Ibid.

107 Harald Kittel notes the influence of translated anthologies on source and target languages in "International Anthologies of Literature in Translation: An Introduction to Incipient Research," in Harald Kittel (ed.), *International Anthologies of Literature in Translation, GBIÜ*, 9 (Berlin: Erich Schmidt, 1995), pp. XV–XVI.

108 Peter Schaeffer, "Baroque Philology: The Position of German in the European Family of Languages," in Gerhart Hoffmeister (ed.), *German Baroque Literature: The European Perspective* (New York: Frederick Ungar, 1983), p. 73.

109 Basil Smallman, "Pastoralism, Parody and Pathos: The Madrigal in Germany, 1570–1630," in *Conspectus Carminis: Essays for David Galliver, Miscellanea Musicologica*, Adelaide Studies in Musicology, 15 (Adelaide: University of Adelaide Press, 1988), p. 15.

Chapter 4

From Pastoral to Prayer: Editing Italian Music for Lutheran Germany

This chapter argues that Luther's views of music influenced editorial strategy and practice in the decades of confessional strife leading up to the Thirty Years War. The years between the Peace of Augsburg (1555) and the outbreak of the Thirty Years War (1618) marked a period of confessionalization into the Lutheran, Calvinist, and Catholic denominations.[1] Music, poetry, and drama formed an important part of this process. Nowhere is this stronger than in the case of the Lutheran faith.

More than any other reformer, Martin Luther proclaimed the value of music for the praise of God, in his letters, liturgical and exegetical writings, and, most importantly, hymnal prefaces. Taken together, they demonstrate his conscious effort to form an approach to worship that granted a special role for music. At its heart is a fundamentally theocentric philosophy of music, that centers on three basic tenets.[2] First, music was a divine gift to humanity, next only to the Word of God or theology. Second, Luther embraced the concept of music's affective and formative power, based ultimately on a Christian interpretation of the Greek ethical teachings of Plato and Aristotle. In 1538 Luther proclaimed "The Holy Ghost himself honors her [music] as an instrument for his proper work ... through her his gifts were instilled in the prophets, namely, the inclination to all virtues. ... On the other hand, she serves to cast out Satan the instigator of all sins."[3] Finally, Luther argued for music's use as a pedagogical and edifying tool, once again following ancient Greek thought, formulated in Plato's *Republic* and Aristotle's *Politics*. Luther granted music an esteemed intellectual and artistic position within the Protestant Latin school curriculum. In the preface to the 1524 Wittenberg hymnal, Luther argues that "the young ... must receive an education in music as well

---

1   The German term *Konfessionalisierung* ["confessionalization"] describes the rise and consolidation of the three main churches, and the formation of confessional identity among the common people. For a useful summary, see Heinz Schilling, "Confessionalization in the Empire: Religious and Societal Change in Germany Between 1555 and 1620," in *Religion, Political Culture and the Emergence of Early Modern Society: Essays in German and Dutch History*, Studies in Medieval and Reformation Thought, 50, ed. Heiko A. Oberman (Leiden: E.J. Brill, 1992), pp. 205–45.

2   The following is based on Dietrich Bartel, *Musica poetica: Musical-Rhetorical Figures in German Baroque Music* (Lincoln: University of Nebraska Press, 1997), pp. 3–9.

3   Martin Luther, "Preface to Georg Rhau's *Symphoniae iucundae* (1538)," trans. Ulrich S. Leupold, in Ulrich S. Leupold (ed.), *Liturgy and Hymns, Luther's Works*, general ed. Helmut T. Lehmann, series ed. Jaroslav Pelikan (Philadelphia: Fortress Press, 1965), vol. 53, p. 323.

as in the other arts if we are to wean them away from carnal and lascivious songs and interest them in what is good and wholesome."[4]

The role of music in the spread of Lutheran ideas in the first half of the sixteenth century is undisputed. In her study of vernacular songs and the Reformation, Rebecca Wagner Oettinger argues that polemical songs, including translations of psalms and musical sermons (many by Luther himself), had a more profound impact on the common people than either his writings or sermons from the pulpit.[5] But music's role in the later phase of Lutheran confessionalization is less clear. As Alexander Fisher observes in his study of the bi-confessional city of Augsburg, "music's contribution to confessionalization ... was hardly straightforward or unambiguous."[6] Part of the ambiguity arose from the pan-European reception of Italian secular song, which formed the basis of Latin motets and spiritual songs for both Catholic and Protestant practices. Further, there was a free mix, at least before the Thirty Years War, of Catholic and Protestant musical personnel employed by cities, courts, and private patrons throughout German-speaking lands.

The work of music editors can shed light on the intersections of Lutheran musical thought and performance during the decades around 1600. This chapter argues that, while the sound of their volumes borrowed heavily from contemporary Italian practices, the editorial selection of images, lyrics, and packaging remained deeply indebted to Luther's theology of music. The Lutheran poet and dramatist Martin Rinckart (1586–1649) replaced the secular texts of the madrigal anthology *Il trionfo di Dori* (Venice, 1592) with sacred ones that champion the power of music, a central theme of Lutheran theology. Rinckart's anthology *Triumphi de Dorothea* (Leipzig, 1619) showcases an early attempt to Germanize madrigalian verse, a goal that continued to inspire poets throughout the seventeenth century. While Rinckart's *Triumphi de Dorothea* looked forward, editor and poet Petrus Neander (1575–1645) brought the Italian canzonetta into direct contact with the tradition of psalm singing, which played an important role in Luther's liturgical and educational reforms and their reception in the first century of the Reformation. Neander superimposed his own paraphrases of psalm texts from the Lutheran Bible onto 36 of Orazio Vecchi's widely popular canzonetta melodies, which he issued in two volumes (1614, 1620). In keeping with their psalm origins, the collections served the needs of Protestant churches, schools, and homes. By focusing on contrafacta, the chapter draws attention to a subject that has suffered from an overriding tendency among scholars to privilege original texts over their later reworkings.[7]

---

4   Walter E. Buszin, "Luther on Music," *The Musical Quarterly*, 32 (1946): 88.

5   Rebecca Wagner Oettinger, *Music as Propaganda in the German Reformation* (Aldershot: Ashgate, 2001), p. 36.

6   Alexander J. Fisher, *Music and Religious Identity in Counter-Reformation Augsburg, 1580–1630* (Aldershot: Ashgate, 2004), p. 17. This ambiguity is demonstrated by the numerous books of music by Catholic composers alongside the significant amount of secular music owned by, and likely performed at, the Protestant church and school of St Anna in Augsburg. See my Chapter 5.

7   For the most part contrafacta have been either ignored or downplayed in the literature. Contrafacta occupy a mere seven pages of Friedrich Blume's monumental study, *Protestant Church Music: A History* (New York: W.W. Norton, 1974), pp. 29–35 of a total 831 pages.

Petrus Neander's Psalm Canzonettas

Neander's *Außerlesene vierstimmige Canzonetten Horatii Vecchi* unites popular melodies with the Lutheran tradition of psalm singing, a tradition that offers insight into how, and in what contexts, the collections may have been used. Psalm texts provided multi-functional material for religious devotion, education, and spiritual pleasure across German-speaking lands. With their simple note-against-note homophony, the Genevan psalm settings of Loys Bourgeois and Claude Goudimel were transplanted to Lutheran Germany by Lucas Osiander, court preacher in Stuttgart, and one of the theological architects of the *Formula Concordiae* (1577), an anthology of documents that defined the Lutheran faith.[8] In his *Psalmen mit vier Stimmen ... für die Schulen und Kirchen* (1586), Osiander positioned the chorale melody in the upper voice part, rather than the tenor (the practice of earlier Lutheran settings). A steady stream of cantional settings followed, by Melchior Frank, Bartholomäus Gesius, Johannes Jeep, Hans Leo Hassler, and Michael Praetorius. Gabriel Husduf's preface to *Melodeyen Gesangbuch* (Hamburg, 1604) makes it clear that the repertory suited a variety of performance contexts. In churches, it formed the basis for both choral and congregational singing:

> For if such Christian songs ring out either from the youth in the choir, or from artful organ playing, or [when] both make a chorus, and the boys sing with the organ, and the organ conversely plays with the hymn (as is now usual in this city ...), hence each Christian may also raise his poor layman's voice [*Leyenstimme*] just confident and loud enough, and thereby [is] not the fifth wheel but rather the justifiable fourth wheel of the music wagon of praise and honor to God's name, pulling along powerfully, and helping to drive up to the most high.[9]

Husduf's metaphor of the music wagon [*Musicwagon*] affirms Luther's promotion of congregational singing. The *Melodeyen Gesangbuch* was equally appropriate for the home: "So when a father with one or two schoolboys, his dear little sons, can hold two or three voices, also the dear housemother and household, yes the murmuring babes, awaiting the descant part so that they can join in."[10] It might even

---

Oettinger's *Music as Propaganda in the German Reformation* has gone a long way to remedy the situation for the first half of the sixteenth century.

8   The *Formula Concordiae* (1577) contained the three historic creeds, Luther's two Catechisms, the Augsburg Confession (1530), and the *Formula Concordiae* itself.

9   "Denn wann solche Christliche Gesenge/ entweder die liebe Jugendt auffm Chor her quinckliret/ oder auch der Organist auff der Orgel künstlich spielet/ oder sie beyde ein Chor machen/ vnd die Knaben in die Orgeln singen/ vnd die Orgel hinwiederumb in den Gesang spielet (als nunmehr in dieser Stadt gebreuchlich/ ...) alsdann mag auch ein jeder Christ/ seine schlechte Leyenstimme nur getrost vnd laut gnug erheben/ vnd also nunmehr nicht als das fünffte/ sondern als das vierdte vnd gar fügliche Radt den Musicwagen des lobes vnd preises Göttliches Namens gewaltiglich mit fortziehen/ vnd biß an den Allerhöbesten treiben vnd bringen helffen" (Gabriel Husduf, *Melodeyen Gesangbuch* [Hamburg: Rüdingen, 1604], exemplar Herzog August Bibliothek Wolfenbüttel: Tl 201, fols 3r–v).

10   "Dann so etwan ein Vater mit einem oder zween Schülerlein seinen lieben Söhnlein/ zwo oder drey Stimmen halten kan/ kan auch die liebe Haußmutter/ vnd das Gesind/ ja die

be useful for "travelers, to give occasion for wholesome reflection" and schoolboys who "with fun can be instructed without their noticing."[11]

Neander advertised his two volumes of psalm-canzonettas with these audiences in mind. On the title page of Book 1, he recommended them "zum bessern vnd nützlichern Brauch in Kirchen an statt deß *Benedicamus*, auch sonderlicher Vbung der Jugendt in Schulen" [for the improvement and more serviceable use in churches in place of the Benedicamus, also more particularly, for practice by the school boys].[12] As substitutes for the Benedicamus, the psalm canzonettas marked the end of vespers, a musically rich service that Neander led at the *Stadtkirche* in Gera, where he served as *Figuralcantor* at the church and at the affiliated Gymnasium Rutheneum from 1608 until his death in 1645.[13] Vespers assumed an important part of Luther's liturgical reforms, replacing the celebration of daily Mass as the principle form of public worship and devotion.[14] They were held daily at five or six in the evening, and included the New Testament Lesson (1–2 chapters read consecutively from day to day), Sermon (on the lesson), Collect, Psalmody, and Benedicamus. The structure and timing of vespers formed a counterpart to the daily matins services, held at four or five in the morning, and featuring readings from the Old Testament. From his examination of church ordinances, Robin Leaver observed the practice on feast days of continuing musical praise after the Benedicamus, with the singing of the *Nunc dimittis*, the *Gloria patri*, the compline hymn *Jesu redemptor seculi*, ending with the appropriate hymns of the day or season.[15] Neander's psalm-canzonettas provided suitable musical material for this distinctly Lutheran spiritual experience.[16]

---

lallenden Kinderlein/ mit abwartung des Discants auch das ihre mit dazu thun" (ibid., fol. 3v).

11   "reisenden Manne zu allerhandt guter andacht vrsach geben" (ibid., fol. 3v) and "mit lust vnd vnuermerckt können beygebracht werden" (ibid., fol. 4r).

12   *Vier vnd Zwantzig Ausserlesener vierstimmige Canzonetten Horatii Vecchi* (Gera: Martin Spiessen Erben, 1614; RISM A/I, V1038), exemplar Staatsbibliothek zu Berlin – Preußischer Kulturbesitz, Musikabteilung mit Mendelssohn-Archiv: Mus. Ant. Pract. V288, fol. 1r. For a transcription of the complete title page, see Appendix A, pp. 199-200.

13   The title *Figuralcantor* indicates that Neander directed polyphonic music, rather than unison singing, which fell under the auspices of the *Musica choralis* (Hans Rudolf Jung, "Ein unbekanntes Gutachten von Heinrich Schütz über die Neuordnung der Hof-, Schul- und Stadtmusik in Gera," *Beiträge zur Musikwissenschaft*, 1 [1962]: 24). 1645 is given as Neander's year of death in Johann Walther's *Musicalisches Lexicon* (Leipzig, 1732; reprint Kassel: Bärenreiter, 1953, p. 438); cf. Hans Rudolf Jung, "Zwei unbekannte Briefe von Heinrich Schütz aus den Jahren 1653/54," *Beiträge zur Musikwissenschaft*, 14 Jahrgang, Heft 3 (1972), 231 n. 6.

14   The following is based on Robin A. Leaver, "Lutheran Vespers as a Context for Music," in Paul Walker (ed.), *Church, Stage, and Studio: Music and Its Contexts in Seventeenth-Century Germany*, Studies in Music, 107, series ed. George J. Buelow (Ann Arbor: UMI Research Press, 1990), pp. 143–61.

15   Ibid., p. 151 n. 38 citing a Lübeck church ordinance of 1531.

16   According to Luther's *Deudsche Messe und Ordnung Gottesdiensts* (late 1525 or early 1526), which formed the basis for many ordinances over the next century, psalms would be suitable as an introductory song before the Kyrie, for the Gradual, after the Gospel reading

Neander intended the psalm-canzonettas to be use both for performance and for teaching. In keeping with Luther's reform of the Latin school curriculum, the repertory that formed the basis of the teaching was also sung in the church to which the school was attached. According to Rector Adam Reinhard's *Stundenplan* [timetable] of 1609, Neander taught students of the third and fourth classes five hours of *Exercitium Musices* per week.[17] The title page to Neander's first volume of psalm-canzonettas recommends their use for schoolboys "...with beautiful spiritual quotations taken mostly from the songs of David, arranged according to the nature and style of the underlaid Italian rhymes" ["mit schönen geistlichen Sprüchen meistentheils auss den Psalmen Davids genommen gezietet nach Art und Weise der Welschen Reime unter gelegt"]. The psalm-canzonettas made ideal models for teaching part-writing and techniques of text-setting; it is easy to imagine students adding their own psalm paraphrases or other texts for practice. Further, Vecchi's melodies may have helped students learn the text and meaning of the psalms. The *Stundenplan* devotes one hour every Friday morning to the Psalms of David—many of which are paraphrased by Neander.[18]

This dual pedagogical and liturgical purpose is reinforced by Neander's dedication of the *Ander Theil Ausserlesener Canzonetten* (Gera: Johann Spiess, 1620) to his students in Gera (transcribed in Appendix A, pp. 207–8). Here Neander followed the German practice of honoring students as dedicatees of sacred music books. Georg Körber addressed his edition of Balthasar Musculus's *Viertzig schöne geistliche Gesenglein mit vier Stimmen* (Nuremberg, 1597) to his students at Nuremberg's Laurentian school, who had already sung the pieces at their music lessons with him. Adam Gumpelzhaimer dedicated his *Neüe Teütsche Geistliche Lieder, mit dreien Stimmen, nach Art der Welschen Villanellen* (Augsburg, 1591), which included many German translations of psalms or biblical passages, to the four *Schulherren* appointed by the Augsburg city council to oversee the schools.[19] Among Neander's dedicatees was his most famous pupil, Heinrich Albert, a cousin of the Dresden chapelmaster Heinrich Schütz. Albert entered the Gymnasium Rutheneum in 1619, two years after Schütz visited Gera to evaluate the court, school, and town music.[20] In his report of 9 December 1617 Schütz praised Neander, the *Directores Musices* of the city's "sehr vornehme Music" [very distinguished music].[21] Schütz's close contact with Neander during this visit may have facilitated Heinrich Albert's future studies with the Gera Cantor.

The dedication of Neander's first volume sheds light on an additional performance context: the court at Gera. Neander addressed the inaugural *Vier und Zwantzig Ausserlesene vierstimmige Canzonetten* (Gera: Martin Spiessen Erben, 1614) to his

---

and during the Communion, which opens up the possibility that Neander's psalm-canzonettas served liturgical functions beyond Benedicamus substitutes.

17   Jung, "Ein unbekanntes Gutachten von Heinrich Schütz," p. 25.

18   Ibid., p. 25.

19   Fisher, *Music and Religious Identity*, p. 75.

20   Albert remained a student at the Gymnasium until 1622 (Jung, "Ein unbekanntes Gutachten von Heinrich Schütz, p. 27).

21   Schütz's report is found at the Landesarchiv Greiz, n. Rep. Gera/K, Kap. LIX, 1 Nr. 1 and is transcribed in its entirety in Hans Rudolf Jung, "Ein neuaufgefundenes Gutachten von Heinrich Schütz aus dem Jahre 1617," *Archiv für Musikwissenschaft*, 18/3–4 (1961): 241–7.

patrons, the Younger Line of the Reuss family, who assumed official residence at Gera in 1564. The date of the volume's printing coincides with Neander's first year of service as *Schloßcantor*. Neander's letter of appointment of 17 January 1614 was written by Heinrich Posthumus von Reuss himself. It required him to:

> instruct the dear youth in the city, and appropriately observe the points and provisions in the appointment thereby established for him. [He will] provide figural music [polyphonic music] not only for the city church but also [for] the choir in our castle church, especially when we have our court removed to Gera; and, otherwise, to attend whenever we have him summoned ... [22]

The timing of Neander's new appointment suggests he used the publication of the *Canzonetten Horatii Vecchi* both to honor his new patron and to provide suitable music for spiritual recreation at court.

The performance contexts for the *Canzonetten Horatii Vecchi* provide a backdrop for examining the contents of the collections (listed in Appendix B, pp. 237–8, 241–2). Vecchi's canzonettas offered Neander ready-made melodies that had already achieved much fame. There was intense interest in the composer and the genre in German-speaking lands, following Vecchi's inclusion in Friedrich Lindner's *Gemma musicalis* anthologies (see ch. 2), and Gerlach and Kauffmann's subsequent volumes devoted to his secular music. Their strophic form, simple internal rhyme scheme, and straightforward melodic lines and harmonies facilitated the reception of Vecchi's canzonettas across northern Europe. Neander's 36 psalm-canzonettas contributed to a total of 150 contrafacta from Vecchi's four books of canzonettas, and from the *Selve di varia ricreatione*, published between 1597 and 1627.[23] The familiarity of Vecchi's melodies made them a powerful vehicle for the circulation of psalm texts.

As a textual model, the Book of Psalms offered an exemplary message for Lutheran audiences. Psalm texts helped justify music's central place in Lutheran

---

22   "die liebe Jugent in der Stadt mit allem gebührenden Vleiß informiren, und sich seiner deswegen mit ihm aufgerichteten Bestallung in allen Puncten und Clauseln gemäß bezeigen. So wohl neben der Stadtkirchen auch den Chor in unßrer Schloßkirchen, vornemblich, wann wier unßer Hoflager zue Gera haben werden, mit der Figural Musica versorgen, und sonsten so oft wier ihn erfordern laßen ..." Landesarchiv Greiz, Consistorium Gera. Fach 49, nr. 1 (quoted in Jung, "Ein unbekanntes Gutachten von Heinrich Schütz," p. 28).

23   There are eight canzonettas by Vecchi with German texts in Georg Körber's edition of Balthasar Musculus's *Viertzig schöne geistliche Gesenglein mit vier Stimmen* (RISM B/I, 1597[7]; reprinted in *Sacra Cithara*, RISM B/I, 1625[6]), nine with German sacred texts in Erasmus Widmann's edition of the same collection (RISM B/I, 1622[15]), three with English texts in Thomas Morley (ed.), *Canzonets, or Little Short Songs for Foure Voyces* (RISM B/I, 1597[23]), three with Italian *lauda* texts in *Nuove laudi ariose della Beatissima Vergine* (RISM B/I, 1600[5]), the complete set of 90 in three books with German texts by Valentin Haussmann (1610), 36 in two books with German Psalm texts by Petrus Neander (1614, 1620), and one with a German Psalm text in Ambrosius Profe's *Extract ... auss dem musicalischen Interim Am[b]rosii Profii* (RISM B/I, 1627[8]) (Orazio Vecchi, *Orazio Vecchi: The Four-Voice Canzonettas. With Original Texts and Contrafacta by Valentin Haussmann and Others*, ed. Ruth I. DeFord, Recent Researches in the Music of the Renaissance, 92–3 [Madison, WI: A-R Editions, Inc. 1993], part 1 [vol. 92], p. 6).

worship. In the preface to his psalm commentaries, Luther praised the Book of Psalms for it contains "such clear prophecies concerning the death and resurrection of Christ, and holds forth such great and gracious promises concerning the kingdom of Christ, the spread of the Gospel, and the state of the whole church."[24] Both Testaments offer evidence of the use of psalm singing in worship and praise. Such passages were quoted often in book prefaces as justification for the glorification of God through music. In the preface to the 1524 *Geistliches Gesangbüchlein* (known as the Wittenberg Hymnal), Luther wrote:

> That it is good and God pleasing to sing hymns is, I think, known to every Christian; for everyone is aware not only of the example of the prophets and kings in the Old Testament who praised God with song and sound, with poetry and psaltery, but also of the common and ancient custom of the Christian church to sing Psalms. St. Paul himself instituted this in I Corinthians 14 [:15] and exhorted the Colossians [3:16] to sing spiritual songs and Psalms heartily unto the Lord so that God's Word and Christian teaching might be instilled and implanted in many ways.[25]

Luther's biblical citations reappear in Johann Walter's lengthy didactic poem *Lob und preis der löblichen Kunst Musica* (Wittenberg: Georg Rhau, 1538): [26]

Die Music braucht Gott stetz also	Thus God always needs music
Beim heilgen Euangelio/	for the Holy Gospel.
Solchs zeuget der Aposteln schriefft	The Apostles' texts testify to this;
Den rechten brauch der Kunst sie trifft/	they address the correct use of the art.
Sanct Pauel spricht/ die Christen sollen	Saint Paul says Christians should,
Wann sie sich selbst vermanen wöln/	when they wish to admonish themselves,
Psalm vnd geistlich lieder singen	sing Psalms and spiritual songs.
Solchs auch sol von hertzen dringen/	These should also come from the heart.

The Book of Psalms promoted the use of music in worship, and hence it remained a recurring source for Lutheran texts.

Neander adopted a self-conscious approach to working with his models. He used German rather than Venetian editions for his musical texts. For his first book

---

24 Martin Luther, *A Manual of the Book of Psalms: or, The Subject-Contents of all the Psalms*, trans. Rev. Henry Cole (London: Bohn, 1847), p. 5. The tradition of Lutheran psalm commentaries dates back to Luther's first series of lectures on the Psalms (*Dictata super Psalterium*), delivered between August 1513 and October 1515.

25 Luther, "Preface to the Wittenberg Hymnal," trans. Paul Zeller Strodach, rev. Ulrich S. Leupold, in *Luther's Works*, vol. 53, pp. 315–16.

26 Exemplar Herzog August Bibliothek Wolfenbüttel: Yn 4° Helmst. Kapsel 1 (1), fol. 9r.

Figure 4.1   *Ach mein Herr ins Himmels Thron,* from Petrus Neander, *Ander Theil Außerlesener Canzonetten Horatii Vecchi* (Gera, 1620), fol. 6v, Staatsbibliothek zu Berlin – Preußischer Kulturbesitz, Musikabteilung mit Mendelssohn-Archiv: Mus. ant. pract. V293

of 1614, Neander drew on Haussmann's three volumes of German-texted secular adaptations of Vecchi's canzonettas (Nuremberg, 1610); Paul Kauffmann's edition of Vecchi's *Canzonette a quattro voci ... raccolte insieme* (Nuremberg, 1600–01) served as the source for Neander's second book of 1620. Neander announced his source in the headline to each setting. He marked each setting in the second volume with the number of the corresponding piece from Kauffmann's edition of Vecchi's canzonettas, and labeled each piece with the corresponding psalm number(s) from the *Luther Bible* (1545) (Figure 4.1).

By identifying his sources, Neander invited comparison between the model and its reworking, thereby highlighting his work as editor and translator. The procedure was followed by Ambrosius Profe, whose *Extract oder erster Theil ... Madrigalien und anmutige Cantiones* (Wittenberg, 1627) included contrafacta of Italian secular songs that indicate the specific chapter from the Book of Psalms used by Profe as the source text.[27] Further, rather than underlaying only the first stanza (a normal practice for strophic forms), Neander set all stanzas of the psalm-canzonettas beneath the music. This made the books easier to use. Singers did not need to recall the melody as they cycled through the verses and students could more readily compare the text and its musical setting.

The process of fitting Vecchi's melodies to the German language required a high degree of textual and musical sophistication. Neander paraphrased the psalm texts with the form, shape, rhyme, and syllable count of his model in mind. At the most basic level, he added rhyme and meter to the prose psalm texts. There was a long tradition of applying meter and rhyme to the psalms to facilitate memorization and congregational singing. The practice dates back to the early years of the Reformed church of the 1530s and 1540s, with the publication of the complete rhyming Psalter (with tunes) by Jakob Dachser (Strasbourg, 1538) and Hans Gambersfelder (Nuremberg, 1542). The most important model for the second half of the century was Clément Marot's rhyming Psalter of 1562, which became the basis for the Calvinist Psalter. Ambrosius Lobwasser translated the Marot Psalter into German in 1573.

As poets, both Vecchi and Neander positioned rhymes mostly in pairs of adjacent lines (AABB). For stanzas of an odd number of lines, however, Neander often departed from Vecchi's rhyme structure (Example 4.1).

Example 4.1 Comparison of Rhyme Structure between Petrus Neander's *Ach mein Herr ins Himmels Thron* (first stanza) and Orazio Vecchi's *Non si sa chi tu sei* (first stanza). The text is published in *Orazio Vecchi: The Four-Voice Canzonettas. With Original Texts and Contrafacta by Valentin Haussmann and Others*, edited by Ruth I. DeFord. 2 vols. (R92 and R93) Recent Researches in the Music of the Renaissance, vol. 92. Madison, WI: A-R Editions, Inc. 1993. Used with permission.

Petrus Neander, *Ach mein Herr ins Himmels Thron*, Book 2, no. 9

Orazio Vecchi, *Non si sa chi tu sei*
RISM A/I, V1030, no. 87

Ach mein HERR ins Himmels Thron,
Zu dir heb ich mein Augen auff Hülff zu thun.
Gleich wie ein Knecht,
Der wil thun recht,
Auff den Herrn sein
Muß sehen allein,
Also sehn auch die Augen auff den Herrn mein.

Non si sa chi tu sei,
C'hora vuoi far la schifa ai desir miei?
Tu mi gridi, tu mi scacci,
Tu mi spregi à piu non posso;
Guarda chi mi vuol far del fiero adosso.

---

27   RISM B/I, 1627[8].

[Oh my Lord in heaven's throne, to you I lift my eyes for help. As a servant who wants to do right must look at his master alone, so my eyes look at my Lord.]

[Who do you think you are to despise my desires like this? You shout at me, you chase me away, you disdain me until I can't stand it. Look who's swaggering behind my back.]

Neander converted Vecchi's five-line rhyme scheme of AABCC into a seven-line pattern of AABBCCC. Like his fellow editor-translators, Neander expanded the textual scope of his model to accommodate the verbosity of the German language.

Vecchi's texts are normally in lines of 7 and 11 syllables, a reflection of the influence of Italian madrigal poetry on the canzonetta. There is a greater variety of line lengths in Neander's texts. In many cases Neander splits up 11-syllable lines into two shorter ones to accommodate the syntax of the German language. In the opening of *Lobt Gott im Heyligthume* (Example 4.2), Neander divides Vecchi's single 11-syllable line into two shorter ones of seven and four syllables.

Example 4.2 Comparison of Petrus Neander's *Lobt Gott im Heyligthume* (excerpt) and Orazio Vecchi's *Amor con ogni impero* (excerpt). The texts are published in *Orazio Vecchi: The Four-Voice Canzonettas With Original Texts and Contrafacta by Valentin Haussmann and Others*, edited by Ruth I. DeFord. 2 vols. (R92 and R93) Recent Researches in Music of the Renaissance, vol. 92. Madison, WI: A-R Editions, Inc. 1993. Used with permission.

Petrus Neander, *Lobt Gott im Heyligthume*
Book 2, no. 12

Orazio Vecchi, *Amor con ogni impero*
RISM A/I, V1030, no. 35

Lobt Gott im Heyligthume;
Gebt ihm Ruhme.

Amor con ogni impero e gran possanza

[Praise God in His holiness; give Him honor.]

[Love, with all authority and great power]

The closing lines of *Mein Seel soll dich, O Gott* offer another example of a bifurcated 11-syllable line, this time divided into 5 + 6 (Example 4.3).

Example 4.3 Comparison of Petrus Neander's *Mein Seel soll dich, O Gott* (first stanza) and Orazio Vecchi's *Hor che'l garrir* (first stanza). The texts are published in *Orazio Vecchi: The Four-Voice Canzonettas. With Original Texts and Contrafacta by Valentin Haussmann and Others*, edited by Ruth I. DeFord. 2 vols. (R92 and R93) Recent Researches in the Music of the Renaissance, vol. 92. Madison, WI: A-R Editions, Inc. 1993. Used with permission.

Petrus Neander, *Mein Seel soll dich, O Gott*	Orazio Vecchi, *Hor che'l garrir*
Book 2, no. 6	RISM A/I, V1030, no. 44

Mein Seel soll dich O GOtt im Himmel loben,	Hor ch'el garrir de gl'Augelletti s'ode,
Der du schön gschmäckt vnd prächtig bist	Et che vestono i prati,
erhoben.	
Wie groß sind deine Wercke,	Novi fioretti e grati,
Und zubereit mit Stärcke,	Amor anch'egli si risent'e gode.
Groß an der Zahle, [5 syllables]	[11 syllables]
Weißlich allzumahle. [6 syllables]	

[May my soul praise you, oh God, in heaven;	[Now that the birds are singing and
you are glorious and adorned with majesty.	the meadows are putting on new flowers,
How great and mighty are your works,	Love, too, is reawakening and rejoicing.]
innumerable and wise.]	

Turning to the musical setting of this passage, it becomes clear that Neander in fact adopts the 5 + 6 division from Vecchi, who isolates the six-syllable segment "si risent'e gode" for a fourfold repetition.

For the first volume, Neander used Haussmann's adaptations of Vecchi's canzonettas as his source. Working with a German-texted model meant that many of the challenges of shifting from an Italian form to a German one had already been resolved by Haussmann. Accordingly, Neander retained the syllable- and line-count of all but two of Haussmann's texts (Example 4.4). In many cases, he used the same rhyme scheme at the end.

Example 4.4 Comparison of Petrus Neander's *Herr, unser Herrscher* (first stanza) and Valentin Haussmann's *Als ich mich hatt* (first stanza). The texts are published in *Orazio Vecchi: The Four-Voice Canzonettas. With Original Texts and Contrafacta by Valentin Haussmann and Others*, edited by Ruth I. DeFord. 2 vols. (R92 and R93) Recent Researches in the Music of the Renaissance, vol. 92. Madison, WI: A-R Editions, Inc. 1993. Used with permission.

Petrus Neander, *Herr, unser Herrscher*
Book 1, no. 2

Herr, unser Herrscher, herrlich ist verhanden
Dein Nam in allen Landen,
Da man dir dancket droben
Im Himmel hoch mit loben.

[Oh Lord, our Lord, your name is glorious in all lands, for you are thanked with praise in heaven above.]

Valentin Haussmann, *Als ich mich hatt*
Book 3, no. 4

Als ich mich hatt an deiner schön versehen,
Da wars vmb mich geschehen.
Mein hertz fieng an zu brinnen;
Wust nicht was ich solt b'ginnen.

[When I saw your beauty, I was done for. My heart began to burn, and I didn't know what to do.]

In *Lobt Gott den Herrn mit schallen*, Neander departs from Haussmann's syllable count for the final line, adopting 11 syllables instead of Haussmann's nine (Example 4.5).

Example 4.5 Comparison of Petrus Neander's *Lobt Gott den Herrn mit schallen* (first stanza) and Valentin Haussmann's *Jungfrau, ich muß euch klagen* (first stanza). The texts are published in *Orazio Vecchi: The Four-Voice Canzonettas. With Original Texts and Contrafacta by Valentin Haussmann and Others*, edited by Ruth I. DeFord. 2 vols. (R92 and R93) Recent Researches in the Music of the Renaissance, vol. 92. Madison, WI: A-R Editions, Inc. 1993. Used with permission.

Petrus Neander, *Lobt Gott den Herrn mit schallen,* Book 1, no. 7

Lobt Gott den Herrn mit schallen;
Das ist ein köstlich Ding, und thut gefallen
Dem allerhöchsten Herren.
Drumb lobet ihn und singet ihm zu Ehren.

[Praise the Lord God with glad sounds; that is a good thing and pleases the highest Lord. Therefore praise Him and sing to honor Him.]

Valentin Haussmann, *Jungfrau, ich muß euch klagen*, Book I, no. 2

Jungfrau, ich muß euch klagen,
Was mich für grosse lieb zu euch thut tragen.
Darnach ich jetzt thu streben;
Muß eurer gnad alleine leben.

[Young lady, I must complain to you of the great love that draws me to you; I live for your mercy alone.]

Neander's solution recalls Vecchi's original, with its final 11-syllable refrain, "Dura mill'anni il giorno amaro mene" [a day lasts a thousand years, alas poor me], from *Mentre io campai contento*, the ultimate source for both Neander and Haussmann. Neander's second and last deviation from Haussmann's syllable count appears in *Meinm lieben Gott und Herrn*, where he replaces the 11-syllable opening line with two shorter ones (6 + 5), and compensates with an extra 11-syllable line of text at the end (Example 4.6).

Example 4.6 Comparison of Petrus Neander's *Meinm lieben Gott und Herrn* (first stanza) and Valentin Haussmann's *Ein wunder schönes Bild* (first stanza). The texts are published in *Orazio Vecchi: The Four-Voice Canzonettas. With Original Texts and Contrafacta by Valentin Haussmann and Others*, edited by Ruth I. DeFord. 2 vols. (R92 and R93) Recent Researches in the Music of the Renaissance, vol. 92. Madison, WI: A-R Editions, Inc. 1993. Used with permission.

Petrus Neander, *Meinm lieben Gott und Herrn*
Book I, no. 20

Valentin Haussmann, *Ein wunder schönes Bild*, Book III, no. 28

Meinm lieben Gott und Herrn
Wil ich dancken gern,
Weil ich lebendig bin auff dieser Erden;
Darnach so mus das himmelreich mir
werden.

Ein wunder schönes Bild hab ich gesehen;
Dafür hab ich kein ruh in meinem hertzen.
Tag und auch nacht bringt sie mir pein
und schmertzen.

[I thank my dear God and Lord gladly,
because I am alive on this earth, and
thereafter the kingdom of heaven shall be
mine.]

[I have seen a most beautiful image,
which has left me no peace in my heart.
It gives me pain and torment day and
night.]

Neander's solution closely follows the syntax of the psalm paraphrase, the opening address answered by a line of praise, while the final line promises eternal life.

Haussmann's Germanization of Vecchi offered a ready-made structural framework for Neander's psalm paraphrases. While Neander retained much of the structural contour of Haussmann's verses, for the most part, Neander's texts inhabit an entirely different world than the love imagery of Vecchi, or even the more chaste tone of Haussmann. Though listeners may have recalled the "original" words upon hearing Neander's psalm contrafacta, there are few cases of intertextuality between Neander's psalm paraphrases and either Vecchi's or Haussmann's secular texts. A more constructive comparison can be made between Neander's spiritual contrafacta and those of Georg Körber, Erasmus Widmann, and Ambrosius Profe. There are sacred contrafacta of eight of Vecchi's canzonettas in Körber's edition of Balthasar Musculus's *Viertzig schöne geistliche Gesenglein mit vier Stimmen* (Nuremberg, 1597), nine in Erasmus Widmann's edition of the same collection (Nuremberg, 1622), and one with a German Psalm text in Ambrosius Profe's *Extract ... auss dem musicalischen Interim Am[b]rosii Profii* (Wittenberg, 1627). Neander, Körber, and Widmann each wrote German sacred texts for Vecchi's *Mentre io campai contento*;

Neander's text is given above in Example 4.5, *Lobt Gott den Herrn mit schallen*, which paraphrases Psalm 92. Like Neander, both Körber and Widmann built on the musical qualities embedded in Vecchi's original (a theme that is not taken up in Haussmann's *Jungfrau, ich muß euch klagen*) (Examples 4.7–4.9).

Example 4.7 Orazio Vecchi, *Mentre io campai contento* (third stanza). The text is published in *Orazio Vecchi: The Four-Voice Canzonettas. With Original Texts and Contrafacta by Valentin Haussmann and Others*, edited by Ruth I. DeFord. 2 vols. (R92 and R93) Recent Researches in the Music of the Renaissance, vol. 92. Madison, WI: A-R Editions, Inc. 1993. Used with permission.

Mentre io campai cantando,	While I lived singing, the days went flying
Li giorni se n'andavano volando,	away, and now that I live in pain, a day lasts
Et mò ch'io vivo in pene,	a thousand years, alas poor me.
Dura mill'anni il giorno amaro mene.	

Example 4.8 Georg Körber (?), *Last uns jetzt frölich singen*. The text is published in *Orazio Vecchi: The Four-Voice Canzonettas. With Original Texts and Contrafacta by Valentin Haussmann and Others*, edited by Ruth I. DeFord. 2 vols. (R92 and R93) Recent Researches in the Music of the Renaissance, vol. 92. Madison, WI: A-R Editions, Inc. 1993. Used with permission.

Last vns jetzt frölich singen,	Let us sing and dance for joy; now that we
Und darzu sein auch guter ding in springen;	are together, let us all sing in God's name.
Weil wir nun sein beisamen,	
So last uns all singen inn Gottes Namen.	

Drumb kehret vleiß an alle,	Let us take care when we run fast that no
Wanns laufft gar gschwind, daß keiner nicht	one falls; otherwise people will laugh at
mög fallen;	us. Everyone look out for himself.
Sonst thut man unser lachen.	
Drumb hab acht ein jeder auff seine Sachen.	

Example 4.9 Erasmus Widmann, *Last uns jetzt frölich singen*. The text is published in *Orazio Vecchi: The Four-Voice Canzonettas. With Original Texts and Contrafacta by Valentin Haussmann and Others*, edited by Ruth I. DeFord. 2 vols. (R92 and R93) Recent Researches in the Music of the Renaissance, vol. 92. Madison, WI: A-R Editions, Inc. 1993. Used with permission.

Last uns jetzt frölich singen,	Let us now sing joyfully and have good
Und alle seyn von hertzen guter dingen.	thoughts in our hearts. Since we are
Weil wir nun seyn beysammen,	together now, let us all praise God's name.
So last uns alle preisen Gottes Namen.	

Lobt ihn und musiciret,	Praise Him and make music, and be
Und frewet euch; im Herren jubiliret.	joyful; rejoice in the Lord. Join together
Allerley Seitenspiele	the playing of all sorts of strings and
Stimmet zusamm und lobt Gott nach	and praise seinem Wille.God
	according to His will.

While Widmann made few changes to Körber's first stanza, he substituted a new text for the second stanza that departed entirely from the earlier edition. The central message of Widmann's piece is embedded in the Latin inscription that heads it: "Plaudite Christicolae: plectra movete manu" [Clap your hands, Christians; move the plectra with your hands]. Here Widmann strengthens the call for voices—and instruments—to join together.

The musicality of Vecchi's *Mentre io campai contento* reflects a central theme of Neander's psalm paraphrases and, in this respect, offers an important (though rare) moment of intertextuality between the original and the contrafactum. As an editor, Neander chose psalms that evoke the art of song itself, literally the "hymns of Israel." The two volumes include nine of the Psalms of David, who is described in the second book of Samuel (2 Samuel 23:1) as "the sweetest psalmist of Israel."[28] The use of King David as a symbol of music and praise recurs in prefaces to Lutheran music books. In his poem *Lob und Preis der löblichen Kunst Musica* (Wittenberg, 1538) Johann Walter singled out David for his psalm performance:[29]

Wenn Dauid itzund leben solt	If David were alive today,
Weil Gottes zusag ist erfüllt/	Because God's commandment was fulfilled,
Er würd die Music hocher ehrn	He would revere music more highly,
kein gelt nicht sparn die Kunst zumehrn/	Spare no expense to further this art,
Dauid solt ein exempel sein	David should be an example
Der Herrn vnd Fursten liecht vnd schein/	For the enlightenment of lords and princes.

Further, there was a long practice of setting the Psalms of David to music. One example is *Der gantz Psalter Dauids, wie derselbig in Teutsche Gesang verfasset* (Tübingen, 1569) by the Würtenberg court chapelmaster Sigmund Hemmeln. In the lengthy *Vorred an den Christlichen Leser*, the Hoffprediger Balthasar Bidenbach extols David's musical virtues:

Sonderlich aber hat Dauid vor andern Königen solche *Musicam* in bester form/ beide mit Singern vnd Instrumentisten/ auffs herzlichst bestellet: Ja selbst sehr vil vnd mancherley Psalmen/ auß eingeben des heiligen Geists darzù gemacht/ daß sie gehörter massen in der Gemein Gottes neben allerley Instrumenten solten gesungen werden. Wie es aber im newen Testament den Christen nicht verweißlich/ sondern löblich/ daß sie die Psalmen Dauids haben/ vnd zù ihrer lehr/ besserung vnd trost gebrauchen: Also ist auch dise liebliche

---

28 *The Holy Bible*, King James Version (New York: Harper, 1995), p. 331.

29 Johann Walter, *Lob und Preis der löblichen Kunst Musica* (Wittenberg: Georg Rhau, 1538), fol. 8r. Exemplar Herzog August Bibliothek Wolfenbüttel: Yn 4° Helmst. Kapsel 1 (1).

Kunst die Musica (wölche eigentlich zù den Psalmen gehörig) im newen Testament ein zierd vnd wol stand/ an denen orten/ vnd in denen Kirchen/ da das heilig Euangelion rein vnd lautter gepredigt würt.[30]

[But in particular David had, more than other kings, the very best of such music, both with singers and instrumentalists, cultivated with the greatest sincerity: yes, he himself fashioned a great many and various Psalms, through the gift of the Holy Spirit, that they might be sung as appropriate among God's people alongside various instruments. Just as in the New Testament it is not objectionable, but rather praiseworthy, for Christians that they have and use the songs of David for their education, improvement, and consolation. Thus also is this charming art of Music (which is integral to the Psalms) an ornament and pleasure in the New Testament, to those places, and in those churches, where the holy Gospel is preached purely and clearly.]

Neander's psalm contrafacta echo a long-standing Lutheran practice.

There are a further 14 psalm canzonettas that make specific reference to music-making.[31] In the opening *Lobet den Herren alle* (Book 1, no. 1), for instance, Neander adds the verb to sing ["Singt ihm"], which is absent from his source text, the Lutheran Bible. For the seventh piece, *Lobt Gott den Herrn mit schallen*, Neander paraphrases Psalm 92, a text infused with musical resonance. The opening two verses call for praise with "glad sounds" ["mit schallen"] and songs "to honor Him" ["singet ihm zu Ehren"]. *Singet dem Herren lieblich* (Book 1, no. 18) calls upon the performers to "sing sweetly to the Lord," a paraphrase of the opening verse of Psalm 147. The request is made again in *Mein Seel soll dich, O Gott* [May my soul praise you, oh God] (Book 2, no. 6) from the second volume, which paraphrases Psalm 104. Neander calls upon "the playing of psalteries" ["Drumb last uns für ihn gehn mit Psalterspiele"] in *Kompt herzu: im Herren fröhlich seyn* (Book 2, no. 4).

The finale of the two-volume series is a paraphrase of Psalm 150, the Doxology marking the end of the Psalter, and thus a fitting conclusion for Neander's series as well. Music-making in *Lobt Gott im Heyligthume* crescendos across the three strophes: the first calls for "glad sounds" ["mit Schalle"]; the second adds instruments, trumpets, and psalteries; and the finale is the musical climax with a full symphony of sound, with strings, cymbals, and pipes. Turning to Vecchi's own canzonetta, we find an example of intertextuality of musical demands between the two texts (Examples 4.10–4.11).

---

30 Sigmund Hemmeln, *Der gantz Psalter Dauids, wie derselbig in Teutsche Gesang verfasset* (Tübingen: Ulrich Morharts Wittib, 1569), fol. 3r. Exemplar: Herzog August Bibliothek Wolfenbüttel: 3.3.3 Musica.

31 Book 1, nos 1, 3, 7, 8, 16, 18, 21, and 22;Book 2, nos 3, 4, 5, 6, 7, and 12.

Example 4.10 Orazio Vecchi, *Amor con ogni impero* (first stanza). The text is published in *Orazio Vecchi: The Four-Voice Canzonettas. With Original Texts and Contrafacta by Valentin Haussmann and Others*, edited by Ruth I. DeFord. 2 vols. (R92 and R93) Recent Researches in the Music of the Renaissance, vol. 92. Madison, WI: A-R Editions, Inc. 1993. Used with permission.

Amor con ogni impero e gran possanza	Love, with all authority and great power,
S'è mosso con furor per assediarmi,	moved in fury to lay siege to me, to the
A suon di Trombe e di Tamburri e d'armi.	sound of trumpets and drums and arms.

Example 4.11 Petrus Neander, *Lobt Gott im Heyligthume*. The text is published in *Orazio Vecchi: The Four-Voice Canzonettas. With Original Texts and Contrafacta by Valentin Haussmann and Others*, edited by Ruth I. DeFord. 2 vols. (R92 and R93) Recent Researches in the Music of the Renaissance, vol. 92. Madison, WI: A-R Editions, Inc. 1993. Used with permission.

Lobt GOtt im Heyligthume;	Praise God in His holiness; give Him honor;
Gebt ihm Ruhme.	praise His great majesty and power. Praise
Preist seine grosse Pracht	Him with glad sounds in all His works.
In der feste seiner Macht.	
Lobt ihn mit schalle	
In seinen Thaten alle.	
Zu loben seydt stäts bereit	Be ready already to praise His glory; praise
Sein Herrligkeit;	Him with a glad heart. Blow the trumpets.
Lobt ihn mit fröhlichm mut.	Rejoice greatly, and praise Him with the
Blaset die Posaunen gut.	sound of the psaltery.
Der Frewden macht viel,	
Und lobet ihn mit Psaltrspiel.	
Lobet den HErren mit Gsang	Praise the Lord with song and the sound of
Und Seyten Klang,	strings, the sweet ringing of cymbals and the
Die Cymbeln lieblich klingn,	happy singing of pipes. Everything that has
Und die Pfeiffen frölich singn.	Breath, praise the Lord always.
Alles was Odm hat,	
Lobe den Herrn früh und spat.	

With its refrain calling for trumpets and drums, *Amor con ogni impero* foreshadows typical sonorous ingredients for Neander as well.

Neander's inclusion of four Psalms of Ascent suggests a more specific message for his Lutheran audiences. Known as the pilgrim songs, psalms 120–34 refer to the pilgrimage to Jerusalem. The narration of this story includes the joyful arrival at Jerusalem, the giving of prayers and thanksgiving, processions, a communion sacrifice, and "a farewell to the Levites at the Temple."[32] By including four of them, Neander distinguishes himself from contemporary psalm editors. Adam Gumpelzhaimer, the Cantor at the Lutheran church of St Anna in Augsburg, for instance, avoids these highly polemic psalm texts in his collection of *Neüe Teütsche Geistliche Lieder* of 1591.[33] Neander includes the first and last of the songs of ascent: Psalm 120, which praises Zion as the pilgrim's goal, and Psalm 134, the liturgy of blessing. Neander paraphrases the second verse of Psalm 120 as "The liars who strip me of my honor and slander me fearlessly with their false tongues."[34] By including an exile's prayer for deliverance from the injustice suffered at the hands of enemies, Neander makes a clear reference to the confessional strife of his time.

In choosing texts, Neander was drawn to traditional texts that emphasized music's role in worship and praise, and that spoke to the Lutheran community more specifically. For the first volume, Neander presented texts from across the Book of Psalms with no respect to their ordering. For the second, he followed the numerical order of the Book of Psalms, concluding the series with the final (150th) psalm. Neander created textual unity by framing the series with the text "Lobt den Herrn." The opening psalm canzonetta is *Lobet den Herren alle* (Psalm 117), echoed by "Lobet den Herren mit Gesang" in the last strophe of the closing psalm-canzonetta in volume two (Psalm 150). Within the first book, this line appears in the third and seventh settings, and is varied as "Lobsinget Gott dem Herren" [Sing praise to God the Lord] in no. 16. In *Mein Seel soll dich, O Gott* (Book 2, no. 6), the text is made more emphatic in the first person: "Ich will den HERREN loben" [I will praise the Lord]. It returns (back in the imperative form) in Book 2, no. 10, *Lobt den Herren, ihr knechte* [Praise the Lord, you servants]. Neander reinforced the central message of the volumes through repetition and strategic placement.

To summarize, Neander used Vecchi's canzonetta melodies to circulate texts central to the Lutheran doctrine of music for praise. Neander guided their use by penning dedications to Lutheran institutions in Gera—the court, church, and its adjoining Latin school.

While Neander turned to the lighter style of the canzonetta for his model, Martin Rinckart's inspiration was the loftier madrigal. In what follows, I examine Rinckart's *Triumphi de Dorothea* (Leipzig, 1619) as an example of Luther's influence on the reworking of one of the most famous madrigal anthologies of the period. Like Neander, Rinckart was fully immersed in Lutheran music and culture. At the age of 15, Rinckart entered the prestigious Thomasschule in Leipzig, where he sang under the direction of Sethus Calvisius.[35] In 1602, he matriculated at the University of Leipzig to study theology and philosophy; he received the Baccalaureate in 1609. In 1610, he accepted the post of Cantor at the Nikolaikirche in Eisleben, the town

---

32　James L. Mays (ed.), *Harper's Bible Commentary* (San Francisco: Harper & Row, 1988), pp. 487–8.

33　Fisher, *Music and Religious Identity*, p. 33.

34　The intervening song of ascent, Psalm 132, is a liturgy commemorating God's choice of Zion and of the Davidic dynasty.

35　Siegmal Keil (Walter Blankenburg), "Rinckart, Martin," *MGG*[2], Personenteil 14, cols. 173–4.

of Luther's birth and death. After promotions to deacon at the Annenkirche (1611) and preacher in nearby Erdeborn (1613), he accepted the post of archdeacon in his native Eilenburg in 1617, where he remained for the rest of his life. Today Rinckart is remembered primarily for his contributions to Lutheran drama.[36] He penned a total of seven Lutheran plays that commemorate key moments in Reformation history. *Indulgentiarius Confusus* marks the jubilee of Luther's nailing of the 95 theses (1617), and *Lutherus Augustus* of 1630 celebrates the 100-year anniversary of the Augsburg Confession. Rinckart enjoyed early recognition for his artistry. He was crowned Poet Laureate in 1615, and received a master's degree the following year. Scholarship has suffered from disciplinary boundaries that overlook the interaction of Rinckart's religious, musical, pedagogical, and literary roles.[37] These roles intersect in the anthology *Triumphi de Dorothea*, with its central themes of praise for music, and for its causes and effects.

Martin Rinckart, *Triumphi de Dorothea* (Leipzig, 1619)

Rinckart announced the themes of *Triumphi de Dorothea* in a rich tapestry of paratextual material. His Lutheran transformation of the *Trionfo di Dori* began with the title of the anthology. The name Dorothea was first associated with the *Trionfo* collection in the two-part *Musicalische Streitkräntzelein ... Triumphi di Dori oder de Dorothea* (Nuremberg, 1612–13) with texts by Johannes Lyttich, where it is offered as a German substitute for the Italian name Dori.[38] The second volume included a Latin epigram signed "Martinus Rinckhart Theologus Isleviensis" [Martin Rinckart, theologian of Eisleben], thus confirming Rinckart's involvement in the series.

The name Dorothea held special meaning in Lutheran circles. Bartholomaeus Gesius included a song of praise for Dorothea in *Ein ander new Opus Geistlicher*

---

36 For works, see Gerhard Dünnhaupt, *Bibliographisches Handbuch der Barockliteratur: Hundert Personalbibliographien Deutscher Autoren des Siebzehnten Jahrhunderts*, Hiersemanns bibliographische Handbücher, 2, 3 vols (Stuttgart: Anton Hiersemann, 1980-81), vol. 3, pp. 1539–54.

37 *Triumphi de Dorothea* often goes unmentioned in works lists and studies of his theology and Lutheran dramas. It is omitted in Karl Dienst, "Rinckart, Martin," *Biographisch-Bibliographisches Kirchenlexikon*, ed. Friedrich Wilhelm Bautz (Herzberg: Traugott Bautz, 1994), vol. 8, cols 367–9; and Richard Erich Schade, "Rinckart, Martin," *Literatur Lexikon. Autoren und Werke deutscher Sprache*, ed. Walther Killy (Gütersloh and Munich: Bertelsmann Lexikon Verlag, 1991), vol. 9, pp. 473–4.

38 *Musicalische Streitkräntzelein: hiebevorn von den allerfürtrefflichsten unnd berhümtesten Componisten, in welscher Sprach, pro certamine, mit sonderlichem Fleiss, und auffs künnstlichst, mit 6. Stimmen auffgesetzt, und dannenhero Triumphi di Dori oder de Dorothea genennet ... und in Druck verfertiget, durch Johannen Lyttichium, ...* (Nuremberg: A. Wagenmann, 1612; RISM B/I, 1612[13]); and *Rest musicalisches Streitkränzleins: hiebevorn von den allerfürtrefflichsten unnd berhümtesten Componisten, in welscher Sprach, pro certamine, mit sonderlichem Fleiss, und auffs künstlichsts, mit 6. Stimmen auffgesetzt, und dannenhero Triomphi di Dori oder de Dorothea genennet. ... in Druck gefördert, durch Salomonem Engelhart, ...* (Nuremberg: B. Scherff, 1613; RISM B/I, 1613[13]).

Deutscher Lieder I (Frankfurt an der Oder, 1605), that offers insight into the associations the name carried in Lutheran Germany (Example 4.12).[39]

Example 4.12 Bartholomaeus Gesius, *Ein Lied von S. Dorothea*[40]

Es war ein Gottfürchtiges/	There was a God-fearing
Vnd Christlichs Jungfräwlein/	And Christian maiden
Gotts Wort vnd Catechismus/	She had studied God's Word
hat sie gelernet fein/	and the catechism.
Ir Name Dorothea/	Her name, Dorothea,
Ist weit vnd breit bekandt/	is known far and wide
Nach ihrem Vatr vnd Mutter/	thus was she named
Wurd sie also genandt.	after her father and mother.
Auff Deutsch ein Gottes Gabe/	In German, a gift from God,
Die Dorothea heist/	is the meaning of Dorothea,
Die doch vom Himmel herabe/	which from Heaven above,
Beschert der heilig Geist.	the Holy Ghost bestows.
Offt bringt ein guter Name/	Often a good name
Ein gute art mit sich/	brings with it a good nature,
Wenns Kind von gutem Samen/	if a child is from a good seed
Gezeuget wird ehrlich.	honorably conceived.

The meaning of Dorothea, as "gift of God," lay at the heart of Rinckart's central message for the 1619 anthology. Rinckart made the link on the title page: *TRIUMPHI DE DOROTHEA ... Von der hochedlen, und recht Englischen Dorothea oder grossen Gottes Gabe; der Frau Musica* [Triumphs of Dorothea ... Of the most noble, and quite angelic Dorothea or the great gift of God; of Lady Music] (Figure 4.2).

Once again, we find a direct link to Luther, who affirmed music's causes and effects in the *Vorrhede auff alle gute Gesangbücher* that prefaced Johann Walter's *Lob und Preis der löblichen Kunst Musica* (Wittenberg, 1538). Building on the tradition of personifying the arts, sciences, and virtues, Luther summarized his attitude toward music in the form of a didactic poem (Example 4.13).[41]

---

39   Bartholomeus Gesius, *Ein ander new Opus, Geistlicher Deutscher Lieder, D. MART. LUTHERI, ... Das erste Theil* (Frankfurt an der Oder: Johann Hartmans, und bey seinem sohn Friederichen, 1605). Exemplar Herzog August Bibliothek Wolfenbüttel: Yv 758 8° Helmst.

40   Bartholomeus Gesius, *Ein ander new Opus, Geistlicher Deutscher Lieder, D. MART. LUTHERI, ... Das erste Theil* (Frankfurt an der Oder: Johann Hartmans, und bey seinem sohn Friederichen, 1605), no. CLII. Exemplar Herzog August Bibliothek Wolfenbüttel: Yv 758 8° Helmst. Thanks to Sharon Krebs for her assistance with the translation of this passage.

41   Luther, "A Preface to All Good Hymnals," trans. Paul Nettl, in *Luther's Works*, vol. 53, pp. 319–20.

Figure 4.2   SLUB Dresden / Abt. Deutsche Fotothek, Title page of Martin Rinckart, *Triumphi de Dorothea* (Leipzig, 1619), Mus. 1-C-2, nr. 527

Example 4.13 Martin Luther, "A Preface to All Good Hymnals (1538)"

Dame Music [speaks:]

Of all the joys upon the earth
None has for men a greater worth
Than what I give with my ringing
And with voices sweetly singing.
There cannot be an evil mood
Where there are singing fellows good,
There is no envy, hate, nor ire,
Gone are through me all sorrows dire;
Greed, care, and lonely heaviness
No more do they the heart oppress.
[...]
Through my bright power the devil shirks
His sinful, murderous, evil works.
[...]
The best time of the year is mine
When all the birds are singing fine.
Heaven and earth their voices fill
With right good song and tuneful trill.
[...]
But thanks be first to God, our Lord,
Who created her by his Word
To be his own beloved songstress
And of *musica* a mistress.
For our dear Lord she sings her song
In praise of him the whole day long;
To him I give my melody
And thanks in all eternity.

Luther's assessment of music's attributes offers a backdrop for Rinckart's own views, over 80 years later.

Rinckart's prefatory material demonstrates that the foundations of music in Lutheran thought remained surprisingly consistent for the first century after the Reformation. Rinckart included different front matter in each of the five surviving partbooks. On the verso of each title page, he excerpted passages from the writings of Luther, church fathers, and ancient Greek philosophers, all in an effort to lend authority to his anthology. The cantus partbook opens with a quotation from one of Luther's most influential statements on music, "Von der himmlischen Kunst Musica," that prefaces the motet collection *Symphoniae iucundae* (Wittenberg, 1538). The preface was translated into German by Johann Walter in 1538;[42] Wolfgang Figulus authored

---

42 The *Vorrede* was published independently, without the music (Wittenberg, 1538). Exemplar Herzog August Bibliothek Wolfenbütel: H Yn Helmst. 4° Kapsel 1 (1). It is

his own German translation in *Cantionum sacrarum* (Frankfurt an der Oder, 1575); Leonhard Lechner paraphrased it in the preface to *Newe Teutsche Lieder, mit Vier und Fünff Stimmen* (Nuremberg, 1577); and Michael Praetorius reprinted it in *Musae Sioniae ... geistliche Concert Gesänge* (Regensburg, 1605). Drawing on arguably the most important document of Lutheran musical culture, Rinckart selected the central message: "next to the Word of God, music deserves the highest praise" [*"Ego nulli Arti post S. S. Biblia, plus tribuo; quàm MUSICÆ"*].[43] The remaining four prefatory quotations in the cantus partbook emphasize music's affective qualities. A passage from Luther's letter of 1530 to composer Ludwig Senfl states: "There should be no seed of virtue in those who do not delight in musical art" [*"Nulla virtutis semina oportet inesse iis; qui Arte non delectantur Musicâ"*].[44] To close, Rinckart excerpted three passages from Luther's *Tischreden* [Table Talk] that praise music's ability to drive out the devil, to bring comfort to whoever knows the art, and to heal.[45]

Praise for music's affective powers dominated Rinckart's selection of passages for the remaining partbooks. In the sexta partbook, he drew on Luther's own authorities, the philosophers of Greek antiquity. Rinckart began with a free paraphrase of Plato's dialogue *Timaeus*, writing: "Music is given to the human race mainly for this reason: that we might consider sweet song and harmonious music as correcting dissonances of the mind, will, and heart."[46] Citations from Quintilian's *De Musice* and Cicero's *Tusculan Disputations* lend weight to the role of musicians in society. A passage from Joachim Camerarius in the quinta partbook makes the case even more forcefully: "Divine music affects not only the minds of people, but their very bodies as well."[47] Music's power to stir the intellectual and physical body caused friction and even fear among early church fathers. Rinckart cites the famous story of St. Augustine (354–430) who, in the autobiographical *Confessions*, reflects on his struggle with the role of music in worship*s*: "How many tears did I shed, as I was deeply stirred by

---

translated in Luther, "Preface to Georg Rhau's *Symphoniae iucundae* (1538)," p. 323.

43   Martin Rinckart, *Triumphi de Dorothea ... geistliches musicalisches Triumph-Cräntzlein* (Leipzig: Lorenz Köber, 1619; RISM B/I, 1619[16]); exemplar SLUB Dresden / Abt. Deutsche Fotothek, Mus. 1-C-2, nr. 527, cantus partbook, fol. 1v.

44   Trans. Harrison Powley III, *"Il trionfo di Dori:* A Critical Edition," 3 vols (Ph.D. diss., University of Rochester, Eastman School of Music, 1974), vol. 2, p. 216. For the complete letter, see Walter E. Buszin, "Luther on Music," *The Musical Quarterly*, 32 (1946): 84–5.

45   RISM B/I, 1619[16], exemplar SLUB Dresden / Abt. Deutsche Fotothek, Mus. 1-C-2, nr. 527, cantus partbook, fol. 1v: "Sie ist ein Labsal [b]eim betrübten Menschen: vnd eine halbe Disciplin= vnd Zuchtmeisterin/ die das Hertz frölich/ vnd die Leute gelinder vnd sanfftmütiger/ sittsamer vnd vernünfftiger macht" [She is a comfort to a person in distress. ... She makes people more gentle and mild, more virtuous and sensible.] (trans. Powley, *"Il trionfo di Dori*, vol. 2, p. 215).

46   RISM B/I, 1619[16], exemplar SLUB Dresden / Abt. Deutsche Fotothek, Mus 1-C-2, nr. 531, sexta partbook, fol. 1v: "MUSICA generi humano hanc ob causam præcipuè data est; ut suavem Cantum et concentum audietes cogitemus de corrigendâ dissonantia mentis, voluntatis & cordis," adapted freely from Plato's *Timaeus* 47D (trans. Powley, *Il trionfo di Dori*, vol. 2, p. 217).

47   RISM B/I, 1619[16], exemplar SLUB Dresden / Abt. Deutsche Fotothek, Mus 1-C-2, nr. 530, quinta partbook, fol. 1v: "DIVINA MUSICA, non tantum Animos hominum, sed et ipsa corpora quodammodo afficit" (trans. Powley, *Il trionfo di Dori*, vol. 2, p. 219).

the voices of Thy church sweetly swelling in the singing of Thy hymns and canticles. Those voices flowed into my ears, and truth was distilled into my heart, and a feeling of piety welled up from it."[48] In the altus partbook music's effects are praised by the philosopher, doctor, politician, and theologian. The Philosopher opens the discourse observing that "Nothing is so void in humanity, that it is not captured by the art and love of Music."[49] "Music is the food of life and sanity," states the Doctor. It is "the key of power and advancement," answers the Politician. The Theologian has the final word: "The musical exercise is the feeling of eternal life."

Rinckart reserved the most extensive prefatory material for the tenor partbook, a practice common to the music print culture of early modern Germany. The Grimma copy of the tenor partbook includes a list of citations from Abraham, Isaac, Jacob, Moses, Aaron, Joshua, David, Salomon, and other Biblical figures noting, "Sie haben MUSICAM gelernet/ vnd geistliche Lieder gedichtet" [They have studied MUSIC and composed spiritual songs].[50] It is followed by a lengthy dedication, dated 2 July 1619, and signed: "M. Mart. Rinckhard Mitarbeiter vnd Diener am Wort Gottes" [M. Mart. Rinckhard Assistant and Servant of the Word of God] (fols 4r–v). Rinckart addressed the volume to "Einer gantzen löblichen Cantorey Gesellschafft zu Eylenberg" [The most laudable church-choir society of Eylenberg], where he served as archdeacon.

After the obligatory bows to his patrons, Rinckart offered his own account of the work.[51] He recounts the history of the first *Trionfo* settings, noting that a number of Italian composers "fell in love" ["inamoriret und verliebet"] with Dorothea, their affection resulting in the collection *Triumphi di Dori*. Yet Rinckart does not believe that his Italian predecessors honor the true Dorothea, but "rather, her Italian and fleshly nature, a shamed Venus," that is, a more debased love of pagan and erotic origins.[52] At best, Rinckart argues, the Italians honor Dorothea involuntarily or unknowingly, just as is the case in Proverbs 17, or in the actions of Caiaphas cited in John 11: 49-52, or in the actions of "Bileams Esel" [Balaam's ass] in Numbers

---

48   RISM B/I, 1619[16], exemplar SLUB Dresden / Abt. Deutsche Fotothek, Mus. 1-C-2, nr. 530, quinta partbook, fol. 1v: "Quantum flevi in Hymnis, & canticis suave sonantis Ecclesiæ vocibus! voces influebant auribus meis; et eliquabatur Veritas in cor meum, & ex ea æstuabat inde affectus Pietatis." Rinckart incorrectly cites the passage as Book 9, Chapter 7 of Augustine's *Confessions*. It is actually found at the end of Chapter 6 (Augustine, *Confessions*, trans. Vernon J. Bourke, *The Fathers of the Church*, 21 [Washington: The Catholic University of America Press, 1966], p. 21, quoted in Powley, *Il trionfo di Dori*, vol. 2, p. 219 n. 3).

49   RISM B/I, 1619[16], exemplar SLUB Dresden / Abt. Deutsche Fotothek, Mus. 1-C-2, nr. 528, altus partbook, fol. 1v: "Nihil est tàm expers humanitatis, quod non arte capiatur et Amore MUSICES" (Philosophus); "MUSICA est vitæ & sanitatis nutrimentum" (Medicus); "MUSICA est clavis Aulæ et promotionis" (Politicus); and "Exercitium Musices, est SENSUS VITÆ ÆTERNÆ" (Theologus).

50   RISM B/I, 1619[16], exemplar SLUB Dresden / Abt. Deutsche Fotothek, Mus. Gri. 23.10 nr. 529, tenor partbook, fol. 1v.

51   The dedication is transcribed in its entirety in Appendix A, pp. 201–4.

52   "sondern ihrer Welschen vnd Fleischlichen art nach/ ein sch[a]ndde VENUS genennet" (RISM B/I, 1619[16], exemplar SLUB Dresden / Abt. Deutsche Fotothek, Mus. Gri. 23.10 nr. 529, tenor partbook, fol. 3r).

22:24.[53] Such erudite citation of Biblical passages typifies prefaces to Lutheran books, and exemplifies Rinckart's interweaving of his professional roles as theologian and poet.

Rinckart's goal was no less than a spiritual renovation of the *Trionfo di Dori*. He aimed to restore the true meaning of the collection, by honoring Dorothea and praising the mercy of the almighty Creator. As he explains, "[I] undertook my well-meant intention to express myself [*exprimiren*] and so now and then, I underlaid one or another [song] with available spiritual texts; until, finally, it is again hoped that through God's mercy and the urging of good people therewith it may come so far that my beloved Dorothea is fully liberated from her Italian ungodliness and thus, praise God, might become pure and Lutheran."[54] Rinckart's goal of purifying the texts justified his use of parody: "the undoubted hope, that they [these songs], not as Jesuitical parodies, but pious parodies [*piam fraudem*] ... will not only generously and amply please you, but that you will also accept them ... for the kindnesses and favors demonstrated before me up to now."[55] Rather than stealing the work of others (a common attack), Rinckart saved these songs, an act he likens to the Hebrew flight from Egypt, or a rescue from captors.

Having defended himself against potential criticism, Rinckart turned his attention to the audience for these pieces, his friends and supporters. His intended audience is two-fold. First, the music is well suited "for the recreation of the senior masters and emeritus musicians and honorable tutors and spectators, and the delight of these same in listening ..."[56] Second, for their children and youth, the collection held a higher purpose. For this group, "they [the songs] may be recommended and assigned for frequent practice," so that the youth will praise God and acquaint themselves with the virtuous Dorothea rather than "with a lush Venus" ["einer uppigen *Venus*"].[57] As

---

53 "so werden sie doch deroselben edlen Gab Gottes/ zum allerwenigsten vnwissend/ vnd gleich wider ihren willen/ wie dort Caiaphas vom HErrn Christo/ Joh. II vnd Bileam/ oder auch Bileams Esel/ Num. 22. 24." (RISM B/I, 1619[16], exemplar SLUB Dresden / Abt. Deutsche Fotothek, Mus. Gri. 23.10 nr. 529, tenor partbook, fol. 3r).

54 "solch mein wolmeynend *intent* zu *exprimiren* mich vnterfangen/ vnd je biß weilen eines vnd das ander mit gegenwertigen geistlichen Texten vnterleget/ biß es endlich wider verhoffen/ durch Gottes Gnad/ vnd guter Leute antreiben damit so weit kommen/ daß meine liebe Dorothea von ihrer Welschen Abgötterey völlig erlediget/ vnd nun mehr/ Gott lob/ gantz lauter vnd Lutherisch worden" (RISM B/I, 1619[16], exemplar SLUB Dresden / Abt. Deutsche Fotothek, Mus. Gri. 23.10 nr. 529, tenor partbook, fol. 3r).

55 "der vngezweiffelten hoffnung/ sie werden ihnen solchen/ nicht Jesuitischen/ sondern recht *piam fraudem* ... nicht allein großgünstig vnd günstig gefallen lassen/ sondern dieselbe auch/ als ein *Umbram gratitudinis*/ vor die mir biß *dato* erzeigte Gut= vnd Wolthaten/ zu ihrem Großgünst. vnd günstigem *Patrocinio* von mir *accepiren* vnd auffnemen" (RISM B/I, 1619[16], exemplar SLUB Dresden / Abt. Deutsche Fotothek, Mus. Gri. 23.10 nr. 529, tenor partbook, fol. 3v).

56 "die Herren *Seniores* vnd *Emeriti Musici tanquam Tutores & spectatores honorum* ihnen zur *recreation* vnd ergetzung dieselbe mit anzuhören ..." (RISM B/I, 1619[16], exemplar SLUB Dresden / Abt. Deutsche Fotothek, Mus. Gri. 23.10 nr. 529, tenor partbook, fol. 3v).

57 "Ihren Kindern aber vnd der jungen Mannschafft zum *liberali exercitio, recommendiret* vnd befolen seyn lassen" (RISM B/I, 1619[16], exemplar SLUB Dresden / Abt. Deutsche Fotothek, Mus. Gri. 23.10 nr. 529, tenor partbook, fol. 3v).

a theologian, Rinckart recognized the power of transmitting "the Word" through familiar tunes. His stance echoed the sentiment of Lutheran commentators since the Reformation. As the Bohemian Brethren argued in a letter of 1574 to the Saxon Elector Friedrich III, it was much more important to preserve the "beautiful melodies," so that people could more easily be brought "to the apprehension of truth through familiar sound."[58]

Rinckart's dedicatory preface is among the longest accounts of editorial work from the period. Such a personal account of faith and work is deeply rooted in Lutheranism, which distinguished itself from Catholicism by emphasizing one's personal relationship with God. *Triumphi de Dorothea* is a statement of Rinckart's own faith, and of the role of music in its expression. The personal nature of the volume is suggested by the inclusion of Rinckart's *symbolum* in the bassus partbook, M.M.R. M.V.S.I.C.A., with the explanation [Magister Martin Rinckart] Mein Vertrawen Steht In Christo Allein [My trust remains in Christ alone].[59] Here Rinckart equates music with the expression of devout faith and piety.

Rinckart retained the theme of music's causes and effects across the volumes, through the use of running heads. The first 18 madrigals use the running heads "*Laus Musicæ â variis causis*" [Praise to music in accordance with various causes] (cantus and quinta partbooks) and versions of "Musicen Lob/ nach allen *causis* vnd Vmbständen/" [Praise to music according to all causes and circumstances] (altus, tenor, and sexta partbooks). Running heads for nos 19–21 vary the message as "*Laus musicæ â variis Effectis*" [Praise to music in accordance with various effects] (cantus and quinta partbooks) and "Musicen Lob/ Musicen krafft vnd Wirkung" [Praise to music (according to) the power and effect of music] (altus and sexta partbooks).[60] Headlines to individual pieces incorporate various calls for "Praise to music" that complement Rinckart's contrafacta (discussed below). For roughly the second half of the anthology, settings 19–31, Rinckart praises music's effects in the running heads and headlines to individual pieces, by incorporating quotations from St. Augustine (no. 22), St. Basil (no. 23), the Bible (nos 8, 21, 24, 29, 30), Aristotle (no. 35), Plato (no. 36), and Luther (nos 37, 38)—all authorities first introduced in the prefaces to the anthology.

Rinckart created a web of references across the paratextual space of the title, title page, prefaces, running heads, and headlines. He interwove quotations from the Bible, ancient Greek philosophers, early church fathers, and reformers. Together, they present a coherent message of praise for music and its causes. Attention now turns to how Rinckart conveyed this message in the accompanying musical settings.

Rinckart modeled his collection on arguably the most famous anthology of madrigals of the late sixteenth century. *Il trionfo di Dori* contains 29 madrigals by as many different composers, yielding one of the most diverse collections from the period. The anthology inspired commercial ventures and artistic inspiration on both

---

58 Blume, *Protestant Church Music*, p. 30.

59 Johannes Linke, *Martin Rinkarts geistliche Lieder* (Gotha: Friedrich Andreas Perthes, 1886), p. 183. The bassus partbook is now missing from Linke's Dresden exemplar. See the list of surviving copies in Appendix A, p. 207.

60 Trans. Powley, *Il trionfo di Dori*, vol. 2, p. 276.

sides of the Alps. It was reprinted once by Angelo Gardano in 1599, and five times by Pierre Phalèse between 1595 and 1628.[61] It inspired an English version in 1601, and German-texted volumes from 1612, 1613, and 1619.[62] Settings of individual madrigals appeared in the Venetian and northern anthologies *Piu e diversi madrigale e canzonette* (Nuremberg, 1594), *Fiori del giardino* (Nuremberg, 1597), *Musica Transalpina II* (London, 1597), *Ghirlanda di madrigali* (Antwerp, 1601), *Trias precum vespertinarum* (Nuremberg, 1602), *Nervi d'Orfeo* (Leiden, 1605), *Hortus musicalis II–III* (Munich, 1609), and *Lieblicher Madrigalien I* (Nuremberg, 1624).[63] Rinckart set all 29 madrigals of the *Trionfo di Dori* (Venice, 1592), along with three additional works by Christian Erbach (set to a Latin text), Luca Marenzio, and Antonio Scandello.

Rinckart's knowledge of *Il trionfo di Dori* was first filtered through the work of earlier German editors. His immediate model was the two-volume series *Musicalische Streitkräntzelein* (Nuremberg, 1612–13), which included all 29 madrigals from the *Trionfo di Dori*, with German secular texts by Johannes Lyttich. Lyttich taught at the Royal Mansfeld Gymnasium, founded in Eisleben by Luther in 1546, and succeeded Rinckart as Cantor at the Nikolaikirche there from 10 April 1611 until his death later that year.[64] For the first volume, Lyttich set the opening 16 madrigals of *Il trionfo di Dori* in their original order. According to the title page of the companion volume, Lyttich's Mansfeld colleague, Salomon Engelhart, "legally acquired [the remaining songs] upon Lyttich's death" ["nach absterben Herrn JOHANNIS LYTTICHII vollendt absolviert"]; he edited madrigals 16–29 along with two works by Hans Leo Hassler and Luca Marenzio, and issued them as *Rest musicalisches Streitkräntzleins*. Lyttich retained the pastoral quality of the original *Trionfo* poems, which tell the story of shepherds and Arcadian nymphs singing praise to the beautiful Dori. Each madrigal ends with the unifying refrain "Viva la bella Dori" [Long live fair Dori]. Title pages note that the contrafacta honored "the excellent authors" ["Den trefflichen *Authoribus*"] and "all chaste German maidens" ["allen Ehrntugentsam(m)en Teutschen Jungfrauen"] with "amusing and artful German texts after the correct alphabetical order of feminine names" ["mit lustigen vnd anmutigen züchtigen Texten/ nach richtiger alphabetischer Weiblicher Namen ordnung"].[65] After an opening song in honor of music, the volumes progress

---

61 For Gardano, see RISM B/I, 1599[10]; for Phalèse, see RISM B/I, 1595[2]; RISM B/I, 1596[9]; RISM B/I, 1601[6]; RISM B/I, 1614[11], and RISM B/I, 1628[12].

62 See RISM B/I, 1601[16]; RISM B/I, 1612[13]; RISM B/I, 1613[13]; and RISM B/I, 1619[16].

63 See Powley, *Il trionfo di Dori*, vol. 1, pp. 211–18.

64 Lyttich could have served only for a short time as teacher at the Mansfeld Gymnasium and Cantor at St Nicolai in Eisleben, for he was not appointed by Grafen Friedrich Christoph until 10 April 1611 (Kurt Gudewill, "Lyttich, Johann," *MGG²*, Personenteil, vol. 11, col. 673).

65 *Musicalische Streitkräntzlein* (Nuremberg, 1612; RISM B/I, 1612[13]), cantus partbook, fol. 1r: "Den fürtrefflichsten *Authoribus* zu vnsterblichen Ehrn/ vnd sonderlich allen Ehrntugentsam[m]en Teutschen Jungfrauen/ vnd derer Tugenden/ ... mit lustigen Politischen Teutschen Texten/ nach richtiger alphabetischer weiblicher Namen ordnung auffgesetzt" (exemplar Staatsbibliothek zu Berlin – Preußischer Kulturbesitz, Musikabteilung mit Mendelssohn-Archiv: Mus. ant. pract. L 1200) and *Rest musicalisches Streitkräntzleins*

in alphabetical order from Annelein to Ursula. Lyttich wrote three verses for each song, effectively transforming the madrigals into strophic canzonettas, each ending with the refrain "Meine Schön ist die Beste" [My love is the best].

The most striking link between *Triumphi de Dorothea* and its German predecessors is Rinckart's retention of the three-strophe structure of Lyttich's 1612–13 set. In other respects, Rinckart departs in significant ways from both Lyttich and the Venetian *Trionfo di Dori*. Rinckart rearranged the order of the contents of the *Trionfo* madrigals to create his own unified message, captured in the new refrain "Unsere Kunst bleibt ewig" [Our art endures eternally]. The contents of *Triumphi de Dorothea* and their relationship to Lyttich's earlier anthologies are given in Appendix B, pp. 239–40. Rinckart freely adapted the musical model by adding extra music at cadential points. Here Rinckart departs from the practice of Haussmann and Lyttich, who generally retain the syllable count of Italian lines, or split them into rhymed couplets. Although the original anthology's pastoral praise of Dori is retained (though in the guise of religious sentiment in honor of Dorothea), Rinckart's poetry in other ways departs from its model, avoiding the rich imagery of Italian madrigal poetry, with its natural inclination for mimetic interpretation. There are but two instances of a direct parallel between the original and Rinckart's reworking. Even in cases of a common theme—such as the opening *Frisch auff ihr Musicanten*, which adopts the motive of singing heard in Baccusi's *Un giorno a Pale sacro*—Rinckart does not align the shared sentiment.[66]

The "Register vnd Ordnung nachfolgender Gesange" [Register and Order of the Songs that follow] (tenor partbook, fols 5r–6v) states the composer and subject matter for each piece, both potential search criteria for Rinckart's consumers (Figure 4.3). Settings 1–12 are unified by their calls to praise God with voices and instruments. Praise for music from the natural world—birds, mountains, and animals—dominates the texts of selections 13–14, while numbers 15–16 focus on what separates the human voice from animals. The third stanza of *O Mensch bedenck dich eben* (set to music by Lodovico Balbi) asks the performer and audience to consider the purpose of the human voice (Example 4.14).

(Nuremberg, 1613; RISM B/I, 1613[13]), tenor partbook, fol. 1r: "Den trefflichen *Authoribus* zu vnsterblichen Ehrn/ vnd allen der Music Liebhabern/ zu günstigem gefallen/ mit lustigen vnd anmutigen züchtigen Texten/ nach richtiger alphabetischer Weiblicher Namen ordnung" (exemplar SLUB Dresden / Abt. Deutsche Fotothek: Mus. gri. 22,2).

66   Rinckart's third line "her/ her/ wer gerne singt" [Come here, who loves to sing] falls earlier than Baccusi's "Chi cantava chi al suono" [Some sang, some to the sound] and hence misses the musical imitation of singing in Baccusi's madrigal (trans. for Baccusi from Harrison Powley [ed. and trans.], *Il trionfo di Dori: The 29 Madrigals of the 1592 Collection for Mixed Voices*, Renaissance Voices [New York: Gaudia Music and Arts, 1990, Schaffner Publishing Co., sole agent], p. 1).

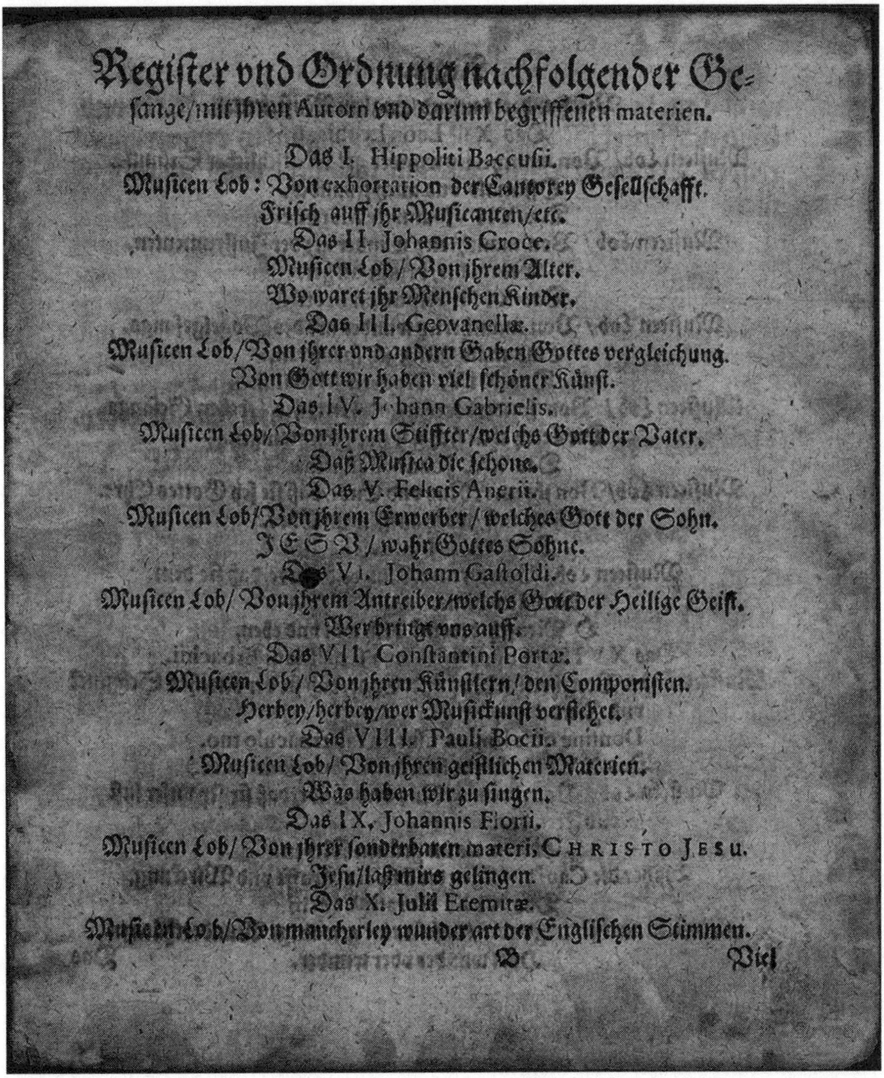
Register vnd Ordnung nachfolgender Ge-
sange/mit jhren Autorn vnd darinn begriffenen materien.
Das I. Hippoliti Baccusii.
Musicen Lob: Von exhortation der Cantorey Gesellschafft.
Frisch auff jhr Musicanten/etc.
Das II. Johannis Croce.
Musicen Lob/Von jhrem Alter.
Wo waret jhr Menschen Kinder.
Das III. Geovanellæ.
Musicen Lob/Von jhrer vnd andern Gaben Gottes vergleichung.
Von Gott wir haben viel schöner Künst.
Das IV. Johann Gabrielis.
Musicen Lob/Von jhrem Stiffter/welchs Gott der Vater.
Daß Musica die schöne.
Das V. Felicis Anerii.
Musicen Lob/Von jhrem Erwerber/welches Gott der Sohn.
JESV/wahr Gottes Sohne.
Das VI. Johann Gastoldi.
Musicen Lob/Von jhrem Antreiber/welchs Gott der Heilige Geist.
Wer bringt vns auff.
Das VII. Constantini Portæ.
Musicen Lob/Von jhren Künstlern/den Componisten.
Herbey/herbey/wer Musickunst verstehet.
Das VIII. Pauli Bocii.
Musicen Lob/Von jhren geistlichen Materien.
Was haben wir zu singen.
Das IX. Johannis Fiorii.
Musicen Lob/Von jhrer sonderbaren materi/CHRISTO JESU.
Jesu/laß mirs gelingen.
Das X. Julii Eremitæ.
Musicen Lob/Von mancherley wunder art der Englischen Stimmen.
B Viel

Figure 4.3 SLUB Dresden / Abt. Deutsche Fotothek, "Register vnd Ordnung nachfolgender Gesange," from Martin Rinckart, *Triumphi de Dorothea* (Leipzig, 1619), tenor partbook, fol. 5r, Mus. Gri. 23.10 nr. 529

Example 4.14 Martin Rinckart, *O Mensch bedenck dich eben* (third stanza)[67]

O Mensch bedenck dich wol und eben/	O human being, consider this well:
warum[b] hat dir Gott geben/	Why has God given you
ein frölich singende Zunge/ Mund vnd Stimme?	A happily singing tongue, mouth and voice?
daß man heul vngezieme?	That you may howl in an unseemly fashion?
sich stetig herm vnd greme?	[That you may] constantly fret and worry?
vnd nicht viel mehr/ daß man im gantzen Leben/	And not rather so that all your life
fein frisch vnd frölich mundwerck von sich gebe/	You may emit fine, bright, and joyous vocal sounds.
sing/ klinge/ jauchtze/ springe/	[May] sing, ring out, rejoice, leap,
im Herren [Herzen] guter dinge/	With a heart full of good cheer,
vn[d] andr auch mit auffbringe/	And uplift others, too,
daß jederman hier zeitlich vnd dort ewig/	Such that everyone here in this time and there [in Heaven] eternally,
Gott lob vnd preise mit vns frisch vnd frölich/	May laud and praise God with us brightly and merrily
denn Vnsere Kunst bleibt im[m]r vnd ewig.	For our art endures forever and ever.

The purpose of the human voice was to praise God, a function that elevated the voice of humankind over the world of animals. For the second half of his anthology, Rinckart turns to an account of music's effects (settings 17–24), once again providing the musical fulfillment of the prefaces. Settings 25–29 praise music, a sentiment most pronounced in the opening lines of no. 25 "O Du hoch edle Musica/ du schön Dorothea/ ... nechst Gott de[m] Herrn dein/ Außerwehltes Engelein" [O Thou high and noble Music, Thou lovely Dorothea ... Next to God, the Lord above, Thou art a chosen angel]. The final two settings (nos 30–31) build on the refrain that ends each piece, "Vnsere Kunst bleibt ewig" [Our art endures eternally]. The Appendix is based on music by Antonio Scandello that is not found in either the Venetian *Trionfo* or the two-part *Musicalische Streitkräntzelein*. With the heading "Das Himlische gebawte Hauß" Rinckart evokes the metaphor of a heavenly house reserved for his Lutheran audience. The theme of God's house is explored in the third stanza (Example 4.15).

---

67   RISM B/I, 1619[16], exemplar SLUB Dresden / Abt. Deutsche Fotothek, Mus. 1-C-2, no. 527, cantus partbook, fols 16r–v. Thanks to Sharon Krebs for her assistance with the translation of this passage.

Example 4.15 Martin Rinckart, *Ich weiß mir Gott lob viel ein schöner Hauß* (excerpt from the third stanza)[68]

Ich weiß mir Gott lob in demselben Hauß,	I know, praise God, in the selfsame house
ein Fräwlein, das kömpt nimmer drauß	Is a maiden who never steps out,
aller Ehr und Tugend voll,	Who's full of virtue and of honor
ihr Lieb und Gunst ich haben muß,	Her love and favor I must have.

Rinckart leaves the performer with a final message at the bottom of the page: "Trieff mich/ Das bitt ich/ Odr laß mich/ Gott bhüt dich" [Affect me, I pray, O leave me, I say, May God protect and guard you].[69]

Rinckart framed the *Triumphi de Dorothea* with pieces that directly address the performers. He begins the anthology with *Frisch auff ihr Musicanten*, a call to musicians "to honor our Lord and His Name" [zu Ehren vnserm Gott/ vnd seinem Namen] (first stanza). It is a contrafactum of Hippolito Baccusi's opening *Un giorno a Pale sacro* [On a day sacred to Pales], which plays a similar role in setting the scene for *Il trionfo di Dori* (1592). The festive mood of Rinckart's text recalls his title page, with its address to "all joyous musicians and music-lovers to their free exercise, delight, and pleasure" [allen Geistfrewdigen Musicanten vnd Music=Liebhabern zum *liberali Exercito*/ lust vnd ergetzung]. The merry tone persists across the first 12 settings with calls to "Dance and jump to Christ our Lord" ("tantzet vnd springet/ Christo dem Herren/" from no. 5, *Jesu wahr Gottes Sohne*) and "Jump and shout, Sing, jump, and ring" ("Jauchtzen vnd springen/ Singt/ sprint vnd klingt," from no. 10, *Viel hundert tausent Englein musiciren*).

The natural world makes a strong presence in Rinckart's anthology, one that recalls the pastoral atmosphere of the Italian *Trionfo di Dori* madrigals. The first stanza of Rinckart's *Eins mals gieng ich spatzieren* evokes a vision of paradise that mimics the natural setting of the *Trionfo* anthology (Example 4.16).[70]

---

68   RISM B/I, 1619[16], exemplar SLUB Dresden / Abt. Deutsche Fotothek, Mus 1-C-2, nr. 527, cantus partbook fols 31r–32r.

69   RISM B/I, 1619[16], exemplar SLUB Dresden / Abt. Deutsche Fotothek, Mus 1-C-2, nr. 527, cantus partbook, fol. 32r.

70   See, for instance, Dom Mauritio Moro's text for Baccusi's opening madrigal *Un giorno a Pale sacro* which is set "in a beautiful and pleasant meadow" ["In un bel prato ameno"]. The full text and translation appear in Powley (ed.and trans.), *Il trionfo di Dori: The 29 Madrigals of the 1592 Collection*, p. 1.

Example 4.16 Martin Rinckart, *Eins mals geing ich spatzieren* (first stanza)[71]

Eins mals gieng ich spatzieren/	Once I went for a walk,
mich zur lustiren/	for my enjoyment
kam auff ein schöne Wiese	I came to a beautiful meadow
gleich eim himlischen Feld/ odr Paradise,	like a heavenly field or paradise.
dahin aus aller Werlet ende/	Whereto from all the ends of the earth
all Vöglein sich gewendet/	All birds had turned
sie hüpten/ sie spru[n]gn/ sich hoch erschwu[n]gn/	They hopped, they jumped, they soared aloft,
all liblich sunge[n]/	they all sang so beautifully
das thet erschallen/	[their songs] rang out
in Wälden/ Bergn vnd Thalen/	In forests, mountains, and valleys,
sie sprungn vnd sungn all frölich/	They all jumped and sang merrily,
Ewere Kunst bleibt ewig.	Your art endures eternally.

Rinckart unites the pastoral and spiritual worlds with praise for the lark (no. 14) that "Above all things, praises God our Lord" ["Lobt Gott vor allen Dingen"] with its "twittering" ["scirliren"] and "amorous speaking" ["lieblichen parliren"]. The text recalls Luther's praise for birds in the preface to *Symphoniae iucundae* (1538):

> Music is still more wonderful in living things, especially birds, so that David, the most musical of all the kings and minstrel of God, in deepest wonder and spiritual exultation praised the astounding art and ease of the song of birds when he said in Psalm 104 [:12], "By them the birds of the heaven have their habitation; they sing among the branches."[72]

Lutheran theology permeates Rinckart's selection of textual themes.

At the mid-point of the anthology Rinckart adds contrafacta based on music by Christian Erbach and Luca Marenzio, music that was not included in the *Dori di Trionfo*. While his contrafactum of Marenzio retains the pastoral quality of settings 13–14, for Erbach's melody, Rinckart substitutes the Latin contrafactum *Domine, quis linguæ usus in tabernaculo tuo?* a paraphrase of Psalm 15 (Psalm 14 in the Vulgate).[73] Psalms 15 and 24 recount the service at the Temple gates, where acceptance is granted for a person once presumed guilty or under suspicion.[74] Accordingly, Rinckart's text adopts a question-and-response format that centers on issues of morality, faith, and charity. It opens, like Psalm 15, with the question: "Lord, who can speak in your tabernacle?" Rather than following the psalm's listing

71   RISM B/I, 1619[16], exemplar SLUB Dresden / Abt. Deutsche Fotothek, Mus 1-C-2, nr. 527, cantus partbook, fols 13v–14v.   Thanks to Sharon Krebs for her assistance with the translation of this passage.

72   Luther, "Preface to Georg Rhau's *Symphoniae iucundae* (1538)," p. 322.

73   Powley, *Il trionfo di Dori*, vol. 1, p. 112.

74   Mays (ed.), *Harper's Bible Commentary*, p. 441.

of faults, Rinckart answers the question with a list of affirmative attributes of those suitable for entry. Each verse asks the audience to be charitable to neighbors: (1) "Who sings for his neighbor, The way of holy devotion" ["qui canit proximo suo viam, piae præ[b]it devotionis"], (2) "Who somehow shows his neighbor the royal road to heaven" ["ostendit proximo suo quænam, via regia sit in cœlum"], and (3) "Who gives good example of pious application to his neighbor" ["Exemplum proximo suo bonum, piæ præbet attentionis"].[75] Rinckart's call for acceptance and trust is particularly striking in the early stage of the confessionally-charged Thirty Years War.

Though this is a unique instance of Rinckart's use of a psalm as the basis for a contrafactum text, psalm singing in broader terms plays a significant role in the anthology. Rinckart's *Wach auff, wach auff mein Ehre* (to music by Palestrina, no. 15) is headed with an abbreviated passage from St. Ambrose's *Hexameron*: "Quis sensum hominis gerens non erubescat sine Psalmorum celebritate diem vel inchoare vel claudere; cum Aves solenni devotione et dulci carmine ortus dierum et noctium prosequantur?"[76] St. Ambrose advocates ending the day with the singing of psalms, in imitation of birds that start and end the day with sweet song. The passage recalls Rinckart's appeal to the pleasures of the natural world (nos 13–14) and David's praise of the song of birds (Psalm 104: 12). The second verse of *Nur weg, nur weit, Teuffel weg* (no. 24, Away, far away, you devil) recounts the power of Davidian psalms and harps to drive away the devil—an ability cited in Luther's *Tischreden*. David is praised again in the headline to no. 26, as "Animorum conciliatrix dulcissima" [the sweetest advisor of souls].[77] References to psalm singing in both the textual and paratextual content of the *Triumphi* connect Rinckart's anthology to Neander's *Canzonetten*—both works validate the importance of psalms for the Lutheran church.

A final group of song texts focuses on music's causes and effects, a thematic shift signaled when a change of running heads calls for praise of music's powers. Rinckart recasts two of the most famous accounts of music's hold on its listeners: the myth of Orpheus, and St. Augustine's struggle. His *Hört Wunder uber Wunder* (no. 19) transforms Orazio Vecchi's madrigal into a strophic song that recounts the myth of Orpheus. The Orphic mood is set by the headline in the cantus partbook: "Music: according to the Greek poet, the most powerful worker of miracles" (Musica:

---

75 RISM B/I, 1619[16], exemplar SLUB Dresden / Abt. Deutsche Fotothek, Mus 1-C-2, nr. 527, cantus partbook, fol. 17r (trans. Powley, *Il trionfo di Dori*, vol. 2, pp. 270–72).

76 The headline appears only in the altus partbook (RISM B/I, 1619[16], exemplar SLUB Dresden / Abt. Deutsche Fotothek, Mus 1-C-2, nr. 528, fol. 15r). The complete passage from St. Ambrose reads: "For what person of natural human sensibility would not blush to [begin and] terminate the day without a ritual singing of the psalms, since even the tiniest bird ushers in the approach of day and night with customary devotion of sweet song?" (Ambrose, *Hexameron, Paradise, and Cain and Abel*, trans. John Savage, The Fathers of the Church, vol. 42 [New York: The Fathers of the Church, 1961], p. 192, quoted in Powley, *Il trionfo di Dori*, vol. 2, p. 263).

77 The headline only appears in the cantus and quinta partbooks (RISM B/I, 1619[16], exemplar SLUB Dresden / Abt. Deutsche Fotothek, Mus 1-C-2, nr. 527, cantus partbook, fol. 26r and Mus 1-C-2, nr. 530, quinta partbook, fol. 23r).

secundum Poëtas Ethnicos Miraculorum Effectrix potentissima). Orpheus is named directly in the second stanza (Example 4.17).

Example 4.17 Martin Rinckart, *Hört Wunder uber Wunder* (second stanza)[78]

Da *Orpheus* Musiciret/	When Orpheus made music,
mit Klang vnd Gsang noch Kunst wie sich gebüret/	With artful singing and ringing as was proper,
hat er Stein/ Stahl vnd Eisn gezungn vnd gbrochen/	He forced and broke stone, steel and iron.
wild Thier sich schmogn vn[d] bogen/	Wild beasts turned and changed their ways,
all Vöglein mit ihm sungen/	All the birds sang along with him,
die Berge hüpfftn vnd sprungen/	The mountains hopped and jumped,
die Bäum im Wald verliessen irn ort vnd Stelle/	The trees in the woodlands left their places,
sie folgtn nach gschwind vnd schnelle/	They followed quickly and swiftly,
vnd sungn all mit ihm frölich/	And all sang happily with him,
Orphei Kunst bleibt ewig.	The art of Orpheus endures eternally.

Rinckart's use of the Orphic myth to explain the miraculous power of music unites the natural, pastoral, and spiritual worlds that figure prominently across the anthology.

Rinckart's *Solt man mit Musiciren* (to a madrigal by Gasparo Zerto, no. 22) adapts the story of St. Augustine, whose views on music were granted special status in Reformation Germany, on account of Luther's own background as an Augustinian monk.[79] Headlines from the cantus and quinta partbooks cite Augustine's conflict with the pleasures of music: "Musica secundum Augustinum, IEHOVÆ victrix blandissima" [Music, according to St. Augustine, the Lord's most pleasant victress].[80] The headline from the altus partbook (fol. 21v) settles the conflict by granting God's approval: "Musica frew dich/ Gott giebt sich" [Music, be happy, for God gives his consent]. Meanwhile the headline from the sexta partbook (fol. 22v) reminds us of music's power of persuasion: "Der nicht zu zwingen/ lest sich gern zwingen/ durch geistlich singen" [Whoever cannot be compelled, loves to be compelled by sacred singing]. According to his *Confessions* (Book X, 33), St. Augustine's "dangerous pleasure" was that he found himself "more moved by the singing than by what

---

78   RISM B/I, 1619[16], exemplar SLUB Dresden / Abt. Deutsche Fotothek, Mus 1-C-2, nr. 527, cantus partbook, fols 19v–20v (trans. Powley, *Il trionfo di Dori*, vol. 2, p. 278).

79   Oettinger, *Music as Propaganda in the German Reformation*, p. 39.

80   Trans. Powley, *Il trionfo di Dori*, vol. 2, p. 286. RISM B/I, 1619[16], exemplar SLUB Dresden / Abt. Deutsche Fotothek, Mus 1-C-2, nr. 527, cantus partbook, fol. 22v; nr. 529, tenor partbook (in German), fol. 26r; and nr. 530, quinta partbook, fol. 19v.

is sung."[81] His struggle is adapted by Rinckart in the first stanza of *Solt man mit Musiciren* (Example 4.18).

Example 4.18 Martin Rinckart, *Solt man mit Musiciren* (first stanza)[82]

Solt man mit Musiciren/	Should one by making music
den allmächtigen Gott	To the almighty God
können so starck *moviren*/	Be moved so strongly
in allem Fall der noth/	In any case of need?
solt man ihn können binden/	Should one bind him in his deeds
vnd vberwinden/	And maybe overcome him
mit was güldenen Ketten?	With what golden chains?
mit so schönen Moteten/	With motets so beautiful,
ja wol/ die wil er hören	Yes, those are what he wants to hear,
willig vnd geren/	Quite eagerly and willing,
hier zeitlich vnd dort ewig/	Temporarily here and eternally there,
des singn wir allzeit frölich/	Evermore we'll joyfully sing,
Vnsere Kunst bleibt ewig.	Our art endures eternally.

Rinckart resolves St. Augustine's turmoil by stating that God himself enjoys song, an argument that reinforces his overriding call for music's place in worship and praise.

Beyond sensory pleasure, Rinckart taps into a venerable tradition of music's medicinal powers to heal and strengthen the body. The metaphor of music as medicine was commonplace in the early modern period, most famously promoted as a cure in Robert Burton's *Anatomy of Melancholy* (1621). Decades earlier, Leonard Lechner welcomed music as a diversion from worries and anxieties over the plague, in the dedication of his *Newe Teutsche Lieder zu drey Stimmen Nach art der Welschen Villanellen* (Nuremberg, 1577). Rinckart establishes the theme in the headline of *Musicen klang und Menschen stimm darneben*, which cites the theologian and physician Joachim Camerarius (1500–74): "Music, according to Camerarius the most effectual quickener of body and soul" ["Musica, secund.(um) Camer. Animorum & corporum Vivificatrix Efficacissima"].[83] The text (to a madrigal by Luca Marenzio) espouses the power of music to heal the body (Example 4.19).

---

81   Albert C. Outler (trans./ed.), *Augustine: Confessions and Enchiridion*, The Library of Christian Classics, 7, gen. eds John Baillie, John T. McNeill, and Henry P. Van Dusen (Philadelphia: The Westminster Press, 1955), p. 231.

82   RISM B/I, 1619[16], exemplar SLUB Dresden / Abt. Deutsche Fotothek, Mus 1-C-2, nr. 527, cantus partbook, fols 22v–23r (trans. Powley, *Il trionfo di Dori*, vol. 2, p. 286).

83   RISM B/I, 1619[16], exemplars SLUB Dresden / Abt. Deutsche Fotothek, Mus 1-C-2, nr. 527, cantus partbook, fol. 20v; Mus 1-C-2, nr. 529, tenor partbook (in German), fol. 24r; and Mus 1-C-2, nr. 530, quinta partbook, fol. 17v (trans. Powley, *Il trionfo di Dori*, vol. 2, p. 280).

Example 4.19 Martin Rinckart, *Musicen klang und Menschen stimm darneben*[84]

MVsicen klang vnd Mensche[n] stim[m] darnebe[n]/
gibt dem Gmüth krafft vn[d] lebe[n],
das in trübsal versuncken/
vertreibt manch Gdancken/
Melancholey/ seltzame Taubn vnd Grillen/
die vns als Fallstrick stellen/
der Teuffl vnd all sein Gsellen/
müssn fliehn von dannen/
MUSICA kan sie bannen/ [...]

The sound of music, together with human voices,
Gives strength and life unto the soul
That may be drowned in sorrow:
And chases ill thoughts far away,
And melancholy thoughts and gloom,
That throw a snare into our life.
The devil and his cohorts
Must at that moment flee,
For music bans them well. [...]

MVsicen klang vnd Seitenspiel darneben/

gibt dem Leib Krafft vnd lebe[n]/
daß nicht in Kranckheit falle/
vertreibt manch Grillen/
macht rein vnd fein/ frölich vnd frisch Geblüte/ [...]

The sound of music, together with the sound of strings
Gives strength and life unto the body,
That it will not fall to any illness;
Chases away the blues,
Makes clean and fine, merry and fresh the blood, [...]

MVsicen klang vnd Menschen stim erfrewet
Leib vnd Seel gantz vernewet/
recht tieff in Hertzen grunde/
vertreibt manch stunde/
viel Zanck vnd Streit/ vbel vnd vnheil mehret/ [...]

The sound of music, with joyful human voice,
Rejuvenates both body and soul
Deep down within the heart,
It makes the hours pass away,
When strife and quarrel, malady and harm occur. [...]

Rinckart's verses reinforce tropes of music's efficacy to cure melancholy, chase away illness, and balance the humors.

Rinckart's most striking example of the healing power of music is his setting of the poet Mutio Manfredi's *Eran ninfe e pastori*, set to music by Alessandro Striggio (no. 23). Each of Rinckart's three verses is devoted to the personification of music as doctor, lawyer, and theologian—connections first introduced in the preface to the altus partbook where Fraw Musica is likened to the professions of doctor, politician, philosopher, and theologian. The metaphor of the doctor is particularly apt for paying tribute to music's affective powers (Example 4.20).

---

84   RISM B/I, 1619[16], exemplar SLUB Dresden / Abt. Deutsche Fotothek, Mus 1-C-2, nr. 527, cantus partbook, fols 20v–21v.

Example 4.20 Martin Rinckart, *Gleich wie ein süsses Zucker* (first stanza)[85]

Gleich wie ein süsses Zucker/	Just as a sweet candy,
nach kunst der *Medicorum* vnd Apotheker/	By the art of the Doctor and Apothecary
herbe Artzney vnd Pillen	Lets bitter pills and drugs
beybringt ohn widerwillen/	Go down without reluctance,
also verzuckert *Musica* der Jugend/	Just so music sweetens youth,
vnd vns die herbe tugend/	And bitter virtue,
so bald man frölich singet/	As soon as one sings happy songs,
steigt auff Hertz/ sin[n] vnd gmüth/ sich	Grows in our heart, mind and soul, and
hoch erschwinget/	rises high,
vnser *DOCTORIN* ist glückselig:	Our lady Doctor is joyful:
ihre *Practic* vnd Kunst bleibt ewig.	Her art and practice endures eternally.

Rinckart may have been inspired by Manfredi's original text, in which nymphs and shepherds produce such sweet sounds and songs that the sun stood still and the grass flowered (Example 4.21).

Example 4.21 Mutio Manfredi, *Eran ninfe e pastori*[86]

Eran Ninfe e Pastori	Nymphs and shepherds
Uniti con le gratie e con gl' Amori,	United with the graces and the gods of love
E di suoni e di canti,	And with music and songs,
Facean tal armonia,	Produced such harmony
Che si fermava il sol l'herba fioria,	That the sun stood still and the grass flowered.
Poi di rose e d'acanti,	Then from roses, acanthus,
Tessevano ghirlande e d'amaranti,	And amaranth they wove garlands
E ne i versi dicean cogliend'i fiori,	And, in their verses, gathering flowers, they said:
Viva la bella Dori.	"Long live fair Doris!"

Rinckart's intertextual reference joins the spiritual world with the mythological one, in a compelling argument for music's affective powers.

Rinckart's Lutheran vision of the *Triumphi de Dorothea* was realized through an intertwining of musical and religious goals. His contrafacta furthered the circulation and performance of Italian madrigals in religious and educational settings. At the same time, the secular melodies promoted the learning, repetition, and memory of the sacred messages.

---

85   RISM B/I, 1619[16], exemplar SLUB Dresden / Abt. Deutsche Fotothek, Mus 1-C-2, nr. 527, cantus partbook, fols 23r–24r.

86   Powley (ed.and trans.), *Il trionfo di Dori: The 29 Madrigals of the 1592 Collection*, p. 143.

Conclusion

Neander and Rinckart thoroughly engaged with their musical and textual models, selecting elements that fit their Lutheran world-view, and ignoring those that did not. Their approach to editorship and translation recalls Peter Burke's concept of *bricolage*, whereby "receivers" of a foreign cultural influence select relevant, attractive, and useful elements from their surroundings, and assimilate them to indigenous traditions they already possess.[87] By critically engaging with their foreign models, Rinckart and Neander created something new and meaningful to their own culture. Lutheran contrafacta of Italian secular song have gone largely unrecognized for their role in the development of German verse. Yet the rich imagery of Neander and Rinckart's settings retained the tradition of Lutheran (predominantly monophonic) song-texts of the mid-sixteenth century, while remaining contemporary with the musical style of the early seventeenth century. Neander and Rinckart infused their texts with local and personal meaning. As we will see in the final chapter, on consumers, such textually relevant collections resulted in the prolonged reception of Italian secular music in Lutheran lands.

---

87   Peter Burke, *The Fortunes of the* Courtier*: The European Reception of Castiglione's* Cortegiano (Oxford: Polity Press, 1995), p. 2.

Chapter 5

German Consumers of Early Modern Music Books

Chapters 2–4 charted various performance contexts for Italian and Italianate music in German-speaking lands, ranging from the patrician music societies of Nuremberg, to the Lutheran school, church, and court at Gera. Alongside its function in performance, listening, and educational contexts, foreign music became an object for collection and display in and of itself. Lorenzo Bianconi dubs the phenomenon musical "collectionism" and likens the creation of music "cabinets" to the formation of "cabinets" of books, portraits, or naturalia.[1] German patricians, merchants, and nobility were all united by a culture of collecting, in their pursuit of consumer and luxury goods. The movement resonated with new ideas about wealth that began to emerge in Italy in the fifteenth and sixteenth centuries. These attitudes were codified and circulated in print, in the writings of the Neapolitan Giovanni Pontano (1426–1503). In *I trattati delle virtù sociali* [A Treatise on Social Virtues], Pontano disseminated a systematic view of consumption that shifted the focus, from public expenditures for communal benefit, to private expenditures to enhance an individual's reputation or purely for enjoyment.[2] Richard Goldthwaite has distinguished three distinct phases that mark this new attention: (1) the tasteful spending of personal wealth; (2) the gradual accumulation of material goods; and (3) the gradual transformation of these goods through the process of specialization.[3] A similar process of self-fashioning occurred in northern Europe in the mid-to-late sixteenth century.[4] The acquisition of Italian luxury goods, including music books, was intimately linked to the creation of an identity. The madrigal and canzonetta were exemplary cultural building blocks.

This chapter uses the terms "consumers" and "consumption" to capture the various types of users, from practitioners to collectors and their multiple modes of using music books, be it performance, collection for a library, acquisition of a printed work for a complete series, or purchase by an agent in a network. This approach builds on the work of Jane Bernstein and Mary Lewis, who distinguish

---

1   Lorenzo Bianconi, *Music in the Seventeenth Century*, trans. David Bryant (Cambridge: Cambridge University Press, 1987), p. 80.

2   See Giovanni Pontano, *I trattati delle virtù sociali*, ed. Francesco Tateo (Rome: Edizioni dell'Ateneo, 1965). See Richard A. Goldthwaite, *Wealth and the Demand for Art in Italy, 1300–1600* (Baltimore: Johns Hopkins University Press, 1993), pp. 208–09.

3   Goldthwaite, *Wealth and the Demand for Art*, pp. 243–55.

4   Stephen Greenblatt, *Renaissance Self-Fashioning: From More to Shakespeare* (Chicago: University of Chicago Press, 1980).

between buyers and collectors, linking the former with a more casual approach to acquisition, and the latter with a more systematic one.[5] The chapter examines the diverse functions of Italian music books, and groups consumers into three broad categories: nobility, merchants, and patricians; music professionals of limited financial resources (teachers, students, musicians, performers); and religious and educational institutions. While their use of music ranged from the practical to the symbolic, the chapter argues that all consumers performed tasks of decision-making, critical evaluation, and interpretation that mimic the editorial process itself. German consumers transformed Italian music once again, giving it a new function and social context.

German Courts

German territorial dukes and princes were among the most avid collectors and among the first to assemble libraries of music. Music books served a practical function at court—they provided repertory for performance. But they also served a symbolic role as a form of social capital. Books enhanced the reputations of their dedicatees and owners. They formed part of a broader, cultural ideal of Renaissance princes, a group Hugh Trevor-Roper characterizes as:

> Patrons of learning and the arts, founders of colleges, chairs, private academies, scientific laboratories, competitors with each other in their ostentatious patronage, sometimes themselves practitioners of learning and the arts—such, in general, is the character, or at least the ideal, of the Renaissance princes.[6]

Landgrave Moritz of Kassel (1572–1632) epitomized this ideal, fashioning himself as a man of learning and civility. An active composer, Moritz surrounded himself with the finest musicians of the day, including Alessandro Orologio, Hans Leo Hassler, Heinrich Schütz, and English instrumentalists; many honored Moritz by addressing

---

5   Mary S. Lewis, *Antonio Gardano, Venetian Music Printer: 1538–1569*, 3 vols (New York: Garland, 1988–2005), vol. 1, p. 9;vol. 3, pp. 19–49; Jane A. Bernstein, "Buyers and Collectors of Music Publications: Two Sixteenth-Century Music Libraries Recovered," in Jessie Ann Owens and Anthony Cummings (eds), *Music in Renaissance Cities and Courts: Studies in Honor of Lewis Lockwood* (Warren, MI: Harmonie Park Press, 1997), pp. 21–34; and Mary S. Lewis, "Manuscripts and Printed Music in the World of Patrons and Collectors," in Angelo Pompilio et al. (eds), *IMS 14th Congress 1987. Round Table IV. Produzione e distribuzione di musica nella società europea del XVI e XVII secolo*, 3 vols (Turin: Edizioni di Torino, 1990), vol. 1, pp. 319–25.

6   Hugh Trevor-Roper, "The Culture of the Baroque Courts," in August Buch, Georg Kauffmann, Blake Lee Spahr, and Conrad Wiedemann (eds), *Europäische Hofkultur im 16. und 17. Jahrhundert*, Vorträge und Referate gehalten anläßlich des Kongresses des Wolfenbütteler Arbeitskreises für Renaissanceforschung und des Internationalen Arbeitskreises für Barockliteratur in der Herzog August Bibliothek Wolfenbüttel vom 4. bis 8. September 1979, Wolfenbütteler Arbeiten zur Barockforschung, 8, 3 vols (Hamburg: Ernst Hauswedell, 1981), vol. 1, p. 14.

printed music books to him.[7] Moritz's patronage of musicians was complemented by an extensive collection of music books. An inventory of 14 February 1613 of "aller Musicalischen bücher" [all music books] numbered 258 entries, divided into printed Latin and German motets, Magnificats, and Masses; Latin, German, and French sacred motets, psalms, and songs; "Madrigalien Canzonetten, villanellen Jn allerley Sprachen" [Madrigals, Canzonettas, Villanellas in all languages]; instrumental music; cantional books; and works by Landgrave Moritz.[8] The section for "Madrigalien" includes both anthologies and single-author volumes, though the brevity of the entries makes it difficult to determine the particular edition in question, a problem that diminishes the value of inventories as evidence for the distribution of particular music books.[9] Italian-texted madrigals and canzonettas dominate the list, with numerous single-author volumes by Orazio Vecchi, Philippe de Monte, Cipriano de Rore, and Marco da Gagliano, and the anthologies *Il trionfo di Dori*, *Musica di Tredici autore Illustri* (Venice), *De fiori del giardino* (Nuremberg), *Melodia olympica* (Antwerp), *Giardino novo I–II* (Copenhagen, 1605–06), and *Gemma musicalis I* (Nuremberg, 1588). The presence of *teutsche Lieder* by Valentin Haussmann paved the way for the dominance of German-texted repertory in the later inventory of 22 January 1638. Here Valentin Haussmann's German editions of Luca Marenzio (1606) and Thomas Morley (1609) are favored over Italian-texted secular songs.[10] The shift from Italian-texted works in the 1613 inventory to German-texted ones in the inventory of 1638 provides further evidence of the changing attitude towards Italian repertory, in the light of the growing interest in German as an artistic language.

Haussmann's anthologies figured prominently in the library assembled by Duke Julius (1528–89) and his son, Heinrich Julius (1564–1613), of Braunschweig-Lüneburg at their residence at Wolfenbüttel.[11] Liborius Otho drew up the first inventory of their library c. 1614. He arranged the books by subject, following the seven liberal arts of grammar, dialectic, rhetoric, music, arithmetic, astronomy, and geometry. The inventory totaled 4,300 volumes; of these, it contained a short list of "Musici Libri" (Figure 5.1).

---

7   A list of music books bearing dedications to Landgrave Moritz can be found in Ernst Zulauf, "Beiträge zur Geschichte der Landgräflich-Hessischen Hofkapelle zu Cassel bis auf die Zeit Moritz des Gelehrten," *Zeitschrift des Vereins für hessische Geschichte und Landeskunde*, Neue Folge, 26 (1903): 93–4.

8   Hess. Staatsarchiv Marburg, 4ᵇ–46ᵃ–nr. 3, Bl. 1–22 (Bl. 16 and 18 are missing). The inventory is transcribed in Zulauf, "Beiträge zur Geschichte der Landgräflich-Hessischen Hofkapelle zu Cassel," pp. 99–115.

9   Hess. Staatsarchiv Marburg, 4ᵇ–46ᵃ–nr. 3, fols 4v–7r, transcribed in Zulauf, "Beiträge zur Geschichte der Landgräflich-Hessischen Hofkapelle zu Cassel," pp. 105–11.

10   Both volumes are listed with books "in 2 schranken nach dem Fenster zu" [in two cabinets by the window] on fol. 12 of the inventory at the Hess. Staatsarchiv Marburg, 4ᵇ–46ᵃ–nr. 5, Bl. 1–27, cited in Zulauf, "Beiträge zur Geschichte der Landgräflich-Hessischen Hofkapelle zu Cassel," p. 122.

11   For a useful account of the library in English, see Wolfgang Milde, "The Library at Wolfenbüttel, from 1550 to 1618," *The Modern Language Review*, 66 (1971): 101–12.

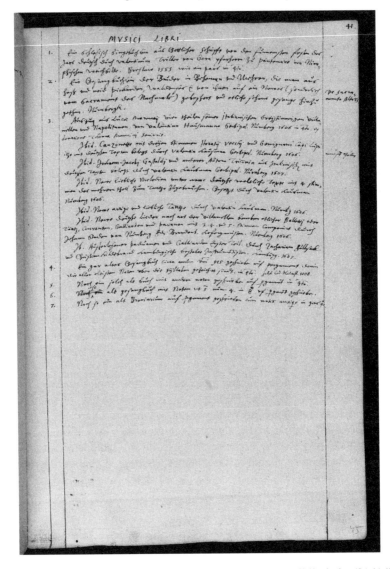

Figure 5.1   Liborius Otho, Katalog der Wolfenbütteler Bibliothek, (?1614), fol. 41r, Herzog August Bibliothek Wolfenbüttel: Codex Guelph. A. Extravagantes

Item three on the list is a binder's copy (printed books bound together to form a single volume) consisting of the following seven books:

1. Valentin Haussmann, *Ausszug auss Lucæ Marentii vier Theilen seiner Italianischen dreystimmigen Villanellen und Napolitanen* (Nuremberg: Paul Kauffmann, 1606; RISM A/I, M611)

2. Valentin Haussmann, *Canzonette, mit dreyen Stimmen, Horatii Vecchi unnd Gemignani Capi Lupi* (Nuremberg: Paul Kauffmann, 1606; RISM A/I, V1034=RISM B/I, 1606[13])

3. Valentin Haussmann, *Johann-Jacobi Gastoldi und anderer Autorn Tricinia* (Nuremberg: Paul Kauffmann, 1607; RISM A/I, GG553a=RISM B/I, 1607[25])

4. Valentin Haussmann, *Neue liebliche Melodien ...mit vier Stimmen* (Nuremberg: Paul Kauffmann, 1606; RISM A/I, H2389 [5th printing])

5. Valentin Haussmann, *Neue artige und liebliche Täntze* (Nuremberg: Paul Kauffmann, 1606; RISM A/I, H2386 [6th printing])

6. Johann Staden, *Neue Teutsche Lieder nach art der Villanellen ... vier und fünff Stimmen* (Nuremberg: Paul Kauffmann, 1606; RISM A/I, S4224)

7. Zacharius Füllsack and Christian Hildebrand, *Ausserlesener Paduanen und Galliarden erster Theil ... zu fünff Stimmen* (Hamburg: P. von Ohr, 1607; RISM B/I, 1607[28]).

The set demonstrates the systematic pattern of preservation and collection that Mary Lewis associates with binder's copies. The books are all upright format, stem from German presses (all but one from the firm of Paul Kauffmann in Nuremberg), and include secular music by German composers printed within the two-year window 1606–07. The cover of the basso partbook contains a handwritten dedication from Thomas Mancinus, the court's first chapelmaster. Mancinus assumed the administration of the library from 1589 (upon the death of Herzog Julius) until the appointment of Johann Adam Lonicerus in 1600, and again in 1611 until the naming of his successor Liborius Otho.[12] Mancinus presented the books as a set to Duke Friedrich Ulrich (1591–1634), son of Heinrich Julius, with the following inscription:

> Illustrissimo, necnon clementissimo principi suo, Domino FRIDERICO ULRICO Duci Brunsuicensi, et Lunæburgensi obtulit, et dono dedit Thomas Mancinus Senior. Anno 1611.

> [Most illustrious, most clement, master Friedrich Ulrich, Duke of Brunswick and Luneburg, dedicated by Thomas Mancinus, Senior. Year 1611][13]

The volume provided performance repertory for the Wolfenbüttel court, which at the time showed a strong interest in English instrumental music, with Füllsack,

---

12 Records of Mancinus's employment are located at the Niedersächsisches Staatsarchiv Wolfenbüttel, shelfmark 3 Alt. 89 and 324, and are discussed in Martin Ruhnke, *Beiträge zu einer Geschichte der deutschen Hofmusikkollegion im 16. Jahrhundert* (Berlin: Merseburger, 1963), pp. 55–6.

13 The dedicatory note appears on the inside cover of the basso partbook (Herzog August Bibliothek Wolfenbüttel: 36.4 Musica Helmst.). Canto and tenore volumes also survive (Herzog August Bibliothek Wolfenbüttel: 36.1, 36.3 Musica Helmst.). Duke Friedrich Ulrich transferred his family's books to the Academia Julia (formerly the University of Helmstedt) in 1618; the collection was returned to the Herzog August Bibliothek in the early twentieth century, with the volumes bearing the signature "Helmst."

Hildebrand, and John Dowland recruited for service in the years around 1600. A taste for Valentin Haussmann's music was established through his prior travel to Wolfenbüttel in 1597, to present Heinrich Julius with a dedicatory copy of the third part of his *deutschen weltlichen Lieder* (Nuremberg, 1597).[14]

The early library at Wolfenbüttel contained a limited number of music books that corroborate what we know about the employment of musicians and performance traditions at the court. A more encyclopedic approach to collection was taken by Duke August the Younger (1579–1666), the youngest son of Herzog Heinrich von Dannenberg of the Lüneburg family line. In 1661, Duke August's library numbered an enormous 116,350 works.[15] Many books reached the library through the Duke's European-wide network of agents, who fitted the court with cultural products, including books, and reported back on current news and events. Others found their way into the collection through the acquisition of entire libraries, purchases from book publishers and dealers, dedicated books and gifts, and books whose printing was sponsored by the ducal court, such as Michael Praetorius's *Syntagma Musicum*. The systematic approach to collecting books was matched by the rigor of their cataloging. Duke August's collection was cataloged in six black bound folio books, known as the "Bücherradkatalog," so named after the wheeled furniture on which it sat.[16] Music books were entered on 27 October 1626, and bear the signature "Musica". Duke August assembled a representative sampling of lute and organ tabulatures, by masters of the mid-sixteenth through early-seventeenth century, including Bernhard Schmidt, Johann Rühling, Johann Woltzen, Samuel Scheidt, Mattias Waissel, Antonio Terzi, and Sebastian Ochsenkhun. His taste in theoretical works combined traditional, now canonical texts—such as *De tutte l'opere del R.M. Gioseffo Zarlino* (Venice, 1589), Heinrich Glarean's *Dodecachordon* (Basel, 1547), and Michael Praetorius's *Syntagma musicum* (1614–19) —with works of regional interest, such as *Erotemata Mvsices Practicæ* (Nuremberg, 1563), by the Braunschweig theorist "Ambrosio Wilphlingsedero." For vocal music in quarto and octavo formats, the Duke favored Italian and Italianate secular songs by Orazio Vecchi, Hans Leo Hassler, Gemignano Capilupi, Luca Marenzio, Giovanni Gastoldi, Paul Sartorius, and motets by Michael Praetorius, Melchior Franck, Orlande de Lassus, and Jean de Castro. Building on the visits of English instrumentalists to the court under Heinrich Julius, Duke August collected volumes of dance music by Thomas Simpson and William Brade, and their German imitators Christian Hildebrandt, Johann Hermann Schein, and Georgium Engelmann.

Duke August's collecting habits suggest a change in the function of what was acquired. His fervent acquisition of madrigal books came at a time when the genre

---

14   See Klaus-Peter Koch, "Documentary Biography," in Robert B. Lynn, *Valentin Haussmann (1565/70–ca.1614): A Thematic-Documentary Catalogue of His Works*, Thematic Catalogues, 25, ed. Barry S. Brook (Stuyvesant, NY: Pendragon Press, 1997), pp. 32–3.

15   Lore Sporhan-Krempel, "Georg Forstenheuser aus Nürnberg 1584–1659: Korrespondent, Bücherrat, Faktor und Agent," *Börsenblatt für den Deutschen Buchhandel*, Frankfurt Edition, 23 (20 March 1970): 722.

16   See Maria von Katte, "Herzog August und die Kataloge seiner Bibliothek," *Wolfenbütteler Beiträge*, 1 (1972): 168–99.

was on the wane in German-speaking lands. By the mid seventeenth century, such repertory was out-of-step with performance tastes at the Wolfenbüttel court, where *Singspiele* and ballets were in vogue. Rather than performance repertory, madrigal books formed part of a larger project of building a universal library. The development of libraries reflected a broader culture of collecting that was closely linked to the formation of *Kunstkammern* across German-speaking lands. Julius von Schlosser's pioneer study of 1908 defined the German *Kunst-* and *Wunderkammer* of the late Renaissance as princely and private gathering places for precious objects, paintings, sculpture, and other cultural artifacts deemed of historic, artistic, or stylistic value.[17] Emperors, princes, theologians, lawyers, doctors, scholars, poets, and artists emerged as a "collecting class" that supported a burgeoning professional class of agents who advised them on how and what to collect. Building on this desire to collect (and thereby domesticate) both foreign and native objects, Duke August was encyclopedic, rather than highly selective, in his collecting style. He collected books on all subjects as a form of information management, with the goal of presenting a universal knowledge. With their exotic titles and foreign composers, Italian music books were ripe for inclusion.

Merchants and Patricians: Germany's Urban Elite

The libraries of wealthy merchants and patricians often rivaled those of territorial princes, and offer important evidence of the collecting habits of the urban elite. The strongest examples come from the imperial cities, particularly those in southern Germany, where commercial and artistic ties with Italy were particularly close. Before 1620, the imperial cities of Augsburg and Nuremberg were among the largest and wealthiest in Germany. Situated at the crossroads of overland trade routes between northern and southern Europe, both cities emerged as centers for commerce and the arts, activities dominated largely by a handful of patrician families and merchants.[18] At the top was the Fugger family of Augsburg, whose library was assembled mainly by brothers Raimund (1528–69) and Georg (1518–69), Georg's son Philipp Edward (1546–1618), and brothers Hans Jakob (1516–75) and Ulrich (1526–84).[19] Raimund

---

17 Julius von Schlosser, *Die Kunst- und Wunderkammer der Spätrenaissance: Ein Beitrag zur Geschichte des Sammelwesens* (Braunschweig [2nd edn]: Klinkhardt and Biermann, 1978, 1st edn Leipzig, 1908). Some conclusions of his encyclopedic study—his differentiation between princely collecting and *Kunstkammern* north of the Alps (exemplified by what he interpreted as the adventurous and unsystematic qualities of the Dresden and Rudolfine collections), and the artistic and monumental collections of Italy—have been subject to revision, emendation, or rejection. See Thomas DaCosta Kaufmann, *The Mastery of Nature: Aspects of Art, Science, and Humanism in the Renaissance* (Princeton: Princeton University Press, 1993), p. 175.

18 See my Chapter 2 and Lewis, *Antonio Gardano, Venetian Music Printer*, vol. 3, p. 21.

19 Most of the collection of Raimund, Georg, and Philipp Edward passed in 1655 into the present Austrian National Library in Vienna, and is the subject of Alfred Noe, *Die Präsenz der romanischen Literaturen in der 1655 nach Wien verkauften Fuggerbibliothek 3:*

Fugger's 1566 catalog of music already numbered 70 madrigal books and some villanella books.[20] For the Fuggers, book acquisition formed part of a larger patronage program. Gregor Aichinger, Giovanni Gabrieli, Hans Leo Hassler, Christian Erbach, Jakob Hassler, Kaspar Hassler, Ferdinand Lassus, Orlande de Lassus, Tiburtio Massaini, Philippe de Monte, Jacob Regnart, Gregorio Turini, and Orazio Vecchi all dedicated music books to Fuggers. Their Augsburg rival, the Welser family, had commercial interests as bankers stretching from South America to the Indies, and boasted a union with the imperial family through the marriage of Philippine Welser to the Archduke Ferdinand of Habsburg. Educated at home under Greek scholar Hieronymus Work, Marcus Welser traveled to Italy, studied Greek, French, Latin, and Italian, and served Augsburg as senator, consul, *septemvir* [the inner circle of councilmen], and *duumvir* or *Stadtpfleger* [the head city warden] from 1600 until his death in 1614. The Welser brothers, Anton (1551–1618), Marcus (1558–1614), and Paul (1555–1620) mainly collected theological and history books, though Paul's library included 34 entries for music, books that were later transferred to the Augsburg City Library.[21] The modest number is deceptive—33 entries are for binder's copies, and the final entry is for "68 ungebundene allerlei gesangbüecher" [68 unbound song books].[22] Paul's interest in madrigals by Venetian-based composers of the mid-sixteenth century—Andrea Gabrieli, Cipriano de Rore, and Adrian Willaert—may have been sparked by his own study trip to Italy. Perhaps the most avid collector in the city was Johann Heinrich Herwart (1520–83), a business associate of the Fuggers, and member of the City Council. Herwart collected over 450 music books, including 200 madrigal and villanella books, which form the bulk of the collection of the present Bavarian State Library.[23]

Like their Augsburg counterparts, the consumption habits of Nuremberg patricians exemplify the new attitudes toward private expenditure detailed in Pontano's *I trattati delle virtù sociali*. Many of Nuremberg's most prominent families made their fortune as industry traders. The increase in personal capital garnered from these mercantile enterprises, and the leisure time this capital afforded, created a demand for consumer goods among Nuremberg's urban elite. The city's close commercial relations with Venice, the international marketplace for these goods, ensured that consumer demand could be readily met. Nuremberg was itself a major craft and industrial center, known for metal wares (everything from clocks to tools and weapons),

---

Die Texte der 'Musicales,' Internationale Forschungen zur Allgemeinen und Vergleichenden Literaturwissenschaft, 21, ed. Alberto Martino (Amsterdam: Rodopi, 1997).

20   Richard Schaal, "Die Musikbibliothek von Raimund Fugger d.J.: Ein Beitrag zur Musiküberlieferung des 16. Jahrhunderts," *Acta Musicologica*, 29 (1957): 126–37.

21   Their collection is the subject of Hans-Jörg Künast, "Welserbibliotheken: Eine Bestandsaufnahme der Bibliotheken von Anton, Marcus und Paulus Welser," in Mark Häberlein and Johannes Burkhardt (eds), *Die Welser: Neue Forschungen zur Geschichte und Kultur des oberdeutschen Handelshauses*, Sonderdruck aus Colloquia Augustana, 16 (Augsburg: Akademie Verlag, 2002), pp. 550–84.

22   Ibid., p. 557 n. 30

23   Upon Herwart's death the collection was purchased by Duke Wilhelm of Bavaria. See H. Colin Slim, "The Music Library of the Augsburg Patrician, Hans Heinrich Herwart (1520–1583)," *Annales musicologiques*, 7 (1964–77): 67–109.

paintings, sculpture, wood carvings, astronomical instruments, and books.[24] In the course of the sixteenth century, these luxury products found their way into private homes and collections. Willibald Imhoff (1519–80) and Paul von Praun II (1548–1616) distinguished themselves as collectors of paintings, copper engravings, and sculptures.[25] The Kress family, Anton Tucker (1457–1524), Willibald Pirckheimer, Paulus Behaim I, and Lukas Friedrich Behaim started family libraries.[26] Hieronymus Baumgartner the Younger, a city councillor, *Kirchenpfleger* [church administrator], and member of the city's music society, assembled the most important private library of music books in the city.[27] Of Baumgartner's Italian music books (Table 5.1), one is immediately struck by the number of Venetian editions, which confirms the importance of the Gardano and Scotto firms as early suppliers of madrigal books to German customers.

24   See Renate Pieper, "The Upper German Trade in Art and Curiosities before the Thirty Years War," in Michael North and David Ormrod (eds), *Art Markets in Europe, 1400–1800* (Aldershot: Ashgate, 1998), pp. 93–102.

25   Horst Pohl, *Willibald Imhoff, Enkel und Erbe Willibald Pirckheimers*, Quellen zur Geschichte und Kultur der Stadt Nürnberg, 24 (Nuremberg: Selbstverlag des Stadtrats zu Nürnberg, 1992) includes a modern edition of Willibald Imhoff's art collection and *Haushaltsbuch*. See also A. Springr, "Inventare der Imhoff'schen Kunstkammer zu Nürnberg," *Mitteilungen der kaiserl. Königl. Central Commission*, 5 (1860): 352–7.

26   See Eva Pleticha, *Adel und Buch:Studien zur Geisteswelt des fränkischen Adels am Beispiel seiner Bibliotheken vom 15. bis zum 18. Jahrhundert*, Veröffentlichungen der Gesellschaft für Fränkische Geschichte series 9, Darstellungen aus der fränkischen Geschichte, 33 (Neustadt a.d. Aisch: Degener, 1983), pp. 50–55.

27   Heinz Zirnbauer's reconstruction of the library of the Nuremberg City Council located 43 volumes bearing the Baumgartner coat of arms (*Der Notenbestand der Reichsstädtisch Nürnbergischen Ratsmusik:Eine bibliographische Rekonstruktion*, Veröffentlichungen der Stadtbibliothek Nürnberg, 1 [Nuremberg: Stadtbibliothek, 1959]).

Table 5.1 Italian Music Books in the Library of Hieronymus Baumgartner the Younger[a]

RISM	COMPOSER	SHORT TITLE	PLACE	DATE
B2593	Bianchi, Pietro Antonio	*Il primo libro de madrigali, 4vv*	Venice	1582
C1518	Casulana, Maddalena	*Il secondo libro de madrigali, 4vv*	Venice	1570
F516	Ferretti, Giovanni	*Il primo libro delle canzoni, 5vv*	Venice	1579
F521	Ferretti, Giovanni	*Il secondo libro delle canzoni alla napolitana, 5vv*	Venice	1578
F525	Ferretti, Giovanni	*Il terzo libro delle napolitane, 5vv*	Venice	1575
F529	Ferretti, Giovanni	*Il quarto libro delle napolitane, 5vv*	Venice	1579
none	Flori, Jacobus	*Canto de floridi virtuosi d'Italia, il primo libro de madrigali, 5vv* (lost)	Venice	1583
none	Flori, Jacobus	*Il secondo libro de madrigali ... de floridi virtuosi, 5vv* (lost)	Venice	1575
G72	Gabrieli, Andrea	*Il secondo libro de madrigali, 6vv*	Venice	1580
1576⁵	Gardano, Angelo (ed.)	*Musica di XIII. autori illustri ... madrigali, 5vv*	Venice	1576
G1840	Gianotti, Giacomo	*Canzoni ... libro primo, 4vv*	Venice	1584
L930	Lassus, Orlande de	*Libro de villanelle, moresche et altre canzoni, 4–6vv, 8vv*	Antwerp	1581
L959	Lassus, Orlande de	*Madrigali: novamente composti, 5vv*	Nuremberg	1585
none	Magghiels, Jean	*Premier livre des chansons nouvelles, 4–6vv*	Douai	1583
M500	Marenzio, Luca	*Il primo libro de madrigali, 6vv*	Venice	1581
M525	Marenzio, Luca	*Madrigali spirituali ... libro primo, 5vv*	Rome	1584
M549	Marenzio, Luca	*Il quarto libro de madrigali, 5vv*	Venice	1584
M1253	Masnelli, Paulo	*Madregali ... libro primo, 4vv*	Venice	1582
M3347	Monte, Philippe de	*Il secondo libro delli madrigali, 6vv*	Venice	1582
M3373	Monte, Philippe de	*Il decimo libro delle madrigali, 5vv*	Venice	1581

RISM	COMPOSER	SHORT TITLE	PLACE	DATE
N382	Nenna, Pomponio	*Il primo libro de madrigali, 5vv*	Venice	1582
1583[15]	Phalèse, Pierre (ed.)	*Musica divina di XIX. autori illustri, … madrigali, 4–7vv*	Antwerp	1583
S6948	Striggio, Alessandro	*Il primo libro de madrigali, 5vv*	Venice	1569
S6956	Striggio, Alessandro	*Il primo libro de madrigali, 6vv*	Venice	1579
V1010	Vecchi, Orazio	*Canzonette … libro primo, 4vv*	Venice	1580
V1040	Vecchi, Orazio	*Madrigali … libro primo, 6vv*	Venice	1583
1584[4]	Vincenti, Giacomo (ed.?)	*Musica de diversi autori illustri … Libro primo*	Venice	1584
V1678 =1583[19]	Vinci, Pietro	*Il primo libro de madrigali, 6vv*	Venice	1583
V1679	Vinci, Pietro	*Il quarto libro de madrigali, 5vv*	Venice	1583
V1682 =1583[20]	Vinci, Pietro	*Il secondo libro de madrigali, 6vv*	Venice	1583
V1684	Vinci, Pietro	*Il primo libro de madrigali, 4vv*	Venice	1583
V1685	Vinci, Pietro	*Il sesto libro de madrigali, 5vv*	Venice	1584
V1686	Vinci, Pietro	*Il settimo libro de madrigali, 5vv*	Venice	1584
W853	Wert, Giaches de	*Modulationum sacrarum … libri tres, in unum volumen redacti, 5–6vv*	Nuremberg	1583

[a]Table 5.1 is assembled from Zirnbauer, *Der Notenbestand der Reichsstädtisch Nürnbergischen Ratsmusik.*

Within the madrigal and related genres, Baumgartner selected volumes on the basis of composer. He favored music by Giovanni Ferretti, Luca Marenzio, and Pietro Vinci, composers who were hailed as models in their day.[28] The strong presence of Venetian music books in private libraries of the mid to late sixteenth century may have given northern printers the confidence to experiment with Italian repertory themselves. The range of Baumgartner's collection also suggests the possibility that private collectors supplied German editors with source material. As church administrator, Baumgartner recruited Friedrich Lindner to the St. Egidien in Nuremberg, and the two maintained contact as members of the music society. It is tempting to link Baumgartner's taste and access to Italian music books with Lindner's editing of *Gemma musicalis I–III* (Nuremberg, 1588–90).

Baumgartner's cultural tastes were shared by fellow members of the Nuremberg City Council, a group that regulated virtually all aspects of commercial, religious, intellectual, and social life in the city. The Nuremberg City Council was famous for "wyse government" and maintaining "civill" society, as the English cotton merchant, historian, and amateur genealogist, William Smith, described in 1594.[29] Michael Praetorius echoed this praise in the dedication of his third volume of *Syntagma musicum* (Wolfenbüttel, 1619) to the Nuremberg City Council, which "always cherished music and held those who practise and foster it in high esteem" ["sondern auch vornemlich, was Musicam anlanget, dieselbe und deroselben Cultores jederzeit veneriret, und hochgehalten"].[30] An important facet of its cultural patronage was the purchase and collection of music books. The Council's holdings in music were at one time housed in the State Archives in Nuremberg prior to their transfer to the Bavarian State Library in Munich in 1894. Heinz Zirnbauer made a reconstruction of the *Ratsmusik* in 1959, based on a catalog of the Bavarian State Library, contemporary inventories (1575, 1598, and two from 1609), and receipts for book dedications found in the "Stadtrechnungsbüchern" [city account books].[31] A comparison of the inventories from 1575, 1598, and 1609 shows a growing interest in Italian music, alongside *teutsche Lieder*, motets, psalm books, and sacred concertos. Many of the Italian volumes bear the coat-of-arms of Hieronymus Baumgartner, whose collection

---

28   Thomas Morley praises Marenzio and Ferretti in *A Plaine and Easie Introduction to Practicall Musicke* (London, 1597) (James Chater: "Marenzio, Luca (4)," *Grove Music Online*, ed. Laura Macy [Accessed 28 May 2006], <http://www.grovemusic.com>, and Iain Fenlon: "Ferretti, Giovanni," *Grove Music Online*, ed. Laura Macy (Accessed 28 May 2006), <http://www.grovemusic.com>); Pietro Cerone deems Vinci among the best madrigalists in his treatise *El melopeo y maestro: tractado de música theorica y pratica* (Naples, 1613) (Paolo Emilio Carapezza and Giuseppe Collisani: "Vinci, Pietro," *Grove Music Online*, ed. Laura Macy (Accessed 7 June 2006), <http://www.grovemusic.com>)

29   Karlheinz Goldmann, "William Smith: A Description of the Cittie of Noremberg (Beschreibung der Reichsstadt Nürnberg) 1594," *Mitteilungen des Vereins für Geschichte der Stadt Nürnberg*, 48 (1958): 216.

30   Hans Lampl, "Michael Praetorius, *Syntagma Musicum:* A Translation," (Ph.D. diss., University of California at Berkeley, 1957), pp. 6–7. For a facsimile, see Michael Praetorius, *Syntagma Musicum Band III. Termini musici Wolfenbüttel 1619*, ed. Wilibald Gurlitt (New York: Bärenreiter, 1958), fols 3v–4r.

31   Zirnbauer, *Der Notenbestand der Reichsstädtisch Nürnbergischen Ratsmusik.*

was transferred to the *Ratsmusik* in 1620.[32] The diversity of the city's collection reflects the multiple functions it served. For the Nuremberg City Council, ownership and patronage of music enhanced its reputation as an artistic and intellectual body. Beyond image-making, music served the civic, social, educational, and religious needs of the city. The Council needed music to service Nuremberg's three religious institutions, the parish churches of St. Sebald and St. Lorenz, and the Frauenkirche. Secular, sacred, and instrumental music was performed at meetings of the city's private music societies (see Chapter 2). Several councillors joined societies in the 1570s, including Hieronymus Baumgartner, Philipp Geuder, and Bartholomaeus Pömer. The city also kept 15 instrumentalists in its employ, adding more for special ceremonies and events. In short, music was considered a "civic work," administered and directed by the Council.

Though the nucleus of the Council's Italian music books came from Baumgartner's library, several volumes found their way into the Council's library directly from the Gerlach-Kauffmann firm, which served as one of the official printers of the City Council. In 1594, the Council purchased four madrigal anthologies from the heirs of Katharina Gerlach: *Sdegnosi ardosi* (Munich, 1585) and all three volumes of Lindner's *Gemma musicalis* (Nuremberg, 1588–90). Four years later, the Council purchased the madrigal anthology *Fiori del giardino* (printed and likely compiled by Paul Kaufmann in 1597) and numerous volumes by Hans Leo Hassler, whom the Council was hoping to secure as music director for the city.[33] The receipt to Paul Kauffmann indicates that his brother David served as the firm's publisher at the time (Figure 5.2).[34]

By far the most significant source of music were the many volumes presented to the City Council by composers active in German-speaking lands. Rather than monetary compensation, composers usually received free copies of music books from printers. Such copies could be presented to patrons in return for a dedicatory stipend. Among the earliest presentation copies from the seventeenth century, one finds an exemplar of Orlande de Lassus's motet collection *Magnum opus musicum* sent to the Nuremberg City Council by his sons Ferdinand and Rudolf on 18 August 1605 (more than a decade after the composer's death, and a year following the volume's printing in Munich).[35] For the *Magnus opus musicum*, Lassus's sons received 12 gulden from the Council; no higher fee was paid by any other south German town. Schweinfurt paid Lassus's sons only seven gulden, Bayreuth six, and

---

32   Bartlett Russell Butler, "Liturgical Music in Sixteenth-Century Nuremberg: A Socio-Musical Study" (Ph.D. diss., University of Illinois at Urbana-Champaign, 1970), p. 515 n. 16.

33   The Ältere Herren met on 12 June 1601 (two weeks after receiving Hassler's second book of motets, which bears a dedication to them), and decided to offer Hassler an annual salary of 200 florins, an unprecedented amount for a musician. Hassler negotiated for 300 florins, and signed a contract on 16 August 1601 (ibid., p. 774 and n. 617). Hassler departed for Ulm on a leave of absence in 1604, and revoked his Nuremberg citizenship in 1605.

34   David Kauffmann is not listed as a bookseller in the city's trade books until 1632, after officially taking over the firm from his brother Paul (Ämterbüchlein 151, Staatsarchiv Nürnberg).

35   Staatsarchiv Nürnberg, Stadtrechnungsbelege, Rep. 54a II, no. 507.

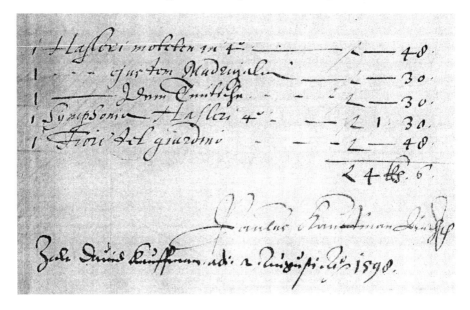

Figure 5.2   Receipt for Music Books Purchased by the Nuremberg City
Council, Staatsarchiv Nürnberg, Rep. 54a II, Reichsstadt Nürnberg,
Stadtrechnungsbelege, Nr. 442

Augsburg ten.[36] The fee made the Nuremberg Council an attractive patronage option
for Melchior Franck, chapelmaster at the Coburg court, who regularly sent volumes
of music to the Council between 1617 and 1635.[37] Anxious to have their works
accepted, composers promoted the practical function of their music in dedicatory
letters. In a dedicatory letter of 21 April 1626, Johann Hermann Schein remarked
that his compositions were equally suited for church and private music-making at
home. [38] After *Opella nova, Ander Theil Geistliche Concerten mit 3. 4. 5. und 6.
Stimmen* (Leipzig, 1626) was reviewed by organist Johann Staden (at the request of
the Council), Schein was sent the generous sum of 20 florins on 22 August 1626.
The dedicatory stipend, as well helping to develop the Council's collection of music,
was an important monetary incentive for encouraging prolonged service to the city.
Johann Staden and his son Sigmund Theophil sent a steady flow of volumes to the
Council, perhaps as leverage for promotions to the positions of organist at St. Sebald
and St. Lorenz, respectively.[39] The Council funded Johann Erasmus Kindermann's
year-long study trip to Italy in 1635, (when he may have met Claudio Monteverdi
and Francesco Cavalli) and in January 1636 Kindermann returned to Nuremberg to

---

36   Harold E. Samuel, *The Cantata in Nuremberg* (Ann Arbor: UMI Research Press,
1982), pp. 6 and 262 nn. 25–8.

37   See Heinz Zirnbauer, "Drei unbekannte Briefe des Coburger Hofkapellmeisters
Melchior Franck," *Jahrbuch der Coburger Landesstiftung*, 4 (1959): 197–208.

38   Staatsarchiv Nürnberg, Stadtrechnungsbelege, Rep. 54a II, no. 702.

39   Zirnbauer, *Der Notenbestand der reichsstädtisch nürnbergischen Ratsmusik*, pp.
35–7.

assume the post of second organist at the Frauenkirche.[40] He showed his gratitude to the Council with a series of *New Jahrsgesang* dedications, beginning the following year.[41]

By the early seventeenth century, German-texted books started to outnumber Italian-texted books in the Council's collection. The libraries of German patricians from these decades confirm a shift toward German-texted music by native composers. A significant case is the library of Egenolf von Schermar (1573–1605) and his son Anton (1604–81), members of a patrician family from Ulm known for collecting music. Anton von Schermar bequeathed around 4,000 manuscripts and music books to the Ulm City Library in his will of 21 March 1681.[42] As Table 5.2 indicates, Schermar's collection of Italian and Italianate music books mirrors the trend toward translations of Italian song and native secular imitations charted in Chapters 3–4:

40   Harold E. Samuel: "Kindermann, Johann Erasmus," *Grove Music Online*, ed. Laura Macy (Accessed 11 May 2006), <http://www.grovemusic.com>

41   Zirnbauer, *Der Notenbestand der reichsstädtisch nürnbergischen Ratsmusik*, p. 18.

42   See Clytus Gottwald, *Katalog der Musikalien in der Schermar-Bibliothek Ulm*, Veröffentlichungen der Stadtbibliothek Ulm, 17 (Wiesbaden: Harrassowitz, 1993).

Table 5.2   Italian and Italianate Printed Music Books in the Schermar Library[a]

RISM	COMPOSER	SHORT TITLE	PLACE	DATE
B812	Banchieri, Adriano	*Canzonette ... [libro I], 3vv*	Venice	1597
B817	Banchieri, Adriano	*La pazzia senile ... libro secondo, 3vv*	Venice	1599
F1663	Franck, Melchior	*Tricinia Nova ... Lieblicher Amorosischer gesänge, 3vv*	Nuremberg	1611
G542 =1607[25]	Gastoldi/Haussmann	*Johann-Jacobi Gastoldi und anderer Autorn Tricinia, 3vv*	Nuremberg	1607
G5129	Gumpelzhaimer, Adam	*Neue Teutsche Geistliche Lieder, 3vv*	Augsburg	1591
H2342	Hassler, Hans Leo	*Lustgarten Neuer Teutscher Gesäng, 4–6, 8vv*	Nuremberg	1610
H2399	Haussmann, Valentin	*Melodien unter Weltliche Texte, 5vv*	Nuremberg	1608
H2402	Haussmann, Valentin	*Außzug Auß ... Tänze ... Venus-Garten, 4–5vv*	Nuremberg	1609
1615[22]	Hassler/Haussmann	*Venusgarten: oder neue lustige liebliche Täntze, 4–6vv*	Nuremberg	1615
J509	Jeep, Johannes	*Studentengärtleins Erster Theil ... Weltlicher Liedlein, 3–5vv*	Nuremberg	1614
J513	Jeep, Johannes	*Studentengärtleins Ander Theil ... Weltlicher Liedlein, 4–5vv*	Nuremberg	1614
L3143	Lyttich, Johannes	*Venus Glöcklein, Oder Neue Weltliche Gesänge, 4–5vv*	Jena	1610
M611	Marenzio/Haussmann	*Ausszug auss Lucae Marentii ... Villanellen und Napolitanen, 3vv*	Nuremberg	1606
M2471	Metzger, Ambrosius	*Venusblümlein, Erster Theil, ... Weltlicher Liedlein, 4vv*	Nuremberg	1611
M8249 =1608[22]	Myller, Andreas	*Newe teutsche Canzonetten ... von den fürtrefflichsten italianischen Componisten, 3vv*	Frankfurt	1608
R751	Regnart, Jacob	*Neue Kurtzweilige Teutsche Lieder, 5vv*[b]	Nuremberg	1580
R2504	Rore, Cipriano de	*Il primo libro de madrigali, 4vv*	Venice	1557
1557[24]	Rore, Cipriano de	*Il secondo libro de madregali ... con una canzon di Gianneto, 4vv*	Venice	1557
S4227	Staden, Johann	*Venus Kränzlein ... Gesäng, 4–5vv*	Nuremberg	1610

RISM	COMPOSER	SHORT TITLE	PLACE	DATE
V1034 =1606[13]	Vecchi/Haussmann/ Capi Lupi	*Canzonette ... Horatii Vecchi unnd Gemignani Capi Lupi*, 3vv	Nuremberg	1613
W1032	Widmann, Erasmus	*Musikalischer Tugendtspiegel ... Gesäng, 5vv ... Däntz*, 4vv	Nuremberg	1613
Z32	Zangius, Nikolaus	*Schöne Neue Auszerlesene Geistliche und Weltliche Lieder*, 3vv	Berlin	1617
Z41	Zangius, Nikolaus	*Ander Theil Deutscher Lieder*, 3vv	Berlin	1617
Z46	Zangius, Nikolaus	*Dritter Theil Neuer Deutschen Weltlichen Lieder*, 3vv	Berlin	1617

[a] Table 5.2 is assembled from Gottwald, *Katalog der Musikalien in der Schermar-Bibliothek Ulm*.

[b] The copy includes a manuscript appendix with German, Latin, and Italian-texted songs including a series of pieces from Antonio Scandello's *Il primo libro delle canzoni Neapolitane* (Nuremberg, 1566) that appear as a unit at the end (Gottwald, *Katalog der Musikalien in der Schermar-Bibliothek Ulm*, pp. 36–45).

Most of the volumes came from German firms; there are four Venetian books, all from before 1600. The collection recalls the contents of Thomas Mancinus's binder's copy presented to Friedrich Ulrich. Both point to a new wave of consumers less familiar with the Italian language. The strong reception of German-texted repertory coincides with the rise in status of German as a language for artistic expression, creating a close link between patterns of musical production and consumption.

Professionals: Musicians, Teachers, and Students

Inventories, account books, and surviving copies confirm that professionals formed an important sector of the book-buying public. Giulio Ongaro has argued that less wealthy amateurs and professionals exercised greater care in their selection of books than encyclopedic collectors like Duke August, which makes their libraries a better gauge of contemporary musical tastes.[43] Beyond their own purchases, professional musicians and teachers may have set an example for others, and possibly recommended books.[44] The "Index Librorum Bibliothecae Raselianae" indicates that Valentin Haussmann's teacher, Andreas Raselius (c.1563–1602), owned an impressive collection, including 115 theological works (with high representation by Luther, Calvin, Erasmus, and Melanchthon), Classics (Petrarch, Virgil, Horatio, Ovid), music theorists (Sethus Calvisius, Heinrich Glarean), and composers (Orlande de Lassus, Alexander Utendal, Jacob Regnart, Jacobus de Kerle, Leonhard Lechner, Jacobus Handl, Johann Knöfel, Henning Dedekind, Christian Hollander, Wolfgang Striccius, Ivo de Vento, Luca Marenzio, Claudio Merulo, and Giovanni Giacomo Gastoldi).[45] The range of Raselius's library reflects his broad interests and duties as assistant master and Cantor at the Gymnasium Poeticum in Regensburg (a post that combined the roles of pastor and teacher), and as author of two treatises on Glarean's twelve-mode system, *Hexachordum seu Questiones musicae practicae* (Nuremberg, 1591) and "Dodechachordi vivi" of 1589 (MS, Regensburg, Bischöfliche Zentralbibliothek, Proske-Musikbibliothek). It is tempting to speculate that Valentin Haussmann first learned of Gastoldi's music through Raselius, who owned a copy of Gastoldi's five-voice *Balletti*.

One of the largest libraries was assembled by Thomas Selle (1599–1663), Cantor and director of music in Hamburg. The city and university librarian Joachim Bloom started an inventory of Selle's collection in 1659, which he completed in May 1663, only six weeks before Selle's death and the donation of his books to the City Library.[46] A study of the inventory reveals that Selle owned volumes of Italian

---

43   Giulio Ongaro, "The Library of a Sixteenth-Century Music Teacher," *The Journal of Musicology*, 12 (1994): 358.

44   Ibid., p. 358.

45   The "Index Librorum Bibliothecae Raselianae" survives at the Stadtarchiv Regensburg. See Karl Schwämmlein, "Die Bibliothek des Andreas Raselius Ambergensis," *Der Eisengau*, 1 (1992): 53–77.

46   Dated 1659, the inventory is housed at the Staats- und Universitätsbibliothek Hamburg, signature Bibliotheksarchiv IV, 1, "Designatio Librorum Philosophicorum et Musicorum, qui ex donatione et liberalitate Clarissimi et Doctissimi Viri ... THOMAE SELLII, Chori Musici

madrigals or canzonettas by Luca Marenzio, Orlande de Lassus, Orazio Vecchi, Cornelis Schuyt, Jakob Hassler, Giovanni Stephani, Giovanni Giacomo Gastoldi, and Claudio Monteverdi. The presence of many older music books suggests Selle's tastes were conservative for his day. Mary Lewis draws the same conclusion about Selle's tastes in sacred music.[47] Perhaps he used the volumes for teaching rather than performance. The library featured a high number of anthologies: *Sdegnosi ardori*, Lindner's three motet anthologies, the first two parts of *Gemma musicalis*, *Musica divina* (Antwerp, 1595), *Harmonia celeste* (Antwerp, 1593), Andreas Myller's *Neue teutsche Canzonetten* (Frankfurt, 1608), and Daniel Friderici's *Servia musicalis prima* (Rostock, 1617). The strong presence of anthologies suggests that frugal purchasers considered them value-packed commodities in the early music-book trade. The importance of collections was noted in Gabriel Naudé's *Advis pour dresser une Bibliothèque* [Advice for Assembling a Library] of 1627, which offers advice and warnings for collectors as they select and assemble their libraries. Naudé addressed the manual to Henri de Mesmes, *president* at the Parlement de Paris, and a fervent book collector. Naudé summed up the benefits of collections containing writing on a single subject by multiple authors, as follows:

> In the first place, they save us the trouble of seeking out an infinite number of highly rare and curious books; secondly, because they leave space for many others and give relief to a Library; thirdly, because they condense for us in one volume and commodiously what we would have to seek with much trouble in several places; and finally, because they bring with them a great saving, being certain that it requires fewer testons [coins worth ten sous] to buy them than it would require écrus if one wanted to have separately all the [works] that they contain.[48]

Anthologies were a pragmatic solution that saved money, time, and space. They appealed to discerning consumers, who purchased on the basis of both genre and composer.

Professional musicians needed music books for teaching, study, and performance. Surviving copies from the library of composer, theorist, and organist Johann Caspar Trost (before 1600–76) confirm that his books were heavily utilized. Trost spent most of his career in the northeastern town of Halberstadt, serving as *Regierungsadvokat* [government lawyer] and organist at the Stadtkirche.[49] His books and manuscripts

---

Hamburgensis Directoris Excellentissimi BIBLIOTHECAE HAMBURGENSI inserti sunt" (Jürgen Neubacher, *Die Musikbibliothek des Hamburger Kantors und Musikdirektors Thomas Selle (1599–1663): Rekonstruktion des ursprünglichen und Beschreibung des erhaltenen, überwiegend in der Staats- und Universitätsbibliothek Hamburg Carl von Ossietzky aufbewahrten Bestandes*, Musicological Studies & Documents, 52, ed. Ursula Günther [Neuhausen: American Institute of Musicology, Hänssler-Verlag, 1997], p. 15).

47   Lewis, *Antonio Gardano, Venetian Music Printer*, vol. 3, p. 31.

48   From a reproduction of the 1644 edition of *Advis pour dresser une bibliothèque* (Paris, 1990), p.57, quoted in Roger Chartier, *The Order of Books: Readers, Authors, and Libraries in Europe between the Fourteenth and Eighteenth Centuries*, trans. Lydia G. Cochrane (Stanford: Stanford University Press, 1994), pp. 65–6.

49   For biography, see Daniela Garbe, *Das Musikalienrepertoire von St. Stephani zu Helmstedt: Ein Bestand an Drucken und Handschriften des 17. Jahrhunderts*, Wolfenbütteler

were integrated into the library of the nearby University of Helmstedt upon his death in 1676.[50] Manuscripts from Trost's library suggest that he had access to books that he did not own, which confirms that the amount of music one experienced was not limited to the contents of one's library (and, conversely, the presence of a volume in a private library does not guarantee that it was consulted). Trost's library includes a single manuscript for the sexta part of madrigals for six to ten voices from the closing decades of the sixteenth century.[51] The 45 madrigals were first printed between 1579 and 1591; many also appeared in German and Antwerp anthologies, including Lindner's *Gemma musicalis I–III,* and Phalèse's *Musica Divina, Harmonia celeste, Symphonia angelica, Melodia olympica* and *Il lauro verde.* [52] None of these printed sources survives in Trost's library, an absence that suggests Trost copied from printed books he did not own. Trost selected madrigals for transcription that best suited his needs as a composer and pedagogue. His rationale for the inclusion and ordering of music presents a striking parallel to that demonstrated by professional editors of anthologies. His transcription of madrigals from the sixteenth century confirms the longevity of the genre as a model for composers of the mid seventeenth century.

Religious and Educational Institutions

Lutheran churches and schools followed Martin Luther's own mandate to collect books. Writing in 1524 "To the Councilmen of All Cities in Germany," Luther argued that

> no effort or expense should be spared to provide good libraries or book repositories, especially in the larger cities which can well afford it. For if the gospel and all the arts are to be preserved, they must be set down and held fast in books and writings (as was done by the prophets and apostles themselves, as I have said above). This is essential, not only that those who are to be our spiritual and temporal leaders may have books to read and study, but also that the good books may be preserved and not lost, together with the arts and languages which we now have by the grace of God. St. Paul too was concerned about this when he charged Timothy to give attention to reading [I Tim. 4:13], and bade him bring with him the parchments from Troas [II Tim. 4:13].[53]

Arbeiten zur Barockforschung, 33, 2 vols (Wiesbaden: Harrassowitz, 1998), vol. 1, pp. 122–7.

50 The libraries of both the Cantorei Sancti Stephani and the University of Helmstedt are now part of the Herzog August Bibliothek.

51 It now survives at Herzog August Bibliothek Wolfenbüttel: Codex Guelf. 334 Mus. Hdschr.

52 Garbe, *Das Musikalienrepertoire von St. Stephani zu Helmstedt,* vol. 1, pp. 51–3, 154–5 and vol. 2, p. 145.

53 Martin Luther, "To the Councilmen of All Cities in Germany That They Establish and Maintain Christian Schools, 1524," in Albert T.W. Steinhaeuser (trans.), rev. Walther I. Brandt, in Walther I. Brandt (ed.), *The Christian in Society II, Luther's Works,* ed. Helmut T. Lehmann (Philadelphia: Muhlenberg Press, 1962), vol. 45, p. 373.

The importance Luther attributed to books inspired the expansion of existing libraries and the creation of new ones across Lutheran lands. The importance ascribed to music collections stemmed from music's prominent role in Lutheran worship and praise (see Chapter 4). Though many music books have not survived, seventeenth-century church inventories document their strong presence in church collections. The Marktkirche, Ulrichskirche, and Moritzkirche in Halle owned 20–30 music titles each.[54] Inventories of the Katharinenkirche in Zwickau (1634, 1661) and the Waldenburg church (1642) list 51 and 50 titles, respectively, from the sixteenth and seventeenth centuries.[55] The collections favored motets and sacred songs by German composers, alongside more confessionally neutral music, relevant both to Catholic and to Lutheran devotional contexts. The volumes provided repertory for both churches and city church-schools. This dual purpose made music books of special interest to city councils. In an effort to build the collections of the *Ratsschule* and the church of St. Wenzel, the Naumburg city council purchased, for 1 Thaler, a "neue Meß" [new mass] by the city's Cantor, Johann Adelsbach (Stadtrechnung 1574), paid Erhard Bodenschatz 12 Groschen for three settings of the Magnificat (Stadtrechnung 1599), and sent 10 Ducats to the sons of Orlande de Lassus for two "Opera Musico Magno" (Stadtrechnungen 1609).[56] The schoolmaster Christophen Vögl made an inventory, dated 28 April 1640, of the Gumpoldskirche music collection, that included mainly motet, psalm, and liturgical books, along with a brief and elusive entry for "Welsche partes Sechs, authore Horatio Vecchi" [Italian music in six parts by Orazio Vecchi] and "Ein grose schwarze Sing Tafel" [A large blackboard for singing].[57]

This last example raises the issue of the presence of secular, Italianate repertory in libraries of Protestant churches. Despite the overriding tendency for religious institutions to collect sacred music books, there is plenty of evidence to suggest a freer mixing of sacred and secular repertories at Catholic and Protestant institutions across Germany.[58] In addition to direct purchases, secular repertory entered religious institutions through donations, both of individual books and of entire private libraries. In 1603, the St. Nikolaikirche in Flensburg acquired the library of Johannes Hartmann, who served from 1569–93 as royal *Amtsschreiber* [official secretary] in the city.[59] Hartmann owned music books from presses across German-speaking

---

54 Garbe, *Das Musikalienrepertoire von St. Stephani zu Helmstedt*, vol. 1, p. 192.

55 Ibid., vol. 1, p. 194.

56 Arno Werner, "Die alte Musikbibliothek und die Instrumentensammlung an St. Wenzel in Naumburg a.d.S.," *Archiv für Musikwissenschaft*, 8/4 (1927): 397, 398, and 400.

57 Herbert Seifert, "Ein Gumpoldskirchner Musikalieninventar aus dem Jahr 1640," *Studien zur Musikwissenschaft*, 39 (1988): 57 (Vecchi) and 60 (Sing Tafel).

58 For an example from a Catholic church, the "Cathalogus omnium Librorum musicalium ad Ecclesiam Cathedralem Frisingensem" [Catalog of all music books of the Cathedral of Freising], of 20 January 1651, included Valentin Haussmann's *Tricinia mit Teutschen Texten*, and madrigals and canzonettas by Bartholomaeus Sorte, Philippe de Monte, Gioseffo Biffi, Giuglielmi Arnoni, Antonio Troilo, Gasparo Torelli, Orazio Vecchi, Jhan Gero, and Orlande de Lassus (K.G. Fellerer, "Ein Musikalien-Inventar des fürstbischöflichen Hofes in Freising aus dem 17. Jahrhundert," *Archiv für Musikwissenschaft*, 6/4 [1924]: 471–83).

59 See Gerhard Kraack, *Die St.-Nikolai-Bibliothek zu Flensburg: Eine Büchersammlung aus dem Jahrhundert der Reformation. Beschreibung und Katalog*, Schriften der Gesellschaft

lands—Nuremberg, Dresden, Munich, Erfurt, Wittenberg, and Mühlhausen—and the foreign centers of Venice, Louvain, and Antwerp. Like many collectors, Hartmann received some books directly from composers. Valentin Haussmann honored him with a handwritten dedication of the manuscript "In Natalem" in 1601.[60] The Flensburg city musician Johannes Liechtwer sent Hartmann a copy of Johannes Regnart's *Il secondo libro delle canzone italiane* (Nuremberg, 1581), with a handwritten note of August 1582 on the title page of the bassus partbook.[61] The volume is bound with copies of Phalèse's *Musica divina* (1583), Andreas Pevernage's *Harmonia celeste* (1583), *Sonetz de Pierre de Ronsard* set by Philippe de Monte (Antwerp, 1575), and Orlande de Lassus's *Madrigali* (Nuremberg, 1587), for four to six voices. The binder's copy provides early evidence of Hartmann's interest in Italian repertory. To this we can add all three volumes of Lindner's *Gemma musicalis* (Nuremberg, 1588–90) and a series of German songs "nach art der Welschen Canzonen" [in the style of Italian songs], by Leonhard Lechner (Nuremberg, 1586), Antonio Scandello (Dresden 1570 and 1575), Wolfgang Striccius (Nuremberg, 1588), and Ivo de Vento (Munich, 1572 and 1575). Hartmann's interest in Italian music and culture may stem from prior service at the Gottorf court of Duke Adolf, and participation in the Seven Years War against Sweden under Daniel Rantzau, whose own passion for Italian culture stemmed from a five-year stay in Italy in the 1550s.

The high quantity of secular Italian music at the Lutheran school and church of St. Anna in Augsburg points to the specific musical tastes of Adam Gumpelzhaimer, who served as the institution's preceptor and Cantor from 1582 until his death in 1625. Gumpelzhaimer's connections with Catholics and Catholic institutions—he studied at the Benedictine school of SS Ulrich and Afra in Augsburg as a boy, and obtained his *Magister* degree from the Jesuit-controlled university in Ingolstadt—apparently caused little concern among those of higher rank at the St. Anna, perhaps on account of the church's financial dependence upon Augsburg's biconfessional city bureaucracy.[62] Gumpelzhaimer's educational background likely influenced his musical tastes as he built the collections of the St. Anna. Alexander Fisher has noted the strong presence of Catholic composers and Marian antiphons, Magnificats, and litanies in the library—an unusual ecumenical trend for Augsburg's most Protestant church.[63] Gumpelzhaimer started an inventory of the library in 1620; his assistant and successor, Johann Faust, continued the inventory in 1625.[64]

---

für Flensburger Stadtgeschichte, e.v., 35 (Schleswig: Schleswiger Druck- und Verlagshaus, 1984), especially pp. 109–17 and 260–64, upon which the following is based.

60 Flensburg, Landeszentralbibliothek Schleswig-Holstein, M MS 7 (5 an: B 427) (Lynn, *Valentin Haussmann*, p. 221).

61 See Kraack, *Die St.-Nikolai-Bibliothek zu Flensburg*, p. 111.

62 Alexander J. Fisher makes this point in *Music and Religious Identity in Counter-Reformation Augsburg, 1580–1630*, St Andrews studies in Reformation history (Aldershot: Ashgate, 2004), pp. 71–84.

63 Ibid., pp. 80–84.

64 The inventory is transcribed in Richard Schaal (ed.), *Das Inventar der Kantorei St. Anna in Augsburg: Ein Beitrag zur protestantischen Musikpflege im 16. und beginnenden 17. Jahrhundert*, Catalogus Musicus, 3 (Kassel: International Musicological Society, 1965).

The inventory reveals much information about book pricing and the layout of the library. The main part of the inventory ends with Gumpelzhaimer's payment records of 1 November 1625 for books he likely purchased from private collections. The inventory opens with "Cantorey Büecher" (fols 1r–11r), consisting of sacred songs, and German and Latin motets. The section includes five single-author volumes by Orlande de Lassus for 6 Florins (fl), 43 Kreuzer (kr), all three of Lindner's motet anthologies for 7 fl, 30 kr, and seven volumes by Michael Praetorius for 11 fl, 15 kr. The second section of the inventory (fols 12r–24r) records books purchased from Johannes Heinrich Hörwart for 40 Gulden (using funds from "Singgelt" [singing money] and "Straffgelt" [fines]).[65] The section freely mixes sacred and secular genres, and features a diverse range of madrigals. It includes Venetian madrigal books by Philippe Verdelot, Vincenzo Ruffo, Cipriano de Rore, and Alessandro Striggio from the mid century, *teutsche Lieder* by Leonhard Lechner, Jacob Regnart, and Abraham Ratz's *Threni amorum ... Lustiger weltlicher Lieder I–II* (Nuremberg, 1595), an edition of Jacob Regnart's two books of five-voice *canzoni alla napolitana* with German texts by Ratz. Northern editions are well represented, with a binder's copy of single-author volumes by Rinaldo del Mel (1588), Bernardino Mosto (1588), Philippe de Monte (1575), and Luca Marenzio (1594), and the anthologies *Harmonia celeste* (1583), *Symphonia angelica* (1585), *Musica divina* (1583), *Melodia olympica* (1591), and *Il lauro verde* (1591)—all for 10 fl, 19 kr.[66] Lindner's *Gemma musicalis I–III* commanded 3 fl, 39 kr, a high price compared to a binder's copy of Italian madrigals, balletti, and canzonettas by Orazio Vecchi, Hans Leo Hassler, Gregorio Turini, Giovanni Ferretti, Costanzo Porta, Giovanni Giacomo Gastoldi, Séverin Cornet, Gioseffo Biffi, Luca Marenzio, a volume of "Neüe teütsche gsang nach art der welschen Madrigalien vnnd Canzonetten," and the anthology *Fiori del giardino* (Nuremberg, 1597), acquired for the more modest sum of 3 fl, 30 kr.[67]

The rich, multi-genre repertory of Lutheran churches and schools coincides with the various functions these institutions served in early modern Germany. In addition to liturgical use and daily observances, the collections served the educational wing of Lutheran churches, and may have functioned as recreational music as well. The efforts of institutions to compile libraries point to the interconnected nature of religious, educational, and civic life in early modern German-speaking lands.

---

65   "Verzeichnus deren Gesangbücher so teils Her' Johannes Heinrich Hörwart Scholarcha ad D. Annae etc. Anno 15.96. vom Singgelt bezalt, als nemblich viertzig gulden teils aber nach und nach vom Straffgelt bezalt worden; Solche Gsangbüecher seind zufinden im Casten mit 2 daden in der Maur zu nechst beim Ofen gegen der Fuggeren garten." Entry dated January 1620, fol. 12r (ibid., p. 29).

66   The two exemplars are housed at the Scholarchatsarchiv der Evangelisch-lutherischen Gesamtkirchenverwaltung Augsburg, Signatur 63a and 63b, and Stadtarchiv Augsburg, Evangelisches Wesenarchiv 1065. *Inventarium Der Gsangbuecher, so den 3. Cantoreyen und inns gmain, inn die Schul zu S. Anna gehoeren*, fol. 21v, transcribed in Schaal, *Das Inventar der Kantorei St. Anna in Augsburg*, p. 48.

67   *Inventarium Der Gsangbuecher, so den 3. Cantoreyen und inns gmain, inn die Schul zu S. Anna gehoeren*, fols 21v and 22v, transcribed in Schaal, *Das Inventar der Kantorei St. Anna in Augsburg*, pp. 48, 50.

Conclusion

The above account contributes to broad debates concerning orality and literacy, the spread of print culture, cultural transfer and vernacularization, and anthologizing as a didactic tool or new organizational rubric. Patterns of acquisition challenge perceived wisdom concerning the circulation of music books in the early seventeenth century. The decline, after 1620, of the printing of single-author volumes and anthologies is well documented.[68] Yet this decline is tempered by the tendency for the publishing cycle of a given book to extend over a period of decades. Consumers acquired music books long after their date of printing, either directly from publishers or from composers, or through the donation, division, and exchange of libraries over the course of the seventeenth century. The longevity of the publishing cycle created overlapping categories of consumers, as music books shifted location, function, and context.

At the same time, the mobility of books suggests a surprisingly stable performance repertory at courts, churches, and schools between the late sixteenth and seventeenth centuries. The medium of print, so long touted as a revolutionary force, may in fact have encouraged the collection (and prolonged use) of old books. First, editors extended the life cycle of repertory, and the diversity of its functions, by anthologizing, revising, and issuing "improved" editions. Their activities kept old repertory in print for decades after its original composition, widening the chronological and geographic gap between composer and later consumer. Second, printers and publishers had a vested interest in promoting old stock. If a printer overestimated initial consumer response, dozens of copies would remain from a given print-run. Georg Willer's catalog of 1622, for instance, included anthologies and madrigal books by Luca Marenzio, Peter Philipps, Felice Anerio, Agostino Agazzari, Orazio Vecchi, and Hans Leo Hassler that had appeared in his Frankfurt bookfair catalogs more than 20 years earlier.[69] Likewise, Kaspar Flurschütz's *Index novus Cantionum ... Italiae Musici compositarum* (Augsburg, 1613) advertised both the new style of Giulio Caccini and Lodovico Viadana with *basso continuo*, and the older style of music dating back to the *Concerti* by Andrea and Giovanni Gabrieli (Venice, 1587), *Concerti* by Claudio Merulo, and three-voice *Canzonette* by Vecchi.[70]

Music publishers promoted a culture of consumption that encouraged long-term interest in the performance and collection of a musical repertory. Their efforts are most tangible in the retrospective stock catalogs of Nicolaus Bassé, Israel Spach, Henning Gross, Johannes Cless, and Georg Draudius.[71] The most prolific compiler was Georg Draudius, who served as editor at the Frankfurt-based firms of Bassé

---

68   Bianconi, *Music in the Seventeenth Century*, pp. 76-7.

69   See Richard Schaal, "Georg Willers Augsburger Musikalien-Katalog von 1622," *Die Musikforschung*, 16 (1963): 127–33.

70   The contents of Flurschütz's seven catalogs are transcribed in Richard Schaal (ed.), *Die Kataloge des Augsburger Musikalien-Händlers Kaspar Flurschütz, 1613–1628*, Quellenkataloge zu Musikgeschichte, 7 (Wilhelmshaven: Heinrichshofen's Verlag, 1974).

71   Entries for music in summary catalogs by Georg Willer, Johannes Cless, and Georg Draudius are extracted in Horst Heussner and Ingo Schultz, *Musikbibliographie in Deutschland bis 1625*, Catalogus Musicus, 6 (Kassel: Bärenreiter-Antiquariat, 1973).

(1590–91) and Verlag-Sigmund-Feyerabend-Erben (1592–99).[72] Between 1610 and 1625, Draudius completed six catalogs of books from the past century, with the suggestive titles *Bibliotheca Exotica* (Frankfurt, 1610; revised 1625), *Bibliotheca Classica* (Frankfurt, 1611; revised 1625), and *Bibliotheca Librorum Germanicorum Classica* (Frankfurt, 1611; revised 1625). Unlike publishers' stock lists, which were organized by performing resources, the structure of retrospective catalogs points to a readership who consulted them for different purposes.[73] Draudius's *Bibliotheca Librorum Germanicorum Classica* (1611, 1625) ends with music books, which he divides alphabetically by genre, ignoring performing resources altogether. Likewise in his *Collectio in unum corpus ... Pars Tertia*, Bassé distinguishes neither by genre nor performing resources; chansons and madrigals for few or many voices are freely mixed. German-texted books are arranged alphabetically by the author's first name, starting with Adam Gumpelzheimer's *Newe teutsche geistliche Lieder* (Augsburg, 1591), and ending with Wolfgang Striccius's *Newe teutsche Lieder* (Nuremberg, 1588). The structure of these "virtual libraries" suggests that users of the catalogs were more interested in categories or species of music than finding suitable repertory for performance.

The longevity of music books in the summary catalogs of bookfair lists suggests that the act of collecting started to change the meaning of what was collected. As the performance of madrigals and *teutsche Lieder* began to fall out of fashion, their function in private and institutional libraries shifted from performance repertory to objects of cultural or historical interest.

---

72   M. Elizabeth C. Bartlet: "Draudius, Georg," *Grove Music Online*, ed. Laura Macy (Accessed 1 May 2006), <http://www.grovemusic.com>

73   Angelo Gardano's stock list of 1591, for instance, starts with "*MVSICA A Due voci*" [Music for two parts], proceeds through three- and four-voice settings (divided by genre), and ends with "*Madrigalia 5 & piu voci*" [Madrigals for 5 & more voices]—a layout designed for practical music-making. It is transcribed and annotated in Richard J. Agee, *The Gardano Music Printing Firms, 1569–1611* (Rochester: University of Rochester Press, 1998), Appendix II.A, pp. 360–83.

Conclusion

This study opened with a quotation from Balthasare Castiglione's *Il libro del cortegiano* (Venice, 1528) that promoted the imitation of models as a viable path to cultural refinement. The German reception of Italian secular song, as charted through the work of editors, demonstrates the complexity of what Castiglione describes with the simple metaphor of the bee. Editing was a highly sophisticated and multifaceted activity that resulted from the collaboration (direct or indirect) of editors, composers, printers, publishers, and consumers. These groups, acting as individuals and in concert, exerted great influence on what was compiled, how it was assembled, and how much editorial adaptation took place.

Case studies from across German-speaking lands signal that editing is a historically-defined practice, whose product, the anthology, is a highly malleable publication-type that is responsive to religious and political currents, the conditions of the local marketplace, the personal taste of an editor, and the perceived tastes of a diverse range of customers. The degree to which editors adapted their material varied considerably. The musical contents, structure, and packaging of anthologies compiled by Friedrich Lindner, Valentin Haussmann, Petrus Neander, and Martin Rinckart demonstrate the variety and flexibility that characterize music-editing in German-speaking lands. Editors approached their sources with different criteria, governed by the particular social, linguistic, religious, and commercial climates in which they worked. Friedrich Lindner relied on Venetian sources to create a large compendium ordered by performance resources and composer. He packaged the anthologies with Latin-texted title pages and dedications, to elevate the contents and to reach a larger audience. Valentin Haussmann arguably engaged with his models on a deeper level, as he translated and adapted Italian texts into German. Martin Rinckart and Petrus Neander significantly altered the original meaning of Italian madrigals and canzonettas, to create works that reflected the religious sensibilities of the Lutheran courts, schools, and churches for which they edited.

Editors performed a range of tasks that, together, had a profound impact on the circulation of music in early modern Europe. From a practical standpoint, they assembled materials, from either local sources or further afield, to bring music to new audiences. Conscious of this role, Friedrich Lindner, on the title page of his *Tertius Gemmae Musicalis liber* (Nuremberg, 1590) advertised madrigals and *canzoni alla napolitana* "Nunc primum in lucem editus" [published for the first time] in Germany.[1] Valentin Haussmann pointed out that Luca Marenzio's three-part villanellas and *canzoni alla napolitana* were "zuvor in Teutschland nicht vil gesehen worden" [previously little known in Germany].[2] In the case of German-speaking

---

1   Canto partbook, Bayerische Staatsbibliothek München, Musikabteilung: 4° Mus. pr. 2718/2, fol. 1r.

2   Valentin Haussmann, *ausszug auss Lucæ Marentii vier Theilen seiner Italianischen dreystimmigen Villanellen und Napolitanen* (Nuremberg: Paul Kauffmann, 1606; RISM A/I,

lands, editorial work explains the shift in buying habits of the northern public, which had little use for the madrigal prior to the period in question. With backgrounds in teaching, court, or religion, editors assured the credibility and accuracy of music books. This was particularly important for anthologies of foreign music—including madrigals and related genres—where consumers needed to be guided through less familiar territory. Editors enhanced the practical value of music books by offering increased performance options to wider audiences. They made texts easier to use by adding indices, contents lists, notes to performers, and commentary (often embedded in a dedication) on the gestation and intended function of the work. The spread of indexing, foliation, and pagination indicates the growing value placed on the visual presentation of texts, in ways that facilitated their consultation and comprehension.[3] Such ordering schemes found a parallel in publishers' catalogs, that organized available stock according to language, performing resources, genre, and composer. These categories complemented those available to consumers when searching for repertory within a given book, suggesting that changes in the presentation of printed texts led to changes of thought patterns among their users.[4]

Anthologies served multiple cultural functions in early modern Germany. Editors provided a practical gathering of performance repertory, assembled it into a value-priced whole, and supplied introductions, commentaries, and indices to educate consumers and ease their use of the book. In addition to providing access to a variety of performance repertory, edited collections fulfilled the needs of elite cultures in search of musical discernment, debate, and refinement, while at the same time providing emblems of display that contributed to cultural image-making. Through the possession of objects—material or sound—the social and educated classes acquired knowledge, while through their display and arrangement, they gained honor and reputation. A conceptual link can be drawn with the German passion for assembling *Kunstkammern* of artistic, foreign, and technological objects. Like their professional counterparts in the world of the *Kunstkammer*, German anthologists gathered and domesticated non-native, foreign objects, and fashioned northern replicas when needed. A parallel also exists with the audiences for these collections: the *Kunstkammern* of the imperial court of Rudolf II, the Saxon Electors, and the smaller courts of Wolfenbüttel, Kassel, and Gottorf, coexisted alongside those of wealthy burghers, thereby mirroring the audiences for collections of foreign music.

The primary tenets for compiling a *Kunstkammer* all have counterparts in the gathering strategies of German music editors. Writing to the Saxon Elector Christian I in 1587, Gabriel Kaltemarckt advised that "all sorts of good paintings

M611), cantus partbook, fol. 1r (Faksimile-Edition Schermar-Bibliothek Ulm, 24 [Stuttgart: Cornetto, 1997]).

3   Brian Richardson, *Printing, Writers and Readers in Renaissance Italy* (Cambridge: Cambridge University Press, 1999), p.131.

4   Ibid. p. 131, citing Walter J. Ong, *Orality and Literacy: The Technologizing of the Word* (London: Routledge, 1982), pp. 123–9; and Elizabeth L. Eisenstein, *The Printing Press as an Agent of Change: Communications and Cultural Transformations in Early Modern Europe*, 2 vols (Cambridge: Cambridge University Press, 1979), vol. 1, pp. 88–107.

and sculptures belong in an art collection."[5] His approach offers a framework for understanding the significance of variety and abundance in large anthologies like the *Gemma musicalis* trilogy, and the strategies for the selection and display of their contents. In the hope of securing employment at the Lutheran court of Christian I, Kaltemarckt promoted Catholic Italy as a source for such works of art and sculpture, while offering a Lutheran rationale for collecting them: "The fact that these arts, as well as music, are the most amiable is generally acknowledged, since music, through hearing, and the visual arts, through sight, arouse man to proper and honest joy, and are nobly given and ordained by God."[6] Kaltemarckt's reasoning echoes Martin Rinckart's defense of setting the madrigals of *Il trionfo di Dori* (Venice, 1592) to Lutheran texts. Both assigned didactic and moral functions to art. The quest for systematic inclusion, evident in Paul Kauffmann's "collected editions" of madrigals by Luca Marenzio and canzonettas by Orazio Vecchi, found a parallel in the efforts of Samuel Quiccheberg (1529–67), a doctor from Antwerp who later served as artistic consultant to Duke Albert V of Bavaria. Quiccheberg's *Inscriptiones vel tituli theatri amplissimi* (Munich: Adam Berg, 1565) presents a systemic approach to cataloging all of the natural, scientific, and artistic objects of the universe.

The medium of print accentuated the impetus to collect, for it allowed the exchange and reordering of things according to different schemata. As compilations of objects drawn from diverse sources, collections bore an inherent tension between the variety of the new whole and the fragmentary nature of each item within, detached from its original context. Print resolved this tension by creating a visual and material framework for transmission.

The German case marks a broader movement, as communities across northern Europe responded to Italian cultural influences. Scholars have long acknowledged the northern fascination with Italian political, social, literary, and artistic models, and, more recently, have examined the activity of northerners in reproducing, reflecting, and engaging with them. For music, the closing decades of the sixteenth century witnessed a relocation of the production base, as northern printers came to rival Venetian ones as suppliers of madrigal and canzonetta books to transalpine audiences. The northern music industry was led from Antwerp by Pierre Phalèse the Younger (c.1545–1629), whose output included more than 60 editions of Italian music. Phalèse marketed his wares to a global audience connected by a tight publishing network that linked Antwerp to virtually all corners of Europe. His efforts to appeal to a wide array of northerners are reflected, not only in the large size of his anthologies, but in their packaging as well. Phalèse's collections have a standardized appearance: their title pages adopt a simple, scroll border, characteristic of all music books from the Phalèse shop. They often include a short dedication, but are otherwise free of prefatory remarks. Phalèse grouped works according to various ensemble sizes, with a strong representation of popular settings and famous Italian composers, peppered with a handful of northern favorites. In their size, physical

---

5   Barbara Gutfleisch and Joachim Menzhausen, "'How a Kunstkammer Should Be Formed': Gabriel Kaltemarckt's Advice to Christian I of Saxony on the Formation of an Art Collection," *Journal of the History of Collections*, 1 (1989): 30.

6   Ibid., p. 8.

layout, and content, Phalèse designed anthologies suitable for music-making in a variety of contexts to appeal to an audience with generic tastes.

By comparison, editors in German-speaking lands were more responsive to their local environments. Though Lindner's trilogy shares many surface features with Phalèse's madrigal anthologies, Lindner's inclusion of lighter canzonettas alongside madrigals suggests a conscious appeal to the German tradition of strophic song. Likewise, Lindner's adherance to textual unity, demonstrated by his tendency to transmit complete settings of a poem, may reflect the strong literary interests of his Nuremberg audience. The translated anthologies of Haussmann, Neander, and Rinckart demonstrate even more strongly the heightened response to musical, linguistic, and religious communities. A more apt comparison can be made with the translated editions of "madrigals Englished" by Nicholas Yonge, Thomas Watson, and Thomas Morley. Both cultures translated the texts of madrigals for native audiences who "either [did] not sing them [Italian songs] at all, or at the least with little delight," as Yonge wrote in his preface to *Musica Transalpina I* (London, 1588).[7] Yonge addressed the volume "To the right honourable Gilbert Lord Talbot," a figure whose status might be compared to a Nuremberg city councillor.[8] Yonge recounts the "Gentlemen and Merchants of good accompt" that gathered for "entertainment of pleasure" at his home, a performance context that mirrors the amateur patricians and merchants of Nuremberg's music societies.[9] This shared social setting explains the common appreciation for the lighter-style works of Orazio Vecchi and Luca Marenzio. But the regions differed significantly in the long-term reception of Italian music and culture. The English love affair with Italy was all but over by the early seventeenth century, as religious tracts advised a turn against the Italians, fearing their Popery. Yet in German-speaking lands, Italian music and poetry continued to play a strong, even nationalist role, as musicians and poets embraced foreign models in their search for an enhanced vernacular.

The role of editors in the revision and repackaging of texts challenges the tendency of musicologists to look back only as far as the nineteenth century for the origins of editorial practice.[10] This bias is rooted in the distinction between practical and scholarly editions, and the implied status of the editors responsible for each type. James Grier writes that the "illustrous history of editorial practice" began in the mid-nineteenth century with the formation of the Bach-Gesellschaft under Johann Nikolaus Forkel, the start of Collected Editions of the most important composers,

---

7   Nicholas Yonge (ed.), *Musica Transalpina* (London: Thomas East, 1588; RISM B/I, 1588[29]), The English Experience: Its Record in Early Printed Books Published in Facsimile, 496 (New York: Da Capo Press, 1972), fol. 2r.

8   Ibid., fol. 2r.

9   Ibid., fol. 2r.

10   See Annette Oppermann, "Die Geburt des Herausgebers aus dem Geist des Widerspruchs Johann Nikolaus Forkel und die *Oeuvres completes de Jean Sebastien Bach*," in Christiane Henkes, Walter Hettche, Gabriele Radecke, and Elke Senne (eds), *Schrift-Text-Edition: Hans Walter Gabler zum 65. Geburtstag*, Beihefte zur editio, 19, ed. Winfried Woesler (Tübingen: Max Niemeyer, 2003), pp. 171–9.

and the creation of national series and collections.[11] These efforts not only made older music accessible, they also contributed to canon formation, both necessary elements for an emerging academic discipline.[12]

Yet, as case studies from German-speaking lands affirm, the commercial, intellectual, and artistic significance of editorial work was vital to the music print industry from the start. Early modern editors and translators developed a verbal discourse for discussing their work methods, boasted of their attention to exact borrowing from musical sources, and promoted the accuracy and correctness of their editions. Like their nineteenth-century counterparts, they shaped the reception of musical genres and styles. German editors made Italian music accessible in larger quantities and to larger audiences than before, thereby reinforcing existing patterns of reception, while expanding them at the same time.

Like their nineteenth-century and modern counterparts, early modern editors played a vital role in the formation of a canon of musical works and genres, by selecting music for long-term circulation and preservation. The vehicle for their work, the anthology, assured that editorial taste and selection would have a lasting influence. Because an anthology was a compilation of material classified by professionals, the music selected gained status from inclusion in it. Presenting musical settings of diverse composers and styles side by side reflected an editor's assessment of quality, and encouraged ranking and evaluation by users. The tabular presentation of contents communicated an editor's asssessment in a single glance.

Editorial selection and ordering are integral processes of canon formation. There is much status granted to composers whose works are anthologized, or placed in a metaphorical rare-book room of collected works.[13] There is a close correlation between the fame and reputation of a madrigalist and his inclusion in German anthologies. It is a mark of status for Luca Marenzio, Orazio Vecchi, Giovanni Giacomo Gastoldi, and Jacob Regnart that editors like Valentin Haussmann and Abraham Ratz were willing to undergo the demanding processes of translating, adapting, and explaining their works. Friedrich Lindner's focus on madrigals by Marenzio and canzonettas by Giovanni Ferretti and Vecchi speak not only to the popularity of these composers, but to the contemporary recognition they received, from theorists, fellow composers, and commentators. Lindner gave his audiences models of composition, works that remain among the best examples of sixteenth-century Italian secular song. That such pieces as Marenzio's *Liquide perle*, Cipriano de Rore's *Anchor che col partire*, Giovanni Pierluigi da Palestrina's *Vestiva i colli*, and Domenico Ferrabosco's *Io mi son giovinetta* remain canonical, attests to the effect of anthologizing on the long-term reception of individual authors and styles.

---

11 James Grier, *The Critical Editing of Music: History, Method, and Practice* (Cambridge: Cambridge University Press, 1996), p. 8.

12 Ibid., p. 8.

13 G. Thomas Tanselle observes that books by "collected" authors often find their way into rare-book collections, furthering their canonicity ("Books, Canons, and the Nature of Dispute (1992)," in his *Literature and Artifacts* [Charlottesville: The Bibliographical Society of the University of Virginia, 1998], p. 284).

Positioned within a historical context, the practice of anthologizing echoed contemporary efforts to establish a hierarchy of composers and works. At the start of the sixteenth century, the music of Josquin was singled out, at first by patrons and later by theorists, as laudable. Orlande de Lassus earned the unique status as the first composer to hold rights to the reproduction and distribution of his music, a legal privilege normally granted to publishers. Print culture encouraged hierarchies by providing forums for debate and discussion. Title pages of anthologies praised compilations of "the best" composers of a particular city, court, or country. Danish madrigalists Hans Nielsen and Mogens Pedersøn, in the prefaces to their first books of madrigals, fashioned a lineage for themselves as students of the Venetian master Giovanni Gabrieli. The rising confessional tensions of the closing decades of the sixteenth century only enhanced this phenomenon, as rival cultures sought to define themselves by forging a distinct national identity (albeit one built from foreign models).

The exigencies of transmission and instruction kept "collected" composers in fashion. The pedagogical function of German anthologies of Italian music heightened the tendency toward canonization. Petrus Neander and Martin Rinckart adapted Italian secular songs to German texts for the education and instruction of schoolboys in Lutheran lands, a sign that the now ubiquitous anthology found its place in the classroom early on. By making Vecchi's canzonettas and the Venetian *Il trionfo di Dori* textually relevant for Lutheran churches and schools, Neander and Rinckart prolonged the use of this music well into the seventeenth century, and enhanced its potential for even longer "survival" in the canon of late Renaissance music. While modern editors are well aware of the danger that anthologizing leads to canonization—and many make bold claims to avoid this tendency—early modern editors, by contrast, boldly advertised the prized objects within, and promoted their gatherings as bastions of scholarly and intellectual values.[14]

The publication and distribution systems for music books furthered the processes of canon formation. Northern editors relied heavily on Venetian music books for source material, selecting madrigals that may have been in circulation for some time. Editors extended the lifespan of this material by reworking and recombining it. While printers continued to print old music, publishers continued to promote it decades after its printing, in stock lists and retrospective catalogs, like Georg Draudius's *Bibliotheca Exotica* (Frankfurt, 1610; revised 1625), *Bibliotheca Classica* (Frankfurt, 1611; revised 1625), and *Bibliotheca Librorum Germanicorum Classica* (Frankfurt, 1611; revised 1625). Such compilations became the impetus for acquiring book collections, both real and virtual. Using Draudius's lists, the

---

14   In his preface to the second edition of the *Norton Anthology of Western Music*, Claude Palisca informs us that "Didactic functionality, historical illumination, intrinsic musical quality rather than 'greatness' or 'genius' were the major criteria for selection" (New York and London: W.W. Norton, 1988), vol. 1, p. xv. Likewise, Allan Atlas's *Anthology of Renaissance Music* is praised for being "carefully selected" and "sensibly organized, avoiding the 'great composer' approach" (Allan W. Atlas [ed.], *Anthology of Renaissance Music: Music in Western Europe, 1400–1600* [New York: W.W. Norton, 1998], book jacket).

Pomeranian pastor Paulus Bolduanus included an 80–page section on music in his *Bibliotheca philosophica*, with 1,299 titles.[15]

The profession of the editor emerged from these interlocking forces of collecting, commercial industry, and authorial focus. The contents of books and their packaging suggest that, in the decades around 1600, editors felt a growing confidence in their work and method. Rather than resurrecting Italian works in their original, pristine state, they allowed linguistic rewriting to take over. Abraham Ratz balanced the twin needs, of, on the one hand, conformity with the original, and, on the other, of relevance to German audiences, by retaining all musical details but translating the text. Musical rather than linguistic purity was deemed essential. Gradually, the fixity of the musical model itself was challenged, as poet-editors like Martin Rinckart freely added notes to accommodate the new German texts, a deviation that reminds us that musical works were considered to be evolving, rather than fixed objects. The processes of selection, ordering, and adaptation adjusted the compositional framework, thereby blurring the distinction between the editor and the composer. The association between authorship and editorship, evident on title pages and in the contents within, was closely linked to the expansion of a market for music that print alone could create.

The conclusions of my study have implications of relevance to the broader processes of cultural transmission and transformation of Renaissance models. German editors imparted interest in a repertory that northerners had had little use for prior to the 1580s. They imposed meaning on what they collected, by categorizing Italian music according to composer, sub-genre, style, and poetic theme. Editorial work joined the professional musical class (of editors, composers, and musicians) to the musically literate public, and to the culturally literate collecting class. The legacy of their work is evident in the continued reliance on editorial judgment and taste that shapes modern reading, musical, and consumer cultures.

---

15 The music section is reproduced in facsimile, with annotations on the facing page, in Donald W. Krummel, *Bibliotheca Bolduaniana: A Renaissance Music Bibliography* (Detroit: Information Coordinators, 1972). Most of the citations can be traced directly to the earlier of the two editions of Draudius's three lists: *Bibliotheca exotica*, *Bibliotheca classica*, and *Bibliotheca librorum germanicorum classica*.

Appendix A

Transcriptions of Title Pages and Prefaces

Transcriptions are followed by a list of locations of surviving copies. An asterisk indicates the copy used as the source for the accompanying transcriptions.

1.   Title page and dedicatory preface to Friedrich Lindner, *Gemma musicalis: selectissimas varii stili cantiones*. Nuremberg: Katharina Gerlach, 1588; RISM B/I, 1588[21].

[voice designation enclosed in decorative frame] *TENORE.* | GEMMA MV- | SICALIS: | SELECTISSIMAS VARII STILI CAN- | TIONES (VVLGO ITALIS MADRIGALI ET NAPOLITANE | DICVNTVR) QVATVOR, QVINQVE, SEX ET PLVRIVM | VOCVM CONTINENS: | *Quæ ex diversis præstantißimorum Musicorum libellis, in Italia excusis, decerptæ, & ingratiam* | *utriusq*[ue] *Musicæ studiosorum, uni quasi corpori insertæ & in lucem editæ sunt, studio & opera* | FRIDERICI LINDNERI *Lignicensis.* | LIBER PRIMVS. | NORIBERGAE, | Imprimebatur in officina typographica Catharinæ Gerlachiæ. | [rule] | *M. D. LXXXVIII.*

DEDICATION, Fol. 2r (all partbooks)

ILLVSTRISSIMO PRINCIPI | AC DOMINO, DOMINO CHRISTIANO, DV- | CI SAXONIAE, SACRI ROMANI IMPERII ARCHIMAR- | schallo & Electori, Landgravio Duringiæ, Marchioni Misniæ, & Burg- | gravio Magdeburgensi, Domino suo clementissimo, | *S. P. D.* | TANTA sunt, Illustrissime, Illustrissimiq[ue]; generis Princeps & Elector, Domine clementissime, Illustriss: C.T. | Patris AVGVSTI Ducis Saxoniæ, Principis Electoris (piæ laudatissimæq[ue]; memoriæ) Domini quondam | mei clementissimi, in me collata beneficia, ut ea silentio sepeliens vix infamiæ, nedum ingratitudinis notam ef- | fugere posse videar. Cum enim adolescens per aliquot annos Illustriss: Celsitud: eius Musicæ Aulicæ qualem- | cunq[ue]; operam, canendo superiorem adolescentibus accommodatam vocem, addixissem, non tantum toto illo | tempore singulare eius clementiss: erga me affectionis studium expertus sum: sed postea quoq[ue];, voce tandem | mea in virilem mutari incipiente, Illustriss: Celsitud: eius sumtibus, primum in celebri Schola Portensi, & deinde | in inclita Academia Lipsensi, ut literis humanioribus operam darem, clementissimè sustentatus sui. Qua Illu- | striss: Celsit: eius in me clementia, ac beneficentia prorsus paterna, me Illustriss: Electorali domui Saxoniæ universæ, inprimis verò | Illustriss: C. T. Princeps Christianissime, quò ad vixero, ad omnia gratitudinis officia præstanda (quod utinam per tenuitatem me- | am liceret) devinctum esse agnosco. Collegi autem hoc tempore, instinctu & monitis quorundam magni nominis Virorum, selectis- | simas quasdam Cantilenas, à præstantissimis nostræ ætatis Musicis compositas, & ex Italia ad me allatas, quæ, quanquam non tam vi- | va voce expeditè cantari, quàm omnis generis instrumentis summo cum artificio & suavitate accommodari possint : nusquam tamen | hactenus, his præsertim in locis visas esse existimo, ut solicite multi de iis inquisiverint. Quæ cum ita se habeant, occasionem mihi | nullo modo negligendam grati animi significationem aliquam ostendendi oblatam esse existimavi, si has cantiones sub Illustriss: C. T. | nomine, insigniis, ac patrocinio in publicum emitterem, eidemq[ue]; inscriberem ac consecrarem. Eas igitur nunc typis editas, Illustriss: | C. T. offero, humilimè debitaq[ue], animi subjectione rogans, ut hanc, licet se indignam dedicationem consueto benignitatis vultu acci- | pere, ipsisq[ue]; Cantionibus inter solennes epulas, propter Autorum saltem excellentiam, ad sui aliorumq[ue]; Magnatum, qui Illustriss: C. T. | crebro ac certatim invisunt, delectationem ac recreationem uti, sibiq[ue]; hunc meum qualemcunq[ue]; laborem commendatum habere di- | gnetur. Ad me quod attinet, sedulam dabo operam, ne Illustriss: Cels: T. reverentiam, obedientiam, sidem in me desiderare possit: | meq[ue]; Il8. | Illustriss: Celsitud: T. | addictissimus servus, | Fridericus Lindenerus Ligniceusis Silesius.

SURVIVING LOCATIONS:

Graz, Universitätsbibliothek (A-Gu), A, B
Vienna, Österreichische Nationalbibliothek (A-Wn), S, A, T, 5 incomplete
Augsburg, Staats- und Stadtbibliothek (D-As), 2 copies
*Bayerische Staatsbibliothek München (D-Mbs), Musikabteilung: 4° Mus. pr. 2718, T
Dresden, Sächsische Landesbibliothek (D-Dl), complete
Flensburg, Bibliothek des Staatlichen Gymnasiums (D-FLs), S
Freiburg i. B., Universitätsbibliothek (D-FR), S, A, 5
Hamburg, Staats- und Universitätsbibliothek (D-Hs), complete
Kassel, Murhardsche Bibliothek (D-Kl), 2 copies
Regensburg, Proskesche Musikbibliothek (D-Rp), complete
Zwickau, Ratsschulbibliothek (D-Z), complete
London, British Library (GB-Lbl), S, 5
Danzig, Biblioteka Polskiej Akademii Nauk (PL-GD), complete
Warsaw, Biblioteka Narodowa (PL-Wn), S, A, 5
Uppsala, Universitetsbiblioteket (S-Uu), complete

2.   Title page and dedicatory preface to Friedrich Lindner, *Liber secundus Gemmae musicalis: selectissimas varii stili cantiones.* Nuremberg: Katharina Gerlach, 1589; RISM B/I, 1589⁸.

LIBER SECVNDVS | GEMMAE MV- | SICALIS: | *SELECTISSIMAS VARII STILI* | *CANTIONES, QVAE MADRIGALI ET NAPO-* | *litane Italis dicuntur, Quatuor,* *Quinque, Sex &* | *plurium vocum, continens.* | Quarum omnium versa pagina accuratissimum Indicem (qui & Musicorum, è quorum monumentis sumtæ sunt, | nomina prodet) exhibebit. Editæ studio & opera FRIDERICI LINDNERI, S.P.Q. NO- | RIBERGENSI à cantionibus. | CANTO. | NORIBERGAE, | EX TYPOGRAPHIA MVSICA CATHA- | RINAE GERLACHIAE. | [rule] | *M. D. LXXXIX.*

DEDICATION, Fols 2r-3r (all partbooks)

MAGNIFICO VIRO, | NOBILITATE GENERIS, OMNI- | BVSQVE VIRTVTVM ORNAMENTIS ET | multiplici rerum usu & experientia prædito, Domino CAROLO | ALBERTINELLO Florentino, Domino | & fautori suo suspiciendo, | S. P. D. | *CVM ANTE MENSES AB HINC NON MVLTOS, CA-* | *ROLE nobilißime, interpellantibus me diversorum loco-* | *rum Musicis atq[ue] cantoribus, primam eius generis can-* | *tionum, quas Madrigaletti & Napolitane vocant, par-* | *tem, ex præcipuorum in Italia artificum, quæ quidem hoc* | *tempore ad nos pervenere, monumentis collectam, edidis-* | *sem; eamq[ue] singulari favore & approbatione Philomusorum exceptam esse* | *animadvertissem: placuit, ut Typographo nostro seduolo efflagitanti morem* | *gererem, & hanc secundam partem, quam non minore studio & delectu ex* | *celebratißimorum totius Italiæ Musicorum exemplaribus collegi, & aliquot* | [fol. 2v] *hactenus non impressarum, non tamen minus suavium cantionum acceßione* | *auxi, typis evulgare: Quæ quidem omnes & ipsæ (meo judicio) ita composi-* | *tæ at que elaboratæ sunt, ut cum primæ partis cantionibus non infeliciter cer-* | *tare, & concentus dulcedine illas si non vincere, æquare saltem videantur.* | *Hanc cantionum secundam partem, sub tui nominis auspicio, eodemq[ue] titulo,* | *cuius tu ipse autor fuisti, Gemmæ nimirum Musicalis, in publicum prodire* | *volui, CAROLE nobilißime; non quod te his egere existimem, qui domi huius-* | *modi deliciarum instructißimum promtuarium habeas, sed quod tibi in huius* | *artis cognitione & usu exercitatißimo, eas summæ semper voluptati fuisse* | *animadverterim. Deinde cum sæpius, si quid eius modi cantionum ex Italia* | *ab amicis accepisti, eas mecum benigne communicaris, & alioquin jam per* | *aliquot annos me pluribus iisque non contemnendis beneficiis afficeris, volui* | *etiam, tua tibi quasi restituendo, hoc testimonio publico meam ergate obser-* | *vantiam & grati animi significationem ostendere. Fortasse etiam tuo exem-* | *plo aliquorum generosi animi accendentur, ut quoties per occupationes neces-* | *sarias licebit, in huius suavißimæ artis exercitio potius, quàm in aliis frivolis* | *rebus, voluptatem delectationemq[ue] quærant. Oro igitur tuam Magnificen-* | [fol. 3r] *tiam quàm officiosißimè, CAROLE nobilißime, ut hoc meum factum in opti-* | *mam partem interpreteris, & me porrò tua benevolentia complecti pergas.* | *Ego quibus potero officiis tuum in me amorem atq[ue] studium demereri conabor.* | *Bene vale, Noribergæ Calendis Februarii, Anno à Christo nato 1 5 8 9.* | *Tuam Magnificent:* | *observans & colens,* | *Fridericus Lindenerus.*

SURVIVING LOCATIONS:

Vienna, Österreichische Nationalbibliothek (A-Wn), S, A, T, 5
Graz, Universitätsbibliothek (A-Gu), A, B
Augsburg, Staats- und Stadtbibliothek (D-As), 2 copies
Dresden, Sächsische Landesbibliothek (D-Dl), complete
*Bayerische Staatsbibliothek München (D-Mbs), Musikabteilung: 4° Mus. pr. 173/4, complete
Flensburg, Bibliothek des Staatlichen Gymnasiums (D-FLs), S
Freiburg i. B., Universitätsbibliothek (D-FR), S, A, 5
Hamburg, Staats- und Universitätsbibliothek (D-Hs), complete
Kassel, Murhardsche Bibliothek (D-Kl), 2 copies
Regensburg, Proskesche Musikbibliothek (D-Rp), complete
Zwickau, Ratsschulbibliothek (D-Z), complete
London, British Library (GB-Lbl), S
Danzig, Biblioteka Polskiej Akademii Nauk (PL-GD), complete
Warsaw, Biblioteka Narodowa (PL-Wn), S, A, 5
Uppsala, Universitetsbiblioteket (S-Uu), complete

3.   Title page and dedicatory preface to Friedrich Lindner, *Tertius Gemmae musicalis liber: selectissimas diversorum autorum cantiones*. Nuremberg: Katharina Gerlach, 1590; RISM B/I, 1590[20].

TERTIVS | GEMMAE MVSI- | CALIS LIBER: | *SELECTISSIMAS DIVERSORVM AVTO-* | *rum cantiones, Italis Madrigali & Napolitane dictas,* | *Octo, Septem, Sex, Quinque & Quatuor vocum* | *continens.* | Nunc primum in lucem editus studio & opera | FRIDERICI LINDNERI. | [within a decorative frame] CANTO. | NORIBERGAE, | Imprimebatur in officina typographica Catharinæ Gerlachiæ. | *M. D. XC.*

DEDICATION, Fols 2r-v (all partbooks)

NOBILITATE GENERIS, | PIETATE, VIRTVTE AC DOCTRINA | ORNATISSIMO DOMINO ONOPHRIO ZOLE- | KOFERO, Patricio Sangallensi, Domino suo offi- | ciosè colendo, S. D. | *ETSI mihi persuaseram, editione duarum partium, quæ* | *titulo Gemmæ Musicalis anno superiore seorsim prodierunt, Amatori-* | *bus Musicæ à me abundè satisfactum, eorumq*[ue] *desiderium ita exsatia-* | *tum fuisse, ut talis mea opera non usq*[ue] *adeo requiri deberet amplius, sicut* | *& omni hoc editionis labore supersedere in posterum, vel hac quoq*[ue]*, de caus-* | *sa decreveram, ne malevolis quibusdam meis (qui ut omnia, ita & hoc* | *meum studium atq*[ue] *laborem carpunt, metuentes scilicet, ne apud Philo-* | *musos gratiolam aliquam ineam) quid amplioris molestiæ inferrem: Quia* | *vero Musicæ Fautores, qui huius nobilißimæ artis suavitate excitati, non hîc tantum, sed & in Ele-* | *ctorum atq*[ue] *Principum Aulis quotidiè augentur, me & scriptis & verbis interpellare non desinunt,* | *hortantes, ut non tertiam tantum, sed & quartam, imo & quintam partem, prioribus, si poßim, ad-* | *jungam, existimavi, eorum me judicia atq*[ue] *autoritatem malevolorum calumniis* *meritò anteferre | debere. Passus igitur sum me impelli, ut tertiæ quoq*[ue] *partis (in qua florem eius modi cantionum com- | plexus mihi videor) collectionem atq*[ue] *editionem adgrederer, præsertim cum intelligam, hoc meum | studium ab ipsis etiam Autoribus in Italia non improbari, ut qui & originalia (ut vocant) ad me | mittant, & exemplaria hîc excusa, magno numero ad se reportari curent. Cogitanti vero mihi, | cui hanc Tertiam partem inscriberem, quò & ipsa, sicut priores duæ, non sine patrono emitteretur, | venit ante alios mihi in mentem tua præstantia, ornatißime Domine Onophri, quòd nobis exercendæ | Musicæ gratia congregatis, sæpenumero depræhenderim te & Autores, quorum opera hac parte con- | [fol. 2v] tinentur, ob singularem in hac arte suavitatem atq*[ue] *usum, vehementer probare, & eorum cantio- | nes, quoties per negocia atq*[ue] *occupationes licet, non canendo tantum, sed & Musicis instrumentis | accommodatas non sine singulari voluptate privatim atq*[ue] *domi tuæ exercere. Deinde cum per annos | aliquot hactenus, ob qualemcunq*[ue] *artis Musicæ usum, me non indignum tua familiaritate judicâris, | & benevolentis animi indicia, non sine multorum in me beneficiorum quasi cumulo, sæpe declarâris, | volui etiam hac de caussa cantiones istas tuo nomini inscribere, ut mei ergate grati animi publica | extaret significatio. Peto igitur à te ornatißime Domine Onophri, ut hoc meum qualecunq*[ue] *studi- | um tuo favore comprobes, meq*[ue]*, si ita mereri videbor, tua benevolentia complecti non desinas. Ego | quibuscunq*[ue] *potero officiis, tuam erga me animi propensionem retinere atq*[ue] *demereri conabor. Vale. | Datum Noribergæ in die Omnium Sanctorum, Anno Christi 1589. | T. Præstantiam | colens & observans, | Fridericus Lindenerus, | Cantor ad D. Ægidii.*

SURVIVING LOCATIONS:

Vienna, Österreichische Nationalbibliothek (A-Wn), S, A, T, 5
Augsburg, Staats- und Stadtbibliothek (D-As), complete
Dresden, Sächsische Landesbibliothek (D-Dl), complete
*Bayerische Staatsbibliothek München (D-Mbs), Musikabteilung: 4° Mus. pr. 2718/2, complete
Flensburg, Bibliothek des Staatlichen Gymnasiums (D-FLs), S
Freiburg i. B., Universitätsbibliothek (D-FR), S, A, 5
Kassel, Murhardsche Bibliothek (D-Kl), 2 copies
Regensburg, Proskesche Musikbibliothek (D-Rp), complete
Zwickau, Ratsschulbibliothek (D-Z), complete
London, The British Library (GB-Lbl), S
Danzig, Biblioteka Polskiej Akademii Nauk (PL-GD), complete
Warsaw, Biblioteka Narodowa (PL-Wn), S, A, 5

4.   Title page and dedicatory preface to Valentin Haussmann, *Ausszug auss Lucae Marentii vier Theilen seiner Italianischen dreystimmigen Villanellen und Napolitanen.* **Nuremberg: Paul Kauffmann, 1606; RISM A/I, M611.**

Außzug | AUß *Lucæ Marentii* vier | Theilen seiner Italianischen dreystim= | migen Villanellen vnd Napolitanen/ so | zuvor in Teutschland nicht vil | gesehen worden. | Dem *Autori* zu Ehren/ vnd de= | nen/ so der Italianischen Sprach nicht | kundig/ zu besserm gebrauch jetzo mit Teutschen | Texten gezieret/ vnnd inn | Truck publiciert | von | *Valentino Haussmanno Gerbipol.* | *CANTVS.* [enclosed in decorative frame] | Gedruckt zu Nürmberg/ durch | Paulum Kauffmann. | [rule] | *M D C V I.*

DEDICATION, fol. 2r (all partbooks)

Dem Ehrnvesten vnd Für= | nemen Wolff Rehlein/ Burgern vnd deß grös= | sern Raths zu Nürnberg/ der löblichen Music sonders | Liebhabern vnd Patronen/ meinem gün= | stigen Herrn. | Ehrnvester vnnd Fürnemer/ Günstiger Herr/ man | findet ihrer viel/ die kein Italianisch wort verstehen/ vnnd | gleichwol inn derselben Sprache die Italianischen Gesänge | gerne singen/ zum theil das solche *Compositiones* für an= | dern gemeiniglich künstlich vnd anmutig/ eins theils auch | daß die Italianisch Sprach an im selbst lieblich ist. Weil es | aber lächerlich vnd seltzam scheinet/ die wort singen/ vnd *mo=* | *re Psittaci* nicht wissen was einer singet/ So habe ich | auß meines guten Freundes deß *Typographi* anleitung | mich bewegen lassen/ vnnd auff deß weitberhümten *Lucæ* | *Marentii* etliche dreystimmige Italianische Liedlein/ dem | *Autori* zu sonderm Rhum/ vnnd denen/ welche der Ita= | lianischen Sprach nicht kundig/ zu besserm gebrauch/ Teutsche Texte gemacht/ vnd inn | Truck übergeben/ damit auch etwas Teutsches von dreyen Stimmen/ der sonst nicht | vil zu finden/ möchte vorhanden sein/ wie ich dann dergleichen Italianische *Tricinia* | mehr für die Hand zu nemen/ vnd mit Teutschen Texten zuverwechßlen/ gesinnet bin/ | wen[n] ich ein angenemes werck hierauß spüren werde. Dises aber deß *Marentii* von mir | mit Teutschen Texten *colligierte* Wercklein Eur Ehrnvest zuzuschreiben hat mich ver= | vrsacht/ nicht das E. E. der Italianischen Sprach/ die sie gar wol verstehet/ vnerfahren | sein solte/ sondern weil sie zu disem Componisten eine grosse beliebung trägt/ vnnd an Teutschen wol geschickten Poetischen Texten ein gefallen hat/ daß ir dise Text vnter | den Marentianischen Noten desto angenemer sein möchten/ Fürnemlich aber E. E. zu- | spüren hette/ es sey die vor zweyen Jaren zu Nürnberg mir erzeigte Gunst vn[d] Gutthat | in kein vergessen gestellt. Wie dann E. E. mein danckbarlich gemüthe hierauß schliessen/ | vnnd dises *Munusculum* vnter frembder *Composition*, biß zu füglicher gelegenheit | meiner eigenen/ für guten willen annemen/ auch mein günstiger Herr vnd Patron/ | deme ich zu ferner Gunst dienstlich hiemit mich befelhen thu/ sein vnnd bleiben wölle. | Gerbstett/ den *12. Iunii, Anno 1606.* | E. Ehrnv. | Dienstgefliessener | Valentinus Haußmann *Gerbipol.*

SURVIVING LOCATIONS:

Basel, Universitätsbibliothek (CH-Bu), T, B
Hamburg, Staats- und Universitätsbibliothek (D-Hs), C, T [2 copies], B

*Ulm, Von Schermar'sche Familienstiftung (D-Usch), complete [Faksimile-Edition Schermar-Bibliothek Ulm, 24 (Stuttgart: Cornetto-Verlag, 1997)]
Wolfenbüttel, Herzog August Bibliothek (D-W), complete
London, The British Library (GB-Lbl), C, T
Budapest, Országos Széchényi Könyvtár (Bibliothèque nationale Széchényi (H-Bn), B
Cracow, Biblioteka Jagiellońska (PL-Kj), complete
Lublin, Biblioteka Katolickiego Uniwersytetu (PL-Lk), T, B

5. **Title page and dedicatory preface to Valentin Haussmann,** *Canzonette,* *mit dreyen Stimmen, Horatii Vecchi unnd Gemignani Capi Lupi.* **Nuremberg: Paul Kauffmann, 1606; RISM A/I, V1034=RISM B/I 1606[13].**

CANZONETTE, | mit dreyen Stimmen/ | *Horatii Vecchi* vnnd *Gemi-* | *gnani Capi Lupi,* zuvor mit Italianischen | Texten/ jetzo aber zu besserm gebrauch denen/ welche | Italianisch nicht verstehen/ mit Teutschen | Texten beleget/ vnd inn | Truck gegeben | Durch | Valentin Haussmann | *Gerbipol.* | *CANTVS.* [enclosed in decorative frame] | Gedruckt zu Nürmberg/ durch | Paulum Kauffmann. | [rule] | *M D C V I.*

DEDICATION, fol. 2r (all partbooks)

Den Ehrbaren vnd Fürne= | men Hanns vnd Georg Losen Gebrüdern/ | Burgern zu Nürmberg/ Meinen günstigen | lieben Herren. | Ehrbare vnnd fürneme insonders günstige liebe | Herren/ Ich habe neulich vnter deß fürtrefflichsten *Lucæ* | *Marentii* dreystimmige *Canzonette* Teutsche Text gesetzt/ | vnd in offnem Truck außgehen lassen. Vnd weil ich gesehen/ | daß vielen der *Music* Liebhabern/ bevorab denen/ so die Wel= | schen Text nicht verstehen/ ein sonders gefallen daran besche= | hen/ Als habe ich mich der fernern mühe vnterfangen/ vnnd vnter deß *Horatii* | *Vecchi* vnnd *Gemignani Capi Lupi Canzonette,* auch dergleichen Text ge= | macht/ vnd in offnen Truck verfertigt. Daß ich sie aber E. E. zuschreibe/ beschicht | der vrsachen/ daß mir wol bewußt/ daß sie ihnen nicht allein die Teutschen Text | wol gefallen lassen/ sonder auch *in Instrumentali & vocali Musica* selbsten wol | geübet/ vnd also sonderliche *Fautores* vnd Liebhaber derselbigen seyen. Bitt der= | wegen dienstlich/ E. E. wöllen solch geringes Werck von mir im besten an vnnd | auffnemen/ auch hinfüro/ wie bißher/ meine günstige Herren vnd Förderer sein | vnd bleiben. *Datum* Gerbstett/ den *24. Augusti, Anno 1606.* | E. Ehrb. | Dienstwilliger |Valentin Haußmann | *Gerbipol.*

SURVIVING LOCATIONS:

Hamburg, Staats- und Universitätsbibliothek (D-Hs), complete
Tübingen, Eberhard-Karls-Universität, Universitätsbibliothek (D-Tu), T
*Ulm, Von Schermar'sche Familienstiftung (D-Usch), complete [Faksimile-Edition Schermar-Bibliothek Ulm, 32 (Stuttgart: Cornetto-Verlag, 1997)]
Wolfenbüttel, Herzog August Bibliothek (D-W), complete
Paris, Bibliothèque nationale (ancien fonds du Conservatoire

national de musique (F-Pc), C, B
Cracow, Biblioteka Jagiellońska (PL-Kj), C, B

6.   Title page and dedicatory preface to Valentin Haussmann, *Johann-Jacobi Gastoldi und anderer Autorn Tricinia*. Nuremberg: Paul Kauffmann, 1607; RISM A/I, GG553a=RISM B/I, 1607[25].

JOHANN-JACOBI | *GASTOLDI* vnd anderer Autorn | *TRICINIA*, | Welche zuvor mit Italiani= | schen Texten componiert/ jetzo aber denen/ so | dieselbige Sprach nicht verstehen/ zu besserm nutz vnd | gebrauch/ mit Teutschen Weltlichen Texten | in Truck gegeben | Durch | Valentinum Haussmann | *Gerbipol*. | *CANTVS I.* [enclosed in decorative frame] | Gedruckt zu Nürmberg/ durch | Paulum Kauffmann. | rule |
M D C V I I.

DEDICATION, fol. 2r (all partbooks)

Dem Erbarn Georg Gru= | ber/ Burgern in Nürmberg/ Meinem | in sonders günstigen vertrauten | lieben Freund. | ERbarer günstiger lieber Freund/ | Was sonderliche lust vnd beliebung ihr zu der | Edlen *Music*, vnnd derselben Zugethanen/ traget/ ist | meniglich vnverborgen. Derwegen nicht vnbillich/ daß | ihr von derselben widerumb geehret vnd geliebet werdet. | Vnd demnach dann auch ich/ inn dere von so vil Jaren | hero gehabten Kunthschafft/ euer geneigtes treuhertziges | Gemüth gegen mir jederzeit gespüret: Als hab ich mich | mit gegenwertigen deß *Gastoldi Triciniis*, darunter ich/ wie hiebevorn vnter deß | *Marentii, Vecchii* vnd *Capi Lupi* beschehen/ Teutsche Text gesetzt/ gegen euch | der mal eines auch danckbar erzeigen wöllen/ mit dienstlicher bitte/ dieselben von | mir im besten an und auffzunemen/ vnnd wie bißher/ also hinfort mein günstiger | Freund vnd Beförderer sein vnd bleiben. Gerbstett am *21. Decembris, An-* | *no 1606.* | Euer guter | Freund | Valentin Haußmann.

SURVIVING LOCATIONS

Frankfurt am Main, Stadt- und Universitätsbibliothek, Musik- und Theaterabteilung (D-F), complete
Hamburg, Staats- und Universitätsbibliothek (D-Hs), complete
Tübingen, Eberhard-Karls-Universität, Universitätsbibliothek (D-Tu), C2
*Ulm, Von Schermar'sche Familienstiftung (D-Usch), complete [Faksimile-Edition Schermar-Bibliothek Ulm, 40 (Stuttgart: Cornetto-Verlag, 1998)]
Wolfenbüttel, Herzog August Bibliothek (D-W), complete
Paris, Bibliothèque nationale (ancien fonds du Conservatoire national de musique) (F-Pc), C1
London, The British Library (GB-Lbl), C2
Cracow, Biblioteka Jagiellońska (PL-Kj), C1, B

7.   Title page and dedicatory preface to Valentin Haussmann, *Liebliche Fröliche Ballette mit 5. Stimmen, welche zuvor von Thoma Morlei unter Italianische Texte gesetzt.* Nuremberg: Paul Kauffmann, 1609; RISM A/I, M3700.

Liebliche Fröliche *Ballette* | mit 5. Stimmen/ welche zuvor von *Thoma* | *Morlei* vnter Italianische texte gesetzt/ jetzo aber/ zu besserm ge= | brauch denen so der Italianischen sprache vnkündig/ mit | vnterlegung Teutscher texte auffs Neue | inn truck gegeben | Durch | Valentinum Haussmann | *Gerbipol.* | *CANTVS.* [enclosed in decorative frame] | Gedruckt zu Nürnberg / bey vnd in ver= | legung Paul Kauffmanns. | rule | *M D C I X.*

DEDICATION, fol. 1v (all partbooks)

Dem Edlen Gestrengen vn[d] | Ehrnvesten Gebharten Johann von Alvenß= | leben/ Erbgesessen auff Eychenparleben vnd Erx= | leben &c. meinem großgünstigen Junckherrn. | EDler/ Gestrenger vn[d] Ehrnvester/ Großgünstiger | Junckher/ es kommen auß Italien vil schöne gesang zu vns | in Teutschla[n]d/ so von dem mehrern theil on verstand der texte | musicirt vnd gesungen werden. Daher ich mich durch guter | freunde anhalten bewegen lassen/ vnter etliche Italianische | gesang Teutsche texte zu legen/ vnd dem *Typographo*, neben andern meiner eig= | nen *composition* biß anhero außgegangenen Wercken mit zu theilen/ wie dann | mit des *Marentii, Vecchi* vnd *Gastoldi Triciniis* von mir geschehen. Weil | dann des *Thomæ Morlei Ballette*, welche sonst in Italianischer sprach auß= | gangen/ aber in Teutschland nicht vil gesehen werden/ eine feine liebliche art vnd | zur frölligkeit nicht undienlich ist/ hab dieselben/ mit vnterlegung Teutscher weltli= | cher texte/ zu besserm nutz denen so der Italianischen sprach nicht kundig/ gleicher | gestalt in truck zu übergeben/ vnd E. Gestr. als der löblichen Music liebhaber/ | fürnemlich auch daß dieselbe meinem gebiettende[n] günstigen Junckherrn Gebhart | von Alvenßleben &c. mit naher Blutfreundschafft verwandt/ zu dediciren/ vnd zu | dero neuem angefangenen Ehestande glück zu wünschen/ ich nicht vnterlassen | wöllen/ der guten zuversicht/ E. Gestr: werde es im besten von mir annemen/ | mein wolmeinend gemüth hierauß vermercken/ vn[d] mein günstiger Junckher sein | vnd bleiben: E. Gestr: hiemit mich dienstlich befehlend. Datum Gerbstett/ | den *26. Martii*, im Jar *1609.* | E. Gestr: | dienstgeflissener | *Valentinus Hausmann. Gerbipol:*

SURVIVING COPIES

Bautzen, Stadt- und Kreisbibliothek (D-BAUk), C, A, T, B
*Hamburg, Staats- und Universitätsbibliothek (D-Hs): 1 an. Scrin. A/580, complete
Tübingen, Eberhard-Karls-Universität, Universitätsbibliothek (D-Tu), A, T, 5
New Haven, Yale University, The Library of the School of Music (US-NH), 5
Cracow, Biblioteka Jagiellońska (PL-Kj), complete
Wroclaw, Biblioteka Uniwersytecka (PL-Wru), A, T, B

8.   Title page to Valentin Haussmann, *Die erste Class, der vierstimmigen Canzonetten Horatii Vecchi*. Nuremberg: Paul Kauffmann, 1610; RISM A/I, V1035=RISM B/I, 1610[19]. [no dedication]

Die erste Claß | DEr vierstim[m]igen *Can-* | *zonetten Horatii Vecchi*, wel= | che zuvor von ime mit Italianischen Texten com= | poniert / vnd ietzo den jenigen/ welchen die Italianische spra= | che nicht bekandt ist/ zu mehrer ergetzligheit vnd besserm gebrauch / | mit unterlegung Teutscher Texte auffs neue | inn Druck gebracht/ | durch | Valentinum Haussmann | *Gerbipol.* | *CANTUS*. [enclosed in decorative frame] | Gedruckt zu Nürnberg/ bey vnd in ver= | legung Paul Kauffmanns. | rule | *M D C X*.

SURVIVING COPIES

Berlin, Staatsbibliothek zu Berlin, Preußischer Kulturbesitz (D-Bsb), C, B
*Göttingen, Niedersächsische Staats- und Universitätsbibliothek (D-Gs): 8
MUS VI, 750: Cantus I, complete
Tübingen, Eberhard-Karls-Universität, Universitätsbibliothek (D-Tu), A, T
Legnica, Biblioteka Towarzystwa Przyjaciól Nauk (PL-Letpn), B
Lublin, Biblioteka Katolickiego Uniwersytetu (PL-Lk), A
Warsaw, Biblioteka Narodowa (PL-Wn), C
The copy of the work at Darmstadt, Hessische Landes- und Hochschulbibliothek, Musikabteilung (D-DS) was destroyed during World War II.

9.   Title page to Valentin Haussmann, *Die ander Class Der vierstimmigen Canzonetten Horatii Vecchi*. Nuremberg: Paul Kauffmann, 1610; RISM A/I, V1036. [no dedication]

Die ander Claß | DEr vierstim[m]igen *Can-* | *zonetten Horatii Vecchi*, wel= | che zuvor von ime mit Italianischen Texten com= | poniert/ vnd ietzo den jenigen/ welchen die Italianische spra= | che nicht bekandt ist/ zu mehrer ergetzligheit vnd besserm gebrauch/ | mit vnterlegung Teutscher Texte auffs neue | inn Druck gebracht/ | durch | Valentinum Haussmann | *Gerbipol.* | *CANTUS*. [enclosed in decorative frame] | Gedruckt zu Nürnberg/ bey vnd in ver= | legung Paul Kauffmanns. | rule | *M D C X*.

SURVIVING COPIES

Berlin, Staatsbibliothek zu Berlin, Preußischer Kulturbesitz (D-Bsb), C, B
*Göttingen, Niedersächsische Staats- und Universitätsbibliothek (D-Gs): 8 MUS
VI, 750: Cantus, 2, complete
Tübingen, Eberhard-Karls-Universität, Universitätsbibliothek (D-Tu), A, T
Legnica, Biblioteka Towarzystwa Przyjaciól Nauk (PL-Letpn), B
Lublin, Biblioteka Katolickiego Uniwersytetu (PL-Lk), A
Warsaw, Biblioteka Narodowa (PL-Wn), C

10. **Title page to Valentin Haussmann,** *Die dritte Class Der vierstimmigen Canzonetten Horatii Vecchi.* **Nuremberg: Paul Kauffmann, 1610; RISM A/I, V1037.** [no dedication]

Die dritte Claß | DEr vierstim[m]igen *Can-* | *zonetten Horatii Vecchi*, wel= | che zuvor von ime mit Italianischen Texten com= | poniert/ vnd ietzo den jenigen/ welchen die Italianische spra= | che nicht bekandt ist/ zu mehrer ergetzligheit vnd besserm gebrauch/ | mit vnterlegung Teutscher Texte auffs neue | inn Druck gebracht/ | durch | Valentinum Haussmann | *Gerbipol.* | *CANTUS.* [enclosed in decorative frame] | Gedruckt zu Nürnberg/ bey vnd in ver= | legung Paul Kauffmanns. | rule | *M D C X.*

SURVIVING COPIES

Berlin, Staatsbibliothek zu Berlin, Preußischer Kulturbesitz (D-Bsb), C, A (incomplete), B
*Göttingen, Niedersächsische Staats- und Universitätsbibliothek (D-Gs): 8 MUS VI, 750: Cantus, 3, complete
Tübingen, Eberhard-Karls-Universität, Universitätsbibliothek (D-Tu), A, T
Legnica, Biblioteka Towarzystwa Przyjaciól Nauk (PL-Letpn), B
Lublin, Biblioteka Katolickiego Uniwersytetu (PL-Lk), A
Warsaw, Biblioteka Narodowa (PL-Wn), C

11. **Title page and dedicatory preface to Petrus Neander,** *Vier und Zwantzig Ausserlesene vierstimmige Canzonetten Horatii Vecchi.* **Gera: Martin Spiessen Erben, 1614; RISM A/I, V1038.**

[title page enclosed in decorative frame] Vier vnd Zwantzig | AUßerlesene vier= | stimmige *Canzonetten Horatii Vecchi,* | so hiebevor/ vnter andern/ von ihme mit Ita= | lianischen Texten *componirt*, vnnd jetzo zum bessern | vnd nützlichern Brauch in Kirchen an statt deß *Benedicamus*, auch son= | derlicher Vbung der Jugendt in Schulen/ mit schönen geistlichen Sprü- | chen/ meistentheils auß den Psalmen Davids genommen/ gezie- | tet/ nach Art vnnd Weise der Welschen Reime vnter | gelegt/ vnd in Druck verfertiget/ | Durch | *PETRVM NEANDRVM Iû-* | *trobocensem,* der Reusischen Plawi= | schen Landtschule zu Geraw *Canto-* | *rem figuralem.* | höchste Stimme. [in decorative frame] | *Ad Coloß. 3. Cap.* | Lehret vnd verwahnet euch selbst/ mit Psalmen vnd Lobsängen/ vnd | Geistlichen lieblichen Liedern/ vnd singet dem HErrn in ewren | Hertzen/ etc. | Gedruckt zu Gera/ durch Martin Spiessen | Erben/ Anno 1614.

DEDICATION, fols 2r-v

Dem Wolgebornen vnd | Edlen Herrn/ Herrn Christiano Schenken/ | Freyherrn
in Lautenburg/ vnd Frawen | Brißnitz/ etc. | Vnd | Dem Wolgebohrnen vnnd Edlen
Herrn/ | Herrn Heinrichen dem andern Jüngern/ Herrn Hein= | richen dem dritten
Jüngern/ Reussen/ Herrn von Plawen/ Herrn zu Graitz/ | Crannichfeld/ Geraw/
Schläitz vnd Lobenstein/ | Meinen gnädigen Herren. | WOlgeborne/ Edle vnd Gnädige
| Herren/ Demnach ich innerhalb sechs | Jahren/ in der Reussischen/ Plawischen |
Landschule zu Geraw/ mancherley *Mu-* | *sices exercitia* mit den jungen Knaben/ |
dadurch sie *ad expeditè canendi scien=* | *tiam* desto ehe möchten erwecket/ ge= |
wehnet vnnd gebracht werden/ vor die | Hand genommen/ Vnter welchen ich | auch
etliche vierstimmige/ hochgefaßte | *Canzonetten Horatii Vecchi*, ihnen *proponiret*,
vnd an der Ta= | [fol. 2v] fel vorgeschrieben/ daraus ich der Knaben schleunige
profectus im | singen gespüret vnd vermercket/ dieselbigen aber mit ihren/ vom
Au- | *tore* zugefügten Italiänischen vnnd amorosischen Texten/ bey den | Knaben in
Schulen nicht/ viel weniger in Kirchen zugebrauchen: | Vnd gleichwol die Jugendt
propter singularem harmoniæ suavi- | *tatem*, dadurch zur Musickunst/ gleichsam
inflammiret, vnnd zu mehrerm Ernst/ Fleiß vnd Beliebung gereitzet vnnd getrieben
wer= | den. |
   Als habe ich zu förderst den Namen Gottes zu loben/ vnd dann | auch zum
nützlichen Gebrauch beydes in Kirchen vnd Schulen/ son= | derlich aber der Jugendt
zum besten/ sich vnter einander selbsten hier= | innen zu üben/ vier vnd zwantzig
Canzonetten, aus gedachtem/ vor= | trefflichem vnnd kunstreichem *Autore* außlesen/
schöne Biblische | Sprûche darunter *accommodiren*, vnd vnter E.E.E.E.G.G. | G.G.
Name vnd *Patrocinio*, dieselbigen in Druck fertigen/ vnnd | E.E.E.E.G.G.G.G. in
Vnterthänigkeit *dediciren*, vnd hiemit | *offeriren* wollen/ der tröstlichen Hoffnung
vnd Zuversicht/ E.E. | E.E.G.G.G.G. werden Ihnen solch mein geringes/ doch
wolge= | meyntes Wercklein/ nicht vnangenehm seyn lassen/ sondernes in al= | len
Gnaden an vnd auffnehmen/ vnd zu Gottes Lob/ Ehr vnd Preiß/ | auch zur Vbung
vnnd Erlangung der Edlen Musickunst Herrlich | gebrauchen/ vnnd meine gnädige
Herren seyn vnd bleiben. Thue | hiemit E.E.E.E.G.G.G.G. sampt und sonderlich in
Gottes All= | mächtigen Schutz vnd Schirm befehlen. *Datum* Geraw/ *Domi-* | *nica
Reminiscere*, Im Jahr nach der Englischen von Hirten gehör= | ten Music/ 1614. |
E.E.E.E.G.G.G.G. | Vnterthäniger | *Petrus Neander Iütrobocensis*, der | Reussischen
Plawischen Landtschule zu | Geraw *Cantor figuralis*.

SURVIVING COPIES[1]

---

   1   As Ruth I. DeFord notes, the RISM entry incorrectly indicates that the "höchste,"
"vierte," and "tiefste Stimme" are present at the Neustadt/Orla Pfarrarchiv, whereas only the

*Staatsbibliothek zu Berlin – Preußischer Kulturbesitz, Musikabteilung mit Mendelssohn-Archiv: Mus. Ant. Pract. V288, C
Neustadt an der Orla, Evangelisch-Lutherische Kirchgemeinde, Pfarrarchiv (D-NA), B

12.   Title page and dedicatory preface to Martin Rinckart, *Triumphi de Dorothea ... geistliches musicalisches Triumph-Cräntzlein*. Leipzig: Lorenz Köber, 1619; RISM B/I, 1619[16].

TRIUMPHI DE DOROTHEA, | *non illâ Italico-Prophanâ; sed Angelico-cœlesti &* im- | *mortali, id est: MUSICA,* | *sive* | *LAUS MUSICÆ;* | *A Præstantißimis Musicorum Italicorum Coryphœis,* | *OLIM, QUASI ALIUD AGENTIBUS;* | *Sub nomine Dorotheœ cujusdam, 6. vocibus, decantata.* | Das ist/ | Geistliches/ Musicalisches | Triumph=Kräntzlein/ | Von der hochedlen/ vnd recht Englischen Dorothea oder grossen | Gottes Gabe; der Fraw *MUSICA;* | Ihrem vortrefflichem Adel; hohem Alter; eigentlichem Vrsprung; | vielfältiger Art vnd Eigenschafft/ vnzehligem/ ewigwehrendem Brauch/ Nutz vnd | frommen/ auch wunderbaren Göttlichen Krafft vnd Wirckung. | Aus dem/ der aller vortrefflichsten Italiänischen *Componisten,* | *Certamine Musico, Triomphi de Dori* entlehnet: Vnd Gott/ vnd der Kunst zu Ehren: | so wol als allen Geistfrewdigen Musicanten vnd Music=Liebhabern zum *liberali Exercitio,* | lust vnd ergetzung auff solche art vnd weise mit gantz newen Deutschen geistlichen | Texten *exorniret,* | Durch | *M. MARTINUM RINCKHARDUM* | *Illebergensem; Musico-philum sempiternum.* | *CANTUS.* | Was lebt vnd shwebt/ sing frölich/ | Vnsere Kunst bleibt ewig. | [rule] | Leipzig/ | Gedruckt bey Lorentz Kober/ in vorlegung Bartholomæi Voigts/ | Im Jahr 1619.

DEDICATION (Tenor partbook only, fols 2v-4v)

Dedication Schrifft.

Ehrwürdige/ Ehrnveste/ Achtbare/ Hoch vnd | Wolgelahrte/ Wolweise/ auch Erbare/ großgünsti= | ge vnd günstige Herren vnd Freunde/ Ewer Acht= | bare/ Ehrwürden/ Ehrenvesten/ Weißh. vnd | Gunsten verehr ich mit gegenwertiger einer erbarn | vnd recht tugentsamen Jungfrawen Dorotheen/ | so ihrer ankunfft vnd herkommens himlisch vnd | Englishes Geschlechts/ doch weiland in *Italia* in zimliche Abgötterey | gerathen/ nun mehr aber durch Gottes Gnad wiederumb darauß er= | rettet/ vn[d] zum wahren Christenthum[m] bracht/ mit solcher gelegenheit.

   Es haben sich vor Jahren ihrer ohn gefehr/ ein oder 30. der al= | ler vortrefflichsten/ mehrentheils Welschen Componisten an jetzt ge= | dachter Jungfraw *inamoriret* vnd verliebet/ also vnd dermassen/ daß | sie darüber in ein ernstes *Certamen* kommen/

---

bass ("vierte und tiefste Stimme") is located there (Orazio Vecchi, *Orazio Vecchi: The Four-Voice Canzonettas. With Original Texts and Contrafacta by Valentin Haussmann and Others*, ed. Ruth I. DeFord, Recent Researches in the Music of the Renaissance, 92-3 [Madison, WI: A-R Editions Inc., 1993], part 1, p. 14)

vnd sich so weit verglie= | chen/ daß ihr ein jeder in einem besondern Meistergesang/ nach seinem | eussersten vnd besten Vermögen/ die *laudes* preisen/ vnd seine Kunst | an ihr beweisen solte vnd wolte: Vnd welcher nun hierinnen vor an= | dern würde das beste thun/ der solte auch den Triumphs Krantz/ zu= | sampt der Jungfraw haben vnd behalten. In welchem *Certamine*, | wie sich ein jeder erzeiget vnd verhalten/ vnd was sie in gesampt vor | Kunst vnd Fleiß *adhibiret* vnd gebrauchet/ ist nicht allein leicht zu er= | achten/ sondern auch nun mehr beydes allhier in diesem *Opusculo*, | (was die *Composition* belanget) so wol als sonsten in offnem Druck | vor Augen: Inmassen sie es denn schon lengsten selber gleich aller | Welt zur *Censur* vnd Urthel vbergeben/ vnd es vmb des gewündsch= | ten Triumphs willen/ *Triomphi di DORI*, oder *Triumphos de DO=* | *ROTHEA intituliret* vnd genennet.

Nun wil man hier von allerley *sententioniren* vnd außgeben/ ja | fast mehr als zu viel darthun vnd beweisen/ es sey von obermelten | künstlern nicht die rechte himlische Dorothea vnd Gottes Gab (die | [fol. 3r] *Musica*) sondern ihrer Welschen vnd Fleischlichen art nach/ ein sch[a]nd= | de *VENUS* genennet vnd angesungen/ welches ich an seinen Ort ge= | stellet seyn lasse. Vnter deß aber/ vnd dieweil die hochgeehrete Doro= | thea (die Musickunst) nicht bey inen damaln befunden/ sondern auch | eben in demselben *Certamine* im werck vnd in der that zum allerhöch= | sten gepreiset vnd beweiset worden: Als bin ich je vnd allezeit die ein= | faltigen/ beständigen Meynung gewesen/ wird auch wol also vnge= | zweiffelt gewiß seyn vnd bleiben/ daß entweder die klugen Weltköpffe/ | ihre Kunst/ die Fraw Musicam/ vnter einer andern/ gleich als fremb= | den vnd irrdischen Dorotheen Namen/ also wissentlich vnd weißlich | verstackt vnd außgegeben/ auff daß sie sich nach Salomonis Regel/ | Prov. 17. verhalten/ vnd nicht selbs so öffentlich loben möchten: oder | aber/ wo das nicht ist/ so werden sie doch deroselben edlen Gab Got= | tes/ zum allerwenigsten vnwissend/ vnd gleich wider ihren willen/ wie | dort Caiphas vom Herrn Christo/ Joh. II. vnd Bileam/ oder auch | Bileams Esel/ Num. 22. 24. dem Volck Gottes das Wort reden/ vnd | die *laudes* haben preisen müssen.

Mit solchen Augen vnd Hertzen hab ich diese Dorotheam/ ihre | Kunst je vnd allezeit angesehen/ mich an irer schöne/ vnd aus der mas= | sen holdseligen Stimme von Hertzen ergetzet/ vnd demnach nicht al= | lein dem allmächtigen Schöpffer vor solche grosse Gnaden Gab in= | niglich gedancket/ sondern auch unlängst mit begebender gelegenheit solch mein wolmeynend *intent* zu *exprimiren* mich vnterfangen/ vnd | je biß weilen eines vnd das ander mit gegenwertigen geistlichen Tex= | ten vnterleget/ biß es endlich wider verhoffen/ durch Gottes Gnad/ | vnd guter Leute antreiben damit so weit kommen/ daß meine liebe | Dorothea von ihrer Welschen Abgötterey völlig erlediget/ vnd nun | mehr/ Gott lob/ gantz lauter vnd Lutherisch worden.

Dieweil denn E. Achtbare/ Ehrw. Ehrnv. Wolw. vnd Gunsten | mit viel vnd ehr ermelten dieser meiner Jungfraw/ theils schon in | [fol. 3v] zimlicher Kundschafft/ allesampt aber mit dero geehrten Vorfahren/ | in recht heiliger *Union* vnd Verbündnüß stehen/ gestalt sie solches mit | ihrer hand *subscription*/ in wolgefasten Cantorey *Legibus* einhellig | bekennen/ wie auch nichts liebers wündschen vnd wollen/

denn daβ gleicher gestalt ihre liebe Kinder vnd Nachkommen/ solche Christliche | *Conjunction* vnd Cantorey Gesellschafft nach vnd mit uns in dem vn[d] | dem zukünfftigen ewigen Frewden Leben glücklich vnd frölich *conti-* | *nuiren* mögen: Als hab ich zu deroselben E. Achtb. Ehrw. Ehrenv. | Wolw. vnd Gunsten/ ich mit diesen/ gleich als *Spoliis Ægyptiacis,* vmb | so viel desto lieber vnd sicherer meinen *recurs* vnd Zuflucht nemen wol= | len/ der vngezweiffelten hoffnung/ sie werden ihnen solchen/ nicht Je= | suitischen/ sondern recht *piam fraudem,* so wol als die mit fug vnd recht | entführte Jungfraw selber/ nicht allein groβgünstig vnd günstig ge= | fallen lassen/ sondern dieselbe auch/ als ein *Umbram gratitudinis/* vor | die mir biβ *dato* erzeigte Gut= vnd Wolthaten/ zu ihrem Groβgünst. | vnd günstigen *Patrocinio* von mir *acceptiren* vnd auffnemen.

Vnd gleich wie diese Meister Gesanglein auff ihrer gantzen *So=* | *cietet* anzahl gerichtet/ vnd einem jeden insonderheit eins/ zu desto | mehrer beliebung vnd Ehrengedächtnüβ *contribuirt* vnd zugeeignet | ist/ wie solches in dieser *Tenor* Stim[m] beym eingang eines jeden zu be= | finden/ Also werden sie auch alle vnd jede nicht allein meine groβgün= | stige vnd günstige Gönner vnd Freunde seyn vnd bleiben/ sondern | auch die viel Ehrengedachte verehrte vnd hiemit *præsentirte* Jung= | fraw/ alle vnd jede/ vnd namhafft die Herren *Seniores* vnd *Emeriti* | *Musici tanquam Tutores & spectatores honorum* ihnen zur *recreation* | vnd ergetzung dieselbe mit anzuhören/ Ihren Kindern aber vnd der | jungen Mannschafft zum *liberali exercitio, recommendiret* vnd befo= | len seyn lassen. Inmassen ich denn mit diesem gantzen Werck auff | die liebe Jugend/ vnd deroselben erbawung vornemlichst gese= | hen/ vnd eben darümb die schöne Englische Locke/ nicht zwar nach | [fol. 4r] Würden/ sondern nach meinem geringen Vermögen/ durch vnd | durch/ von der Fuβsolen an biβ auff die Scheitel/ in allen Stücken | vnd Texten/ *secundum causas & effecta,* höchstes fleisses *commendiret* | vnd gepreiset/ nicht zu dem ende/ daβ sie oder ihre *cultores* sich dessen | vor andern Gaben Gottes vbernemen solten vnd köndten: sondern | dahin ists alles gemeynet vnd gerichtet/ daβ Gott vnd seine Gaben/ | schüldige vnd billiche Ehre/ die liebe studirende Jugend aber/ auch all= | hier bey vns/ wie heutiges Tages/ Gott lob/ allenthalben reichlich vnd | vberflüssig vrsach vnd anlaβ haben möchte/ sich an so Engel=schönem | Frewlein bey zeit zu verlieben/ vnd mit ihr mehr vnd eher/ als mit ei= | ner vppigen *Venus* Kund= vnd Freundschafft zu machen. Auff wel= | chen und keinen andern Zweck auch gleicher gestalt / beschlieβlich und | *protestando* zu gedencken der Geistfrewdige *general-*Schluβ gehet: | Unsere Kunst bleibt ewig / so durch vnd durch behalten / vnd | zum theil gerichtet ist / *ad imitationem illam Italicam,* do sie allezeit se= | tzen: *Viva la bella Dori, id est,* Unsere Dorothea leb vnd bleib ewig: | Zum theil aber vnd viel mehr auff vnsern recht Lutherischen vnd vn= | zweiffelhafften Glauben / daβ wir nicht zweiffeln / sondern fest gläuben | und gewiβ wissen / so gewiβ als wir hier mit gläubigem vnd beständi= | gem Mund vnd Hertzen die *Laudes Dei* anstimmen / so gewiβ vnd | warhafftig werden wir sie dort mit allen außerwehlten im höhern | Chor / frewdig vnd ewig hinauβ singen.

In welcher frewdigen Betrachtung ich E. Achtb. Ehrw. | Ehrenv. Wolw. vnd Gunsten/ diese meine *Primitias Æternita-* | *tis* vnd himlische Jungfraw nochmaln zu trewen händen/ vns | sämptlichen aber mit ir Gott dem allmächtigen zu ewigen Gna=

| den befehle. Eylenberg/ Anno 1619. den 2. Julii/ an wel= | [fol. 4v] chem Tage vorzeiten die hochgebenedeyete Sangmeisterin vnd | Gottes Mutter Maria/ dieses vnser himlisches vnd ewigwe= | rendes Triumph Liedlein glücklich *intoniret* vnnd angestim= | met. | Ewer Achtbarn/ Ehrw. Ehrnv. Wolw. | vnd Gunsten | Dienstgefl. | *M. Mart. Rinckhard* Mitarbeiter | vnd Diener am Wort Gottes.

PREFACES TO PARTBOOKS

CANTUS, fol. 1v

LUTHERUS.

Ego nulli Arti post S.S. Biblia, plus tribuo; quàm | MUSICÆ.

Idem:

Nulla virtutis semina oportet inesse iis; qui Arte | non delectantur Musicâ.

Idem:

Der schönsten/ herrlichsten vnd vortrefflichsten Ga= | ben Gottes/ vnd besten Künste eine ist die Musi= | ca: Der Teuffel erwart ihr nicht/ er ist ihr spin= | nen feind.

Idem:

Sie ist ein Labsal eim betrübten Menschen: vnd eine | halbe Disciplin= vnd Zuchtmeisterin/ die das | Hertz fröhlich/ vnd die Leute gelinder vnd sanfftmü= | tiger/ sittsamer vnd vernünfftiger macht.

Idem:

Musicam hab ich allegeit lieb gehabt. Wer diese | Kunst kan/ der ist gutter art/ vn[d] zu allem geschickt.

ALTUS, fol. 1v

PHILOSOPHUS.

Nihil est tàm expers humanitatis, quod non arte | capiatur et Amore MUSICES.

MEDICUS.

MUSICA est vitæ et sanitatis nutrimentum.

POLITICUS.

MUSICA est clavis Aulæ & promotionis.

THEOLOGUS.

Exercitium Musices, est SENSUS VITÆ | ÆTERNÆ.

TENOR, fols 1v–2r

Fol. 1v

Sirach am 44. & *seq.*

Die berühmeten Leute/ vnd vnsere Väter | nacheinander: als

Enoch/	Noe/	Abraham/	v. 16. 17. 20
Isaac/	Jacob/	Mose/	v. 24. 25. *cap.* 45. v. 1.
Aaron/	Pinchas/	Josua/	v. 7. 28. *cap.* 46. v. 1.
Caleb/	Samuel/	Nathan/	v. 9. 16. *cap.* 47. v. 1.
David/	Salomon/	Elias/	v. 2. 14. *cap.* 48. v. 1.
Elisæus/	Ezechias/	Josias/	v. 13. 19. *cap.* 49. v. 1.
Jeremias/	Hesefiel/	Sorobabel/	v. 9. 10. 13.
Jesus/	Nehemias/	Joseph/	v. 14. 15. 17.

Die Richter/ Könige vnd Propheten/ *cap.* 46. v. 12. *cap.* 48. v. 17. *cap.* 49. v. 12. | ia auch Seth/ Sem vnd Adam/*cap.* 49. v. 19. 10.

Sie haben *MUSICAM* gelernet/ vnd geistliche | Lieder gedichtet.*cap.* 44. v. 5.

Fol. 2r

Denen Ehrwürdigen/ Achtbarn/ Hoch vnd Wolgelar= | ten/ Wolweisen/ auch Erbarn vnd Ehren Wolgeachten/ | Einer gantzen löblichen Cantorey. Gesell= | schafft zu Eylenberg/etc. | Meinen großgünstigen Herren/ geneigten Förderern/ freundlichen *Colle* | *gen/* auch Schwagern Gevattern/ vnd guten Freunden/ etc. | So der Zeit waren:

Dn. Fridricus Lyserus, S. S. Th. D. Superatt.
Dn. Paulus Jenisius Quæstor.
Dn. Adam Papa. [Consules]
Dn. Joannes Müller. [Consules]
Dn. Caspar Zwirner. [Consules]

[Dn.] *Elias Ruthenius Collab.*
[Dn.] *Matthias* Riecheld. *Org.*
[Dn.] *M. Andreas Gödiccus.*
[Dn.] *M. David* Mühlpfort.
[Dn.] *Georgius Fridrich.*

Dn. Jonas Pesserlus, Med. D.

D. M. Nicolaus Bojemus Past. in Monte.

Dn. M. Johannes Heinrici, Diac. in Urbe.

Dn. M. Donatus Borisch. Diac. in Monte.

Dn. Nathanael Roth, Past. Zschepl.

Dn. M. Vvolgangus Phemelius, Curiæ Act.

Dn. Johann Rüdel. [Senatores]

Dn. Johann Röber. [Senatores]

Dn. Sebast. Schubart [Senatores]

Dn. M. Ioann Müller Ludimod.

Dn. Georgius Ulman, Cantor.

[Dn.] *Iohannes* Steinborn.

[Dn.] *Ioachimus* Osterhold.

[Dn.] *Georgius* Hertzog.

[Dn.] *Nicolaus Pönick.*

[Dn.] *Samuel* Vollgnad.

[Dn.] *Christoph* Förster.

[Dn.] *Ieremias* Hund.

[Dn.] *Tobias* Hund.

[Dn.] *Iacobus Alesius.*

[Dn.] *Ambrosius* Kemniß.

[column two bracketed with the inscription: *Cives honoratissimi.*]

QUINTA, fol. 1v

Camerarius

DIVINA MUSICA, non tantum Animos homi- | *num, sed et pisa corpora quodammodo affi-* | *cit.*

Lutherus in Commens. f. 419.

Ein Schuelmeister muß singen konnen/ sonst sehe | ich ihn nicht an.

Augustinus lib. 9. Confes. cap. 7.[2]

Quantum flevi in Hymnis, & canticis suave sonan- | *tis Ecclesiæ vocibus! voces influebant auribus* | *meis*; & *eliquabantur Veritas in cor meum, et ex* | *ea æstuabat inde affectus Pietatis.*

---

2   Powley notes that this passage is incorrectly cited. It is found at the end of chapter 6 (not 7) of the *Confessionum* (Edward Harrison Powley III, "*Il trionfo di Dori*: A Critical Edition," [3 vols, Ph.D. diss., Eastman School of Music, 1974], vol. 2, p. 219).

SEXTA, fol. 1v

Plato in Timæo.

MUSICA generi humano hanc ob causam præci- | *puè data est; ut suaves Cantum* & *concentum* | *audientes cogitemus de corrigendâ dissonan-* | *tia mentis, voluntatis* & *cordis.*

Cicero & *Quintil.*

Quis ignorat, Musicen tantum jam illis antiquis | *temporibus, non studii modò, verùm etiam* | *VENERATIONIS habuisse, ut idem Musici,* | & *Vates* & *Sapientes judicarentur.*

Hinc [Cicero]

Themistocles, cum in Epulis recusasset Lyram, habi- | *tus est indoctior.*

SURVIVING COPIES

*Dreseden, Sächsische Landesbibliothek (D–DI): Mus. 1-C-2, nrs 527–8 (C, A), Mus. 1-C-2, nrs 530–31 (5, 6); Mus. Gri. 23, 10, nr. 529 (T)
Leipzig, Leipziger Städtische Bibliotheken, Musikbibliothek (D-LEm), T (incomplete), 5, 6

13.   Title page and dedicatory preface to Petrus Neander, *Ander Theil Ausserlesener Canzonetten Horatii Vechii*. Gera: Johann Spiess, 1620; RISM A/I, V1039.

[title page enclosed in decorative frame] Ander Theil | AUßerlesener *CAN-* | *ZONETTEN HORATII VECHII,* | zu besserm Brauch vnd Vbung der studierenden Ju= | gend/ mit schönen Psalmen Davids nach Art vnd weise der | Italianischen Verse vnd Reime vntergelegt | vnd in Druck gegeben. | Von | *PETRO NEANDRO,* der Reussischen | Plawischen Landschule *Cantore* | *Figurali.* | [voice designation enclosed in decorative frame] Dritte Stimme. | Singet frölich GOtte der vnser Stärcke ist/ Jauchtzet dem | Gott Jacob/ nehmet die Psalmen/ vnd gebet her die Pau= | cken/ liebliche Harffen mit Psalmen/ etc. Ps. 81. | Werdet voll Geistes vnd redet vnter einander von Psalmen | vnd Lobgesängen vnd Geistlichen Liedern/ Eph. 5. | Gedruckt zu Gera an der Elster/ durch | Johann Spieß/ Im Jahr/ | *M. DC. XX.*

DEDICATION, fols 1v-2r

Nobilibus ac optimæ indolis ac spei adolescen= | *tibus & discipulis.*

Wolffgango Frider. ab Ende.	*Heinrico Meyero.*
Iohanni Heinrico â Zedvvitz.	*Friderico Ammelungie.*
Heinrico Alberti.	*Balduino Conradi.*
Ieremiæ Glasero.	*Tobiæ Habermann.*
Iohanni Dresselio.	*Iosepho Frölichio.*
Martino Enckio.	*Iohanni Conradi.*
Valerio Bohemio.	*Iohanni Erhardo.*
Iohanni Lehr.	*Christiano Reisken.*
Iosepho Graul.	*Christiano Frölichio.*
Esaiæ Amelungio.	*Adamo Auerbachio.*

EDele/ gehorsame vnd vielgeliebte *discipuli*: | Daß die *Musica* vnd Singekunst durch
state vnnd | fleissige Vbung gelernet vnnd erlanget werden muß/ | habt ihr zum theil
genugsam vermerckt vnnd erfahren/ darzu | denn künstliche/ liebliche/ vnnd der
Jugend Stimmen nach be= | queme *Cantiones*/ darinnen sie sich selbsten daheime
exerciren | vnd vben können/ müssen erkohren/ vnd der Jugendt vorgege= | ben
werden.

    Weil mir denn künstlichere/ lieblichere/ vnd ewren Stim= | men vnd
Qualiteten bequemere *Compositiones 4. Vocum* | als gegenwertigen Authoris/ so wol
bey den *Extraneis* als | *Nostratibus Musicis* noch niehe vorkommen. Ob schon |
sonsten allerley schöne vnd kunstreiche *Psalmi, Cantiones* | vnd Fugen/ mit zwo/
drey oder mehr Stimmen von vortreffli= | chen Musicis deutscher Nation sind
außgangen/ vnd zum theil | [fol. 2r] mit grosser Mühe/ bißhero zur Vbung/ an der
Taffel euch vor= | geschrieben worden: So können doch dieselbe nicht so füglich
| ohne den General oder *continuo Basso harmonicè* von | euch gebraucht/ noch
von allen Discipeln *ob iudicij infirmi=* | *tatem* recht abgeschrieben vnd gesungen
werden.

    Als habe ich nochmals/ ewren Vnvermögen *in deicri=* | *bendo* vorzukommen/
etliche Canzonetten *Horatij Vechij,* | weil auß dem vorigen theil schleunige *profectus*
bey vielen | gespürt worden) zu elegiren/ denselben schöne Geistliche Psal= | men
vnd Texte/ nach Art der Italianischen Reime zu vnterle= | gen/ in öffendlichen Druck
zu geben/ vnd euch/ als meinen ge= | liebten Discipeln zu offeriren vnnd dediciren
vor rahtsam | geachtet.

    Offerire/ dedicire vnd befehle demnach euch *amoris er=* | *gò* dieselbe
hiermit/ gantz trewlich vermahnende/ ihr wollet | euch darinnen/ damit ihr/ *iuxta
Dictum D. Bernhardi: Qui* | *corde cantat bis orat,* Gott den HERrn mit Hertz
vnnd | Mund auch zwiefach preisen vn[d] loben/ darzu auch desto schleu= | niger
vn[d] ehe *ad benè canendi perfectionem* gelangen möget/ stäts | vben/ vnnd mich
in gebührenden ferrner achten/ wie ich mit | mehrerm euch jederzeit meine/ auch

lieben. Göttlicher prote= | ction euch sämptlichen/ beneben ewren geliebten Eltern | vnnd Angewandten/ hiermit befehlende. | Datum Gera/ den 25. Augusti/ | Anno *1620.*

SURVIVING COPIES[3]

*Staatsbibliothek zu Berlin – Preußischer Kulturbesitz, Musikabteilung mit Mendelssohn-Archiv: Mus. Ant. Pract. V293, T

---

3   As Ruth I. DeFord notes, RISM incorrectly gives the surviving partbook from this source as the bass (Orazio Vecchi, *Orazio Vecchi: The Four-Voice Canzonettas*, vol. 92, p. 14).

Appendix B

Contents of Music Anthologies

1. *Gemma musicalis ... Liber primus* (Nuremberg, 1588)

COMPOSER	FIRST LINE	FOLIO[a]	EARLIEST PRINTED CONCORDANCE	
			RISM	SHORT TITLE
Twelve-Voice Settings				
Andrea Gabrieli	Ecco Vinegia bella	3v	G58 =1587[16]	Concerti, I–II, Venice
Ten-Voice Settings				
Giovanni Gabrieli	A dio, dolce mia vita. Dialogo	5v	1587[16]	Concerti, I–II, Venice
Alessandro Striggio	D'un si bel foco belta m'incende	7v	none	
Eight-Voice Settings				
Giovanni Gabrieli[b]	A le guancie di rose, ai crin di fila d'oro. Dialogo	9v	1587[16]	Concerti, I–II, Venice
Andrea Gabrieli	Pront'era l'alma mia, pront'il mio amore	10v	1587[16]	Concerti, I–II, Venice
Andrea Gabrieli	E cert'anco di ciò già non mi doglio (seconda parte)	11r	1587[16]	Concerti, I–II, Venice
Andrea Gabrieli	Tirsi, che fai così dolente? Dialogo	11v	1587[16]	Concerti, I–II, Venice
Giovanni Gabrieli	Lieto godea sedendo l'aura che tremolando. Per cantar et sonar	12v	1587[16]	Concerti, I–II, Venice
Alessandro Striggio	Già ninfa, hor voce delle membra scossa e della voce altrui (Amalteo)	13v	none	
Seven-Voice Settings				
Andrea Gabrieli	Io mi sento morir quando non miro. Dialogo	14v	1587[16]	Concerti, I–II, Venice

COMPOSER	FIRST LINE	FOLIO[a]	EARLIEST RISM	PRINTED CONCORDANCE SHORT TITLE
Andrea Gabrieli[c]	Dolce nemica mia, perchè mi vieti. Dialogo	15v	1587[16]	Concerti, I–II, Venice
Andrea Gabrieli	Tirsi morir volea, gl'occhi mirando. Dialogo (Guarini)	16v	1587[16]	Concerti, I–II, Venice
Six-Voice Settings				
Orlande de Lassus	S'io esca vivo (Petrarca)	17v	1579[2]	Corona de madrigali, Venice
Alessandro Striggio	Nasce la pena mia non potendo mirar mio vivo sole	18v	S6950 =1560[22]	Madregali, I, 6vv
Benedetto Pallavicino	Tirsi morir volea, gli occhi mirando di colei ch'adora (Guarini)	19v	P773	Madrigali, I, 5vv, Venice, 1581
Benedetto Pallavicino	Frenò Tirsi il desio ch'havea (seconda parte)(Guarini)	20v	P773	Madrigali, I, 5vv, Venice, 1581
Benedetto Pallavicino	Così moriro i fortunati amanti (terza parte) (Guarini)	21v	P773	Madrigali, I, 5vv, Venice, 1581
Lelio Bertani	Stese la mano Filli, il bel volto tinta di vermiglio	22r	B2115	Madrigali, I, 6vv, Venice, 1585
Lelio Bertani	Mia vita, io non so dire dove s'annid'amore, o ne la fronte vostra	22v	B2115	Madrigali, I, 6vv, Venice, 1585
Lelio Bertani	Cara mia Dafne, a dio, disse partendo a l'apparir del sole	23v	B2115	Madrigali, I, 6vv, Venice, 1585
Lelio Bertani	Qui nacqu'il gran Maron. L'udir quest'onde cantar	24v	B2115	Madrigali, I, 6vv, Venice, 1585
Lelio Bertani	Fortunato terren, cui dat'è in sorte (seconda parte)	25v	B2115	Madrigali, I, 6vv, Venice, 1585
Lelio Bertani	Amatemi, ben mio, perchè sdegn'il mio core ogn'altro cibo	26v	B2115	Madrigali, I, 6vv, Venice, 1585
Lelio Bertani	Tu moristi in quel seno, piccoletta zanzara (Tasso)	27r	B2115	Madrigali, I, 6vv, Venice, 1585
Giovanni de Macque	Vola, vola pensier fuor del mio petto, vanne veloce (Tasso)	27v	M87	Madrigaletti, 6vv, Venice, 1581

COMPOSER	FIRST LINE	FOLIO	EARLIEST PRINTED RISM	CONCORDANCE SHORT TITLE
Five-Voice Settings				
Andrea Gabrieli	Rimanti amor in Sempriterno oblio	28v	1576^5	XIII. autori, 5vv, Venice
Giaches de Wert	D'un si bel foco (Tansillo)	29v	1576^5	XIII. autori, 5vv, Venice
Giaches de Wert	Scorgo tant'alto il lume (Tansillo) (seconda parte)	30r	1576^5	XIII. autori, 5vv, Venice
Claudio Merulo	Io non potria goder	30v	1576^5	XIII. autori, 5vv, Venice
Alessandro Striggio	Le vag' herbette e l'amorose fronde	31v	1576^5	XIII. autori, 5vv, Venice
Giaches de Wert	Sorgi et rischiara al tuo apparir il cielo. Nelle nozze del Prencipe di Mantova	32v	W884	Madrigali, VII, 5vv, Venice, 1581
Giaches de Wert	Scendi, Imeneo. Copia di te si degna (seconda parte)	33v	W884	Madrigali, VII, 5vv, Venice, 1581
Giovanni Pierluigi da Palestrina	Vestiva i colli (Calilupi)	34v	1566^3	Desiderio, II, 5vv, Venice
	Cosi le chiome mie (seconda parte) (Calilupi)	35r	1566^3	Desiderio, II, 5vv, Venice
Luca Marenzio	Liquide perle amor da gl'occhi sparse (L. Pasqualino)	35v	M530	Madrigali, I, 5vv, Venice, 1580
Luca Marenzio	Quando sorge l'aurora ridon l'herbett'e i fiori	36r	M539	Madrigali, II, 5vv, Venice, 1581
Luca Marenzio	Tirsi morir volea, gl'occhi mirando di colei ch'adora (Guarini)	36v	M530	Madrigali, I, 5vv, Venice, 1580
Luca Marenzio	Frenò Tirsi il desio ch'havea (seconda parte) (Guarini)	37r	M530	Madrigali, I, 5vv, Venice, 1580
Luca Marenzio	Cosi moriro i fortunati amanti (terza parte) (Guarini)	37v	M530	Madrigali, I, 5vv, Venice, 1580
Luca Marenzio	Dolorosi martir, fieri tormenti, duri ceppi, empi lacci (Tansillo)	37v	M530	Madrigali, I, 5vv, Venice, 1580

COMPOSER	FIRST LINE	FOLIO	EARLIEST RISM	PRINTED CONCORDANCE SHORT TITLE
Luca Marenzio	Che fà hoggi il mio sole, che fà il mio canto e'l mio suono	38v	M530	Madrigali, I, 5vv, Venice, 1580
Luca Marenzio	Cantava la più vaga pastorella che mai premesse fiori	39r	M530	Madrigali, I, 5vv, Venice, 1580
Luca Marenzio	Deggio dunque partire, lasso, dal mio bel sol che mi dà vita	39v	M539	Madrigali, II, 5vv, Venice, 1581
Luca Marenzio	Io partirò, ma il core si resterà (seconda parte)	40r	M539	Madrigali, II, 5vv, Venice, 1581
Luca Marenzio	Ma voi, caro ben mio, caso che'l corpo (terza parte)	40v	M539	Madrigali, II, 5vv, Venice, 1581
Luca Marenzio	Spuntavan già, per far il mond'adorno, vaghi fioretti	41r	M530	Madrigali, I, 5vv, Venice, 1580
Luca Marenzio	Quando'l mio vivo sol perch'io(seconda parte)	41v	M530	Madrigali, I, 5vv, Venice, 1580
Luca Marenzio	Itene a l'ombra degl'ameni fàggi pasciute pastorelle (Sannazaro)	42v	M539	Madrigali, II, 5vv, Venice, 1581
Luca Marenzio	La bella ninfa mia, ch'al Tebro infiora co'piè le sponde(Molza)	43r	M539	Madrigali, II, 5vv, Venice, 1581
Luca Marenzio	Strider faceva le zampogna a l'aura il pastorel di Filli	43v	M539	Madrigali, II, 5vv, Venice, 1581
Luca Marenzio	Non fu mai cervo sì veloce, Sestina (Sannazaro)	44v	M525	Spirituali, I, 5vv, Venice, 1584
Luca Marenzio	Fallace, incerta e momentanea (seconda parte) (Sannazaro)	45v	M525	Spirituali, I, 5vv, Venice, 1584
Luca Marenzio	Se s'acquetasse l'amorosa (terza parte) (Sannazaro)	46v	M525	Spirituali, I, 5vv, Venice, 1584
Luca Marenzio	Ma lass'io sento che'l pungente (quarta parte) (Sannazaro)	46v	M525	Spirituali, I, 5vv, Venice, 1584
Luca Marenzio	Tal'hor dal cor si mov'un (quinta parte) (Sannazaro)	47v	M525	Spirituali, I, 5vv, Venice, 1584
Luca Marenzio	Signor, tu vedi quant'è oscuro (sesta parte)	48r	M525	Spirituali, I, 5vv, Venice, 1584

COMPOSER	FIRST LINE	FOLIO	EARLIEST RISM	PRINTED CONCORDANCE SHORT TITLE
Luca Marenzio	Dal di ch'io presi il corso (settima parte) (Sannazaro)	48v	M525	Spirituali, I, 5vv, Venice, 1584
Giovanni Maria Nanino	Mentre ti fui si grato (Alamanni)	49r	1582[4]	Dolci affetti, 5vv, Venice
Giovanni Moscaglia	Mentri ti fui si cara (seconda parte) (Alamanni)	49v	1582[4]	Dolci affetti, 5vv, Venice
Luca Marenzio	Hor pien d'alto desio (terza parte) (Alamanni)	50r	1582[4]	Dolci affetti, 5vv, Venice
Giovanni de Macque	Hor un laccio un'ardore (quarta parte) (Alamanni)	50v	1582[4]	Dolci affetti, 5vv, Venice
Francisco Soriano	Lasso dunque che fia (quinta parte) (Alamanni)	51r	1582[4]	Dolci affetti, 5vv, Venice
Annibale Zoilo	Benché senza mentire (sexta parte) (Alamanni)	51v	1582[4]	Dolci affetti, 5vv, Venice
Giovanni Pierluigi da Palestrina	O bella ninfa mia	52r	1582[5]	Il lauro secco, I, 5vv, Ferrara
Giovanni Pierluigi da Palestrina	Io son ferito hai lasso	52v	1561[10]	Muse, III, 5vv, Venice
Four-Voice Settings				
Domenico Ferrabosco	Io mi son giovinetta	53v	1542[17]	Diversi autori, I, 4vv, Venice
Cipriano de Rore	Anchor che col partire io mi sento morire (Alfonso d'Avalos)	54v	R2513	Madrigali, 4vv, Venice, 1577
Baldassaro Donato	O dolce vita mia non mi far guerra ch'io mi ti rendo	55r	D3404	Napollitane, 4vv, Venice, 1550
Baldassaro Donato	Tu mi farai morir ch'io me n'aveggio. Meglio è ch'io muti	55v	D3404	Napollitane, 4vv, Venice, 1550
Baldassaro Donato	Chi dirà mai ch'in donna sia fermezza è matt' in tutt'et dice la busia	56r	D3404	Napollitane, 4vv, Venice, 1550

COMPOSER	FIRST LINE	FOLIO	EARLIEST PRINTED CONCORDANCE RISM	SHORT TITLE
Orazio Vecchi	Mentr'io campai contento, correvano li giorno più che'l vento	56v	V1010	Canzonette, I, 4vv, Venice, 1580
Orazio Vecchi	Occhi ridenti, io moro	57r	V1010	Canzonette, I, 4vv, Venice, 1580
Orazio Vecchi	Son questi i crespi crini e quest'il viso, ond'io rimang' ucciso	57v	V1010	Canzonette, I, 4vv, Venice, 1580
Orazio Vecchi	Chi mira gl'occhi tuoi e non sospira puoi, credo che non è vivo	58r	V1010	Canzonette, I, 4vv, Venice, 1580
Orazio Vecchi	Cosa non vada più come solea, poi che quel nodo (Bembo)	58v	V1010	Canzonette, I, 4vv, Venice, 1580
Orazio Vecchi	Il cor che mi rubasti homai	59r	V1010	Canzonette, I, 4vv, Venice, 1580
Orazio Vecchi	Vaghe ninfe e pastori, lasciat'i primi ardori	59v	V1017	Canzonette, II, 4vv, Venice, 1580
Orazio Vecchi	Hor ch'io son gionto quivi, fra questi boschi et rivi	60r	V1017	Canzonette, II, 4vv, Venice, 1580
Orazio Vecchi	Se pensand'al partire, io mi sento morire	60v	V1017	Canzonette, II, 4vv, Venice, 1580
Orazio Vecchi	Con voce dai sospiri interrotta, dicea un pastor dolente (Zuccarini)	61r	V1022 =1585[35]	Canzonette, III, 4vv, Venice
[Gaspari Pratoneri][d]	Dolce contrade o chius'e cheti valli	61v	1566[2]	Desiderio, I, 4vv, Venice
Hubert Waelrant	Vorria morire per uscir di guai	62r	1585[19]	Symphonia angelica, Antwerp

[a] Foliation follows the tenor partbook, Bayerische Staatsbibliothek München, Musikabteilung: 4° Mus. pr. 2718.

[b] Lindner misattributes the madrigal to Andrea Gabrieli in the Index, fol. 2v. Headline indicates A8; NV1046 indicates A7.

[c] Lindner misattributes the madrigal to Giovanni Gabrieli in the Index, fol. 2v.

[d] Listed as "D'incerto" (implying anonymous) in the Index, fol. 3r.

2. *Liber secundus Gemmae musicalis* (Nuremberg, 1589)

COMPOSER	FIRST LINE	FOLIO[a]	EARLIEST PRINTED CONCORDANCE	
			RISM	SHORT TITLE
Twelve-Voice Settings				
Giovanni Gabrieli	Sacri di Giove augei, sacre fenici	4v	G85 =1587[16]	Concerti, I–II, Venice
Andrea Gabrieli	O passi sparsi, o pensier vaghi (Petrarch)	6v	1587[16]	Concerti, I–II, Venice
Ten-Voice Settings				
Andrea Gabrieli	Del gran tuonante la sorella e moglie	7v	1587[16]	Concerti, I–II, Venice
Andrea Gabrieli	Quei, vinto dal furor, tutto s'asconde (seconda parte)	8v	1587[16]	Concerti, I–II, Venice
Giovanni Croce	Ecco l'alma beata à cui donò	9v	1586[1]	Musica spirituale, 5vv, Venice
Luca Marenzio	Basti fin qui le pen'e i duri affanni (Sannazaro)	10v	M577	Madrigali, I, 4–6vv, Venice, 1588
Eight-Voice Settings				
Andrea Gabrieli	Ecco la vaga aurora e il sol ch'a noi vien	12v	1587[16]	Concerti, I–II, Venice
Andrea Gabrieli	Quand'havrà fin amore. Dialogo	13v	1587[16]	Concerti, I–II, Venice
Andrea Gabrieli	O dea, che tra le selv'a chi ti chiama. Risonanza di Echo	14v	1587[16]	Concerti, I–II, Venice
Andrea Gabrieli	Hor che nel suo ben seno lieto e tranquillo il mar d'Adria	15v	1587[16]	Concerti, I–II, Venice

COMPOSER	FIRST LINE	FOLIO	EARLIEST PRINTED CONCORDANCE RISM	SHORT TITLE
Seven-Voice Settings				
Andrea Gabrieli	Dunque fia vero, o cara mia fenice. Dialogo	16v	1587[16]	Concerti, I–II, Venice
Andrea Gabrieli	Dunqu'il consenti amor (seconda parte)	17r	1587[16]	Concerti, I–II, Venice
Orazio Vecchi	Ond'avien che di lagrim'et di pianto, ninfa gentil, innondi. Dialogo	17v	none	
Giaches de Wert	In qual parte si ratto i vanni muove il vincitor augel. Dialogo	18v	W884	Madrigali, VII, 5vv, Venice, 1581
Giaches de Wert	Tirsi morir volea, gl'occhi mirando di colei ch'adora. Dialogo (Guarini)	19v	W884	Madrigali, VII, 5vv, Venice, 1581
Six-Voice Settings				
Andrea Gabrieli	In nobil sangue vita humile e questa et in alto (Petrarch)	20r	1587[16]	Concerti, I–II, Venice
Giovanni Gabrieli	Amor s'è in lei con honestate aggiunto (seconda parte) (Petrarch)	21r	1587[16]	Concerti, I–II, Venice
Andrea Gabrieli	Chiaro sol di virtute, onde deriva	21v	1587[16]	Concerti, I–II, Venice
Andrea Gabrieli	Al chiaro suon d'i dolci accenti (seconda parte)	22r	1587[16]	Concerti, I–II, Venice
Andrea Gabrieli	Nel bel giardin entrate, felici alme ben nate	22v	1587[16]	Concerti, I–II, Venice
Andrea Gabrieli	Ma pria odorate il vicin spico (seconda parte)	23r	1587[16]	Concerti, I–II, Venice
Andrea Gabrieli	I'vo piangendo i miei passati tempi (Petrarch)	23v	1587[16]	Concerti, I–II, Venice
Andrea Gabrieli	Si che s'io vissi in guerra (seconda parte) (Petrarch)	24r	1587[16]	Concerti, I–II, Venice

COMPOSER	FIRST LINE	FOLIO	EARLIEST RISM	PRINTED CONCORDANCE SHORT TITLE
Luca Marenzio	Qual vive salamandra in fiamma ardente e ne gioisce poi	24v	M500	Madrigali, I, 6vv, Venice, 1581
Luca Marenzio	Al suon de le dolcissime parole et agl'ultimi accenti	25r	M500	Madrigali, I, 6vv, Venice, 1581
Luca Marenzio	Nel più fiorito aprile cantano in vario suon dolc'e gentile	25v	M500	Madrigali, I, 6vv, Venice, 1581
Luca Marenzio	Occhi sereni e chiari, al cui divin splendore	26r	M500	Madrigali, I, 6vv, Venice, 1581
Luca Marenzio	Cantate, ninfe leggiadrette e belle, i miei novelli ardori	26v	M500	Madrigali, I, 6vv, Venice, 1581
Luca Marenzio	L'aura serena, che tra verdi fronde mormorando (Petrarch)	27r	M500	Madrigali, I, 6vv, Venice, 1581
Luca Marenzio	Le quali ella spargea sì dolcemente (seconda parte) (Petrarch)	27v	M500	Madrigali, I, 6vv, Venice, 1581
Luca Marenzio	Bianchi cigni e canori che de la secca fronde cantaste	28r	1583[10]	Il lauro verde, 6vv, Ferrara
Luca Marenzio	Alzate il nuovo lauro oltra le stelle (seconda parte)	28v	1583[10]	Il lauro verde, 6vv, Ferrara
Luca Marenzio	Guidate dolci et amorosi balli a gara (terza parte)	29v	1583[10]	Il lauro verde, 6vv, Ferrara
Cavallier Antinori	Giovan real se pensa humana	30r	none	
Ippolito Sabino	Io son ferito, ahi lasso, e chi mi diede accusar pur vorrei	30v	S47 =1581[11]	Madrigali, II, 6vv, Venice
Ippolito Sabino	S'io t'ho ferito, non t'ho però morto. Riposta	31v	S47	Madrigali, II, 6vv, Venice, 1581
Giovanni Ferretti	Un pastor chies' ad una ninfa amore et ella diss'a lui	32v	F531	Canzoni, I, 6vv, Venice, 1573

COMPOSER	FIRST LINE	FOLIO	EARLIEST PRINTED CONCORDANCE RISM	SHORT TITLE
Giovanni Ferretti	Dolc'amorose, leggiadrette ninfe, che col vostro cantar	33r	F531	Canzoni, I, 6vv, Venice, 1573
Giovanni Ferretti	Fuggimi quanto voi, faccia mia bella, e celami so volt'a tutte l'hore	33v	F531	Canzoni, I, 6vv, Venice, 1573
Giovanni Ferretti	Pascomi sol di piant'e vivo in pene, dopoi che mi legasti	34r	F531	Canzoni, I, 6vv, Venice, 1573
Giovanni Ferretti	O felice, o beato, o glorioso quel ch'è ligato in servitù d'amore	34v	F531	Canzoni, I, 6vv, Venice, 1573
Giovanni Ferretti	Angelica tua mano, per cui son fatt'insano, deh per pietà	35r	F531	Canzoni, I, 6vv, Venice, 1573
Giovanni Ferretti	Un tempo sospirava, piangev'e lacrimava sol per volere bene	35v	F531	Canzoni, I, 6vv, Venice, 1573
Giovanni Ferretti	Quando mirai sa bella facia d'oro con s'occhi ladri	36r	F531	Canzoni, I, 6vv, Venice, 1573
Five-Voice Settings				
Luca Marenzio	Lasso, ch'io ardo e'l mio bel sole ardente	36v	M530	Madrigali, I, 5vv, Venice, 1580
Luca Marenzio	Amor, io non potrei haver da te se non ricca mercede (Ariosto)	37r	M539	Madrigali, II, 5vv, Venice, 1581
Luca Marenzio	Fillida mia più ch'i ligustri bianca (Sannazaro)	37v	M539	Madrigali, II, 5vv, Venice, 1581
Luca Marenzio	Al vago del mio sole lucido raggio, che'l bel Mincio honora	38r	M539	Madrigali, II, 5vv, Venice, 1581

COMPOSER	FIRST LINE	FOLIO	EARLIEST PRINTED CONCORDANCE RISM	SHORT TITLE
Luca Marenzio	Amor, poi che non vuole la bella donna, a cui nol dir giurai (Parabosco)	38v	M539	Madrigali, II, 5vv, Venice, 1581
Luca Marenzio	Chi strinse mai più bella mano (seconda parte) (Parabosco)	39r	M539	Madrigali, II, 5vv, Venice, 1581
Luca Marenzio	Già torna a rallegrar l'aria e la terra il giovenetto april	39v	M539	Madrigali, II, 5vv, Venice, 1581
Luca Marenzio	Occhi lucenti e belli, com'esser può ch'in un medesmo	40v	M546	Madrigali, III, 5vv, Venice, 1582
Luca Marenzio	Mentre l'aura spirò nel verde lauro, con che m'acces'il core	41v	1582⁵	Il lauro secco, I, 5vv, Venice
Luca Marenzio	Hor perchè lasso ohimè secco ti vedo (seconda parte)	42r	1582⁵	Il lauro secco, I, 5vv, Venice
Philippe de Monte	Tirsi morir volea gl'occhi mirando di colei ch'adora (Guarini)	42v	M3379	Madrigali, XI, 5vv, Venice, 1586
Gioseffi Biffi	Ohimé dolce ben mio	43v	none	
Gioseffi Biffi	Tra bei rubini e perle, che spiran aura di celeste (Amalteo)	44r	none	
Gioseffi Biffi	Da indimanti (seconda parte) (Amalteo; cf. NV)	44v	none	
Giaches de Wert	Amorose viole ch'havete il nome	45r	1583¹²	Li amorosi ardori, I, 5vv, Venice
Giaches de Wert	Quanto lieto vi miro (seconda parte)	45v	1583¹²	Li amorosi ardori, I, 5vv, Venice
Claudio Merulo	Mirami vita mia mirami un poco	46r	1583¹²	Li amorosi ardori, I, 5vv, Venice

COMPOSER	FIRST LINE	FOLIO[a]	EARLIEST PRINTED CONCORDANCE	
			RISM	SHORT TITLE
Girolamo Conversi	Io vo gridando, come spiritato, la notte'l giorno	46v	C3545	Canzoni, I, 5vv, Venice, 1572
Girolamo Conversi	Alma, guidott'amar colei ch'ogn'hora lieta ridendo	47r	C3545	Canzoni, I, 5vv, Venice, 1572
Girolamo Conversi	Ma se tempo giamai verrà che sciolta (seconda parte)	47v	C3545	Canzoni, I, 5vv, Venice, 1572
Girolamo Conversi	Poi che m'hai tolto la tua dolce vista, non far ch'io resti almen	48r	C3545	Canzoni, I, 5vv, Venice, 1572
Girolamo Conversi	Quando mi miri con quess'occhi ladri, divento rosso	48v	C3545	Canzoni, I, 5vv, Venice, 1572
Girolamo Conversi	Stanott'io mi sognava con dolcezza che tu eri contenta	49r	C3545	Canzoni, I, 5vv, Venice, 1572
Girolamo Conversi	Se vi spiace ch'io v'ami, o mia guerriera	49v	C3546	Canzoni, I, 5vv, Venice, 1573
Giovanni Ferretti	Sei tanto gratiosa e tanto bella, che chi ti mira	50v	F512	Canzone, [I], 5vv, Venice, 1567
Giovanni Ferretti	Donna crudel, tu m'hai rubat'il core e mai non manchi	51r	F512	Canzone, [I], 5vv, Venice, 1567
Giovanni Ferretti	Come poss'io morir se non ho vita? Dunqu'a che darmi	51v	F512	Canzone, [I], 5vv, Venice, 1567
Giovanni Ferretti	Hiersera andai da la mia manza bella, solo soletto	52r	F527	Napolitane, IV, 5vv, Venice, 1571
Cavallier Antinori	Son lasso ne piu sento	52v	none	
Four-Voice Settings				
Germano Pallavicino	Vorrei donna scoprirui	53r	none	
Germano Pallavicino	Chi sarà in terr'homai	53v	none	
Germano Pallavicino	Laura soave vita	54r	none	

COMPOSER	FIRST LINE	FOLIO	EARLIEST PRINTED CONCORDANCE RISM	SHORT TITLE
Costanzo Antegnati	Dolce mio ben	54v	none	
Costanzo Antegnati	Io mi sento morir (seconda parte)	55r	none	
Noë Faignient	Basciami vita mia	55v	1583^{14}	Harmonia celeste, Antwerp
Orazio Vecchi	Rendemi il gentil viso, amor, ch'un temp'amai, e teco lo conduci	56v	V1017	Canzonette, II, 4vv, Venice, 1580
Orazio Vecchi	Mi vorrei trasformare, gri, gri, grillo, sol per cantare et farmi	57r	V1022	Canzonette, III, 4vv, Venice, 1585
Felice Anerio	O tu che mi dai pene, dolcissimo mio bene, perché mi dai martire	57v	A1085	Canzonette, I, 4vv, Venice, 1586
Anonymous[b]	Luci sereni e chiare	58r	none	
Anonymous	La piagha ch'he nel cor	58v	none	
Anonymous	Viva viva Baccho	59r	none	
Anonymous	Jay veule cerf du bois sallir	59v	none	
Anonymous	Chantons buvons soyons	59v	none	
No attribution	Fantasia Capriccio. 2. Toni	60r	none	

[a] Foliation follows the canto partbook, Bayerische Staatsbibliothek München, Musikabteilung: 4° Mus. pr. 173/4.
[b] Headlines for the following five pieces state "D'incerto."

3. *Tertius Gemmae musicalis liber* (Nuremberg, 1590)

COMPOSER	FIRST LINE	FOLIO[a]	EARLIEST PRINTED CONCORDANCE	
			RISM	SHORT TITLE
Eight-Voice Settings				
Giaches de Wert	Cara Germania mia, quanto ti deggio, quanto ti deggio, cara Italia mia. Dialogo	4r	W875	Madrigali, IV, 5vv, Venice, 1567
Giaches de Wert	Ch'io scriva di costei ben m'hai tu detto. Dialogo (Bembo)	4v	W855	Madrigali, I, 5vv, Venice, 1558
Giulio Eremita	O misero mio core, poi che si parte amore	5r	E745	Madrigali, II, 5vv, Venice, 1589
Filippo Duc	Dite, signori miei, qual speranza v'invita a far. Dialogo	5v	D3611	Madrigali, I, 4,8vv, Venice, 1570
Filippo Duc	Sacra Muse beate, che con le vostre voci. Dialogo	5v	D3612	Vergini, I, 6, 8vv, Venice, 1574
Seven-Voice Settings				
Giaches de Wert	Che nuovo e vago sol, ch'ardente luce è questa. A Lucretia Ancisa	6v	W878	Madrigali, V, 5–7vv, Venice, 1571
Bartholomeo Spontini	Alma, se stato fossi a pien accorta. Dialogo (Bembo)	7v	1566[17]	Rore, madrigali, V, 5vv, Venice
Six-Voice Settings				
Orazio Vecchi	Gitene, canzonette, al mio signore e'l cor mio gli porgete	8r	V1026	Canzonette, I, 6vv, Venice, 1587
Orazio Vecchi	Saltavan ninfe, satiri e pastori fra gli odorati fiori	8v	V1026	Canzonette, I, 6vv, Venice, 1587
Orazio Vecchi	Deh lascia, Filli, i fiori, che cogli per Damon, tuo fid'amante	9r	V1026	Canzonette, I, 6vv, Venice, 1587

COMPOSER	FIRST LINE	FOLIO	EARLIEST PRINTED CONCORDANCE RISM	SHORT TITLE
Orazio Vecchi	Dicea Damet'a Cloride piangendo: non sai che tu mi struggi	9v	V1026	Canzonette, I, 6vv, Venice, 1587
Orazio Vecchi	A dio, voglio partir, ti lascio, Aminta. Non dubitar, cor mio	10r	V1026	Canzonette, I, 6vv, Venice, 1587
Orazio Vecchi	Io son restato qui sconsolato e un'altr'amante coglierà'l fiore	10v	V1026	Canzonette, I, 6vv, Venice, 1587
Orazio Vecchi	Io v'ho servita, dolce mia vita, molti e molt' anni, congravi affanni	11r	V1026	Canzonette, I, 6vv, Venice, 1587
Orazio Vecchi	E vivere e morire mi fai, quando ti veggio, o faccia bella	11v	V1026	Canzonette, I, 6vv, Venice, 1587
Orazio Vecchi	O sole, o stelle, o luna, o cielo, o terr'o mar, o mia fortuna	12r	V1026	Canzonette, I, 6vv, Venice, 1587
Benedetto Pallavicino	In dir che sete bella scemo le vostre lodi. Prudentia (Tansillo)	12v	P776	Madrigali, II, 5vv, Venice, 1584
Benedetto Pallavicino	I capei de l'aurora, gl'occhi del sol (seconda parte) (Tansillo)	13v	P776	Madrigali, II, 5vv, Venice, 1584
Giaches de Wert	Un bacio solo a tante pene, ahi cruda, un bacio a tanta fede (Guarini)	14v	W887	Madrigali, IX, 5–6vv, Venice, 1588
Giaches de Wert	Mesola, il Po da lato e'l mar a fronte, et intorno le mura (Tasso)	15v	W887	Madrigali, IX, 5–6vv, Venice, 1588

COMPOSER	FIRST LINE	FOLIO	EARLIEST PRINTED RISM	CONCORDANCE SHORT TITLE
Five-Voice Settings				
Benedetto Pallavicino	Destossi fra'l mio gelo fiamma sì dolc'al core	16v	P776	Madrigali, II, 5vv, Venice, 1584
Benedetto Pallavicino	Come poss'io, madonn'il bel desio, che di voi si m'accese	17v	P776	Madrigali, II, 5vv, Venice, 1584
Benedetto Pallavicino	Da ind'in qua tra mille nodi stretto (seconda parte)	18v	P776	Madrigali, II, 5vv, Venice, 1584
Benedetto Pallavicino	O saette d'amor, ch'a mill'a mille quinci movete e non vi s'ha	19v	P776	Madrigali, II, 5vv, Venice, 1584
Benedetto Pallavicino	Dolce mia caro mano, con cui lo strale e'l foco m'aventa	20v	P776	Madrigali, II, 5vv, Venice, 1584
Benedetto Pallavicino	Tu ninfa di beltà sei fior e fonte perchè dal somm'Iddio	21v	P776	Madrigali, II, 5vv, Venice, 1584
Benedetto Pallavicino	Mentre che qui d'intorno l'aura soave spira	22v	P785	Madrigali, IV, 5vv, Venice, 1588
Benedetto Pallavicino	Sì, mi dicesti, et io quel dolcissimo sì mandai nel core (Guarini)	23v	P785	
Benedetto Pallavicino	Non mirar, non mirare di questa bella imago (F. Alberti)	24v	P785	Madrigali, IV, 5vv, Venice, 1588
Benedetto Pallavicino	Non mi ferir più, amore, che già da mille lati	25v	P785	Madrigali, IV, 5vv, Venice, 1588
Benedetto Pallavicino	Tutto eri foco, amore, quand'arsi prima (Guarini)	26v	P785	Madrigali, IV, 5vv, Venice, 1588
Benedetto Pallavicino	Arte mi siano i crini di puro oro lucenti	27v	P785	Madrigali, IV, 5vv, Venice, 1588
Giaches de Wert	Donna, se ben le chiom'ho già ripiene d'algente neve (Tasso)	28v	W884	Madrigali, VII, 5vv, Venice, 1581

COMPOSER	FIRST LINE	FOLIO	EARLIEST PRINTED CONCORDANCE	
			RISM	SHORT TITLE
Giaches de Wert	Ben s'el petto tal hor mi ripercuote (seconda parte) (Tasso)	29v	W884	Madrigali, VII, 5vv, Venice, 1581
Giaches de Wert	Valle, che di lamenti miei sei piena (Petrarch)	30v	W887	Madrigali, IX, 5–6vv, Venice, 1588
Giaches de Wert	Ben riconosco in voi l'usate forme (seconda parte)	31v	W887	Madrigali, IX, 5–6vv, Venice, 1588
Giulio Eremita	Io seguo ardente fiamma, che mi fugge e fuggendo mi strugge	33r	E745	Madrigali, II, 5vv, Venice, 1589
Giulio Eremita	Fuggi, se sai fuggire, fera al mio cor crudele	33v	E745	Madrigali, II, 5vv, Venice, 1589
Giovanni Gastoldi	Dolce d'amor sirena, che le note e i sospiri mesci	34v	G548	Madrigali, II, 5,7,10vv, Venice, 1589
Giovanni Gastoldi	A nobil mensa del celeste ardore, che da due lumi amorosetti	35v	G548	Madrigali, II, 5,7,10vv, Venice, 1589
Giovanni Gastoldi	Filli vezzosa e lieta hor guarda, hor geme, hor tace	36v	G548	Madrigali, II, 5,7,10vv, Venice, 1589
Giulio Renaldi	Se di dolor io potessi morire, donna crudele. Napolitana	37r	R1157	Madregali, 5vv, Venice, 1576
Giulio Renaldi	O dolce vita mia, perchè mi sei tanto spietata. Napolitana	37v	R1157	Madrigali, 5vv, Venice, 1576
Giovanni Gastoldi	Donna, l'ardente fiamma e la pena e'l tormento cresce in me tanto	38r	G547	Madrigali, I, 5vv, Venice, 1588
Giovanni Gastoldi	Signor, la vostra fiamma e la pena e'l tormento. Risposta	38v	G547	Madrigali, I, 5vv, Venice, 1588
Giovanni Gastoldi	O com'è gran martire l'esser in foc'e nol poter scoprire	39v	G547	Madrigali, I, 5vv, Venice, 1588

COMPOSER	FIRST LINE	FOLIO	EARLIEST PRINTED CONCORDANCE RISM	SHORT TITLE
Sessa d'Aranda	Milla, ben mio, rispondi dolcemente a chi t'adora (four voices)	40v	S2842	Madrigali, I, 4vv, Venice, 1571
Benedetto Pallavicino	Ahimè quell'occhi suoi, ahimè i sguardi, ahimè le guancie	41r	P776	Madrigali, II, 5vv, Venice, 1584
Benedetto Pallavicino	Hor veggio chiar che ricoperte alquanto e non già tutte spente	41v	P776	Madrigali, II, 5vv, Venice, 1584
Benedetto Pallavicino	Nè lo star, nè'l fuggir, nè'l mutar loco (seconda parte)	42v	P776	Madrigali, II, 5vv, Venice, 1584
Benedetto Pallavicino	Non dispregiate i miserelli amanti ch'esser non dè beltate (Martelli)	43v	P776	Madrigali, II, 5vv, Venice, 1584
Benedetto Pallavicino	Misero te, non vedi ch'io son finta? In van chiedi soccorso	44v	P776	Madrigali, II, 5vv, Venice, 1584
Benedetto Pallavicino	Natura non mi fè com'io vorrei (seconda parte)	45v	P776	Madrigali, II, 5vv, Venice, 1584
Philippe de Monte	Sogliono i chiari spirti, sacri ad Apollo (six voices)	46v	M3377	Madrigali, V, 6vv, Venice, 1584
Four-Voice Settings				
Giovanni Gastoldi	Amor, tu che congiungi con lieti e cari nodi	47v	1588[18]	Novelli ardori, I, 4vv, Venice
Giovanni Gastoldi	Potrai dunque partire	48v	1588[18]	Novelli ardori, I, 4vv, Venice
Annibale Coma	Cantavan tre leggiadre pastorelle in sì soavi accenti	49v	C3478	Madrigali, II, 4vv, 1588
Annibale Coma	Ond'io, per meglio udire così grata armonia (seconda 50r parte)		C3478	Madrigali, II, 4vv, 1588

| COMPOSER | FIRST LINE | FOLIO | EARLIEST PRINTED CONCORDANCE | |
			RISM	SHORT TITLE
Paolo Marni	Aura dolce e soave	50v	1588[18]	Novelli ardori, I, 4vv, Venice
Paolo Marni	Ma'ahime che piu m'alla	51r	1588[18]	Novelli ardori, I, 4vv, Venice
Francesco da Cedraro	Gentil mia donn' il dissi e dirò sempre	51v	S2842	Madrigali, I, 4vv, Venice, 1571
	"Di Francesco dal Cedraro Discipulo del Sessa"			

[a] Foliation follows the canto partbook, Bayerische Staatsbibliothek München, Musikabteilung: 4° Mus. pr. 2718/2.

4. Valentin Haussmann, *Die erste Class, der vierstimmigen Canzonetten Horatii Vecchi* (Nuremberg, 1610)

FIRST LINE/HAUSSMANN	FOLIO[a]	EARLIEST PRINTED MUSICAL CONCORDANCE [position in Vecchi's volume][b]	VECCHI'S TEXT
Die Canzonetten wir vorehrn euch, Venusknaben	2r	none	[original text by Haussmann]
Ach ihr liedlein der Liebe	3r	Canzonette I, 1580 [1]	Canzonette d'Amore
Jungfrau, ich muß euch klagen	3v	Canzonette I, 1580 [2]	Mentre io campai contento
Weil du verlachst mein schmertzen	4r	Canzonette I, 1580 [3]	Occhi ridenti

FIRST LINE/HAUSSMANN	FOLIO	EARLIEST PRINTED MUSICAL CONCORDANCE [position in Vecchi's volume]	VECCHI'S TEXT
Du hast dich hören lassen	14r	Canzonette I, 1580 [10]	Raggi, dov'è'l mio bene
Eur schöne jugent	14v	Canzonette I, 1580 [11]	Se'l vostro volto
Sagt mir, Jungfrau, ohn wancken	15r	Canzonette I, 1580 [12]	Quando l'aurora
Wie der wind so geschwind sindt dein gedancken	15v	Canzonette I, 1580 [22]	Trà le chiome de l'oro
Amor, du gibst mir tag und nacht zu schaffen	16r	Canzonette I, 1580 [14]	Amor spiega l'insegna
Da ich zu erst meins Bulen schein wardt innen	16v	Canzonette I, 1580 [13]	Corse alla morte

[a] Foliation follows the cantus partbook, Göttingen, Niedersächsische Staats- und Universitätsbibliothek: 8 MUS VI, 750: Cantus, I.

[b] Concordances with Vecchi and the positioning of works in his volumes are taken from Orazio Vecchi, *Orazio Vecchi: The Four-Voice Canzonettas. With Original Texts and Contrafacta by Valentin Haussmann and Others*, ed. Ruth I. DeFord, Recent Researches in the Music of the Renaissance, 92–3 (Madison, WI: A-R Editions, Inc. 1993), part 1 (vol. 92).

5. Valentin Haussmann, *Die ander Class der vierstimmigen Canzonetten Horatii Vecchi* (Nuremberg, 1610)

FIRST LINE/HAUSSMANN	FOLIO[a]	EARLIEST PRINTED MUSICAL CONCORDANCE [position in Vecchi's volume][b]	VECCHI'S TEXT
Ach Gott, wie grossen schmertz	2r	Canzonette II, 1580 [7]	Non ti fuggir da me
O außerwehlte Frau von feinen sitten	2v	Canzonette II, 1580 [6]	O donna ch'a mio danno
Du vilgeplagtes hertze	3r	Canzonette II, 1580 [21]	Rendimi il gentil viso
Amor hat unverdrossen	3v	Canzonette III, 1585 [6]	Guerriera mia Costante
O süsser trost, o meine edle Krone	4r	Canzonette III, 1585 [4]	Lucretia mia
Meine noth muß ich euch mit seufftzen klagen	4v	Canzonette III, 1585 [5]	S'io potessi raccore
Ich habe mich mit lieb zu dir gekehret	5r	Canzonette III, 1585 [7]	Donna, se vaga sei
Von euch hab ich verstanden	5v	Canzonette IV, 1590 [2]	Mentre io vissi in dolore
Jungfrau, gedencket, was lieb bey uns beyden	6r	Canzonette II, 1580 [18]	Fa una Canzone senza note nere
Jungfrau, dein Lieb mich brinnet	6v	Canzonette II, 1580 [19]	Lucilla, io vo morire: Dialogo
Mit trauren muß ich meine zeit vertrieben	7r	Canzonette II, 1580 [20]	Opache selve
Du hast ein steinen hertze	7v	Canzonette III, 1585 [12]	Il Cocodrillo geme
Jungfrau, es nimmt mich wunder	8r	Canzonette II, 1580 [8]	Neriglia, anima mia
Mein Lieb hat mich verstossen	8v	Canzonette II, 1580 [9]	Mentre il buon Tirsi dice
Gehab dich wol, mein hertze	9r	Canzonette II, 1580 [10]	Vostri vivaci lumi
Zu dir hab ich mein liebe	9v	Canzonette III, 1585 [10]	Sarà possibil mai
Von dir bin ich verlassen	10r	Canzonette II, 1580 [13]	Non è cosa ch'io miri
Die grosse liebe	10v	Canzonette II, 1580 [17]	Non son già sguardi

FIRST LINE/HAUSSMANN	FOLIO	EARLIEST PRINTED MUSICAL CONCORDANCE [position in Vecchi's volume]	VECCHI'S TEXT
Cupido hat mein hertze	11r	Canzonette III, 1585 [9]	Sia benedetto Amore
Die Liebe sey verfluchet	11v	Canzonette III, 1585 [8]	Sia maledetto Amore
Ach schatz, last mich vernemen	12r	Canzonette III, 1585 [11]	Se tu vuoi pur ch'io mora
Venus thut mich anfassen	12v	Canzonette II, 1580 [15]	Lasso ch'io son costretto
In dir bin ich verliebet	13r	Canzonette II, 1580 [11]	Se giusto innamorato
Amor, ich geb mich deiner macht gefangen	13v	Canzonette II, 1580 [12]	Amor con ogni impero
Nichts liebers wünsch ich mir auff diser Erden	14r	Canzonette III, 1585 [1]	Hor che'l garrir
Meine lieb hab ich dir zu g'müth geführet	15r	Canzonette III, 1585 [2]	Core mio, tu mi lasciasti
Einen Vogel ich weiß	15v	Canzonette III, 1585 [3]	Mentr'il Cuculo
Bey meinem Buln war ich an einem orte	16v	Canzonette II, 1580 [16]	Lieva la man di qui

a Foliation follows the cantus partbook, Göttingen, Niedersächsische Staats- und Universitätsbibliothek: 8 MUS VI, 750: Cantus, 2.

b Concordances with Vecchi and the positioning of works in his volumes are taken from Orazio Vecchi, *Orazio Vecchi: The Four-Voice Canzonettas*, part 1 (vol. 92).

6. Valentin Haussmann, *Die dritte Class Der vierstimmigen Canzonetten Horatii Vecchi* (Nuremberg, 1610)

FIRST LINE/HAUSSMANN	FOLIO[a]	EARLIEST PRINTED MUSICAL CONCORDANCE [position in Vecchi's volume][b]	VECCHI'S TEXT
Liebliche zier meins hertzen	2r	Canzonette III, 1585 [14]	Porgimi, cara filli
Jungfrau, seht ihr die flammen	2v	Canzonette III, 1585 [15]	L'antiche mie fiammelle
Nun hab ich mich besunnen	3r	Canzonette IV, 1590 [1]	Udit', udite, Amanti: Proemio
Als ich mich hatt an diener schön versehen	3v	Canzonette IV, 1590 [3]	Se da le treccie mie
Feins lieb, erfrisch mein hertze	4r	Canzonette IV, 1590 [4]	Dove s'intese mai
Amor, laß deine Pfeile	4v	Selva di varia ricreatione	Damon e Filli
Ich bitt, Jungfrau, betrachtet meine seufftzen	5r	Canzonette III, 1585 [13]	Con voce da i sospiri
Du holdselige schone	5v	Selva di varia ricreatione	Che fai, Dori
Ach Schatz, ihr wolt betrachten	6r	Selva di varia ricreatione	Deh prega, Amor
Alle mein freud	6v	Canzonette IV, 1590 [5]	Partirò si
O süsser trost meins hertzen	7r	Canzonette IV, 1590 [6]	Non sarò piu ritrosa
O liebliches gesichte	7v	Canzonette IV, 1590 [22]	Dolcissimo ben mio
Amor in seim gebiete	8r	Canzonette III, 1585 [20]	Amor, se vuo'ch'io porti
Wenn ich an die gedencke	8v	Canzonette III, 1585 [22]	Chi vuol veder l'Aurora
Ach allerschönst auf Erden	9r	Canzonette IV, 1590 [10]	Il cor ch'io ti rubai
Wenn soll von liebes schmertze	9v	Canzonette IV, 1590 [11]	Cor mio, se per dolore
In schweren tieffen g'dancken	10r	Canzonette IV, 1590 [12]	Ombre del cieco Averno
O Jungfrau zart, laß mich zu frieden stellen	10v	Canzonette IV, 1590 [13]	Le chiome d'or
Cupido, Gott der liebe	11r	Canzonette IV, 1590 [17]	Io soffrirò, cor mio

FIRST LINE/HAUSSMANN	FOLIO	EARLIEST PRINTED MUSICAL CONCORDANCE [position in Vecchi's volume]	VECCHI'S TEXT
Durch dein anblick bin ich inamoriret	11v	Canzonette IV, 1590 [18]	Tuo cor non hò per furto
Jungfrau, ich werd verdrossen	12r	Canzonette III, 1585 [16]	Caro dolce mio bene
Ach du liebseeligs Bilde	12v	Canzonette III, 1585 [17]	Amante, se ti piace
Wenn ich dir mein anlign gedenck zu klagen	13r	Canzonette III, 1585 [19]	Se si vede abruciar
Ich hab ein rath gefunden	13v	Canzonette IV, 1590 [15]	Raggi, dov'è'l mio male
Durch Venus list bin ich gefangn geschwinde	14r	Canzonette IV, 1590 [16]	Un batter d'occhi
Meine liebliche, schone	14v	Canzonette IV, 1590 [19]	Vivo in foco amoroso
Wenn ich deß nachts soll schlaffen	15r	Canzonette III, 1585 [18]	Mi vorrei trasformare
Ein wunder schönes Bild hab ich gesehen	15v	Canzonette III, 1585 [21]	Ecco novello Amor
Ich hab mich eines dinges unternommen	16r	Canzonette IV, 1590 [8]	Non ha, finto amator
Meins hertzen leid und plage	16v	Canzonette IV, 1590 [9]	Se son quest'occhi tuoi
Die pfeil der liebe thu ich jetzt entpfinden	18r	Canzonette IV, 1590 [14]	Non ti ricordi
Du hast dich mir in allen	18v	Canzonette IV, 1590 [20]	Mirate com'Amore
Nun wirdt mein gut gedichte	19r	Canzonette IV, 1590 [21]	Non si sa chi tu sei
Frölich in ehren	19v	Canzonette IV, 1590 [7]	Trista novella

[a] Foliation follows the cantus partbook, Göttingen, Niedersächsische Staats- und Universitätsbibliothek: 8 MUS VI, 750: Cantus, 3.

[b] Concordances with Vecchi and the positioning of works in his volumes are taken from Orazio Vecchi, *Orazio Vecchi: The Four-Voice Canzonettas*, part 1 (vol. 92).

7. Petrus Neander, *Vier und Zwantzig Ausserlesene vierstimmige Canzonetten Horatii Vecchi* (Gera, 1614) and Its Sources

PETRUS NEANDER	FOLIO[a]	PSALM[b]	VALENTIN HAUSSMANN'S TEXTS	ORAZIO VECCHI'S TEXTS
1. Lobet den Herren alle	3r	117	Liebliche zier meins Hertzen	Porgimi, cara filli
2. Herr, unser Herrscher	3r	8	Als ich mich hatt	Se da le treccie mie
3. Last uns von Hertzen singen	3v	147	Jungfrau, seht ihr die Flammen	L'antiche mie fiammelle
4. Erhebet ewre Hertzen	3v	147	Nun hab ich mich besunnen	Udit', udite, amanti
5. Herr, lehre uns bedencken	4r	91	Amor, laß deine Pfeile	Damon e filli
6. Herr, der du gnädig warst	4r	85	Der jungen Mäidlein sinn	Madonna, io v'hò da dir
7. Lobt Gott den Herrn mit schallen	4v	92	Jungfrau, ich muß euch klagen	Mentre io campai contento
8. Ich wil dem Herren dancken	4v	57, 146	So oft wir z'sammen kommen	Ne gl'occhi d'Angioletta
9. Ach Gott, thu dich erbarmen	5r	15	Ach Schatz, ihr wolt betrachten	Deh prega, Amor
10. O Gott, O unser Herre	5r	143	O süsser Trost	Non sarò piu ritrosa
11. Wie lang in meiner Seelen	5v	91	In dir bin ich verliebet	Se giusto innamorato
12. Ach Herr, straffe mich nichte	5v	1, 143	Du holdselige Schone	Che fai, Dori
13. Nicht uns, nit uns, Herr	6r	115	Eur schöne Jugent	Se'l vostro volto
14. Auff meinem lieben Gotte	6r	71	Du hast dich hören lassen	Raggi, dov'è'l mio bene
15. Ich frewe mich der Reden	6v	122	Sagt mir, Jungfrau, ohn wancken	Quando l'aurora
16. Jauchtzet Gotte, alle Land	6v	66	Die mir mein Hertz besessen	Se pensando al partire
17. Wie der Hirsch rennet	7r	42	Die grosse Liebe	Non son già sguardi
18. Singet dem Herren lieblich	7r	147	Wie kan ich dich verlassen	Chi mira gli occhi tuoi
19. Herre, ich trawe auff dich	7v	31	Ach Schatz, last mich vernemen	Se tu vuoi pur ch'io mora
20. Meinm lieben Gott und Herrn	7v	146	Ein wunder schönes Bild	Ecco novella Amor

PETRUS NEANDER	FOLIO[a]	PSALM[b]	VALENTIN HAUSSMANN'S TEXTS	ORAZIO VECCHI'S TEXTS
21. Frolocket Gott, ihr Völcker	8r	74	Die Liebe sey verfluchet	Sia maledetto Amore
22. Herr Gott, mit diesem Gesang	8r	74	In schweren tieffen g'dancken	Ombre del cieco Averno
23. Ich wende meine Augen zu dem Herren	8v	21	Mein Hertz mit Liebesbrunst	Son questi i crespi crini
24. Her sey dem Vater schone	8v			Amor, se vuo'ch'io porti

[a] Foliation follows the cantus partbook ["Höchste Stimme"], Staatsbibliothek zu Berlin – Preußischer Kulturbesitz, Musikabteilung mit Mendelssohn-Archiv: Mus. Ant. Pract. V288.

[b] Psalm sources are taken from Orazio Vecchi, *Orazio Vecchi: The Four-Voice Canzonettas*, part 1 (vol. 92).

8. Martin Rinckart, *Triumphi de Dorothea* (Leipzig, 1619) and Its German Predecessors[a]

COMPOSER	TEXT AND PLACEMENT BY MARTIN RINCKART (RISM B/I, 1619[16])	TEXT AND PLACEMENT BY JOHANNES LYTTICH (RISM B/I, 1612[13] and RISM B/I, 1613[13])
Ippolito Baccusi	I Frisch auff ihr Musicanten	I (1612) Artlich vnnd wol formiret
Giovanni Croce	II Wo wart ihr Menschenkinder	XVI (1612) MARGARETHA Edles Perlein I (1613) KAETCHEN, mein Mägdichen
Ruggiero Giovanelli	III Von Gott wir haben	VIII (1613) SIe will Studenten haben [SIBYLLA]
Giovanni Gabrieli	IV Das Musica die schone	IV (1612) BLANDINA meine Schöne
Felice Anerio	V Jesu wahr Gottes Sohne	VI (1613) Regiert auch wieblich Geblüte [REBECCA]
Giovanni G. Gastoldi	VI Wer bringt uns auff	XII (1613) SO kommt nun all' vnd thut euch præsentiren [SOPHIA]
Costanzo Porta	VII Herbey wer Musickunst	XIII (1613) SCHOnt thut andere nicht so hoch erheben [SCHOLASTICA]
Paolo Bozzi	VIII Was haben wir zu singen	XI (1612) Ey lieber rath ihr Schwestern [EVA]
Giovanni Florio	IX Jesu laß mir gelingen	IV (1613) MARIÆ MAGDALENÆ
Giulio Eremita	X Viel hndert tausent Englein musiciren	XIV (1612) Her ihr Edlen Jäger alle [HELENA]
Leone Leoni	XI Oftmals und auch jetzunder	V (1613) MARgreth, du edle Perle
Giovanni de Macque	XII Bringet her ihr Lautenisten	VII (1612) Christlich, from[m] und Gottseelig [CHRISTINA]
Alfonso Preti	XIII Eins mals gieng ich spatzieren	V (1612) Bey dir ist freud vnd wonne [BEATA]
Tiburtio Massaino	XIV Die Lerch thut sich gar hoch erschwingen	XII (1612) Forthin wil ich alls trawren legen [FORTUNA]
G.P. Palestrina	XV Wach auff mein Ehre	XIV (1613) SAgt einer viel von seiner [SABINA]
Lodovico Balbi	XVI O Mensch bedenck dich eben	XI (1613) Sagt mir mir ihr lieben Schwestern [SALOME]

COMPOSER	TEXT AND PLACEMENT BY MARTIN RINCKART (RISM B/I, 1619[16])	TEXT AND PLACEMENT BY JOHANNES LYTTICH (RISM B/I, 1612[13] and RISM B/I, 1613[13])
Luca Marenzio	XVIII Eins mals im grünen Meyen	XVI (1613) EINs mals im grünen Mayen [EINICH MEINE]
Orazio Vecchi	XIX Hört wunder vber wunder	III (1612) AGNES ist teusch vnd stille
Luca Marenzio	XX Musicen klang vnd Mensche[n] stim[m] darnebe[n]	VI (1612) BARBARA komm inn deinen schönen Garten
Gasparo Costa	XXI Da Israel den Herre[n]	IX (1613) SUSANNA keusch vnd reine
Gasparo Zerto	XXII Solt man mit Musiciren	VII (1613) REGINA hoch geboren
Alessandro Striggio	XXIII Gleich wie ein süsses Zucker	III (1613) MARTHA hat viel zu schaffen
Annibale Stabile	XXIV Nur weg Teuffel weg	X (1612) Elend hat sich verkehret [ELISABETH]
Ippolito Sabino	XXV O du hoch edle Musica	II (1612) ANNELEIN Zuckermündelein
Pietro Andrea Bonini	XXVI Sihe, wie fein vnd lieblich ist es	II (1613) LUCRETIÆ ihr Tugend
Philippe de Monte	XXVII O wie viel armer Knaben	XV (1612) Jungfräulein ewrent wegen [JUSTINA]
Giovanni Cavaccio	XXVIII Hoch thewr vnd werth sind alle freye Künste	IX (1612) DOROTHEA Gottes gabe
Giammateo Asola	XXIX Gleich wie ein edel Gsteine	XIII (1612) Getrewes hertz inn ehren [GERTRAUT]
Orazio Columbani	XXX Wolauff, wolauff mein Ehre	VIII (1612) Clar scheint die liebe Sonne [CLARA]
Lelio Bertani	XXXI Fahr hin, fahr hin, fahr mein Klage	X (1613) SARA, Sara liebe Sara

Present only in Rinckart

Christian Erbach	XVII Domine, quis linguæ usus in tabernaculo tuo?	
Antonio Scandello	Appendix, Ich weiß mir Gott lob viel ein schöner Hauß	

COMPOSER	TEXT AND PLACEMENT BY MARTIN RINCKART (RISM B/I, 1619[16])	TEXT AND PLACEMENT BY JOHANNES LYTTICH (RISM B/I, 1612[13] and RISM B/I, 1613[13])

Present only in Lyttich (XV 1613)

Hans Leo Hassler URania tritt auff [URSULA]

[a] The Table is based on the exemplars Berlin – Preußischer Kulturbesitz, Musikabteilung mit Mendelssohn-Archiv: Mus. ant. pract. L 1200, cantus partbook (RISM B/I, 1612[13]); SLUB Dresden / Abt. Deutsche Fotothek: Mus. gri. 22,2, tenor partbook (RISM B/I, 1613[13]); and SLUB Dresden / Abt. Deutsche Fotothek: Mus. 1-C-2, nr. 527, cantus partbook (RISM B/I, 1619[16]).

9. Petrus Neander, *Ander Theil Ausserlesener Canzonetten Horatii Vecchi* (Gera, 1620) and Its Sources

PETRUS NEANDER	FOLIO[a]	PSALM[b]	VALENTIN HAUSSMANN'S TEXTS	ORAZIO VECCHI'S TEXTS
1. Der Herr ist mein trew Hirte	2v	23	Venus thut mich anfassen	Lasso ch'io son costretto
2. Gott sey uns gnädig allen	3r	67	Jungfrau, es nimmt mich Wunder	Neriglia, anima mia
3. Eyle zu mir, Herr Gott	3v	70	Da ich zu erst meins Bulen schein	Corse alla morte

PETRUS NEANDER	FOLIO	PSALM	VALENTIN HAUSSMANN'S TEXTS	ORAZIO VECCHI'S TEXTS
4. Kompt herzu: im Herren fröhlich seyn	4r	95	Meine Lieb hab ich dir	Core mio, tu mi lasciasti
5. Jauchtzet dem Herren alle	4v	100	Feins Lieb, erfrisch mein Hertze	Dove s'intese mai
6. Mein Seel soll dich, O Gott	5r	104	Nichts liebers wünsch ich	Hor che'l garrir
7. Gebet dem Herren Ehr	5v	118	Ach Gott, wie grossen Schmertz	Non ti fuggir da me
8. Ich ruff zu dir, Herr	6r	120	O Jungfrau zart	Le chiome d'or
9. Ach mein Herr ins Himmels Thron	6v	132	Nun wirdt mein gut Gedichte	Non si sa chi tu sei
10. Lobt den Herren, ihr knechte	7r	134	Meine liebliche, Schone	Vivo in foco amoroso
11. Ich schrey	7v	142	O du bedrängtes Hertze	O tu che vai per via
12. Lobt Gott im Heyligthume	8r	150	Amor, ich geb mich	Amor con ogni impero

[a] Foliation follows the tenor partbook ["'Dritte Stimme'"], Staatsbibliothek zu Berlin – Preußischer Kulturbesitz, Musikabteilung mit Mendelssohn-Archiv: Mus. Ant. Pract. V293.

[b] Psalm sources are taken from Orazio Vecchi, *Orazio Vecchi: The Four-Voice Canzonettas*, part 1 (vol. 92).

Bibliography

Archival and Manuscript Sources

Nuremberg State Archives: Stadtrechnungsbelege, Rep. 54a II, nos 442, 507, 702.

Otho, Liborius, "Katalog der Wolfenbütteler Bibliothek [?1614]." Herzog August Bibliothek Wolfenbüttel: Codex Guelf. A. Extravagantes.

Staatsarchiv Nürnberg: Ämterbüchlein, nos 151–6.

Stadtarchiv Nürnberg: Heiratsnotelbuch, Rep. B 14/III, nr. 2, 1566–1600.

Trost, Johann [copyist]. Sexta partbook, Madrigals, 6-10vv. Herzog August Bibliothek Wolfenbüttel: Codex Guelf. 334 Mus. Hdschr.

Printed Primary Sources

Berg, Johann vom, *Tertia pars magni operis musici … Quatuor vocum* (Nuremberg: Berg & Neuber, 1559). Exemplar Staatsbibliothek zu Berlin – Preußischer Kulturbesitz, Musikabteilung mit Mendelssohn-Archiv: Mus. ant. Pract. B 440-3.

Bodenschatz, Erhard. *Florilegi Musici Portensis … Pars altera* (Leipzig: A. Lamberg, 1621). Exemplar Bayerische Staatsbibliothek München, Musikabteilung: 4° Mus. pr. 1560.

Diezel, Valentin, *Erster Theil lieblicher, welscher Madrigalien* (Nuremberg: S. Halbmayer, 1624). Exemplar Uppsala, Universitetsbiblioteket: Utl. vok. Mus. i tr. 184.

Engelhart, Salomon [ed. Lyttich], *Rest musicalisches Streitkränzleins* (Nuremberg: B. Scherff, 1613). Exemplar SLUB Dresden / Abt. Deutsche Fotothek: Mus. gri. 22,2.

Gesius, Bartholomeus, *Ein ander new Opus, Geistlicher Deutscher Lieder, D. MART. LUTHERI, … Das erste Theil* (Frankfurt an der Oder: Johann Hartmans, und bey seinem sohn Friederichen, 1605). Exemplar Herzog August Bibliothek Wolfenbüttel: Yv 758 8° Helmst.

Haussmann, Valentin, *Ausszug auss Lucae Marentii vier Theilen seiner Italianischen dreystimmigen Villanellen und Napolitanen* (Nuremberg: Paul Kauffmann, 1606). Exemplar Ulm, Von Schermar'sche Familienstiftung, Faksimile-Edition Schermar-Bibliothek Ulm, 24 (Stuttgart: Cornetto-Verlag, 1997).

——, *Canzonette, mit dreyen Stimmen, Horatii Vecchi unnd Gemignani Capi Lupi* (Nuremberg: Paul Kauffmann, 1606). Exemplar Ulm, Von Schermar'sche

Familienstiftung, Faksimile-Edition Schermar-Bibliothek Ulm, 32 (Stuttgart: Cornetto-Verlag, 1997).

——, *Johann-Jacobi Gastoldi und anderer Autoren Tricinia* (Nuremberg: Paul Kauffmann, 1607). Exemplar Ulm, Von Schermar'sche Familienstiftung, Faksimile-Edition Schermar-Bibliothek Ulm, 40 (Stuttgart: Cornetto-Verlag, 1998).

——, *Liebliche Fröliche Ballette mit 5. Stimmen, welche zuvor von Thoma Morlei unter Italianische Texte gesetzt* (Nuremberg: Paul Kauffmann, 1609). Exemplar Hamburg, Staats- und Universitätsbibliothek: 1 an. Scrin. A/580.

——, *Die erste Class, der vierstimmigen Canzonetten Horatii Vecchi* (Nuremberg: Paul Kauffmann, 1610). Exemplar Göttingen, Niedersächsische Staats- und Universitätsbibliothek: 8 MUS VI, 750: Cantus I.

——, *Die ander Class Der vierstimmigen Canzonetten Horatii Vecchi* (Nuremberg: Paul Kauffmann, 1610). Exemplar Göttingen, Niedersächsische Staats- und Universitätsbibliothek: 8 MUS VI, 750: Cantus, 2.

——, *Die dritte Class Der vierstimmigen Canzonetten Horatii Vecchi* (Nuremberg: Paul Kauffmann, 1610). Exemplar Göttingen, Niedersächsische Staats- und Universitätsbibliothek: 8 MUS VI, 750: Cantus, 3.

Hemmeln, Sigmund, *Der gantz Psalter Dauids, wie derselbig in Teutsche Gesang verfasset* (Tübingen: Ulrich Morharts Wittib, 1569). Exemplar Herzog August Bibliothek Wolfenbüttel: 3.3.3 Musica.

Herrer, Michael. *Hortus musicalis ... Liber primus* (Passau: M. Nenninger, 1606). Exemplar Bayerische Staatsbibliothek München, Musikabteilung: 4° Mus. pr. 24.

Hildebrand, Christian, *Ander Theil, ausserlesener lieblicher Paduanen* (Hamburg: P. von Ohr Erben, 1609). Exemplar Herzog August Bibliothek Wolfenbüttel: 1.3.5 Musica (13).

Husduf, Gabriel, *Melodeyen Gesangbuch* (Hamburg: Rüdingen, 1604). Exemplar Herzog August Bibliothek Wolfenbüttel: Tl 201.

Lechner, Leonhard, *Newe Teutsche Lieder ... mit fünff Stimmen gesetzet durch Leonardum Lechnerum Athesinum* (Nuremberg: Katharina Gerlach, Johann Bergs Erben, 1579). Exemplar Herzog August Bibliothek Wolfenbüttel: 18.1 Mus. Coll. Inc. (11).

Lindner, Friedrich, *Gemma musicalis: selectissimas varii stili cantiones* (Nuremberg: Katharina Gerlach, 1588). Exemplar Bayerische Staatsbibliothek München, Musikabteilung: 4° Mus. pr. 2718.

——, *Liber secundus Gemmae musicalis: selectissimas varii stili cantiones* (Nuremberg: Katharina Gerlach, 1589). Exemplar Bayerische Staatsbibliothek München, Musikabteilung: 4° Mus. pr. 173/4.

——, *Tertius Gemmae musicalis liber: selectissimas diversorum autorum cantiones* (Nuremberg: Katharina Gerlach, 1590). Exemplar Bayerische Staatsbibliothek München, Musikabteilung: 4° Mus. pr. 2718/2.

Lyttich, Johann, *Musicalische Streitkräntzelein* (Nuremberg: A. Wagenmann, 1612). Exemplar Berlin – Preußischer Kulturbesitz, Musikabteilung mit Mendelssohn-Archiv: Mus. ant. pract. L 1200.

Marenzio, Luca, *Madrigalia quinque vocum* (Nuremberg: Paul Kauffmann, 1601). Exemplar Herzog August Bibliothek Wolfenbüttel: 2.2.7 Musica.

Neander, Petrus, *Vier und Zwantzig Ausserlesene vierstimmige Canzonetten Horatii Vecchi* (Gera: Martin Spiessen Erben, 1614). Exemplar Staatsbibliothek zu Berlin – Preußischer Kulturbesitz, Musikabteilung mit Mendelssohn-Archiv: Mus. Ant. Pract. V288.

——, *Ander Theil Ausserlesener Canzonetten Horatii Vechii* (Gera: Johann Spiess, 1620). Exemplar Staatsbibliothek zu Berlin – Preußischer Kulturbesitz, Musikabteilung mit Mendelssohn-Archiv: Mus. Ant. Pract. V293.

Ratich, Wolfgang, *Bericht von der Didactica oder Lehrkunst* (Magdeburg: Pohl, 1621). Exemplar Herzog August Bibliothek Wolfenbüttel: 34.1 Gram (2).

Ratz, Abraham, *Threni Amorum, Der erste Theil* (Nuremberg: Paul Kauffmann, 1595). Exemplar Berlin – Preußischer Kulturbesitz, Musikabteilung mit Mendelssohn-Archiv: Mus. ant. pract. R 255.

Regnart, Jacob, *Il primo libro delle canzone italiane a cinque voci* (Nuremberg: [Katharina Gerlach], 1580). Exemplar Bayerische Staatsbibliothek München, Musikabteilung: 4° Mus. pr. 162.

Rinckart, Martin, *Triumphi de Dorothea* (Leipzig: Lorenz Köber, 1619). Exemplar SLUB Dresden / Abt. Deutsche Fotothek: Mus. 1-C-2, nrs 527–8, 530–31; Mus. Gri. 23, 10, nr. 529.

Sattler, Johann, *Teutsche Orthographey* (Basel: König, 1607). Exemplar Herzog August Bibliothek Wolfenbüttel: 51.7–51.8 Gram.

Walter, Johann, *Lob und preis der löblichen Kunst Musica* (Wittenberg: Georg Rhau, 1538). Exemplar Herzog August Bibliothek Wolfenbüttel: Yn 4° Helmst. Kapsel 1 (1).

Zacharia, Cesare de, *Soave et dilettevole canzonette a quattro voci ... Liebliche und kurtzweilige Liedlein mit vier Stimmen* (Munich: Adam Berg, 1590). Exemplar Bayerische Staatsbibliothek München, Musikabteilung: 4°. Mus. pr. 88.

Secondary Sources (including modern editions)

Agee, Richard J., *The Gardano Music Printing Firms, 1569–1611* (Rochester: University of Rochester Press, 1998).

Ameln, Konrad, "Ein Nürnberger Verlegerplakat aus dem 16. Jahrhundert," in Richard Baum and Wolfgang Rehm (eds), *Musik und Verlag: Karl Vötterle zum 65. Geburtstag am 12. April 1968* (Kassel: Bärenreiter, 1968), pp. 132–42.

——, "Lechner, Leonhard," *New Grove II*, vol. 14, pp. 441–4.

Anderson, Gunilla, "Drama Translation," in Mona Baker (ed.), *Routledge Encyclopedia of Translation Studies* (New York: Routledge, 1998), pp. 71–4.

Applegate, Celia and Pamela Potter (eds), *Music and German National Identity* (Chicago: University of Chicago Press, 2002).

Arnold, Denis, *Giovanni Gabrieli and the Music of the Venetian High Renaissance* (London: Oxford University Press, 1979).

Atlas, Allan W. (ed.), *Anthology of Renaissance Music: Music in Western Europe, 1400–1600* (New York: W.W. Norton, 1998).

Auer, J., "M. Andreas Raselius Ambergensis, sein Leben und seine Werke," *Beilage zu den Monatsheften für Musikgeschichte*, 24 (1892): 1–48.

Bacon, Francis, *New Organon* [1620], trans. Michael Silverthorne, Cambridge Texts in the History of Philosophy (Cambridge: Cambridge University Press, 2000).

Barezzani, Maria Teresa Rosa, "Le villanelle e la loro diffusione in Italia e all'estero," in Maria Teresa Rosa Barezzani and Manella Sala (eds), *Luca Marenzio musicista europeo*, Fondazione Civiltà Bresciana, 2 (Brescia: Edizioni di Storia Bresciana, 1989), pp. 115–63.

Bartel, Dietrich, *Musica poetica: Musical-Rhetorical Figures in German Baroque Music* (Lincoln: University of Nebraska Press, 1997).

Bartlet, M. Elizabeth C., "Draudius, Georg," *Grove Music Online*, ed. Laura Macy (Accessed 1 May 2006), <http://www.grovemusic.com>

Benedict, Barbara M., *Making the Modern Reader: Cultural Mediation in Early Modern Literary Anthologies* (Princeton: Princeton University Press, 1996).

Bernstein, Jane A., "Buyers and Collectors of Music Publications: Two Sixteenth-Century Music Libraries Recovered," in Jessie Ann Owens and Anthony Cummings (eds), *Music in Renaissance Cities and Courts: Studies in Honor of Lewis Lockwood* (Warren, MI: Harmonie Park Press, 1997), pp. 21–33.

——, *Music Printing in Renaissance Venice: The Scotto Press, 1539–1572* (New York: Oxford University Press, 1998).

Bianconi, Lorenzo, *Music in the Seventeenth Century*, trans. David Bryant (Cambridge: Cambridge University Press, 1987).

Blackburn, Bonnie J., "Petrucci's Venetian Editor: Petrus Castellanus and His Musical Garden," *Musica disciplina*, 49 (1995): 15–45.

Blankenburg, Walter/Norburt Dubowy, "Riccio, Teodore," *Grove Music Online*, ed. Laura Macy (Accessed 10 September 2006), <http://www.grovemusic.com>

Blume, Friedrich, *Protestant Church Music: A History* (New York: W.W. Norton, 1974).

Boorman, Stanley, "Printed Music Books of the Italian Renaissance from the Point of View of Manuscript Study," *Revista de musicologia*, 16/5 (1993): 2587–2602.

Bradshaw, Murray C., "Zacharia, Cesare de," *Grove Music Online*, ed. Laura Macy (Accessed 22 February 2006), <http://www.grovemusic.com>

Braun, Werner, *Britannia Abundans: Deutsch-Englisch Musikbeziehungen zur Shakespearezeit* (Tutzing: Hans Schneider, 1977).

Brett, Philip, "Morley, Thomas," *Grove Music Online*, ed. Laura Macy (Accessed 1 April 2006), <http://www.grovemusic.com>

Brown, Howard Mayer, "Emulation, Competition, and Homage: Imitation and Theories of Imitation in the Renaissance," *Journal of the American Musicological Society*, 35 (1982): 1–48.

——, *Instrumental Music Printed Before 1600: A Bibliography* (Cambridge: Harvard University Press, 1965; reprint London: iUniverse.com, 2000).

Brusniak, Friedhelm, "Nürnberger Schülerlisten des 16. Jahrhunderts als Musik-, Schul- und Sozialgeschichtliche Quellen," *Mitteilungen des Vereins für Geschichte der Stadt Nürnberg*, 69 (1982): 1–109.

Bryant, David, "Gabrieli, Andrea," *Grove Music Online*, ed. Laura Macy (Accessed 28 May 2006), <http://www.grovemusic.com>

——, "Gabrieli, Giovanni," *Grove Music Online*, ed. Laura Macy (Accessed 20 February 2006), <http://www.grovemusic.com>

Bullock, Walter L., "The Precept of Plagiarism in the Cinquecento," *Modern Philology*, 25 (1928): 293–312.

Burke, Peter, "The Uses of Italy," in Roy Porter and Mukuláš Teich (eds), *The Renaissance in National Context* (Cambridge: Cambridge University Press, 1992), pp. 6–20.

——, *The Fortunes of the* Courtier: *The European Reception of Castiglione's* Cortegiano (Cambridge, UK: Polity Press, 1995).

Burmeister, Joachim, *Musical Poetics*, trans. Benito V. Rivera, Music Theory Translation Series, ed. Claude V. Palisca (New Haven: Yale University Press, 1993).

Buszin, Walter E., "Luther on Music," *The Musical Quarterly*, 32 (1946): 80–97.

Butler, Bartlett R., "Liturgical Music in Sixteenth-Century Nuremberg: A Socio-Musical Study" (Ph.D. diss., University of Illinois at Urbana-Champaign, 1970).

Carapezza, Paolo Emilio and Giuseppe Collisani, "Vinci, Pietro," *Grove Music Online*, ed. Laura Macy (Accessed 7 June 2006), <http://www.grovemusic.com>

Cardamone, Donna G., *The Canzone Villanesca alla Napolitana and Related Forms, 1537–1570*, 2 vols (Ann Arbor: UMI Research Press, 1981).

——, "Villanella," *Grove Music Online*, ed. Laura Macy (Accessed 30 May 2006), <http://www.grovemusic.com>

Carter, Tim, "Music-Selling in Late Sixteenth-Century Florence: The Bookshop of Piero di Giuliano Morosi," *Music and Letters*, 70 (1989): 483–504.

Castiglione, Baldesar, *The Book of the Courtier*, trans. George Bull (New York: Penguin, 1967; reprint 1976).

Cave, Terence, *The Cornucopian Text: Problems of Writing in the French Renaissance* (Oxford: Clarendon, 1979).

Charteris, Richard, *Giovanni Gabrieli (ca. 1555–1612): A Thematic Catalogue of his Music with a Guide to the Source Materials and Translations of his Vocal Texts*, Thematic Catalogues, 20, general ed. Barry S. Brook (Stuyvesant, NY: Pendragon Press, 1996).

Chartier, Roger (ed.), *The Culture of Print: Power and the Uses of Print in Early Modern Europe*, trans. Lydia G. Cochrane (Princeton: Princeton University Press, 1987).

——, *The Order of Books: Readers, Authors, and Libraries in Europe between the Fourteenth and Eighteenth Centuries*, trans. Lydia G. Cochrane (Stanford: Stanford University Press, 1994).

——, *Forms and Meanings: Texts, Performances and Audiences from Codex to Computer* (Philadelphia: University of Pennsylvania Press, 1995).

Chater, James, *Luca Marenzio and the Italian Madrigal, 1577–1593*, Studies in British Musicology, ed. Nigel Fortune, 2 vols (Ann Arbor: UMI Research Press, 1981).

——, "*Il pastor fido* and Music: A Bibliography," in Angelo Pompilio (ed.), *Guarini, la musica, i musicisti*, Con Natazioni, 3, series ed. Paolo Fabbri (Lucca: Libreria Musicale Italiana Editrice, 1997), pp. 157–83.

——, "Marenzio, Luca (4)," *Grove Music Online*, ed. Laura Macy (Accessed 28 May 2006), <http://www.grovemusic.com>

Claes, Franz, *Bibliographisches Verzeichnis der deutschen Vokabulare und Worterbücher, gedruckt bis 1600* (Hildesheim: Georg Olms Verlag, 1977).

Compagnon, Antoine, *La Seconde Main ou le travail de la citation* (Paris: Editions du Seuil, 1979).

Corns, Thomas N., "The Early Modern Search Engine: Indices, Title Pages, Marginalia and Contents," in Neil Rhodes and Jonathan Sawday (eds), *The Renaissance Computer: Knowledge Technology in the First Age of Print* (London: Routledge, 2000), pp. 95–105.

Cox, Virginia. *The Renaissance Dialogue: Literary Dialogue in its Social and Political Contexts, Castiglione to Galileo* (Cambridge: Cambridge University Press, 1992).

Cusick, Suzanne C., *Valerio Dorico: Music Printer in Sixteenth-Century Rome*, Studies in Musicology, 43 (Ann Arbor: UMI Research Press, 1981).

——, "Balletto (2)," *Grove Music Online*, ed. Laura Macy (Accessed 22 February 2006), <http://www.grovemusic.com>

——, "Imitation," *Grove Music Online*, ed. Laura Macy (Accessed 22 February 2006), <http://www.grovemusic.com>

Darnton, Robert, *The Kiss of Lamourette: Reflections in Cultural History* (New York: W.W. Norton, 1990).

DeFord, Ruth I., "Musical Relationships between the Italian Madrigal and Light Genres in the Sixteenth Century," *Musica Disciplina*, 39 (1985): 107–67.

——, "The Influence of the Madrigal on Canzonetta Texts of the Late Sixteenth Century," *Acta Musicologica*, 59 (1987): 127–51.

——, "Marenzio and the *villanella alla romana*," *Early Music*, 27 (1999): 535–52.

——, "Canzonetta," *Grove Music Online*, ed. Laura Macy (Accessed 20 February 2006), <http://www.grovemusic.com>

Dienst, Karl, "Rinckart, Martin," *Biographisch- Bibliographisches Kirchenlexikon*, ed. Friedrich Wilhelm Bautz (Herzberg: Verlag Traugott Bautz, 1994), vol. 8, cols 367–9.

Dillon, Emma, *Medieval Music-Making and the* Roman de Fauvel (Cambridge: Cambridge University Press, 2002).

Dürr, Walther, "Die italienische Canzonette und das deutsche Lied im Ausgang des XVI. Jahrhunderts," in *Studi in onore di Lorenzo Bianchi* (Bologna: Zanichelli, 1960), pp. 71–102.

Dumont, Sara, "Valentin Haussmann's Canzonettas: The Italian Connection," *Music and Letters*, 63 (1982): 59–68.

——, *German Secular Polyphonic Song in Printed Editions, 1570–1630*, 2 vols (NewYork: Garland, 1989).

Dünnhaupt, Gerhard, *Bibliographisches Handbuch der Barockliteratur: Hundert Personalbibliographien Deutscher Autoren des Siebzehnten Jahrhunderts*, Hiersemanns bibliographische Handbücher, 2, 3 vols (Stuttgart: Anton Hiersemann, 1980–81).

Edwards, Rebecca, "Claudio Merulo: Servant of the State and Musical Entrepreneur in Later Sixteenth-Century Venice (Ph.D. diss., Princeton University, 1990).

Eichhorn, Holger, "Der Deutsche Gabrieli: Zur Überlieferung des Spätwerks von Giovanni Gabrieli unter vorrangigem Betracht deutscher Rezeption und Quellenlage im 17. Jahrhundert," *Giovanni Gabrieli: Quantus vir*, Musik-Konzepte, 105 (1999): 35–58.

Einstein, Alfred, "Claudio Merulo's Ausgabe der Madrigale des Verdelot," *Sammelbände der Internationalen Musikgesellschaft*, 8/2 (1907): 220–54

——, *The Italian Madrigal*, 3 vols (Princeton: Princeton University Press, 1949).

Eisenstein, Elizabeth, *The Printing Press as an Agent of Change: Communications and Cultural Transformations in Early Modern Europe*, 2 vols (Cambridge: Cambridge University Press, 1979).

Fallows, David, "Carmen," *Grove Music Online*, ed. Laura Macy (Accessed 30 May 2006), <http://www.grovemusic.com>

Febvre, Lucien and Henri-Jean Martin, *L'apparition du livre* (Paris: Editions Albin Michel, 1958), trans. David Gerard, *The Coming of the Book: The Impact of Printing 1450–1800* (London: Verso, 1976).

Feldman, Martha, *City Culture and the Madrigal at Venice* (Berkeley: University of California Press, 1995).

——, "Authors and Anonyms: Recovering the Anonymous Subject in *Cinquecento* Vernacular Objects," in Kate van Orden (ed.), *Music and the Cultures of Print*, Critical and Cultural Musicology, 1, ed. Martha Feldman (New York: Garland, 2000), pp. 163–99.

Fellerer, K.G., "Ein Musikalien-Inventar des fürstbischöflichen Hofes in Freising aus dem 17. Jahrhundert," *Archiv für Musikwissenschaft*, 6/4 (1924): 471–83.

Fenlon, Iain, *Music, Print and Culture in Early Sixteenth-Century Italy: The Panizzi Lectures 1994* (London: The British Library, 1995).

——, "Ferretti, Giovanni," *Grove Music Online*, ed. Laura Macy (Accessed 28 May 2006), <http://www.grovemusic.com>

Finscher, Ludwig (ed.), *Die Musik des 15. und 16. Jahrhunderts*, Neues Handbuch der Musikwissenschaft, 3/2, series ed. Carl Dahlhaus (Laaber: Laaber-Verlag, 1990).

——, "Lied and Madrigal, 1580–1600," in John Kmetz (ed.), *Music in the German Renaissance: Sources, Styles, and Contexts* (Cambridge: Cambridge University Press, 1994), pp. 182–92.

Fisher, Alexander J., *Music and Religious Identity in Counter-Reformation Augsburg, 1580–1630*, St Andrews studies in Reformation history (Aldershot: Ashgate, 2004).

Forney, Kristine K., "Tielman Susato, Sixteenth-Century Music Printer: An Archival and Typographical Investigation" (Ph.D. diss., University of Kentucky, 1979).

——, "Antwerp's Role in the Reception and Dissemination of the Madrigal in the North," in Angelo Pompilio et al. (eds), *IMS 14th Congress 1987. Round Table IV. Produzione e distribuzione di musica nella società del XVI e XVII secolo*, 3 vols (Turin: Edizioni di Torino, 1990), vol. 1, pp. 239–53.

——, "Pevernage, Andreas," in *New Grove II*, vol. 19, pp. 530–31.

Foucault, Michel, "Qu'est-ce qu'un auteur?" *Bulletin de la Société française de Philosophie*, 44 (July-September 1969): 73–104, trans. as "What Is an Author?"

in Donald F. Bouchard (ed.), *Language, Counter-Memory, Practice: Selected Essays and Interviews* (Ithaca: Cornell University Press, 1977), pp. 113–38.

Frank, Armin Paul, "Towards a Cultural History of Literary Translation: 'Histories,' 'Systems,' and Other Forms of Synthesizing Research," in Harald Kittel (ed.), *Geschichte, System, Literarische Übersetzung / Histories, Systems, Literary Translations, GBIÜ*, 5 (Berlin: Erich Schmidt, 1992), pp. 369–82.

Freedman, Richard, *The Chansons of Orlando di Lasso: Music, Piety, and Print in Sixteenth-Century France*, Eastman Studies in Music, ed. Ralph P. Locke (Rochester: University of Rochester Press, 2000).

Fromson, Michelle, "A Conjunction of Rhetoric and Music: Structural Modelling in the Italian Counter-Reformation Motet," *Journal of the Royal Musical Association*, 117 (1992): 208–46.

Gabrieli, Andrea, *Andrea Gabrieli: Complete Madrigals 9–10*, ed. A. Tillman Merritt, Recent Researches in the Music of the Renaissance, vols 49–50 (Madison, WI: A-R Editions, Inc. 1983).

——, *Andrea Gabrieli: Complete Madrigals 12*, ed. A. Tillman Merritt, Recent Researches in the Music of the Renaissance, vol. 52 (Madison, WI: A-R Editions, Inc.1984).

Garbe, Daniela, *Das Musikalienrepertoire von St. Stephani zu Helmstedt: Ein Bestand an Drucken und Handschriften des 17. Jahrhunderts*, 2 vols, Wolfenbütteler Arbeiten zur Barockforschung, 33 (Wiesbaden: Harrassowitz, 1998).

Gattuso, Susan, "16th-Century Nuremberg," in Iain Fenlon (ed.), *The Renaissance: From the 1470s to the End of the 16th Century* (Englewood Cliffs, NJ: Prentice Hall, 1989), pp. 286–303.

Genette, Gerard, *Seuils* (Paris: Editions du Seuil, 1987).

——, *Paratexts: Thresholds of Interpretation*, trans. Jane E. Lewin (Cambridge: Cambridge University Press, 1997).

Giuliani, Marco, "Antologie, miscellanee, edizioni collettive nei secc. XVI–XVII," *Nuova Rivista Musicale Italiana*, 22/1 (1988): 70–76.

Goldmann, Karlheinz, "William Smith: A Description of the Cittie of Noremberg (Beschreibung der Reichsstadt Nürnberg) 1594," *Mitteilungen des Vereins für Geschichte der Stadt Nürnberg*, 48 (1958): 194–245.

Goldthwaite, Richard A., *Wealth and the Demand for Art in Italy, 1300–1600* (Baltimore: Johns Hopkins University Press, 1993).

Gottwald, Clytus, *Katalog der Musikalien in der Schermar-Bibliothek Ulm*, Veröffentlichungen der Stadtbibliothek Ulm, 17 (Wiesbaden: Harrassowitz, 1993).

Grafton, Anthony, "Notes from Underground on Cultural Transmission," in Anthony Grafton and Ann Blair (eds), *The Transmission of Culture in Early Modern Europe* (Philadelphia: Univeristy of Pennsylvania Press, 1990), pp. 1–7.

——, "Correctores corruptores?: Notes on the Social History of Editing," in Glenn W. Most (ed.), *Editing Texts/Texte edieren*, Aporemata. Kritische Studien zur Philologiegeschichte, 2 (Göttingen: Vandenhoeck & Ruprecht, 1998), pp. 54–76.

Greenblatt, Stephen. *Renaissance Self-Fashioning: From More to Shakespeare* (Chicago: University of Chicago Press, 1980).

Greene, Thomas, *The Light in Troy: Imitation and Discovery in Renaissance Poetry* (New Haven: Yale University Press, 1982).

Grier, James, *The Critical Editing of Music: History, Method, and Practice* (Cambridge: University of Cambridge Press, 1996).

Gudewill, Kurt, "Lyttich, Johann," *MGG*[2], *Personenteil* 11, cols 673–4.

Gustavson, Royston Robert, "Hans Ott, Hieronymus Formschneider, and the *Novum et insigne opus musicum* (Nuremberg, 1537–1538)" (Ph.D. diss., University of Melbourne, 1998).

Gutfleisch, Barbara and Joachim Menzhausen, "'How a Kunstkammer Should Be Formed': Gabriel Kaltemarckt's Advice to Christian I of Saxony on the Formation of an Art Collection," *Journal of the History of Collections*, 1 (1989): 3–32.

Hamm, Charles and Jerry Call: "Sources, MS, §IX, 21: 16th-century German sources of Catholic music," *Grove Music Online*, ed. Laura Macy (Accessed 20 February 2006), http://www.grovemusic.com

Harrán, Don, *Word-Tone Relations in Musical Thought: From Antiquity to the Seventeenth Century*, Musicological Studies & Documents, 40, ed. Armen Carapetyan (Stuttgart: American Institute of Musicology/Hänssler-Verlag, 1986).

Hausmann, Frank-Rutger, *Bibliographie der deutschen Übersetzungen aus dem Italienischen von den Anfängen bis 1730*, 2 vols (Tübingen, Niemeyer, 1992).

Heuchemer, Dane O., "Pinello di Ghirardi, Giovanni Battista," *Grove Music Online*, ed. Laura Macy (Accessed 22 February 2006), <http://www.grovemusic.com>

———, "Scandello, Antonio," *Grove Music Online*, ed. Laura Macy (Accessed 10 September 2006), <http://www.grovemusic.com>

Heussner, Horst and Ingo Schultz, *Musikbibliographie in Deutschland bis 1625*, Catalogus Musicus, 6 (Kassel: Bärenreiter-Antiquariat, 1973).

Helms, Mary W., "Essay on Objects: Interpretations of Distance Made Tangible," in Stuart B. Schwartz (ed.), *Implicit Understandings: Observing, Reporting, and Reflecting on the Encounters between Europeans and Other Peoples in the Early Modern Era* (New York: Cambridge University Press, 1994), pp. 355–77.

Henning, Aegidius, *Gepriesener Büchermacher, Oder Von Bückern / und Bücher machen [Frankfurt, 1666]*; reprint in *Das Buchwesen im Barock* (Munich: Kraus, 1981).

Hermans, Theo, "Renaissance Translation between Literalism and Imitation," in Harald Kittel (ed.), *Geschichte, System, Literarische Übersetzung/Histories, Systems, Literary Translations*, GBIÜ 5, (Berlin: Erich Schmidt, 1992), pp. 95–116.

Hoffman, Georg, "Writing without Leisure: Proofreading as Work in the Renaissance," *Journal of Medieval and Renaissance Studies*, 25 (1995): 17–31.

Holub, Robert C., *Reception Theory* (London: Methuen, 1984).

Hornschuch, Hieronymus, *Orthotypographia 1608*, ed. and trans. Philip Gaskell and Patricia Bradford (Cambridge: The University Library, 1972).

The Holy Bible, King James Version (New York: Harper, 1995).

Iser, Wolfgang. *The Act of Reading: A Theory of Aesthetic Response* (Baltimore: Johns Hopkins University Press, 1978).

Jackson, Susan, "Johann vom Berg and Ulrich Neuber: Music Printers in Sixteenth-Century Nuremberg" (Ph.D. diss., City University of New York, 1998).

Jardine, Lisa, "Humanistic Logic," in Quentin Skinner and Eckhard Kessler (eds), *The Cambridge History of Renaissance Philosophy* (Cambridge: Cambridge University Press, 1988), pp. 173–98.

Jauss, Hans-Robert, *Toward an Aesthetic of Reception*, trans. Timothy Bahti (Minneapolis: University of Minnesota Press, 1982).

Judd, Cristle Collins, *Reading Renaissance Music Theory: Hearing with the Eyes* (Cambridge: Cambridge University Press, 2000).

Jung, Hans Rudolf, "Ein neuaufgefundenes Gutachten von Heinrich Schütz aus dem Jahre 1617," *Archiv für Musikwissenschaft*, 18/3–4 (1961): 241–7.

——, "Ein unbekanntes Gutachten von Heinrich Schütz über die Neuordnung der Hof-, Schul- und Stadtmusik in Gera," *Beiträge zur Musikwissenschaft*, 1 (1962): 17–36.

——, "Zwei unbekannte Briefe von Heinrich Schütz aus den Jahren 1653/54," *Beiträge zur Musikwissenschaft*, 14 Jahrgang, Heft 3 (1972): 231–6.

Katte, Maria von, "Herzog August und die Kataloge seiner Bibliothek," *Wolfenbütteler Beiträge*, 1 (1972): 168–99.

Kaufmann, Thomas DaCosta, *The Mastery of Nature: Aspects of Art, Science, and Humanism in the Renaissance* (Princeton: Princeton University Press, 1993).

——, *Court, Cloister, and City: The Art and Culture of Central Europe, 1450–1800* (Chicago: University of Chicago Press, 1995).

——, *Toward a Geography of Art* (Chicago: Chicago University Press, 2004).

Kerman, Joseph, *The Elizabethan Madrigal: A Comparative Study* (New York: American Musicological Society, 1962).

Kirwan, A Lindsey, "Vincentius, Caspar," *New Grove II*, vol. 26, pp. 652–3.

Kittel, Harald, "International Anthologies of Literature in Translation: An Introduction to Incipient Research," in Harald Kittel (ed.), *International Anthologies of Literature in Translation*, GBIÜ, 9 (Berlin: Erich Schmidt, 1995), pp. IX–XXVII.

Kleinstäuber, Christian Heinrich, "Geschichte des evangelischen reichstädtischen Gymnasii poetici, part 1 (1538–1811)," *Verhandlungen des historischen Vereins von Oberpfalz und Regensburg*, 35–6, Neue Folge, 27–8 (1880; 1882): 1–152.

Koch, Klaus-Peter, "Documentary Biography," in Robert B. Lynn, *Valentin Haussmann (1565/70–ca.1614): A Thematic-Documentary Catalogue of His Works*, Thematic Catalogues, 25, ed. Barry S. Brook (Stuyvesant, NY: Pendragon Press, 1997), pp. 1–52.

Kraack, Gerhard, *Die St.-Nikolai-Bibliothek zu Flensburg: Eine Büchersammlung aus dem Jahrhundert der Reformation. Beschreibung und Katalog*, Schriften der Gesellschaft für Flensburger Stadtgeschichte, e.v. nr. 35 (Schleswig: Schleswiger Druck- und Verlagshaus, 1984).

Krautwurst, Franz, "Lindner, Friedrich," in *MGG*, 8 (1960), cols. 894–97.

Krieg, Walter, *Materialien zu einer Entwicklungsgeschichte der Bücher-Preise und des Autoren-Honorars vom 15. bis zum 20. Jahrhundert* (Vienna: Herbert Stubenrauch, 1953).

Kristeller, Paul Oskar, "The European Diffusion of Italian Humanism," *Italica*, 39 (1962): 1–20.

Krummel, Donald W., *Bibliotheca Bolduaniana: A Renaissance Music Bibliography* (Detroit: Information Coordinators, 1972)

Künast, Hans-Jörg, "Welserbibliotheken: Eine Bestandsaufnahme der Bibliotheken von Anton, Marcus und Paulus Welser," in Mark Häberlein and Johannes Burkhardt (eds), *Die Welser: Neue Forschungen zur Geschichte und Kultur des oberdeutschen Handelshauses*, Sonderdruck aus Colloquia Augustana, 16 (Augsburg: Akademie Verlag, 2002), pp. 550–84.

Lampl, Hans, "Michael Praetorius, *Syntagma Musicum:* A Translation," (Ph.D. diss., University of California at Berkeley, 1957).

Lasso, Orlando di, et al., *Canzoni villanesche and villanelle*, Donna Cardamone (ed.), Recent Researches in the Music of the Renaissance, 82–3 (Madison, WI: A-R Editions, Inc. 1991).

Leaver, Robin A., "Lutheran Vespers as a Context for Music," in Paul Walker (ed.), *Church, Stage, and Studio: Music and Its Contexts in Seventeenth-Century Germany*, Studies in Music, 107, series ed. George J. Buelow (Ann Arbor: UMI Research Press, 1990), pp. 143–61.

Leopold, Silke, "Madrigali sulle egloghe sdrucciole di Iacopo Sannazaro," *Rivista italiana di musicologia*, 14 (1979): 75–127.

Lesure, François and Claudio Sartori, *Bibliografia della musica italiana profana, nuova ed. interamente rifatta e aumentata con gli indici dei musicisti, poeti, cantanti, dedicatari e dei capoversi dei testi letterari*, 3 vols (Pomezia: Staderini-Minkoff, 1977).

Lesure, François (ed.), *Recueils imprimés XVIe-XVIIe siècles*, RISM B I/1 (Munich: G. Henle Verlag, 1960).

Leuchtmann, Horst and A. Lindsey Kirwan, "Herrer, Michael," *New Grove II*, vol. 11, p. 438.

Lewis, Mary S., *Antonio Gardano, Venetian Music Printer, 1538–1569: A Descriptive Bibliography and Historical Study*, 3 vols (New York: Garland, 1988–2005).

——, "Manuscripts and Printed Music in the World of Patrons and Collectors" in Angelo Pompilio et al. (eds), *IMS 14th Congress 1987. Round Table IV. Produzione e distribuzione di musica nella società europea del XVI e XVII secolo*, 3 vols (Turin: Edizioni di Torino, 1990), vol. 1, pp. 319–25.

——, "The Printed Music Book in Context: Observations on Some Sixteenth-Century Editions," *Notes*, 46 (1990): 899–918.

——, "Twins, Cousins, and Heirs: Relationships among Editions of Music Printed in Sixteenth-Century Venice," in John Knowles (ed.), *Critica Musica: Essays in Honor of Paul Brainard* (Amsterdam: Gordon and Breach, 1996), pp. 193–224.

Lindberg, John Edward, "Origins and Development of the Sixteenth Century Tricinium" (Ph.D., diss., University of Cincinnati, 1989).

Linke, Johannes, *Martin Rinkarts geistliche Lieder* (Gotha: Friedrich Andreas Perthes 1886).

Lipsius, Justus, *Epistolica Institutio*, eds and trans R.V. Young and M. Thomas Hester (Carbondale: Southern Illinois University Press, 1996).

Losse, Deborah N., *Sampling the Book: Renaissance Prologues and the French Conteurs* (Lewisburg: Bucknell University Press, 1994).

Love, Harold, *Scribal Publication in Seventeenth-Century England* (Oxford: Clarendon Press, 1993).

Luther, Martin, *A Manual of the Book of Psalms: or, The Subject-Contents of all the Psalms*, trans. Rev. Henry Cole (London: Bohn, 1847).

——, "To the Councilmen of All Cities in Germany That They Establish and Maintain Christian Schools, 1524," trans. Albert T.W. Steinhaeuser, rev. Walther I. Brandt, in Walther I. Brandt (ed.), *The Christian in Society II*, *Luther's Works*, ed. Helmut T. Lehmann (Philadelphia: Muhlenberg Press, 1962), vol. 45, pp. 339–78.

——, "Preface to Georg Rhau's *Symphoniae iucundae* (1538)," in Ulrich S. Leupold (ed.), *Liturgy and Hymns*, *Luther's Works*, general ed. Helmut T. Lehmann, series ed. Jaroslav Pelikan (Philadelphia: Fortress Press, 1965), vol. 53, pp. 321–4.

——, "Preface to the Wittenberg Hymnal," in *Liturgy and Hymns*, *Luther's Works*, vol. 53, pp. 315–16.

——, "A Preface to All Good Hymnals (1538)," trans. Paul Nettl in *Luther's Works*, vol. 53, pp. 319–20.

Lynn, Robert B., *Valentin Haussmann (1565/70–ca.1614): A Thematic-Documentary Catalogue of His Works*, Thematic Catalogues, 25, ed. Barry S. Brook (Stuyvesant, NY: Pendragon Press, 1997).

Marenzio, Luca, *I cinque libri di Canzonette, Villanelle et arie alla Napolitana a tre voci di Luca Marenzio (in tre quaderni)*, ed. Marco Giuliani (Trent: Edizioni Nova Scuola Musicale, 1995–96).

Martin, Uwe, "Die Nürnberger Musikgesellschaften," *Mitteilungen des Vereins für Geschichte der Stadt Nürnberg*, 49 (1959): 185–225.

Martino, Alberto, *Die italienische Literatur im deutschen Sprachraum: Ergänzungen und Berichtigungen zu Frank-Rutger Hausmanns Bibliographie, Chloe*. Beihefte zum Daphnis, 17 (Amsterdam: Rodopi, 1994).

Marvin, Clara, *Giovanni Pierluigi da Palestrina: A Guide to Research*, Composer Resource Manuals, 56 (New York: Routledge, 2002).

Mays, James L. (ed.), *Harper's Bible Commentary* (San Francisco: Harper & Row, 1988).

McGann, Jerome J., *A Critique of Modern Textual Criticism* (Chicago: University of Chicago Press, 1983).

McKenzie, Donald Francis, *Bibliography and the Sociology of Texts*, *The Panizzi Lectures* (London: The British Library, 1986).

McKitterick, David, *Print, Manuscript and the Search for Order, 1450–1830* (Cambridge: Cambridge University Press, 2003).

Meconi, Honey, "Does Imitatio Exist?" *Journal of Musicology*, 12 (1994): 152–78.

Milde, Wolfgang, "The Library at Wolfenbüttel, from 1550 to 1618," *The Modern Language Review*, 66 (1971): 101–12.

Moore, Stephen Thomson, "*Il vago alboreto* (Antwerp, 1597): An Edition and Commentary on the Unpublished Works," (DMA, Stanford University, 1982).

Morricone, Clotilde and Adriana Salottolo, "Valentin Haussmann trascrittore e le canzonette italiane in Germania," *Rivista di musicologia*, 5 (1970): 73–98.

Moss, Ann, *Printed Commonplace-Books and the Structuring of Renaissance Thought* (Oxford: Clarendon Press, 1996).

Neubacher, Jürgen, *Die Musikbibliothek des Hamburger Kantors und Musikdirektors Thomas Selle (1599–1663): Rekonstruktion des ursprünglichen und Beschreibung des erhaltenen, überwiegend in der Staats- und Universitätsbibliothek Hamburg Carl von Ossietzky aufbewahrten Bestandes*, Musicological Studies & Documents, 52, ed. Ursula Günther (Neuhausen: American Institute of Musicology, Hänssler-Verlag, 1997).

Niemöller, Klaus Wolfgang, "Parodia-Imitatio: Zu Georg Quitschreibers Schrift von 1611," in Annegrit Laubenthal (ed.), *Studien zur Musikgeschichte: eine Festschrift für Ludwig Finscher* (Kassel: Bärenreiter, 1995), pp. 174–80.

Noe, Alfred, "Cesare Zaccarias Zweisprachige Canzonetten-Sammlung von 1590," in Norbert Bachleitner, Alfred Noe, and Hans-Gert Roloff (eds), *Beiträge zu Komparatistik und Sozialgeschichte der Literatur: Festschrift für Alberto Martino, Chloe*. Beihefte zum Daphnis, 26 (Amsterdam: Rodopi, 1997), pp. 211–32.

——, *Die Präsenz der romanischen Literaturen in der 1655 nach Wien verkauften Fuggerbibliohek 3: Die Texte der 'Musicales'*, Internationale Forschungen zur Allgemeinen und Vergleichenden Literaturwissenschaft, 21, ed. Alberto Martino (Amsterdam: Rodopi, 1997).

Oettinger, Rebecca Wagner, *Music as Propaganda in the German Reformation* (Aldershot: Ashgate, 2001).

Ong, Walter J., *Ramus: Method and the Decay of Dialogue: From the Art of Discourse to the Art of Reason* (Cambridge: Harvard University Press, 1958).

——, *Orality and Literacy: The Technologizing of the Word* (London: Routledge, 1988; reprint of London: Methuen, 1982).

Ongaro, Giulio, "Venetian Printed Anthologies of Music in the 1560s and the Role of the Editor," in Hans Lenneberg (ed.), *The Dissemination of Music: Studies in the History of Music Publishing* (USA: Gordon and Breach, 1994), pp. 43–69.

——, "The Library of a Sixteenth-Century Music Teacher," *The Journal of Musicology*, 12 (1994): 357–75.

Oppermann, Annette. "Die Geburt des Herausgebers aus dem Geist des Widerspruchs Johann Nikolaus Forkel und die Oeuvres complettes de Jean Sebastien Bach," in Christiane Henkes, Walter Hettche, Gabriele Radecke, and Elke Senne (eds), *Schrift – Text – Edition. Hans Walter Gabler zum 65. Geburtstag*, Beihefte zur Editio, 19, ed. Winfried Woesler (Tübingen: Max Niemeyer, 2003), pp. 171–9.

Outler, Albert C. (trans. and ed.), *Augustine: Confessions and Enchiridion*, The Library of Christian Classics, 7, general eds. John Baillie, John T. McNeill, and Henry P. Van Dusen (Philadelphia: The Westminster Press, 1955).

Palisca, Claude, *Norton Anthology of Western Music*, 2d edn (New York: W.W. Norton, 1988).

Pass, Walter, "Regnart, Jacob," *New Grove II*, vol. 21, pp. 118–19.

Pieper, Renate, "The Upper German Trade in Art and Curiosities before the Thirty Years War," in Michael North and David Ormrod (eds), *Art Markets in Europe, 1400–1800* (Aldershot: Ashgate, 1998), pp. 93–102.

Pigman, G.W. III, "Versions of Imitation in the Renaissance," *Renaissance Quarterly*, 33/1 (1980): 1–32.

Pike, Lionel, *Pills to Purge Melancholy: The Evolution of the English Ballett* (Aldershot: Ashgate, 2004).

Piperno, Franco, *Gli 'Eccellentissimi musici della città di Bologna', con uno studio sull'antologia madrigalistica del Cinquecento* (Florence: Olschki, 1985)

——, "Polifonisti dell'Italia Meridionale nelle Antologie Madrigalistiche d'Oltralpe (1601–1616)," *La musica a Napoli durante il Seicento. Atti del Convegno Internazionale di Studi Napoli*, Miscellanea Musicologica, 2 (Rome: Edizioni Torre d'Orfeo, 1987), pp. 77–92.

——, "Madrigal Anthologies by Northern Printers and Monteverdi," in Silke Leopold (ed.), *Claudio Monteverdi und die Folgen: Bericht über das Internationale Symposium Detmold 1993* (Kassel: Bärenreiter, 1998), pp. 29–50.

Pleticha, Eva, *Adel und Buch: Studien zur Geisteswelt des fränkischen Adels am Beispiel seiner Bibliotheken vom 15. bis zum 18. Jahrhundert*, Veröffentlichungen der Gesellschaft für Fränkische Geschichte series 9, Darstellungen aus der fränkischen Geschichte, 33 (Neustadt a.d. Aisch: Degener, 1983), pp. 50–55.

Pogue, Samuel F., *Jacques Moderne: Lyons Music Printer of the Sixteenth Century* (Geneva: Librarie Droz, 1969).

——, "A Sixteenth-Century Editor at Work: Gardane and Moderne," *Journal of Musicology*, 1 (1982): 217–38.

Pohl, Horst, *Willibald Imhoff, Enkel und Erbe Willibald Pirckheimers*, Quellen zur Geschichte und Kultur der Stadt Nürnberg, 24 (Nuremberg: Selbstverlag des Stadtrats zu Nürnberg, 1992).

Pontano, Giovanni, *I trattati delle virtù sociali*, ed. Francesco Tateo (Rome: Edizioni dell'Ateneo, 1965).

Powers, Harold S., "Tonal Types and Modal Categories in Renaissance Polyphony," *Journal of the American Musicological Society*, 34 (1981): 428–70.

Powley III, Harrison, "*Il trionfo di Dori*: A Critical Edition," 3 vols (Ph.D. diss., University of Rochester, Eastman School of Music, 1974).

——, (ed. and trans.), *Il trionfo di Dori: The 29 Madrigals of the 1592 Collection for Mixed Voices*, Renaissance Voices (New York: Gaudia Music and Arts, 1990, Schaffner Publishing Co., sole agent)

Praetorius, Michael, *Syntagma Musicum Band III. Termini musici Wolfenbüttel 1619*, ed. Wilibald Gurlitt (New York: Bärenreiter, 1958).

——, *Syntagma Musicum III*, ed./trans. Jeffery Kite-Powell, Oxford Early Music Series (Oxford: Oxford University Press, 2004).

Price, Leah, *The Anthology and the Rise of the Novel: From Richardson to George Eliot* (Cambridge: Cambridge University Press, 2000).

Regnart, Jacob, *Deutsche dreistimmige Lieder nach Art der Neapolitanen, nebst Leonhard Lechner's fünfstimmiger Bearbeitung*, ed. Robert Eitner, Publikation Aelterer Praktischer und Theoretischer Musikwerke, 19 (New York: Boude Brothers, 1966; reprint of Leipzig, 1895).

Richardson, Brian, *Print Culture in Renaissance Italy: The Editor and the Vernacular Text, 1470–1600*, Cambridge Studies in Publishing and Printing History, eds Terry Belanger and David McKitterick (Cambridge: Cambridge University Press, 1994).

——, *Printing, Writers and Readers in Renaissance Italy* (Cambridge: Cambridge University Press, 1999).

Roche, Jerome, "'Aus den berühmbsten italiänischen Autoribus': Dissemination North of the Alps of the Early Baroque Italian Sacred Repertory through Published Anthologies and Reprints," in Silke Leopold and Joachim Steinheuer (eds), *Claudio Monteverdi und die Folgen: Bericht über das Internationale Symposium Detmold 1993* (Kassel: Bärenreiter, 1998), pp. 13–28.

—— and Elizabeth Roche (eds), *Light Madrigals and Villanellas*, The Flower of the Italian Madrigal, vol. 3, trans. Barbara Reynolds (New York: Gaudia Music and Arts, 1995, Schaffner Publishing Co., sole agent).

Röder, Thomas, "Lindner, Friedrich," *MGG²*, *Personenteil*, vol. 11, cols. 161–2.

Rosand, Ellen, "Music in the Myth of Venice," *Renaissance Quarterly*, 30 (1977): 511–37.

Rouse, Mary A. and Richard H. Rouse, "*Statim invenire*: Schools, Preachers, and New Attitudes to the Page," in Robert L. Benson and Giles Constable (eds), *Renaissance and Renewal in the Twelfth Century* (Cambridge: Harvard University Press, 1982), pp. 201–25.

Rubsamen, Walter H., "The International 'Catholic' Repertoire of a Lutheran Church in Nürnberg (1574–1597)," *Annales Musicologiques*, 5 (1957): 229–327.

Ruhnke, Martin, *Beiträge zu einer Geschichte der deutschen Hofmusikkollegion im 16. Jahrhundert* (Berlin: Merseburger, 1963).

——, "Zum Wort-Ton-Verhältnis in den mehrstrophigen Villanellen von Luca Marenzio und ihren Umtextierungen durch Valentin Haußmann," in Martin Just and Reinhard Wiesend (eds), *Liedstudien: Wolfgang Osthoff zum 60. Geburtstag* (Tutzing: Hans Schneider, 1989), pp. 137–51.

Samuel, Harold E., *The Cantata in Nuremberg* (Ann Arbor: UMI Research Press, 1982).

——, "Kindermann, Johann Erasmus," *Grove Music Online*, ed. Laura Macy (Accessed 11 May 2006), <http://www.grovemusic.com>

Schaal, Richard, "Die Musikbibliothek von Raimund Fugger d.J.: Ein Beitrag zur Musiküberlieferung des 16. Jahrhunderts," *Acta Musicologica*, 29 (1957): 126–37.

——, "Georg Willers Augsburger Musikalien-Katalog von 1622," *Die Musikforschung*, 16 (1963): 127–33.

—— (ed.), *Das Inventar der Kantorei St. Anna in Augsburg: Ein Beitrag zur protestantischen Musikpflege im 16. und beginnenden 17. Jahrhundert*, Catalogus Musicus, 3 (Kassel: International Musicological Society, 1965).

—— (ed.), *Die Kataloge des Augsburger Musikalien-Händlers Kaspar Flurschütz, 1613–1628*, Quellenkataloge zu Musikgeschichte, 7 (Wilhelmshaven: Heinrichshofen's Verlag, 1974).

Schade, Richard Erich, "Rinckart, Martin," *Literatur Lexikon. Autoren und Werke deutscher Sprache*, ed. Walther Killy (Gütersloh and Munich: Bertelsmann Lexikon Verlag, 1991), vol. 9, pp. 473–4.

Schaeffer, Peter, "Baroque Philology: The Position of German in the European Family of Languages," in Gerhart Hoffmeister (ed.), *German Baroque Literature: The European Perspective* (New York: Frederick Ungar Publishing Co., 1983).

Scharnagl, August, "Raselius, Andreas," *MGG*, vol. 11, cols 1–3.

Schilling, Heinz, "Confessionalization in the Empire: Religious and Societal Change in Germany Between 1555 and 1620," in *Religion, Political Culture and the Emergence of Early Modern Society: Essays in German and Dutch History*, Studies in Medieval and Reformation Thought, 50, ed. Heiko A. Oberman (Leiden: E.J. Brill, 1992), pp. 205–45.

Schlager, Karlheinz (ed.), *Einzeldrucke vor 1800*, RISM A/1, 9 vols (Kassel: Bärenreiter, 1971–81).

Schlosser, Julius von, *Die Kunst- und Wunderkammer der Spätrenaissance: Ein Beitrag zur Geschichte des Sammelwesens* (Leipzig, 1908; 2nd edn Braunschweig: Klinkhardt and Biermann, 1978).

Schmalzriedt, Siegfried, *Heinrich Schütz und andere zeitgenössische Musiker in der Lehre Giovanni Gabrielis* (Neuhausen: Hänssler-Verlag, 1972).

Schmidt, Georg, "Die frühneuzeitliche Idee "deutsche Nation": Mehrkonfessionalität und säkulare Werte," in Heinz-Gerhard Haupt and Dieter Langewiesche (eds), *Nation und Religion in der Deutschen Geschichte* (Frankfurt: Campus, 2001), pp. 33–67.

Schnell, Dagmar, *In lucem edidit: Der deutsche Notendruck der ersten Hälfte des 17. Jahrhunderts als Kommunikationsmedium. Dargestellt an den Vorreden* (Osnabrück: Der Andere Verlag, 2003).

Schuetze, George C. (ed.), *Settings of* Ardo si *and Its Related Texts*, Recent Researches in the Music of the Renaissance, 78–9 (Madison, WI: A-R Editions, Inc. 1990).

Schwämmiein, Karl, "Die Bibliothek des Andreas Raselius Ambergensis," *Der Eisengau*, 1 (1992): 53–77.

Schwartz, Rudolf, "Hans Leo Haßler unter dem Einfluß der italiänischen Madrigalisten," *Vierteljahrsschrift für Musikwissenschaft*, 9 (1893): 51–61.

Schwarz, Werner, "The Theory of Translation in Sixteenth Century Germany," *The Modern Language Review*, 40 (1945): 289–99.

Seifert, Herbert, "Ein Gumpoldskirchner Musikalieninventar aus dem Jahr 1640," *Studien zur Musikwissenschaft*, 39 (1988): 55–61.

Simpson, Percy, *Proof-Reading in the Sixteenth, Seventeenth, and Eighteenth Centuries* (London: Oxford University Press, 1935; reprint 1970).

Slim, H. Colin, "The Music Library of the Augsburg Patrician, Hans Heinrich Herwart (1520–1583)," *Annales musicologiques*, 7 (1964–77): 67–109.

Smallman, Basil, "Pastoralism, Parody and Pathos: The Madrigal in Germany, 1570–1630," in *Conspectus Carminis: Essays for David Galliver, Miscellanea Musicologica*, Adelaide Studies in Musicology, 15 (Adelaide: University of Adelaide Press, 1988), pp. 6–20.

Smyth, Adam, *'Profit and Delight': Printed Miscellanies in England, 1640–1682* (Detroit: Wayne State University Press, 2004).

Snyder, Kerala J., "Text and Tone in Hassler's German Songs and Their Sacred Parodies," in Nancy Kovaleff Baker and Barbara Russano Hanning (eds), *Musical Humanism and Its Legacy: Essays in Honor of Claude V. Palisca* (Stuyvesant: Pendragon Press, 1992), pp. 253–77.

Spahr, Blake Lee, "The Letter as a Literary Sub-Genre in the German Baroque," *Chloe*, 6 (Amsterdam: Rodopi, 1987): 653–60.

Sponheim, Kristin M., "The Anthologies of Ambrosius Profe (1589–1661) and the Transmission of Italian Music in Germany" (Ph.D. diss., Yale University, 1995).

Sporhan-Krempel, Lore, "Georg Forstenheuser aus Nürnberg 1584–1659: Korrespondent, Bücherrat, Faktor und Agent," *Börsenblatt für den Deutschen Buchhandel*, Frankfurt Edition, 23 (20 March 1970): 705–43.

Springr, A., "Inventare der Imhoff'schen Kunstkammer zu Nürnberg," *Mitteilungen der kaiserl. Königl. Central Commission*, 5 (1860): 352–7.

Steele, John, "Antonio Barré: Madrigalist, Anthologist and Publisher in Rome— Some Preliminary Findings," in Richard Charteris (ed.), *Essays on Italian Music in the Cinquecento* (Sydney: Frederick May Foundation for Italian Studies and the Italian Institute for Culture, 1990), pp. 82–112.

Steiner, Harald, *Das Autorenhonorar – seine Entwicklungsgeschichte vom 17. bis 19. Jahrhundert* (Wiesbaden: Harrassowitz, 1998).

Strauss, Gerald, *Nuremberg in the Sixteenth Century: City Politics and Life between Middle Ages and Modern Times* (Bloomington: Indiana University Press, 1976).

Suleiman, Susan R. and Inge Crosman (eds), *The Reader and the Text: Essays on Audience and Interpretation* (Princeton: Princeton University Press, 1980).

Tanselle, G. Thomas, "Books, Canons, and the Nature of Dispute (1992)," in G. Thomas Tanselle, *Literature and Artifacts* (Charlottesville: The Bibliographical Society of the University of Virginia, 1998), pp. 275–90.

Teramoto, Mariko and Armin Brinzing, *Katalog der Musikdrucke des Johannes Petreius in Nürnberg*, Catalogus Musicus, 14 (Kassel: Bärenreiter, 1993).

Tilmouth, Michael and Richard Sherr, "Parody (i)," *Grove Music Online*, ed. Laura Macy (Accessed 22 February 2006), <http://www.grovemusic.com>

Tomlinson, Gary, *Monteverdi and the End of the Renaissance* (Berkeley: University of California Press, 1987).

—, "The Web of Culture: A Context for Musicology," *19th-Century Music*, 7 (1983– 84): 350–62.

Trevor-Roper, Hugh, "The Culture of the Baroque Courts," in August Buch, Georg Kauffmann, Blake Lee Spahr, and Conrad Wiedemann (eds), *Europäische Hofkultur im 16. und 17. Jahrhundert*, Vorträge und Referate gehalten anläßlich des Kongresses des Wolfenbütteler Arbeitskreises für Renaissanceforschung und des Internationalen Arbeitskreises für Barockliteratur in der Herzog August Bibliothek Wolfenbüttel vom 4. bis 8. September 1979, Wolfenbütteler Arbeiten zur Barockforschung, 8, 3 vols (Hamburg: Ernst Hauswedell, 1981), vol. 1, pp. 11–23.

Vassalli, Antonio and Angelo Pompilio, "Indice delle rime di Battista Guarini poste in musica," in Angelo Pompilio (ed.), *Guarini, la musica, i musicisti*, Con Natazioni, 3, series ed. Paolo Fabbri (Lucca: Libreria Musicale Italiana Editrice, 1997), pp. 185–225.

Vecchi, Orazio, *Orazio Vecchi: The Four-Voice Canzonettas. With Original Texts and Contrafacta by Valentin Haussmann and Others*, ed. Ruth I. DeFord, Recent Researches in the Music of the Renaissance, 92–3 (Madison, WI: A-R Editions, Inc. 1993).

Velten, Rudolf, *Das Ältere Deutsche Gesellschaftslied unter dem Einfluss der Italienischen Musik*, Beiträge zur Neueren Literaturgeschichte, Neue Folge, Heft 5 (Heidelberg: Carl Winters Universitäts-Buchhandlungen, 1914).

Vogel, Emil, *Bibliothek der gedruckten weltlichen Vocalmusik Italiens, aus den Jahren 1500–1700* (Berlin, 1892; reprint Hildesheim: Georg Olms, 1962) [New Vogel].

Wade, Mara R. and Glenn Ehrstine, "Der, die, das Fremde: Alterity in Medieval and Early Modern German Studies," *Daphnis*, 33 (1–2) (2004): 5–32.

Walther, Johann, *Musicalisches Lexicon* (Leipzig, 1732; reprint Kassel: Bärenreiter, 1953).

Weaver, Robert, *Waelrant and Laet: Music Publishers in Antwerp's Golden Age* (Warren, MI: Harmonie Park Press, 1995).

——, "Waelrant, Hubert," in *New Grove II*, vol. 26, pp. 923–6.

Weiss, Roberto, *The Spread of Italian Humanism* (London: Hutchinson, 1964).

Werner, Arno, "Die alte Musikbibliothek und die Instrumentensammlung an St. Wenzel in Naumburg a.d.S.," *Archiv für Musikwissenschaft*, 8/4 (1927): 390–415.

Whenham, John, *Duet and Dialogue in the Age of Monteverdi* (Ann Arbor: UMI Research Press, 1982).

Will, G.A., *Nürnbergisches Gelehrten-Lexicon*, vol. 4 (Nuremberg, 1758; Neustadt an der Aisch: Schmidt, 1997).

Willer, Georg, *Die Messkataloge Georg Willers [1564–1600]*, ed. Bernhard Fabian, Die Messkataloge des sechzehnten Jahrhunderts, 5 vols (Hildesheim: Georg Olms, 1972–2001).

Wolf, Lothar, *Terminologische Untersuchungen zur Einführung des Buchdrucks im französischen Sprachgebiet*, Beihefte zur Zeitschrift für romanische Philologie, 174, series ed. Kurt Baldinger (Tübingen: Max Niemeyer, 1979).

Wolff, Christoph with Daniel R. Malamed (eds), *Anguish of Hell and Peace of Soul/ Angst der Hellen und Friede der Seelen, compiled by Burckhard Grossmann (Jena, 1623)*, Harvard Publications in Music, 18 (Cambridge: Harvard University Press, 1994).

Yonge, Nicholas (ed.), *Musica Transalpina* (London, 1588), The English Experience: Its Record in Early Printed Books Published in Facsimile, 496 (New York: Da Capo Press, 1972).

Zarlino, Gioseffo, *On the Modes: Part Four of* Le Istitutioni Harmoniche*, 1558*, trans. Vered Cohen, Music Theory Translation Series, ed. Claude V. Palisca (New Haven: Yale University Press, 1983).

Zirnbauer, Heinz, *Der Notenbestand der Reichsstädtisch Nürnbergischen Ratsmusik: Eine bibliographische Rekonstruktion*, Veröffentlichungen der Stadtbibliothek Nürnberg, 1 (Nuremberg: Stadtbibliothek, 1959).

——, "Drei unbekannte Briefe des Coburger Hofkapellmeisters Melchior Franck," *Jahrbuch der Coburger Landesstiftung*, 4 (1959):197–208.

Zulauf, Ernst, "Beiträge zur Geschichte der Landgräflich-Hessischen Hofkapelle zu Cassel bis auf die Zeit Moritz des Gelehrten," *Zeitschrift des Vereins für hessische Geschichte und Landeskunde*, Neue Folge, 26 (1903): 1–144.

Index